MILTON'S LITERARY MILIEU

Milton's LITERARY MILIEU

By

GEORGE WESLEY WHITING

Chapel Hill
The University of North Carolina Press
1939

PRINTED IN THE UNITED STATES OF AMERICA BY THE SEEMAN PRINTERY,
DURHAM, N. C.; BOUND BY L. H. JENKINS, INC., RICHMOND, VIRGINIA

PREFACE

BECAUSE of the renaissance in the study of Milton, informed readers are discarding the traditional notion that he was merely the sheltered, austere, and lonely poet of Puritanism. From recent discoveries and just evaluations of old records Milton emerges in his true character: a great poet, devoted to his art but also intensely interested in current religious and political problems; an artist whose work springs from a strong character, powerfully molded by but transcending his age; a protestant humanist of profound convictions and broad culture. In the light of modern scholarship, one is scarcely justified in roundly declaring that Milton's education was "a too careful, a too ideal education under parental supervision and control," an education in which religion predominated, a special and cloistered discipline which spoiled him for contact with the rough and ready world. It is further from the truth to say that Milton was an almost complete embodiment of the ascetic, not only disciplined and self-restrained, but also characterized by an instinctive severity, a natural repulsion from the amusements, the occupations, the sins of the world. It is not true to say that he dwelt in a kind of moral solitude, neither tempted himself nor appreciating the temptations of others. It is certainly wrong to insist that Milton was a lonely recluse: lonely in his isolated youth; lonely in middle age, "waiting on the Muse, seated alone, in the loneliness of London"; lonelier even than Dante and Virgil, who were lonely men; an old man, "lonely and musical, seated at his chamber organ, sliding upon the key-board a pair of hands pale as its ivory in the twilight of a shabby lodging of which the shabbiness and the gloom molest not him; for he is blind—and yet he sees." These statements are not altogether false; as half-truths they are indeed plausible. But without qualification they are, in effect, quite misleading.

29555

Milton was, of course, studious and sincerely religious; but he was neither an ascetic nor a narrow Protestant. As Mr. Tillyard has aptly said, recent scholarship has destroyed "the notion of Milton as a fundamentalist who also wrote poetry."[1] His education was genuinely liberal, humanistic in the best sense, not predominantly religious. Unbiased study of Milton's life has revealed his fundamental humanity. Modern scholarship has made particularly valuable contributions to the understanding and enjoyment of Milton's work. We are finally beginning to realize that to his friends Milton was a very human person; in Mr. C. G. Osgood's words, "his intimates of today find him a most actual and modern fellow-man, and a singer who poured into his song perennial music, fadeless splendors, and ideas of healing for the ills of all times, especially this of ours."[2] Unfortunately, the field of study has been invaded by the zealous scholar intent at all costs upon establishing some cherished theory: that Milton suffered from physical degeneration, that he was a cabalist, that he was not a Puritan, that he was overwhelmingly indebted to this or that source. Although some of this work is of dubious value, from the clash of opinion emerges a clearer understanding of Milton's character, thought, and art.

On its higher levels literary criticism is a rare and, indeed, an indispensable art, which demands of the critic powers of perception, analysis, judgment, and expression granted only to the elect. Criticism of this high order, which may reveal literary values ignored even by discriminating readers, must consider literature as in part the product of the age. If the critic ignores the writer's milieu or distorts his relation thereto, his remarks may be interesting and illuminating but must inevitably be incomplete and unsound. Fully to understand a poet one must understand his age; and the greater the poet the more essential is the just comprehension of the age which he reflects and by which he is conditioned. This is particularly true of Milton, of whom an eminent scholar has recently said: "No

[1] *The Miltonic Setting Past & Present* (Cambridge, 1938), p. 61.
[2] *The Poetical Works of John Milton* (New York, 1936), p. xviii.

great poet has more completely written himself into his work; none has felt more powerfully the influences of his age; none has embodied more richly the traditions of human culture."[3] And again, with reference to *Paradise Lost:* "The poem is, indeed, in one aspect, a kind of cyclopedia of the science of Milton's time . . . Milton's mind had ranged through the whole realm of speculation. Ancient philosophy, Biblical and Patristic thought, Reformation theology in all its varieties, the philosophic movements and religious heterodoxies of his own day—all were familiar to him and from them he culled the elements of his own eclectic system."[4] Moved by a keen realization of the truth of these mature conclusions and by a profound distrust of many studies intended to prove that Milton was deeply indebted to specific sources, I have tried in the present volume to survey somewhat systematically and comprehensively the contemporary setting of Milton's work. I have, of course, not succeeded in treating all phases of this vast and complex subject.

I wish to forestall misunderstanding. Although some remarks in the volume may seem uncharitable, I have no desire to disparage the able work of other scholars. I am obviously indebted to many Milton editors and critics, whose names I delight to honor. If I am obliged to disagree with certain details in some works, I do it in the spirit of Vives when he ventured to correct Politian: "I would not haue any man thinke this spoken in derogation from the glory of so great a scholler; . . . My words ayme at the profit of the most, not at detraction from him or any." I am not interested in controversy *per se* and regret that in the interest of truth controversial subjects cannot be entirely avoided. Again, I am primarily interested not in discovering sources, but in tracing the currency of ideas. I hope to show that a number of Milton's ideas, by some scholars attributed to specific sources, were

[3] *The Poems of John Milton.* With Introduction and Notes by James Holly Hanford (New York, 1936), p. xxx.

[4] James Holly Hanford, *A Milton Handbook.* Revised Edition (New York, 1938), pp. 200, 211.

shared by his contemporaries, some of whose works have been ignored or only cursorily examined in relation to Milton.

In defending Milton from the persistent heresy that he was a sort of inspired plagiarist lifting the great bulk of his ideas from a few sources or literally following first one source and then another, I have occasionally been forced to draw conclusions that are not altogether complimentary to some writers. In such cases, it seemed to me, silence would have betrayed the cause of Milton and of truth, to which I appeal. After all, the proof of the wide currency of the ideas embodied in Milton's work and of the astonishing breadth of his culture is the best refutation of his less generous critics.

It may be well to state more precisely both what the volume does not attempt and what it does attempt to do. It does not deal with biography as such. It does not attempt to supply impressionistic criticism. It does not deal systematically with religion and politics, which are admirably treated in Mr. G. N. Clark's *The Seventeenth Century* and Mr. Godfrey Davies's *The Early Stuarts 1603-1660*, to mention only two recent works. It does not attempt to define Milton's relation to the broad trends of science, philosophy, and literature, subjects ably surveyed in Sir H. J. C. Grierson's *Cross Currents in English Literature of the XVIIth Century* and Mr. Basil Willey's *The Seventeenth Century Background*, not to mention a number of important special studies by French, Gilbert, Greenlaw, Hanford, McColley, Nicolson, Taylor, and others. The definite purpose of this volume is to compare certain ideas in Milton's poetry and prose with those in contemporary writing, hexaemeral, historical, cartographical, psychological, theological, poetical, and controversial. To support the thesis that Milton's work is intimately related to and perhaps in some cases indebted to important contemporary literature is not, of course, to deny the prominence of classical or neo-classical elements in Milton's culture and art. No real student of Milton is likely to underestimate his indebtedness in thought and craftsmanship to Greek, Latin, and Italian literature. This is a well-known influence, stressed, and perhaps overstressed, in such statements as the following: "Virgil and Tasso guided his hand, and behind them Homer; indeed, the whole of *Paradise Lost* is so full of the spirit of Homer that the poem might be called a Christian Μῆνις, the Wrath of God for the sin of man." And again, in *Paradise Lost* "Milton had rewritten the Bible in the style of Homer."[5] On the other hand, careful comparison reveals the fact that many of Milton's ideas are similar to those in contemporary works, broadly defined, which doubtless form part of his background of fact and fancy.

In its emphasis on various aspects of the contemporary scene, this volume attempts in a sense to explore middle ground. This is obvious when it is compared with such important studies in Milton's poetry and prose as Mr. Hanford's "The Youth of Milton," in *Studies in Shakespeare, Milton, and Donne*, Mr. Tillyard's *Milton*, Mr. Fletcher's *Milton's Rabbinical Readings*, Mr. Taylor's *Milton's Use of Du Bartas*, various articles by Mr. McColley,[6] certain chapters on Milton's pamphlets in Masson's *Life*, and various statements and particularly the section on "Milton's Reputation and Influence, 1643-1647" in Mr. Haller's *Tracts on Liberty in the Puritan Revolution 1638-1647*. Discounting the value of the biographical and historical detail in Masson's ponderous work for the investigation of the evolution of Milton's genius, Mr. Hanford quite properly directs attention to the evidence in the poet's self-expression, to the autobiographical passages in the poetry and prose, only occasionally referring to literary relations. Mr. Tillyard also strictly limits his study to Milton's writings, excluding all others except for occasional references. On the other hand, Mr. Fletcher, Mr. Taylor (whose book has an extremely valuable chapter on the medieval and the Renaissance commonplaces in *Paradise Lost*), and Mr. McColley

[5] Mario Praz, "Milton and Poussin," *Seventeenth Century Studies* (Oxford, 1938), pp. 205, 207.
[6] See especially "Milton's Dialogue on Astronomy: The Principal Immediate Sources," *PMLA*, LII, 728-762; and "The Epic Catalogue of Paradise Lost," *ELH*, IV, 180-191.

respectively insist that some large divisions and even many details in Milton's major epic derive immediately from rabbinical
commentaries, Sylvester's *Du Bartas,* and certain works by
Bishop Wilkins and by Alexander Ross. Masson and Mr.
Haller diverge widely in their treatment of Milton as a controversialist. Familiar as he was with seventeenth-century
pamphleteering, Masson compiled a mass of information regarding Milton's prose, but, as has been said, he sins "egre-
giously from the Carlylean attitude of mind by which he was
obsessed." On the other hand, Mr. Haller, whose work is a
valuable source-book of the prose of the Puritan Revolution,
concludes that Milton exerted little contemporary influence.
The first two scholars focus attention upon Milton's work;
the next three on the whole insist upon Milton's indebtedness
to particular sources; of the last two writers, the former represents Milton as a sort of hero or literary dictator in his own
age, and the latter concludes that in the years from 1643 to
1647 Milton was of little note. In fairness to Mr. Taylor,
I should add that although he emphasizes Milton's debt to
Du Bartas, he does not deny his debt to others.

As the direct expression of his character Milton's work
should, of course, receive primary consideration. In a real
sense, poems are not created by influences and movements but
come immediately "from the living hearts of men." However, writers who remember that as poet and pamphleteer Milton was essentially a man of his age do well to investigate
his contemporary literary relations, which seem to have been
extraordinarily rich and complex. As Mr. A. F. Leach has
said, Milton's "alarms and excursions were those of the mind
out of the body."[7] On almost every page that Milton wrote
there is some evidence of his wide reading. In our study it
is well to bear in mind Mr. Hanford's dictum: "Obviously
no account of the sources of Milton's epic can be considered
as exhaustive, for the poem holds as it were in solution the

[7] "Milton as Schoolboy and Schoolmaster," *Proceedings of the British
Academy 1907-1908* (London, n.d.), p. 295.

whole of his immense reading."[8] Appreciation of this truth
should prevent that undue concentration upon specific indebtednesses which may rob one of a sense of proportion and impair
the worth of conclusions drawn from laborious study. The
present work, holding to a middle course and including a rather
wide scope, does not hope to avoid all the pitfalls lying in the
path of the student of contemporary literary relations but perhaps contains within itself the material for the correction of
its own faults as well as some of those in more limited studies.
Realizing the dangers of undiscriminating parallel-hunting, I
recognize the validity of comparisons between artists working
in the same materials or in the same stage of history and gain
confidence from Mario Praz's brilliant analysis of the neo-
classicism of Milton and Poussin.[9] Not being primarily interested in sources, I have as a rule no wish to substitute my
sources for others. Occasionally I emphasize evidence that
indicates indebtedness. On the whole, relationship, not indebtedness, is the theme.

The first part of this volume examines the relation of
Milton's poetry to certain contemporary works and older
works that were then available: a number of stories of creation, three histories of the world, various atlases (especially
Ortelius's *Theatre of the World*), Burton's *Anatomy of Melancholy*, several accounts of pagan deities, Erasmus's *Encomium
Moriae*, and a poetical narrative of Samson's life. The second
part analyses the relation of some of Milton's pamphlets to
contemporary controversial writing. In the past, literary critics have often condemned Milton's prose epoch as a deplor-
able interruption of his poetic career. In the words of Sir
Walter Raleigh, "The labours of the twenty prime years of
his manhood have been copiously bewailed." The truth, as
we now realize, is that Milton's prose is a vital, if occasionally
crude, expression of his thought and character, intimately related not only to contemporary controversy but also to his
poetry. Without apology, therefore, one may supplement an

[8] *A Milton Handbook*, p. 218.
[9] *Seventeenth Century Studies*, pp. 192-210.

investigation of the literary milieu of the poetry with a similar analysis of the prose.

In this volume Milton's poetry is quoted from Beeching's
text, *The Poetical Works of John Milton,* and his prose, as a
rule, from *The Works of John Milton,* published by the Columbia University Press. For the convenience of the reader,
translations of Diodorus Siculus, Pliny, Plutarch, St. Augustine, and others are used. In the discussion, as in that on
Milton's use of maps, the variety of forms of proper names
is due to the repetition of particular spellings used by diverse
authorities. To the editors of *Modern Language Notes, Pub-
lications of the Modern Language Association, Review of English Studies,* and *Studies in Philology* I am indebted for permission to republish articles which here appear in revised form.
To the directors of the Henry E. Huntington Library and Art
Gallery I am grateful for the privilege of study and for permission to use material in their valuable collections. The Li-
brarian of The Rice Institute provided for my use a number
of indispensable books. I sincerely thank Professors James
Holly Hanford and George Coffin Taylor for reading my
manuscript and for their helpful suggestions. To my wife, for
her steady encouragement, ready sympathy, and shrewd criticism, I owe the greatest debt. To conclude, "I commit to
your wonted favour this our Poet, and what is here done, for
the Poet's sake."

The Rice Institute   G. W. W.
Houston, Texas
December 20, 1938

CONTENTS

PREFACE   v

PART I: *Poetry*

I. THE STORY OF CREATION   3

II. THREE HISTORIES OF THE WORLD   36

III. THE USE OF MAPS   94

IV. A COMPLEXION INCLINED TO MELANCHOLY   129

V. PAGAN DEITIES   177

VI. BELIAL AND SATAN   218

VII. *Comus* AND *Encomium Moriae*   242

VIII. THE HISTORY OF SAMSON   251

PART II: *Prose*

IX. BACON AND MILTON   267

X. MILTON AND DIGBY   282

XI. A REPLY AND A DEBT   293

XII. MILTON AND CANNE   311

XIII. THE WRITING OF *Eikonoklastes*   324

XIV. CONCLUSION   354

APPENDIX   368

"The Grim Woolf"   368

Satan and the Serpent   374

BIBLIOGRAPHY   378

INDEX   391

ILLUSTRATIONS

facing page

Frontispiece from Sir Walter Raleigh's *History of the World* 40

Map "Aevi Veteris, Typus Geographicus" in Ortelius's *The Theatre of the World* (1606), Fol. vi 100

Chart of God's Garden, Bishop's Bible (1568) 108

Chart of the Grove of Daphne in Ortelius's *The Theatre of the World* (1606), Fol. xxxvii 110

Map "Presbiteri Iohannis, Sive, Abissinorum Imperii Descriptio" in Ortelius's *The Theatre of the World* (1606), Fol. 113 120

Table V in Ptolemy's *Geographia* (1605) 124

MILTON'S LITERARY MILIEU

Part I: Poetry

CHAPTER I

THE STORY OF CREATION

ENLIGHTENED by recent discoveries in astrophysics and convinced that our home in space was originally a globe of intensely hot gas which through aeons assumed a condition suitable for the advent of life, the modern reader of *Paradise Lost* is impressed by the orthodoxy as well as the beauty of the account of creation, which follows the story of "Warr so neer the Peace of God in bliss" and of Christ's overwhelming defeat of Satan and his hosts. Obeying the command of the Father and invisibly accompanied by Him, the Son and the Holy Ghost, borne upon the wings of cherubim, journey far into the vast abyss of Chaos and there circumscribe and create the universe, with the earth at its center and with man as the crown of creation. Then, accompanied by angelic symphonies, the great Creator returns with his retinue to the Empyrean, where harp and voice acclaim his triumph. In vastness of scope, in vividness of detail, in appeal to the imagination, this account is indeed unique. That it is not altogether orthodox, that for its just appreciation some knowledge of the great body of hexaemeral literature is necessary, the casual reader does not realize. Milton's invocation of the Heavenly Muse, Raphael's consent to gratify Adam's desire of knowledge "within bounds," the conception of creation from first to last as the act of God—all this, in broad outline, apparently indicates that Milton strictly obeyed the spirit, if not the letter, of Scripture. Even repeated readings of the epic may reveal to the uninitiated no material that is unorthodox.

The solution of the problem, which involves the study not only of Milton's work but also of other discussions of this subject, will aid in determining Milton's relation to his literary

milieu. Milton, it is well known, was far from being a fundamentalist. Years ago complacent faith in Milton's orthodoxy
was destroyed by the publication of *De Doctrina Christiana,*
which is intimately related to *Paradise Lost.* Recent studies have
argued that for his physics and in particular for his conception of
the universe Milton was greatly indebted to various unorthodox
sources: to the Neoplatonism of Spenser,[1] to cabalistic and materialistic sources,[2] and to various rabbinical commentaries on the
Bible.[3] More recently, it has been said that Milton deliberately
attempted to enlarge the Mosaic account of creation and at the
same time to "correlate it with the scientific ideas that he favored."[4] Most recently, a valuable study of hexaemeral material
urges that Milton and other writers, such as Browne and Raleigh,
depended for hexaemeral information not upon ultimate sources,
but upon such well-known treatises as Pererius's *Commentatorum
et Disputationum in Genesim* and Mersenne's *Quaestiones
Celeberrimae in Genesim.*[5] Varying widely in purpose, these
valuable studies, which generally insist upon the particular
provenance of Milton's ideas, have two common tendencies:
they as a rule ignore other sources of the ideas considered; they
sometimes exaggerate Milton's unorthodoxy. The inevitable
result is some distortion of idea and relationship. To reach a just
understanding we must study Milton's relation to the *entire
background*—an obvious task, it would seem, but one that in the
search for special sources has been ignored.

We may briefly survey the problem. The question of the
origin of the world is, as Lambertus Danaeus says, an ancient
one, which for a long time has troubled the philosophers and
"in the end by reason of the diverse judgments of men hath
rested so doubtfull, that many grave writers coulde not tell what

---

[1] Edwin Greenlaw, "A Better Teacher than Aquinas," *Studies in Philology,* XIV,
196-217; Edwin Greenlaw, "Spenser's Influence on *Paradise Lost,*" *Studies in Philology,* XVII, 320-359.

[2] Denis Saurat, *Milton Man and Thinker,* pp. 286, 305, *passim;* Denis Saurat,
Milton et le matérialisme chrétien en Angleterre, pp. 29, 33, *passim;* Marjorie H.
Nicolson, "Milton and the *Conjectura Cabbalistica,*" *Philological Quarterly,* VI, 1-18.

[3] Harris F. Fletcher, *Milton's Rabbinical Readings* (Urbana, 1930).

[4] Katharine B. Collier, *Cosmogonies of our Fathers* (New York, 1934).

[5] Arnold Williams, "Commentaries on Genesis as a Basis for Hexaemeral Material
in the Literature of the Late Renaissance," *Studies in Philology,* XXXIV, 191-208.

to determine therein."[6] Danaeus holds that in the contradictory opinions of philosophers, men ignorant of God's truth, there is no sound doctrine. Purchas declares that there is nothing wherein a man may make a greater show with a little learning, "decking and pruning himselfe, like *Aesops* Iay, or *Horace* his Chough, with borrowed feathers; than in this matter of the Creation, written of (after their manner) by so many, Iewes, Ethnickes, Heretikes, and Orthodoxe Christians . . . a cloud of Authors, both for their number, and the varietie of their opinions, the most of them covering, rather than discovering that Truth (which can bee but one) and more to be beleeved in their confuting others, then proving their owne assertions."[7] Declaring that their "store through this disagreeing is become a sore, and burthen, whiles we must consult with many, and dare promise to our selves no surer footing," Purchas draws as near as possible to the sense of Moses' words, omitting "the endlesse and divers interpretations of others, obtruding allegoricall, anagogicall, mysticall" commentaries. This is especially urgent, for, as Danaeus says, Christians have been "stuffed, beewitched and deceived" with heathen philosophy, which is repugnant to the Word of God, our only sure guide.

Even if it were possible, there is no need to survey here the entire course of hexaemeral literature and the extent to which philosophical elements became incorporated with Biblical exegesis, a subject admirably surveyed in F. E. Robbins's *The Hexaemeral Literature* (1912). It may suffice to say that the first philosopher notably to influence hexaemeral literature was Plato, who declared that a deity created the world, in which material things conform to ideal forms; that matter is stubborn and recalcitrant; that time was made with the universe; that in creation the elements of primeval chaos were united in a bond of friendship. By some Christians Plato's world-soul was identified with God. Besides Plato, Aristotle and the Stoics exerted a considerable influence upon the hexaemera, in the theory of the interaction of the elements, in

---

[6] Epistle dedicatory of *The Wonderfull Woorkmanship of the World* (1578).

[7] *Pilgrimage* (1626), p. 5.

the doctrine of qualities, the fifth essence, and the division of the soul into various faculties, in the theory of the Logos or Word exerting a creative force upon formless matter. Origen, for example, lays stress upon the Word or Wisdom, which contains all the forms of things to be created. "After Origen, the use of the terms Son, Word, and Wisdom, equivalent to Logos, persisted throughout the course of the tradition."[8]

To reform the errors of philosophy by the Word of God is the avowed purpose of Danaeus in *The Wonderfull Woorkmanship of the World*, which as a careful synthesis of the views of the Fathers on creation and an admirable statement of the orthodox points of view may here be summarized. Natural philosophy Danaeus defines as "the true knowledge or discourse concerning the Creation and distinction of this whole worlde with the partes thereof, of the causes by which it was so wrought, and likewise of the effectes which followe thereon, apperteining to the praise of God the Creatour." Natural philosophy is contained in Scripture and is the handmaid of divinity. The world is the workmanship of God alone, who in his Word teaches us how it was framed and ordered. Through faith we understand that the world was made by the hand of God. Moses was an inspired historian. Who will believe Aristotle and Plato rather than Moses, "who first received the thinges that he wrote, by most secret revelation from God?"[9] Christian and heathen natural philosophy are contrasted. Christians recognize and praise God as the Creator. The philosophers speak of an uncertain force, Nature, to which is attributed the origin of all things and which is present in all things. The philosophers make God subject to man's wit and capacity. They hold that the matter whereof He made all things was ready to His hand from everlasting; that at length form joined itself to this matter, which was at first rude and formless; and that this matter and form are the first principle of all things. The philosophers differ, some beginning with a certain first matter, others with the four elements, others with a confusion and the distinction thereof,

---

[8] Robbins, *op. cit.*, pp. 15-16.   [9] *Op. cit.*, p. 9.

others with a bottomless depth always boiling forth. But Christians, relying upon Scripture, are assured that God alone is the Creator.

We should observe a number of particulars in Danaeus's account. He rejects Plato's doctrine of ideas or patterns. Things in this world are not the shadows of true natures which remain in God's mind. A bodily thing cannot be the image of spiritual things. According to Plato's doctrine, the world is a fantasy: our meats are imaginary, men are mere shadows, Christ himself and his passion are only dreams. There is no ideal world. God needed no pattern in creating the world. There is not a multitude of worlds. There is but one world and one God. The world is finite; heaven and earth are the bounds thereof. The world does not have one soul, although Aristotle taught that it had. The proof of this statement follows: the parts of the world are separated by space, but the soul cannot be divided; some parts of the world have life, and some, as the sun, moon, and stars, do not; some parts of the world, as beasts, are mortal, but others, as men, are immortal. How could this singular and indivisible soul admit such contrary and repugnant qualities? The world was made in time and is not eternal. It was created by God, Son, and Holy Ghost. The Father created by his will, the Son by his working and bringing forth, the Holy Spirit by implanting strength and nature and by giving motion and life. The action of the Spirit is compared to that of a bird warming and nourishing its young. The world was made of nothing. God did not bring forth the world from a certain disordered heap of matter that had previous existence. As a rule, nothing is made of nothing: "Take away yron from the Smith, timber from the Carpendour, yearne from the Weaver, what other good can they doe but stand still gaping in their shoppes. . . ."[10] But God, the incomparable architect, needed no material for his work. Danaeus denounces the opinion "that first and alwaies there was existing a certein whole masse, and that rude and confused, which was the heape of all the principall partes

[10] *Op. cit.*, p. 40.

and thinges of the worlde which now are existing and fourmed,
but then disorderly mingled togither, which they call *Chaos*.
And in this opinion *Hesiodus* folowed in his *Theogonia*, which
Ovid describeth in his *Metamorphosis* in these wordes.

Beefore the sea and lande were made, the heaven that all doth hide,
In all the worlde one onely face of nature did a̶p̶p̶e̶r̶e̶,
Which *Chaos* hight, an huge rude heape, and n̶o̶t̶h̶i̶ng else but eeven.
An heavie lumpe and clottred clod of seedes togither driven:
Of thinges at strife amonge themselves for want of order due.
No sunne as yet with lightsome beames the shapelesse worlde did
    viewe. &c."[11]

Then Danaeus explains that in creation there was first prepared
a certain rude matter from which the ordered universe was
created. This matter was not single. At the beginning God
created two sorts of matter, the heavenly and the earthly,
which are sharply distinguished. The matter of which the
world was created was good. Referring to St. Augustine's
De Natura Boni, Danaeus declares that the Manichees and the
Valentinians were deceived in thinking that the world was the
effect of a certain foul imperfection and ignorance in God. As
created, before it was defaced by sin, the world was perfect. As
to the means and instruments by which God created the world,
it is foolish to inquire; the whole work was plainly miraculous.
Four things only are to be observed: the world was created
by the word of God; light was necessary as the source of heat
and light; God worked without any pain or weariness at all;
the world was created in six days. As the world began, so
will it end. We live in the crooked age of the world, which
sighs and groans, looking for the restoring of the sons of God.

Such is the orthodox view of creation, which is, of course,
frequently encountered. It is well illustrated in Sylvester's
Du Bartas His Devine Weekes and Workes,[12] which has recently been described as the dominant influence upon *Paradise
Lost*, as Milton's quarry, as the one work from which a great
body of conventional material passed into Milton's major

---

[11] *Op. cit.*, p. 43.
[12] I use the edition of 1611, "Now thirdly corrected & augm."

epic.[13]   Naturally, Mr. Taylor does not contend that Du
Bartas was the only source in shaping the conventional ideas
in the poem; he declares that Milton consulted special works
on the themes that he developed.   Although Milton may have
got an "amazing number of details" of creation from Du Bartas, it is not necessary, says Mr. Taylor, to assume that he
"got them all from Du Bartas," for many of them "might
have been acquired by Milton from various and sundry sources,
such as medieval or Renaissance bestiaries, lapidaries, botanies,
or from Pliny's *Natural History*."[14]   Mr. Taylor concludes,
however, that Milton's use of Du Bartas here "is very, very
great."   It is obvious that Milton may have been influenced
by the orthodoxy of Du Bartas, who, guided by his Muse,
"trained in true Religion," declares that the world was created
in time by the wisdom of the eternal God, with his Son and
Spirit, who also existed from eternity; that without any idea
or pattern the "Worlds goodly frame" was created from nothing; that matter as at first created was a chaos, without beauty,
soul, or motion, and "Full of Disorders and fell Mutinies";
that the Spirit of God "brooding upon this Gulf" warmed this
shapeless mass and endowed it with life; that God first created
light and then in six days all other things; that there is but
one world, which is finite; that there is no fifth essence; that
the Universe will ultimately perish but that man's soul is immortal and destined to "Euer-lasting Happiness or Horror."
There is, however, in Milton's account of creation considerable heterodoxy which has other sources.

With the orthodox doctrine of Danaeus and Du Bartas
one may compare the thought of Francis Bacon in his interpretation of the myths of Cupid and Coelum,[15] in which Bacon
formally pays tribute to the Christian God but explains creation as a natural process.   Cupid was the most ancient of all
things except Chaos, which was coeval with him.   He was

[13] George C. Taylor, *Milton's Use of Du Bartas* (Cambridge, 1934),
p. xv.   [14] *Ibid.*, p. 92.
[15] "De Principiis atque Originibus," *The Works of Francis Bacon*, ed.
Spedding, Ellis, and Heath, V, 461-500; "Coelum; or the Origin of Things,"
op. cit., VI, 723-725.

without parents and united with Chaos to beget the gods and all things. Some say that Chaos came from an egg laid by Nox. Chaos signifies the rude mass of matter; but matter itself, the force and nature thereof, is shadowed in Cupid. Of this primary matter there can be no cause in nature, "for we always except God." It is the "ultimate force and primary law of nature"; but the manner in which this force proceeds is very obscure. Atoms or seeds are of a dark and hidden nature; man "cannot find out the work that God worketh from the beginning to the end." But Bacon declares that in the atom are the elements of all bodies, the original virtue of all virtues. In the following statement he describes this primary matter:

Now that the first matter had some form is demonstrated in the fable by making Cupid a person; yet so that matter as a whole, or the mass of matter, was without form; for Chaos is without form; Cupid is a person. And this agrees well with Holy Writ; for it is not written that God in the beginning created matter, but that he created the heaven and the earth.[16]

Obviously Bacon, as well as Milton, believed that the world was created from a pre-existing chaos. He wished to show too that primary matter had an intrinsic virtue, but out of his regard for Holy Writ, and perhaps Natali Conti's *Mythologiae*, as has recently been indicated,[17] he also said that matter in the aggregate lacked this virtue. In Bacon's interpretation of Coelum, Saturn is matter that always remained the same, suffering neither increase nor diminution, in a period when agitation resulted in vain attempts to create worlds. This stage corresponds to chaos. Then, putting an end to this confusion, Jupiter introduced concord and stability—an era of creation— when change proceeded gradually, leaving the total fabric of the world undisturbed. Thus after notable confusions in the heavens and the lower regions a durable state of peace ensued. But the world may relapse into ancient chaos. Some-

---

[16] "De Principiis atque Originibus," *op. cit.*, V, 468.
[17] Charles W. Lemmi, *The Classic Deities in Bacon* (Baltimore, 1933), pp. 57-58.

what perfunctorily Bacon adds, "We know (through faith) that all such speculations are but the oracles of sense which have long ceased and failed; the world, both matter and fabric, being in truth the work of the Creator."[18] The conclusion may be a sop to Christianity or an illustration of Bacon's medievalism—for in spite of his efforts Bacon had not thrown off the chains of scholasticism. "He fought an enemy whom he had not yet conquered in himself."[19] But we may recognize in his interpretation of the myths the manifestation of a sincere rationalistic spirit unfettered by a dominant theology which, as Geoffrey Bullough has said, fostered a devout ignorance and discouraged secular learning.[20]

In this preliminary survey we may notice, finally, Henry More's *Conjectura Cabbalistica. Or, A Conjectural Essay Of Interpreting the minde of Moses, according to a Threefold Cabbala: Viz. Literal, Philosophical, Mystical, or, Divinely Moral* (1653), which attempts to reconcile the Mosaic and the philosophical accounts of creation. This work, which More describes as the dictate of the free reason of his mind, "heedfully considering the written Text of Moses, and carefully canvasing the Expositions of such Interpreters as are ordinarily to be had upon him,"[21] attempts to explain the profound and mysterious meaning of the Biblical text, to meet the criticism of atheists, and to justify "the more noble results of free Reason and Philosophy from the vulgar suspicion of Impiety and Irreligion." The literal cabbala is merely an expanded paraphrase of the Biblical story of creation, describing, for example, the earth on the first day as "a rude and desolate heap, . . . a deep miry abysse," covered with waters; the firmament as a hollow expanse, firm and transparent, supporting the waters above; the garden of Eden as an ever-springing paradise where all of Adam's senses were gratified in innocence. The philosophical cabbala presents an allegorical interpretation of

[18] *Op. cit.*, VI, 725.
[19] Rudolf Metz, "Bacon's Part in the Intellectual Movement of his Time," *Seventeenth Century Studies* (Oxford, 1938), p. 27.
[20] "Bacon and the Defence of Learning," *Seventeenth Century Studies* (Oxford, 1938), pp. 4-5.   [21] The Preface to the Reader.

Genesis, in which heaven and light signify the intellectual souls of men and beasts and the seminal forms of all things, and earth is the potentiality of the existence of the outward creation. The earth is described as nothing but "Solitude and Emptinesse . . . a deep bottomlesse capacity of being whatever God thought fit to make of it." The Spirit of God is "the *Vehicle* of *Eternal Wisdome*." Light is the "*inexhaustible Treasury of Light and Form*." By His will and power God created real or corporal matter which lies on the border between fluid possibility and seminal forms; this act resulted in "this immensely diffused matter," which was then actuated by the Spirit. By the union of the active and the passive principle, drawing in virtue from the world of life, a vital congruity between parts was established. Every act of creation is thus described as a union of the active and the passive principle, which is also termed masculine and feminine. Creation is the result of the "seminal Forms and Souls of Animals insinuating themselves into the prepared matter," vigor and motion being imparted from the world of life to the immense body of the universe. The creation of man, as Miss Nicolson has said, is thus described:

For after he had prepared the matter for so noble a guest as a humane Soul, the *world of life* was forced to let go what the rightly prepared matter so justly called for. And man appeared upon the stage of the earth, Lord of all living creatures. For it was just that he that bears the Image of the invisible God, should be the Supreme Monarch of this visible world. And what can be more like God than the soul of man, that is so free, so rational, and so intellectual as it is?[22]

There are two Adams: the ethereal Adam is the more perfect and masculine being, whose faculties carried him toward virtue and the holy intellect; the feminine faculty in Adam is the principle of "vital joy and complacency to the matter." It is the "feminized Adam" that the Serpent assailed. In Paradise, Adam's soul is the ground that God had blessed; the Tree of Life is the essential will of God; the Tree of Knowl-

[22] *Op. cit.,* p. 31.

edge is Adam's will; the Serpent is the inordinate desire of pleasure. The moral cabbala deals with the creation of the microcosm: it is the story of the evolution of individual morality. By divine aid man may be raised from one degree of spiritual life to another until he attains full perfection in the life of God. In this way More justifies the Biblical story. The Biblical text, which complies "with the meer rude and ignorant conceits of the Vulgar," is supplemented by the traditional doctrine of the cabbala, which reveals "very choice and singular theorems of natural philosophy and metaphysics." More always assumes that philosophy and the Bible, correctly interpreted, are in perfect accord. This principle is laid down: "there is no considerable truth of *Nature* or *Divinity*, that *Moses* was ignorant of." Philosophy is not an enemy of the divine life. Pythagoras, Plato, Plotinus, Philo Judaeus, even Descartes lend their support to the cabbala. The truth of Scripture is asserted. Controversial questions, which are treated in the defence of the cabbala, are not stressed. More implies that the matter of which the world was made did not previously exist. He does not plainly declare that this matter was good; it was merely passive in creation, and apparently all of its virtues were due to the action of the heavenly principle. It is not, as in Milton, a part of God himself; it is distinct from light or the heavenly principle. Obviously More believed that there were two substances, not one of various degrees, which is Milton's doctrine. In More, the soul, an ethereal substance or principle, introduced from without, corresponds to the spirit which God directly inspired in man. On the whole, despite his profession of reason and his earnest attempt to reconcile Scripture and philosophy, More remains fundamentally orthodox.

Before reviewing the imaginative picture of creation and of matter in *Paradise Lost*, we may against the background already sketched profitably summarize Milton's ideas of creation as abstractly expressed in *De Doctrina Christiana*, in which, as he says, he writes "under the guidance of Scripture." Milton insists that it is the height of folly to inquire into God's actions

before the foundation of the world, which may recall Bacon's
statement that philosophy has been corrupted by seeking after
the parents of Cupid. Milton declares: "That the world was
created, is an article of faith." Creation is defined as "that
act whereby God the Father produced every thing that exists
by his Word and Spirit, that is, by his will, for the manifestation of the glory of his power and goodness."[23] The Father
is the principal cause, the Son is the main agent, and the Spirit
a subordinate minister. The world was created out of pre-
existing matter; the orthodox idea that it was formed of nothing is "a basis as unsubstantial as that of their own theory." It
was necessary that previously there should have existed matter "capable of receiving passively the exertion of the divine
efficacy." But matter did not exist independently of God; all
things are of God. Original matter was intrinsically good "and
the chief stock of every subsequent good." This matter, which
was at first confused and formless, was afterwards "adorned
and digested into order by the hand of God." Creation is a
process of bestowing form and order and life. The highest
heaven, including the angels, probably existed before the creation of the world. The apostasy of the angels, which caused
their expulsion from bliss, probably took place before the world
was created. The angels are spirits, created in perfect holiness
and righteousness, and are immortal. In the visible world, all
living things, including man, are animated from one and the
same source of life. Thus there is in all creation one soul as
there is in essence one matter. Human souls are not the individual creation of God. The common notion that man is composed
of two distinct natures, soul and body, is erroneous. The whole
man is soul, and the soul is man. The soul of man is not an
exception to the general law of creation; God breathed the
breath of life into all living creatures. Milton's unorthodoxy
is apparent: God is omnipotent, and the Son and the Holy
Spirit, his agents, are not essentially one with him; the world
was created from pre-existing matter, which is of God; in its

[23] *The Works of John Milton*, ed. F. A. Patterson . . . (New York,
1933), XV, 5.

essence matter is indestructible; one soul pervades the universe; in man the soul and the body are one.)

Against this background and in relation to several other contemporary accounts of creation, the study of the parts of *Paradise Lost* dealing with matter and creation should throw light upon Milton's indebtedness to specific sources and upon the contemporary validity of his ideas. For comparison with *Paradist Lost* one may take, in addition to the material already cited, the accounts of creation in three works that enjoyed considerable popularity in the seventeenth century—Sir Walter Raleigh's *History of the World,* Purchas's *Pilgrimage,* and Hexham's translation of the Mercator-Hondius *Atlas,* with all three of which Milton was probably familiar. By noting in this comparison the traditional and the distinctive elements in Milton's account of God, Chaos, the plan of creation, the act of creation, the stages or processes, the scale of life, the relation of God to man, we may arrive at a better understanding of Milton's relation to this age.

In *Paradise Lost* creation presupposes the existence of God and Chaos: of God, omnipotent, infinite, just, prescient but not coercive, the "Fountain of Light," invisible but present in all things, immutable, immortal, and through the Son and the Holy Spirit, who are but manifestations of his power and love, the "Author of all being"; of Chaos, a wild abyss, a dark and boundless ocean, where Night and Chaos, ancestors of nature, hold eternal anarchy, a space that is not separate from God, who fills infinitude, and that is filled with a confused matter not lifeless, for it is "The Womb of nature." Chaos is primary matter, created by God and through Him the source of all created things, which, if not depraved, tend towards divinity. As Raphael says,

> O *Adam,* one Almightie is, from whom
> All things proceed, and up to him return,
> If not deprav'd from good, created all
> Such to perfection, one first matter all,
> Indu'd with various forms, various degrees
> Of substance, and in things that live, of life;

> But more refin'd, more spiritous, and pure,
> As neerer to him plac't or neerer tending
> Each in thir several active Sphears assignd.[24]

In this passage the essence of Milton's unorthodoxy appears—the conception of God, the pre-existence of chaos, the virtue of matter, the unity of all life. Although in conformity with the conventions of the epic God is endowed with certain personal qualities, he remains in the story of creation scarcely more than the personification of an intelligent and vital force, a world soul, disguised in part by the conventional religious symbols.

Consider briefly these ideas in the other works. Of innumerable statements of God's qualities the following in Raleigh's *History* may be unique only by reason of its grave eloquence. In its cadences[25] and in its thought there are perhaps certain anticipations of *Paradise Lost:*

God, whom the wisest men acknowledg to be a Power uneffable, and Vertue infinite, a Light by abundant clarity invisible; an Understanding which it self can onely comprehend; an Essence eternal and spiritual, of absolute pureness and simplicity; was, and is pleased to make himself known by the Work of the World: in the wonderful magnitude whereof (all which he embraceth, filleth, and sustaineth) we behold the Image of that glory which cannot be measured, and withal, that one, and yet universal Nature, which cannot be defined. In the glorious Lights of Heaven, we perceive a shadow of his Divine Countenance; in his merciful provision for all that live, his manifold goodness: and lastly, in creating and making existent the World universal, by the absolute Art of his own Word, his Power and Almightiness. . . .[26]

Raleigh declares that primary matter was created to form the world; he subscribes to the orthodox belief that the world was created *ex nihilo.* He describes briefly an imperfect, formless matter, the first condition of creation, from which, he

---

[24] V, 469-477.

[25] Edward Thompson believes that the real proof of Raleigh's influence on Milton "lies in the cadence, the mingling of imagination and of personal pathos" (*Sir Walter Ralegh,* p. 236). Cf. the leading article, "Sir Walter Ralegh's Prose," *The Times Literary Supplement,* January 31, 1935.

[26] P. 1 of the edition of 1687.

says, the ancient poets had their notion of Demogorgon and Chaos. He quotes Ovid's description of this Chaos. In time Raleigh's Chaos does not agree with that of *Paradise Lost*, in which Chaos precedes creation and extends boundlessly on all sides of the universe. Purchas agrees with Raleigh: at first heaven and earth were without form and void, "a darkened depth and waters; a matter of no matter, and a forme without forme; a rude and indigested *Chaos*. . . ."[27] He believes that the world was created of nothing; chaos is merely the first stage of creation. In various chapters and especially in that entitled "Of the Nature, and Forme of Chaos, or Primary Matter," Mercator's *Atlas* describes at length the condition of this primary matter, "this huge masse, which was without forme, rude, and confused," from which God afterwards drew all the parts of the world. Chaos was "the matter and mother of all things that were to be created." It is described as an abyss, a pure solitude, "having nevertheless in it the species, from which all things which are now might be deduced and formed." It is insisted that this matter is not dead. How can God, who is a "forme forming all formes, a pure light, a pure vertue and efficacie, a pure life," produce anything void and dead? "Hee who conceived to create man after his owne Image, how should hee begin a sluggish and dead foundation . . . ?"[28] Chaos "was the first of all things, having in its Essence, the seed of all qualities and formes." It was like the Creator in this, that as God had all things in himself "which are expressed actually in the Word, and shed abroad by the holy Ghost" so Chaos "comprehended all the formes of things, Substances and Qualities, secretly within her bowels, and intrinsick Essence, according to the Seminary and Radicall power" that God had implanted. Again and again the seminary virtue of this primary matter is emphasized; it is not merely passive. In creation the cooperation of God is essential, but matter has an intrinsic virtue. The analogy with Milton's system is unmistakable: in the epic and *Atlas*, primary matter is formless but vital; in both, creation is the result of the warming and

[27] *Pilgrimage*, pp. 6-7.   [28] P. 8.

shaping influence of God. In the *Atlas*, however, Chaos is the first condition of creation, the first stage.

Tracing the influence of Spenser's philosophy on Milton and attempting to define a "relationship almost without parallel, unless it be conceived on such terms as we apply to the relationship between Plato and his master Socrates," a brilliant scholar some years ago argued very cogently that Spenser's philosophy of nature, his theory of the origin of life, of Chaos and Night and the Abyss whence came the world greatly influenced Milton.[29] That Milton was deeply indebted to Spenser no one would deny. But Spenser's idea that Chaos was the mother of the world, that

> This Worlds still moving mightie masse
> Out of great Chaos ugly prison crept

is a common one in the seventeenth century. Again, Spenser's idea that

> The seedes, of which all thinges at first were bred,
> Shall in great Chaos wombe againe be hid

is said to have suggested Milton's concept of Chaos as

> The Womb of nature and perhaps her Grave.[30]

In the Chaos of Spenser, as of Milton, "were elements that, if not kept in bounds, would speedily destroy the universe." The idea in the *Zohar* that before creating the world God created and destroyed several others has been suggested as the origin of Milton's idea that the world might be destroyed and become a portion of these lost worlds of primeval chaos.[31] We have already encountered this theory in Bacon's interpretation of the myth of Coelum. We meet it again in the *Atlas:* Chaos "having been the first beginning of all things, in this all things are finallie resolved, according to Ecclesiastes. chap. 3."[32] According to Scripture, which must be regarded as Milton's primary source, dust and oblivion are the fate of all things.

---

[29] Edwin Greenlaw, "Spenser's Influence on *Paradise Lost*," *Studies in Philology*, XVII, 320-359.   [30] *Ibid.*, p. 335.
[31] Denis Saurat, *Milton Man and Thinker*, pp. 285-286.
[32] P. 8.

In seventeenth-century accounts of creation chaos, the first state of primary matter, is generally present. Milton's Chaos is merely more ancient than that of his contemporaries, except Bacon's.

It may seem unnecessary to emphasize the fact that God had a plan of creation, as Milton briefly indicates at the close of Book VII. The Creator returns to Heaven,

> Thence to behold this new created World
> Th' addition of his Empire, how it shew'd
> In prospect from his Throne, how good, how faire,
> Answering his great Idea.[33]

The orthodox marginal commentary of Du Bartas should be recalled: "God, needing no Idea, nor premeditation, nor Patterne of his work, of nothing made all the World." Involved is the Platonic doctrine of Ideas or Patterns, to which orthodox Christians objected. Mercator's *Atlas* discusses the matter at length. In the chapter entitled "Of God, the beginning and workmaster of all things, according to the Platonists," the author explains that Platonic theology has more appearance of divinity than all others and seems to come nearest to the Mosaic truth, but that even the Platonists erred and ministered matter of erring to others. He expounds the beliefs of the Platonists: the One is a simple essence, the beginning of life, present in all things and containing all things, infinite and omniscient; the Spirit or Intellect is the second God, the Word of God, the Image of God, from whom all life acquires its essence. "Plato calleth it *Idea*, because it comprehendeth in its essence, the Patterne and sole individuall species of all things." The Soul is an act from this Intellectual Spirit. The author then explains the Mosaic theology, offering perhaps a refutation of Platonic theories. By reason of his immense goodness God created man and the world and "digested it into that order, nature, and proportion, according to that Idea, which he from all Eternitie had conceived. . . ." The point is emphasized.

[33] VII, 554-557.

But because that God hath not created the world, either by Chance, or through ignorance, searching the meanes how, or without wisdom, but with a great deale of Prudence and Wisdome, it cannot be denied, but that from all Eternitie, hee hath conceived some certaine modell, and all the Ideas of his works, to which wee give not beginning in the word, as Plato doth, but to the Parent of the word, considering that whatsoever the Sonne hath, hee hath it from his Father. . . .[34]

The idea is reiterated, as in the following: "It is well knowne and usuall, that every good workman, before he begins his worke, conceiveth a certaine Idea thereof, by the contemplation of which, he beginneth and accomplisheth it." This idea is inherent in the work. "So God as by himselfe, being the most wise, most mighty, and the most skilfull Architect of the world, hath created all things no otherwise, than by a most good and exquisite reason. It is necessary therefore, that hee of himselfe from all eternity had conceived an Idea most requisite for his worke. . . ."[35] God, who is all-wise and almighty, had, in the fountain of his essence, pondered all things from the beginning, and had "this increated Idea, shining forth in all things, and possessed it eternally. . . ." This emphasis upon the idea or plan of God is doubtless the effect of and a vain attempt to refute Platonic theories. Rejecting the idea of patterns, the doctrine emphasizes God's wisdom and foresight, for which there is ample warrant in Scripture.

An attempt has been made to identify Milton's Muse Urania with the third Sephira, Intelligence, of the *Zohar*. "Wisdom in Milton is, by name, the Wisdom of Kabbalah: Urania then is the third Sephira, Intelligence, the sister of the second, as Milton well knows, and Milton addresses this Intelligence, which he disguises as Urania, so that he may be inspired by her—the proper power of inspiration."[36] And it has even been said that Milton ascribes to the divine acts "the

---

[34] P. 4.   [35] P. 10.
[36] Saurat, *op. cit.*, p. 291.

sexual character which is so well marked in the *Zohar*."[37] The interpretation is based upon the following lines:

> Thou with Eternal wisdom didst converse,
> Wisdom thy Sister, and with her didst play
> In presence of th' Almightie Father, pleas'd
> With thy Celestial Song.[38]

The theory that relates these lines to the *Zohar* is evidently unsound, for the passage will not bear the interpretation put upon it. Besides, in Scripture wisdom is an inseparable quality of God; and Urania is the well-known Christian Muse, the literary symbol of sacred poetry.[39] Another interpretation relates Urania to Ben Gerson's commentary on Scripture. Explaining that in Milton and Ben Gerson creation is the result of planning, that there is no Biblical authority for this idea, that in rabbi and poet the conceptions of the plan are similar, the advocate of this view insists that Milton derived the idea from Ben Gerson, in whose commentary wisdom and understanding were present with God at creation. In *Paradise Lost*, he declares, Milton without Biblical warrant represents *two spirits as present with the Son of God at creation*. The interpretation is based upon the following lines:

> The King of Glorie in his powerful Word
> And Spirit coming to create new Worlds.[40]

This is said to mean that the Son "was accompanied by two Spirits at and during Creation."[41] The lines should not be thus interpreted. Milton plainly says that God in His Son and Spirit came to create the world. Milton refers to the Trinity.

It is clear that this matter of God's Idea and Wisdom is merely conventional. In connection with Mr. Larson's argument that Servetus influenced Milton's Platonism, Mr. Taylor pertinently cites Du Bartas's lines regarding the Almighty's Idea in creation, and he again reminds us that this matter of the creation is a commonplace in the writings of the Middle

[37] *Ibid.*, p. 291. [38] VII, 9-12.
[39] Lily B. Campbell, "The Christian Muse," *The Huntington Library Bulletin*, Number 8, pp. 29-70. [40] VII, 208-209.
[41] Harris F. Fletcher, *Milton's Rabbinical Readings*, p. 112.

Ages and the Renaissance.[42] The present investigation merely
confirms this criticism. Whatever the source, Milton's reference to God's Idea is partly Platonic, his insistence upon God's
Wisdom is not cabalistic but Scriptural, his Muse is not rabbinical but conventional.

After the bounds of the universe have been set, the initial
act of creation is in *Paradise Lost* represented as the brooding
of the Holy Spirit upon the waters:

> but on the watrie calme
> His brooding wings the Spirit of God outspred,
> And vital vertue infus'd, and vital warmth
> Throughout the fluid Mass. . . .[43]

The idea is a very common one. Raleigh's *History* describes
the act as follows:

After the Creation of Heaven and Earth, then void and without
form, the Spirit of God moved upon the Waters. The *Seventy Interpreters* use the word *superferabatur*, moved upon or
over: *incubabat* or *fovebat* (saith *Hierome*) out of *Basil*; and *Basil*
out of a Syrian Doctor; *Equidem non meam tibi, sed viri cujusdam
Syri sententiam recensebo* (saith *Basil*:) which words *incubare* or
fovere, importing warmth, hatching, or quickning, have a special
likeness. *Verbum translatum est ab avibus pullitiei suae incubantibus,
quamvis spirituali, & plane inenarrabili, non autem corporali modo;
The word is taken of birds hatching their young, not corporally,
but in a spiritual and unexpressible manner.*[44]

Purchas remarks that the Spirit of God moved upon the waters
"as the Hen sitteth on her egges to cherish and quicken, as
Hierome interpreteth the word." And he adds:

This interpretation of the Spirit moving upon the Waters, agreeth
with that opinion which some attribute to the Stoickes. That all
things are procreated and governed by one Spirit, which *Democritus*
calleth the soule of the world, *Hermes* and *Zoroaster*, and *Apollo
Delphicus* call Fire, the maker, quickner, and preserver of all things;
and *Virgill* most elegantly and divinely singeth, seeming to paraphrase on *Moses* words:

[42] *Op. cit.*, p. 52. See also p. 91.
[43] VII, 234-237.   [44] P. 4.

. . . .
Heaven first, and Earth, and Watrie plaines,
Bright Moone, of Starres those twinckling traines,
The Spirit inly cherisheth,
Loves, moves, great body nourisheth;
Through all infus'd this all containes.[45]

Part of William Lauder's charge against Milton was that he
took from Du Bartas this figure of the brooding Holy Spirit.[46]
· The idea of creation as a natural process is also apparent
in Mercator's *Atlas*. The author explains that we "will place
the Father first, as the Seminary reason of the world, the
Sonne, the force vigetative, the H. Ghost the vertue Produc-
tive, & animative, the which with him proceeding from the
Father and being shed out by the Sonne, it passeth into a
worke."[47] He goes on to say that the Holy Ghost awakens
this inexhaustible fountain of the Father, that the immense fecundity of the Son incites Him, and that consequently the
Father begets the world, which He then gives to His Son "as
hee who properly expresseth the Father," and that by act of
the Son the world is brought forth, which is then by the Holy
Ghost "animated in all things according to the proper Idea
of every one of them." The idea of natural engendering is
expressed in the following excerpt:

Two things ought principally to be observed in the Creation: first
of all, that it proceede, by the order of things most imperfect, and
most ignoble, to the most perfect and most noble, as first of all,
from the Chaos, to the Earth, then to the Water, from thence
to the Heavens, and so consequently. Secondlie, that it institute
the nature of all things, their power, actions, order, the manner of
doing, the beginnings, and the ends, and the periods of every of
them, and the universall law of nature, such in the Creation, which
hee would have to be perpetually. Willing then, that the inferiour
world, which ought to be engendred, and that the Superiour, was
the Father endowed with masculine vertue, that is, willing to
ordayne a seminary reason in the Elements, . . . presently after

---

[45] *Op. cit.*, p. 7.
[46] *An Essay on Milton's Use and Imitation of the Moderns, in his Paradise Lost* (London, 1750), p. 141.   [47] P. 4.

that hee began to extract the Elements, hee extracted the matter
of the heavens, to the end, that the father, and the mother might
grow up together, that the power, and all the vertue of the one
and the other, might receive engendring, his lawes and rules in
the same Creation.[48]

The idea of creation as a natural, a sexual, process has been
attributed to cabalistic influences and particularly to the *Zohar*,
which has been declared to be the source of the fundamental
philosophy of *Paradise Lost*.[49] In the *Zohar*, however, creation is made possible by God's withdrawal. This is not the
case in *Paradise Lost*, where the process is similar to that explained in Mercator. At any rate, there is no need to assume
that Milton resorted to occult philosophy for a conception that
seems to have been generally circulated in a popular atlas.

In *Paradise Lost*, although the acts of God are immediate,
creation is described as a gradual process extending over six
days, as in *Genesis*. On the first day the earth was created and
"self-ballanc't on her Center hung." The idea expressed here
has recently been ascribed to Ben Gerson's commentary. It is
said that the connection of the idea of the earth being hung
over nothingness, found in the text of Job, and Milton's idea
of the earth hanging self-balanced from its own center "is to
be found in Ben Gerson's commentary" on *Job* xxvii,7.[50] In
Mercator's *Atlas* the chapter entitled "To what end this Chaos
was created, and of the foundation and forme thereof" explains
the line, if explanation is needed of an idea implicit in the geocentric system. The *Atlas* explains that God assigned "a place
for the Earth, and the Chaos, to wit, a point in the midst of
the void, upon which it rested, and beyond which it is not
permitted to moove."[51] The greatest miracle of all nature is
that so ponderous a weight should subsist hanging in the midst
of the heavens. But as God willed so it was done. "So this
Chaos, and above all, that which is the heaviest in it, to wit,
the Earth, desireth uncessantly the point, which is assigned to
it in this vacuity, and is moved towards him . . . till it hath

---

[48] P. 13.

[49] Saurat, *op. cit.*, pp. 281 ff.

[50] Fletcher, *op. cit.*, p. 137.

[51] P. 6.

obtained a like resting place on all parts. . . . This is the nature of the Earth, and so likewise of the Chaos, and the sympathy, which it hath with all other creatures, which he subjecteth to all in the seate, which he hath appointed to it, which is the *Center* of the world, and being settled firme, round about the Center, resteth, and beareth up all other things. . . ."

In *Paradise Lost* the other acts of creation correspond to those in *Genesis*. Consider the creation of light. Milton writes:

> Let there be Light, said God, and forthwith Light
> Ethereal, first of things, quintessence pure
> Sprung from the Deep, and from her Native East
> To journie through the airie gloom began,
> Sphear'd in a radiant Cloud, for yet the Sun
> Was not; shee in a cloudie Tabernacle
> Sojourn'd the while.[52]

On the fourth day the sun, with the moon and stars, was created:

> For of Celestial Bodies first the Sun
> A mightie Spheare he fram'd, unlightsom first,
> Though of Ethereal Mould: . . . . .
> Of Light by farr the greater part he took,
> Transplanted from her cloudie Shrine, and plac'd
> In the Suns Orb.[53]

Milton's account of the creation of light and its transference to the sun preserves an interpretation common in the seventeenth century. Raleigh explains that light was first created and "afterwards (in the fourth day) gathered and united, and called the Sun, the Organ and Instrument of created light." Light may be called "the Chaos, or material substance of the Sun, and other Lights of Heaven." Moses, says Raleigh, "repeateth twice the main parts of the Universal: first, as they were created in matter; secondly, as they were adorned with form. . . . So the Sun, although it had not its formal perfection, his circle, beauty, and bounded magnitude, till the fourth day, yet was the substance thereof in the first day (under the

[52] VII, 243-249.   [53] VII, 354-361.

name Light) created; and this light formerly dispersed, was in the same fourth day united, and set in the Firmament of Heaven: for, to Light created in the first day God gave no proper place or fixation; and therefore the effects named by *Anticipation* . . . were precisely performed, after this Light was congregated and had obtained life and motion."[54] Purchas summarizes a number of interpretations of the nature and form of original light:

some interpreting this of the Sunne, which they will have then created; some of an immaterial qualitie, after received into the Sunne and Starres; some of a cloud formed of the waters, circularly moved, and successively lighting either Hemisphere, of which afterwards the Sunne was compact; from which they differ not much, which thinke it the matter of the Sunne, then more diffused and imperfect, as the waters also were earthlie, and the Earth fluible, till God by a second worke perfected and parted them. And (to let passe them which apply it to Angels or men) others understand it of the fiery Element, the essential property of which is to enlighten.[55]

With indifference Purchas adds, "Let the Philosophers determine this when they doe other doubts. . . ." Observe that the second and the third interpretations in Purchas are present in Milton's account. Mercator's *Atlas* explains that light, created first and "ordayned for the Sunne," began immediately to gather itself "and to enter within the Globe of the Sunne; so that about ten howres after the Creation . . . it gave light to the world." Later it is said that the creation of light was not perfected until the fourth day, when the substance of the sun, which was at first dispersed, was finally collected and reduced to form. The sun is light organized and concentrated. In Milton, as in the others, an attempt is made to rationalize the Scriptural story.[56]

Insisting that Rashi's commentary throws important light upon Milton's story of creation and that, in fact, many of the

---

[54] Pp. 5-6.   [55] P. 7.

[56] Mr. Taylor (*op. cit.*, p. 93) believes that Milton adopted one of the ideas in Du Bartas's summary of sundry opinions concerning the matter and creation of light.

details in *Paradise Lost* were derived from Rashi, the advocate of Milton's debt to rabbinical commentary explains that Milton, like Rashi, represents creation as an instantaneous act in which were created all things, which were then put in their places during the six days of creation. It is said that in *Paradise Lost* the sun was created on the first day but was "kept hidden until it was transplanted" to its permanent place on the fourth day.[57] This idea, it is truly said, is not found in the Bible; but, it is declared, Rashi's commentary "expressly accounts for just such a procedure with the sun, indeed, with all the luminaries of heaven." This is an obvious misinterpretation of Milton, who distinctly says that the sun did not exist on the first day when light was created but was formed on the fourth day, when the light was transferred to its sphere. Misinterpretation of Milton will not convince us that he "used Rashi's commentary to a very great extent."

Here we may notice Milton's apostrophe to light, although it is not a part of his account of creation. Part of the beautiful passage follows:

> Hail holy light, ofspring of Heav'n first-born,
> Or of th' Eternal Coeternal beam
> May I express thee unblam'd? since God is light,
> And never but in unapproached light
> Dwelt from Eternitie, dwelt then in thee,
> Bright effluence of bright essence increase.[58]

In accounts of creation praise of light is common. Observe the following excerpt from Raleigh's *History:*

Surely, if this Light be not spiritual, yet it approacheth nearest unto spirituality; and if it have any corporality, then of all other the most subtle and pure; for howsoever, it is of all things seen, the most beautiful, and of the swiftest motion, of all other the most necessary and beneficial. For it ministreth unto man, and other creatures all celestial influences; it dissipateth those sad thoughts and sorrows, which the darkness both begetteth and maintaineth; it discovereth unto us the glorious works of God, and carrieth up with an angelical swiftness, our eyes unto Heaven, that by the

[57] Fletcher, *op. cit.*, p. 149.   [58] III, 1-6.

sight thereof, our minds being informed of his visible marvels, may continually travel to surmount these perceived Heavens, and to find out their omnipotent Cause and Creator.

Lastly, If we may behold in any creature, any one spark of that eternal fire, or any far-off dawning of Gods glorious brightness, the same in the beauty, motion, and virtue of this Light, may be perceived. Therefore was God called *Lux ipsa*; and the Light, by *Hermes*, named *Lux sancta;* and Christ our Saviour said to be *that Light which lightneth every man that cometh into the world.*[59]

Recall also Purchas's eulogy of light:

Even this light is more then admirable; life of the Earth, ornament of the Heavens, beautie and smile of the World, eye to our Eyes, ioy of our Hearts: most common, pure and perfect of visible creatures; first borne of this World, and endowed with a double portion of earthly and heavenly Inheritance, shining in both; which contayneth, sustayneth, gathereth, severeth, purgeth, perfecteth, renueth, and preserveth all things; repelling dread, expelling sorrows, *Shaking the wicked out of the Earth*, and lifting up the hearts of the godly to looke for a greater and more glorious light; greatest instrument of Nature, resemblance of Grace, Type of Glorie, and bright Glasse of the Creators brightnesse.[60]

Milton's lines, a supremely beautiful and poignant expression of the blind poet's longing for light, are a remarkable adaptation of conventional material to his individual need. Eulogy of light is a commonplace; eulogy of it by a blind poet holds an unrivaled pathos.

Recall now Milton's description of the Firmament:

> Again, God said, let ther be Firmament
> Amid the Waters, and let it divide
> The Waters from the Waters: and God made
> The Firmament, expanse of liquid, pure,
> Transparent, Elemental Air, diffus'd
> In circuit to the uttermost convex
> Of this great Round: partition firm and sure,
> The Waters underneath from those above
> Dividing. . . .[61]

[59] P. 6.
[60] Pp. 7-8.
[61] VII, 261-269.

Similar is Raleigh's description of the Firmament:

For the waters above the firmament, are the waters in the Ayr above us, where the same is more solid and condense, which God separated from the neather waters by a firmament, that is, by an extended distance and vast space: the words *Raquia* . . . and *Shamajim*, being indifferently taken for the Heaven and for Ayr, . . . and the waters above the firmament, exprest in the word *Majim*, are in that tongue taken properly for the waters above the Ayr, or in the uppermost Region of the same.[62]

Purchas explains that the Firmament is an *expansum*, a stretching out, a vast and wide space, filled with watery clouds and lights, a region of air separating the upper from the lower waters.[63] In the *Conjectura Cabbalistica* the Firmament is explained as a firm and transparent partition, a diaphanous canopy, stretched like a tent over the whole pavement of the earth.[64] As is stated in Newton's edition of *Paradise Lost*, the Firmament is called a "partition firm and sure" for "its certainty not solidity."[65] Endeavoring to relate Milton's Crystalline Sphere to Ben Gerson's Heavens, Mr. Fletcher declares that Milton's " 'expanse of liquid, pure' was made up of the waters, which were stiffened, at the same time forming a firm partition between the Universe and Chaos," and explains that Milton's "statement describing the extent of this sphere of waters implied the uttermost limits of the Visible Universe. Thus, the Firmament marked the farthest extent of the Cosmos as Milton thought of it."[66] This explanation, it seems, confuses Milton's Firmament with his Crystalline Ocean. The Firmament, as Milton and Raleigh explain, is air; the Crystalline Ocean is water, and is not stiffened. Raleigh, who discards the traditional Crystalline Heavens, explains Milton's Crystalline Ocean: "But these waters, separate above this Extension, which the Latine Translation calleth *firmamentum*, or *expansum* . . . are not the Crystalline Heavens created in the imaginations of men . . . for my self, I am perswaded, that the waters

[62] P. 7.
[63] *Pilgrimage*, p. 8.
[64] P. 3.
[65] II, 28.
[66] *Op. cit.*, p. 135.

called, The waters above the Heavens, are but the Clouds and waters engendred in the uppermost Air." Again we observe that there is no analogy with rabbinical commentary when Milton's lines are correctly interpreted.

In his statement of the continuity of life—of the *scala naturae,* the principle of which was first suggested by Aristotle and which with its characteristic Plotinian definition became the "essential conception of the Neoplatonic cosmology" and was accepted by many philosophers and indeed by nearly all educated men "through the Middle Ages and down to the late eighteenth century"[67]—Milton rejects most emphatically the dualism of orthodox Christian theology. The complete passage presenting the scale follows:

> O *Adam,* one Almightie is, from whom
> All things proceed, and up to him return,
> If not deprav'd from good, created all
> Such to perfection, one first matter all,
> Indu'd with various forms, various degrees
> Of substance, and in things that live, of life;
> But more refin'd, more spirituous, and pure,
> As neerer to him plac't or neerer tending
> Each in thir several active Sphears assignd,
> Till body up to spirit work, in bounds
> Proportiond to each kind. So from the root
> Springs lighter the green stalk, from thence the leaves
> More aerie, last the bright consummate floure
> Spirits odorous breathes: flours and thir fruit
> Mans nourishment, by gradual scale sublim'd
> To vital Spirits aspire, to animal,
> To intellectual, give both life and sense,
> Fansie and understanding, whence the soule
> Reason receives, and reason is her being,
> Discursive, or Intuitive: . . . .
> . . . . time may come when men
> With Angels may participate, and find
> No inconvenient Diet, nor too light Fare:
> And from these corporal nutriments perhaps

[67] Arthur O. Lovejoy, *The Great Chain of Being* (Cambridge, 1936), pp. 55, 59, 63, *passim.*

Your bodies may at last turn all to Spirit,
Improv'd by tract of time, and wingd ascend
Ethereal, as wee, or may at choice
Here or in Heav'nly Paradises dwell; [68]

And, plainly relying on the Platonic idea of patterns, Milton suggests that earth may be but the shadow of heaven and "Each to other like, more then on earth is thought." This scale, linking the Other-World and This-World of Plato in an unbroken series, is also found in Mercator's account of creation, including the figure of the plant or tree, which from root to flower symbolizes the range of life:

In summe, if any man will search more diligently the order of things, and consider the communion and difference of *species*, he will perceive that the creation of things (beginning with the more base and ignoble *species*) so almost ascended upward, as the tree hath at first but onely a trunke, wherein all things which are from the roote to the very top, are but one and the same thing by the communion of species, every one of the parts in the meane time having their veines therein: but when they begin to have any difference among themselves, the first division of the trunk is made into branches, after . . . is made the second division, and so consequently untill wee come to the last branches and fruits. So the *Chaos* is the onely trunk of all the species to bee created, having his roote and beginning in the universall Idea, Creatrix, which is the minde and divine will. . . . Furthermore, as this universall Idea, . . . by the division of the species into their determinate number and forme, ascending by little and little, doth divide it selfe, so of one simple species of Chaos without forme, the difference of species by little and little do arise, . . . But that is to be remembered, that those things which are of a more high degree are more slowly perfected. [69]

Notice especially the following excerpt:

Seeing then they were most wisely created for the use and service of man, as well in the superiour, as in the inferiour world, what a faire harmony was there then? when the lower things did accord with the highest; and expected help from them; and the highest communicated their gifts to the lowest, and all things served man,

[68] V, 469-500. See also V, 414-426. [69] P. 22.

untill he should be translated of God into his heavenly habitation. This correspondencie, this beautie of state had continued inviolable, if Adam had not sinned. . . .[70]

According to the *Atlas*, original virtue was not wholly destroyed by Adam's sin. There are yet in the world "the reliques of that matter, of which the celestiall and supercelestiall things were created" and a natural sympathy between the higher and the lower world. In man the rational soul is the image of the divine essence. In this condition man still may hope for salvation.

Dismissing for the present the succeeding days, some of the details of which will be discussed in the following chapter, we come to the crowning work of all, the creation of man, who, endowed with reason and guarded by the Deity, was in Milton's age undwarfed by cosmic immensity and unenslaved by mechanical forces. Made of the dust of the ground and in the image of God, who breathed into his nostrils the breath of life, man became "a living Soul." This is apparently the traditional account, which, however, acquires added significance in the light of the explanation in *De Doctrina Christiana* that the soul is created with the body, that the whole man is soul and the soul is man. In the *Atlas* it is explained that even the spirit of man is extracted out of the first matter. The evolution of man epitomizes the entire order of creation. The soul is engendered by the parents, but as the most noble quality is the last perfected. On the other hand, Raleigh accepts the orthodox point of view: "Into this frame and carcasse God breathed the breath of life; and the man was a living soule: (that is) God gave to a Bodie of earth and of corruptible matter, a Soule Spirituall and incorruptible; . . . this Spirit, which God breathed into man, which is the reasonable soule of man, returneth againe to God that gave it, as the body returneth unto the earth, out of which it was taken, according to *Ecclesiastes*. . . ."[71] Purchas, who says that in the creation of man God showed "his counsaile and wisdome most appar-

[70] P. 25.   [71] P. 16.

ently," explains that man was created by the Trinity and adds: "The manner of his working was also in this Creature, singular; both in regard of his body, which, as a Potter his clay, hee wrought and framed of the dust into this goodly shape; and of his soule, which he immediately breathed into his nostrils."[72] Raleigh discusses at some length the phrase "Image and Similitude of God," so much disputed among the Fathers and later writers. He emphasizes man's reason, quoting St. Augustine to the effect that "man that is endued with right reason is said to resemble God," and that "God made man in respect of the intellect after his own image and similitude." With an imposing array of authorities he explains *Mens*, which is the faculty or gift of God, that divine understanding which although not of the essence of God's understanding is "illuminated by the true and eternal light." Purchas also emphasizes man's primary wisdom. In respect to gifts and natural endowments, the soul received directly from God "a Diuine impression, and Character, in that knowledge, whereby she measureth the heauens, bringeth them to the earth, lifteth up the earth to heauen, mounteth aboue the heauens to behold the Angels, piercheth the center of the earth in darkenesse, to discerne the infernall Regions and Legions, beneath and aboue them all, searcheth into the diuine Nature. . . ."[73] Without study, Adam was the greatest philosopher and the greatest divine (except the second Adam) "that euer the earth bare." It has been said that "Rashi's discussion of Adam's intelligence before the Fall, becomes in *Paradise Lost* one of the most important ideas of the whole medial portion of the epic."[74] But, as Mr. Taylor has pointed out, Adam's unique mental endowment was emphasized by many writers. Du Bartas writes of Adam's busy intellect, of his "mature and settled Sapience." Adam's sin was due not to ignorance but to disobedience; his will was not subject to God.

Our three authorities also hold that in the original state man's will was free.[75] Before the Fall, says Purchas, the will

[72] Pp. 15-16.   [73] P. 16.   [74] Fletcher, *op. cit.*, p. 207.
[75] Mr. Taylor's references (*op. cit.*, p. 20) show that this opinion was widespread.

"in the free choice of the best things, in righteous disposition towards man, and true holinesse towards God" was obedient to God. Raleigh explains that God's foreknowledge is not a cause, that it does not impose any necessity. In creation God gave man "a free and unconstrained will" with the free choice of all things save one. "God set before him, a mortal and immortal life, . . . God gave man to himself, to be his own Guide, his own Workman, and his own Painter, that he might frame or describe unto himself what he pleased, and make election of his own form. *God made man in the beginning,* (saith *Siracides*) *and left him in the hands of his own counsel.*" Mercator's *Atlas* thus justifies the ways of God to man:

Life and death are offered unto man, good and evil which he pleaseth shall be given unto him . . . God did all things well and like a Father. It was his favour, that man was adorned with such excellent gifts of minde, that he might easily obey so small a commandement, and man of right ought to have been thankfull for so great gifts by obeying his creatour. He could therefore as Ecclesiasticus saith, have stoode if he would, but that he fell it was the fault of himselfe, not of God predestinating or willing; for God had created all things very good, and Fatherly ordred them.[76]

As God foresaw, Adam sinned; and then, lest so wise a creation should be in vain, it pleased God through Christ to repair the Fall of man. God therefore "so finished the creation of all things, that in both estates, of obedience, and the fall, he preserved for man the meanes to obtaine eternall life, so that nothing was made of God in vaine, onely the death of the flesh remained, which was due to originall sinne, untill that was taken away from man altogether, and he being wholly pure, as he was created, might come to God, according to the end wherefore he was created."

Review and analysis of typical examples of the contemporary literary background of Milton's account of creation enable us not only to test the claims of specific indebtednesses but also to show, as Mr. Tillyard has recently stated,[77] that Milton

[76] Pp. 29-30.

[77] "Milton and the English Epic Tradition," *Seventeenth Century Studies* (Oxford, 1938), pp. 211 ff.

was not isolated from his age. It is clear that Milton's profoundly religious story includes many points present in the predominantly orthodox accounts of Danaeus, Du Bartas, Purchas, More, and Raleigh but that Milton's narrative asserts its individuality, which is a matter of substance as well as of style. In his emphasis upon a divine life force, an existing chaos, the virtue of matter, and the interrelation of all life (including the soul of man), Milton agrees most intimately with the account of creation in Mercator's *Atlas*. It is not, however, urged that Milton was specifically indebted to Mercator. His relation to contemporary thought is an extraordinarily complicated one that persistently evades dogmatic description and definition. Whatever his specific indebtednesses were—and perhaps it would have been difficult for Milton himself to indicate some of these—it is obvious that his account of creation curiously blends the Neoplatonic and the Christian. As has been said, Milton's God is Plato's Self-Sufficing Perfection and his Self-Transcending Fecundity. Through the Demiurge, his Son, Plato's Timeless and Incorporeal One (not the orthodox Trinity) becomes, without necessity, the source of the universe which is temporal, beautiful, and, before sin, beneficent. Dealing with traditional religious material, Milton preserved the general features of the Mosaic narrative but enriched them with literary allusions and philosophical ideas that were fundamental in his culture. There are, as has recently been remarked,[78] cross-currents and strains in the epic resulting from the conflict between Milton's essential humanistic temper and his sense of God's arbitrariness. Thus, as is entirely natural, his account of creation is typical of his mind and of the transitional period in which he lived. Not Oreb or Sinai or the Aonian Mount or any other one locale was the haunt of Milton's Muse.

[78] Lovejoy, *op. cit.*, pp. 160 ff.

CHAPTER II

THREE HISTORIES OF THE WORLD

MILTON, who was no pedant, gave to those critics intent upon discovering the precise sources of his poetry little direct aid. Except for his *Commonplace Book* and occasional references in his prose, he left no definite account of his literary background. If he had written for *Paradise Lost* such elaborate and learned notes as those with which Abraham Cowley equipped his *Davideis,* he might have anticipated or invalidated the labors of modern scholars. Emulating Cowley, Milton might by the example of Homer and Virgil have justified the use of invocation and hyperbole; he might have cited his authorities for making Beelzebub one of the chief devils, referred to Diodorus Siculus's description of Babylon, declared that according to Aristotle winds are an exhalation from the earth, that according to the ancients stars were nourished by vapors from the sea, that witches by muttering charms caused eclipses of the moon, that all ages have had hard opinions of comets, which cause drought, pestilence, and wars. He might have explained that Rabba was the metropolis of the Ammonites; that the river Arnon, which discharges into the Dead Sea, rises in the land of the Amorites; that Esebon was a famous strong city twenty miles from the Jordan; that Nebo was a part of the mountain Abarim in the land of Moab; that Ophir was a country in the East Indies, which Josephus and Jerome call the Golden Country; that Moloch, the God of the Ammonites, was, according to Arias Montanus, Mercury, or more probably, according to Macrobius and Diodorus Siculus, Saturn; that Astarte was Venus Urania, the moon, to whom men sacrificed in the habit of women and women in the habit of men; that the Ethiopians worshiped two calves, Apis and

Mnevis, the one dedicated to Osiris (the sun) and the other to Isis (the moon); that the purple of the ancients was taken from the shell-fish Purpura, whose blood, according to Pliny, yields the true purple, and that the greatest fishing for these Purples was at Tyre; that it was great pity that Josephus, who said he saw it, did not describe the statue of Lot's wife; that the stones in Samuel's breastplate, disposed as God appointed, were Urim and Thummim or Truth and its Manifestation; that Gabriel is the minister of God's mercies and Michael of his justice; and so on *ad infinitum*. But Milton, not choosing to rival Cowley's learning, left the explanation of his poems to scholars, some of whom in the name of scholarship have rendered him rather dubious service. Because *Paradise Lost* deals with a common theme and embodies conventional material, some critics, from Voltaire and Lauder to the most recent, have maintained that Milton, if not an outright plagiarist, was very heavily indebted to certain predecessors. We might do well to bear in mind Newton's reply to the charge that Milton had borrowed freely from Marsenius and other modern authors:

it is all a pretence, he made use of all authors, such was his learning; but such is his genius, he is no copyer, his poem is plainly an original, if ever there was one. His subject indeed of the fall of Man together with the principal episodes may be said to be as old as Scripture, but his manner of handling them is entirely new, with new illustrations and new beauties of his own; and he may as justly boast of the novelty of his poem, as any of the ancient poets bestow that recommendation upon their works . . . [1]

Ignoring Milton's boast that in his major epic he pursues "Things unattempted yet in Prose or Rhime," some investigators, intent upon specific sources, have minimized Milton's use of other material and in particular the information available in certain universal histories.

In his preface to *Gondibert* (1651), Sir William Davenant, pleading the cause of the poet against those who would fetter him in the shackles of an historian, asks, "For why should a

[1] *Paradise Lost* (London, 1749), I, 8.

Poet doubt in story to mend the intrigues of Fortune by some delightfull conveyances of probable fictions, because austere Historians have enter'd into bond to truth?" Davenant declares that truth "narrative and past, is the Idol of Historians, (who worship a dead thing) and truth operative, and by effects continually alive, is the Mistress of Poets, who hath not her existence in matter, but in Reason."[2] In his answer to this preface, Hobbes supports Davenant's thesis. Although he protests against the exorbitancy of fiction (impenetrable armor, enchanted castles, flying horses, and so on), he lays down the principle that "as truth is the bond of the Historical, so the Resemblance of truth is the utmost limit of Poetical Liberty. . . . Beyond the actual works of Nature a Poet may now go; but beyond the conceived possibility of Nature, never."[3] Doubtless Milton subscribed wholeheartedly to the doctrine that the poet is free from the strict rules of historians, that in the interest of beauty and vital truth he may venture beyond the bounds of historical fact; but clearly he also believed that the subject of *Paradise Lost* prescribed certain limitations of the fancy and a decent regard for philosophical and natural truth, as it was then understood. To achieve objectivity, beauty, and interest in his elaboration of the epic, Milton, it seems probable, recalled part of the rich body of material available in certain universal histories, which, to be sure, embody a large amount of pure fancy and speculation. As Raleigh, quoting Diodorus, writes: *"Nam in Priscis rebus Veritas non ad Unguem querenda. In Ancient Things we are not to require an exact Narration of the Truth."*[4]

Many editors of Milton have, of course, included references to these histories. In Newton's edition, Pliny is cited in connection with the justling rocks of Bosporus, the Assyrian mount, the Sabean odors of Arabia, Egyptian Thebes, the serpent's love of fennel and goat's milk, the Cronian sea, and strange serpents. In addition to these, Verity cites Pliny with reference to the Pyramids, the moon's being affected by magic,

---

[2] *Op. cit.*, p. 10.
[3] *Op. cit.*, p. 59.   [4] *History of the World*, p. 238.

the griffins and the Arimaspians, the Phoenix, the migrations
of birds, the Garden of Adonis, the fig tree in India, and ravenous fowl. Newton refers to Raleigh and Pliny in connection
with the Nyseian isle. Verity refers to Diodorus in connection
with the Serbonian bog. Later editors add a few other references. In Gilbert's valuable *Geographical Dictionary* there are
references to and some quotations from Diodorus and Pliny.
As a summary of and a supplement to these guides it seems
desirable in this chapter to assemble relevant information from
these histories, which may be regarded not primarily as sources
but as background of Milton's poetry.

Milton was not yet six when, in March, 1614, one of the
most famous books of the seventeenth century was published.
The work was *The History of the World;* the author, Sir
Walter Raleigh, then languished in the Tower under sus-
pended sentence of death. The immediate and prolonged success of the *History* is in sharp contrast with the almost complete neglect of it today: ten editions appeared between 1614
and 1687; two continuations and three abridgments were issued; scholars esteemed it an authority and critics praised its
style.[5] By a host of illustrious persons and by the general
public it was enthusiastically hailed as a classic. Dr. Peter
Heylyn called it "Primus in Historia"; it is said to have been
Cromwell's favorite book. It was especially valued because
of the theological spirit of the work and because of Raleigh's
fame as a martyr. Smarting under Stuart misgovernment, the
seventeenth century "revered the name of Ralegh (himself the
victim of a Stuart) as the champion and martyr of national
liberty."[6] Puritans found in the *History* abundant examples
of the Puritan doctrine that history illustrates the working of
divine Providence. Although Raleigh took account of second
causes, his fundamental thesis is this: "For it is God, that only

[5] Charles H. Firth, "Sir Walter Raleigh's *History of the World*," *Proceedings of the British Academy 1917-1918*, p. 431; Sir Charles Firth, *Essays
Historical and Literary* (Oxford, 1938), pp. 50-51.
[6] *The Discoverie of the large and bewtiful Empire of Guiana By Sir
Walter Ralegh*, ed. V. T. Harlow (1928), pp. xvi-xvii.

disposeth of all things according to his own Will, and maketh of one Earth, *Vessels of Honour and Dishonour.*"

Besides the probability that as a Puritan and man of letters Milton would have been acquainted with this famous *History,* two proofs of his interest in Raleigh should be recorded. In his *Commonplace Book,* under "De Matrimonio," Milton entered the statement of "Sir Walter Raughleigh" regarding the Christian attempt to enforce monogamy in the Congo.[7] In 1658, Raleigh's *Cabinet-Council* was published by Milton, with the following statement:

Having had the *Manuscript* of this *Treatise,* Written by Sir *Walter Raleigh,* many years in my hands, and finding it lately by chance among other Books and Papers, upon reading thereof, I thought it a kinde of injury to withhold longer the work of so eminent an Author from the Publick; it being both answerable in Stile to other Works of his already Extant, as far as the subject would permit, and given me for a true Copy by a Learned Man at his Death, who had collected several such peices.   John Milton.

Relying on a comparison of the writings of the two men, some critics believe that Raleigh's influence upon Milton was considerable. Sir Charles H. Firth suggests a comparison of the site and the topography of Paradise in *Paradise Lost* with the relevant chapters in the *History* and declares that the first map in the *History* would form an admirable illustration of Milton's epic.[8] Others think that behind Milton's description of Eden "shakes also the remembered tapestry of Ralegh's pictures of the kindly plains of Guiana" and that the "Gilded Man had an apotheosis in the Shining Ones who inhabited a City more splendid than Manoa."[9] Mr. Edward Thompson asserts that the real proof of Raleigh's influence upon Milton "lies in the cadence, the mingling of imagination and of personal pathos."[10] In the first chapter of the present work are noted certain resemblances between Raleigh's and Milton's accounts of creation. A somewhat more thorough comparison of

[7] P. 18.   [8] *Proceedings,* p. 440; *Essays,* p. 52.
[9] "Sir Walter Ralegh's Prose," *The Times Literary Supplement,* January 31, 1935, pp. 53-54.
[10] *Sir Walter Ralegh* (London, 1935), p. 236.

FRONTISPIECE FROM SIR WALTER RALEIGH'S
HISTORY OF THE WORLD

the *History* and *Paradise Lost* would seem to promise interesting and valuable results. Realizing that Milton's reading
was very thorough, that he and Raleigh drew upon a common
fund of information, and that many things may be credited to
the poet's imagination, I do not argue that every illustration
cited below is proof of direct relationship between the *History*
and the epic. It is merely suggested that the evidence on
the whole shows that the *History* may be one of the quarries
from which Milton derived some of the material for his masterpiece.

In Raleigh's *History* there is much conventional material
analogous to that in *Paradise Lost*, and the temper of mind
and the general attitude revealed in Raleigh's and Milton's
works have a good deal in common. Consider, for example,
the following passage in the *History*, in which denunciation of
ambition is linked with the theme of *Paradise Lost:*

Such is Humane Ambition, a Monster that neither feareth God
(though all powerful, and whose Revenges are without Date and
for Everlasting) neither hath it respect to Nature, which laboureth
the Preservation of every Being; but it rageth also against her,
though garnished with Beauty that never dyeth, and with Love that
hath no end. All other Passions and Affections by which the
Souls of Men are tormented, are by their Contraries oftentimes
resisted or qualified. But Ambition, which begetteth every Vice,
and is it self the Child and Darling of *Satan*, looketh only towards
the ends by it self set down, forgetting nothing (how fearful and
inhumane soever) which may serve it; remembring nothing, whatsoever Justice, Piety, Right or Religion can offer and alledge to
the contrary. It ascribeth the lamentable effects of the like attempts, to the errour or weakness of the Undertakers, and rather
praiseth the Adventure than feareth the like success. It was the
first Sin that the World had, and began in Angels, for which they
were cast into Hell, without hope of Redemption. It was more
ancient than Man, and therefore no part of his natural Corruption. The Punishment also preceded his Creation, yet hath the
Devil which felt the smart thereof, taught him to forget the one,
as out of date, and to practise the other, as befitting every Age,
and Mans Condition.[11]

[11] *The History of the World* (London, 1687), p. 246.

The theme, which is of course conventional, is fundamental in *Paradise Lost*. Ambition is the darling sin of Satan, who

> with ambitious aim
> Against the Throne and Monarchy of God
> Rais'd impious War in Heav'n and Battel proud
> With vain attempt.[12]

By inciting in Eve an ambitious desire for knowledge such as angels have, Satan persuades her to violate God's command. Milton leaves no doubt as to his contempt for epics celebrating the ambitious deeds of men:

> Not sedulous by Nature to indite
> Warrs, hitherto the onely Argument
> Heroic deem'd, chief maistrie to dissect
> With long and tedious havoc fabl'd Knights
> In Battels feign'd; the better fortitude
> Of Patience and Heroic Martyrdom
> Unsung.[13]

As Michael explains, the highest reach of glory in the world, which is

> To good malignant, to bad men benigne,

will be

> to be styl'd great Conquerours,
> Patrons of Mankind, Gods, and Sons of Gods,
> Destroyers rightlier call'd and Plagues of men.
> Thus Fame shall be achiev'd, renown on Earth,
> And what most merits fame in silence hid.[14]

Although one would hesitate to say that Milton was indebted to the passage quoted from the *History*, there is great probability that he had read it and that he was impressed by its powerful and grave eloquence.

Consider also in the *History* the orthodox statements regarding fortune and necessity. Destiny is obedient to God's providence. Fortune or chance is the god of fools. That which seems the most casual and accidental "is yet disposed by the

[12] I, 41-44.
[13] IX, 27-33.   [14] XI, 691-695.

ordinance of God." To the incomprehensible wisdom which we call God the philosophers sometimes "gave the title of Necessity or Fate, because it bindeth by inevitable ordinance." With this compare Milton's entire conception of God's omnipotence and in particular the following lines:

Necessitie and Chance
Approach not mee, and what I will is Fate.[15]

But, as already indicated, neither Raleigh nor Milton literally accepts the concluding statement. They both reject foreordination. They both declare that the will of man is free or was free in the original state of innocence. Raleigh insists that in his creation man had from God "a free and unconstrained will." I do not need to remind the reader that the free will of man is the cornerstone of Milton's justification of God. Milton certainly approved Raleigh's comments on the temptation and the fall. Adam was "betrayed and mastered by his affections" (Milton uses the word *passion*) and scarcely looked into "the miseries and sorrows incident" to his disobedience. Satan made use of "the unquiet vanity of the Woman." Because Adam hearkened to the voice of his wife "contrary to the express commandment of the living God, Mankind by that her incantation became the subject of labour, sorrow, and death: the Woman being given to Man for a comforter and companion, but not for a Counsellor."[16] Adam yielded to Eve's persuasion for the same reason "which hath moved all Men since to the like consent, namely an unwillingness to grieve her and make her sad, lest she should pine and be overcome with sorrow." In *Paradise Lost* Adam and Eve are equally human. There also Eve, "opportune to all attempts," was betrayed by her vanity and the Serpent's glozing arguments; and Adam, drawn by the bond of nature and unable to forego sweet converse with his beloved wife, did not scruple against his better judgment to eat the forbidden fruit. In short, Man's fall was not the result of God's decree; it was the consequence of his own frailty, of his violation of God's law.

[15] VII, 172-173.   [16] *Op. cit.*, p. 39.

In his discussion of fate, Raleigh refers to the ancient belief in astral influence, which, according to him, is dependent upon God's purposes. Although we do not know the precise workings of the celestial bodies, Raleigh is fully convinced that the stars have decided effects:

And certainly it cannot be doubted, but the Starrs are instruments of far greater use, than to give an obscure light, and for men to gaze on after Sunset: it being manifest, that the diversity of seasons, the Winters, and Summers, more hot and cold, are not so uncertained by the Sun and Moon alone, who alway keep one and the same course; but the Stars have also their working therein.[17]

If, as we cannot deny, God gives virtues to springs and fountains, to plants, stones, and minerals, "why should we rob the beautiful Stars of their working powers?" Just as every herb, fruit, and flower adorning the face of the earth has its peculiar virtue and was not created merely to beautify the earth and "to cover and shadow her dusty face," so were these uncountable and glorious heavenly bodies created, not merely to adorn the firmament, but for "instruments and Organs of his divine Providence, so far as it hath pleased his just will to determine." With this may be compared Adam's answer to Eve's question, "Why do the stars shine when we sleep?" Adam explains that the stars have to finish their courses and to guard against the return of total darkness, lest it

> extinguish life
> In Nature and all things, which these soft fires
> Not only enlighten, but with kindly heate
> Of various influence foment and warme,
> Temper or nourish, or in part shed down
> Their stellar vertue on all kinds that grow
> On Earth, made hereby apter to receive
> Perfection from the Suns more potent Ray.[18]

There is a marked resemblance here, which may, of course, be due not to any literary influence at all, but merely to the fact that Raleigh and Milton shared the belief in a mild form of astrology.

[17] *Op. cit.*, p. 8.   [18] IV, 666-673.

From these important but general resemblances turn now to more specific ones and first, as Sir Charles H. Firth suggests, to the boundaries and descriptions of Eden and Paradise. According to Milton, Paradise was planted in the east of Eden, which

> stretchd her Line
> From *Auran* Eastward to the Royal Towrs
> Of Great *Seleucia*, built by *Grecian* Kings,
> Or where the Sons of *Eden* long before
> Dwelt in *Telassar*.[19]

The site of Paradise was much disputed. For example, Purchas, who reproduces Mercator's map of Paradise, summarizes various interpretations and says, "Now the place cannot bee found in Earth, but is become a common place in men's brains, to macerate and vexe them in the curious search hereof."[20] Purchas locates Paradise in that part of Babylonia which Ptolemy called Auranitis or Audanitis, a site that is illustrated in several contemporary Bibles, as will be explained in the next chapter. Raleigh, insisting that "the Seat of Paradise is greatly mistaken" and that even the Fathers of the Church have erred therein, recites and rejects a number of strange opinions: that Paradise had merely an allegorical sense; that it was the whole earth; that it was under the Equinoctial Line; that it was in some high and remote region of the air. Meeting the objection that it is needless and "a kind of curiosity to enquire so diligently after this place of *Paradise*," Raleigh declares that the truth of the story is confirmed by the evidence that the terrestrial Paradise was an actual, determinate place, plainly described by Moses and the Prophets and defined "by the Kingdoms and Provinces bordering it, by the Rivers which watered it, and by the Points of the Compass upon which it lay."[21] Because of the fertility of the soil, of the many beautiful rivers, and the trees that never shed their leaves, the general region was called Eden, "which signifieth in the *Hebrew*, Pleasantness, or delicacy." As "Florida" signifies "flour-

[19] IV, 210-214.
[20] *Pilgrimage*, p. 15.   [21] *Op. cit.*, p. 19.

ishing," so "Eden" signifies "pleasure"; both are the proper names of countries.

Describing the general situation and the unrivaled fertility of Eden, Raleigh writes:

the Region of *Eden*, in which *Paradise* was, lay Eastward from *Judea* and *Canaan*: for the Scriptures always called the people of those Nations, the Sons of the East which inhabited *Arabia, Mesopotamia, Chaldea,* and *Persia*: of which *Ovid,*

> Eurus ad Auroram, Nabathaeaq: regna recessit,
> Persidaque, & radiis juga subdita matutinis.

> The East wind with Aurora hath abiding
> Among th' Arabian and the Persian Hills,
> Whom Phoebus first salutes at his first rising.

From the Scriptural Paradise are derived Homer's Gardens of Alcinous, the Elysian Fields of the Greeks, and the Golden Age, described by Ovid:

> Ver erat aeternum; placidique tepentibus auris,
> Mulcebant Zephiri natos sine semine flores.

> The joyful Spring did ever last,
>   And Zephyrus did breed
> Sweet flowers by his gentle blast,
> Without the help of Seed.[22]

With this compare Milton:

>   aires, vernal aires,
> Breathing the smell of field and grove, attune
> The trembling leaves, while Universal *Pan*
> Knit with the *Graces* and the *Hours* in dance
> Led on th' Eternal Spring.[23]

To illustrate the fertility of the Babylonian soil, the site of Paradise, Raleigh quotes Herodotus, whom he translates thus:

Where Euphrates runneth out into Tigris, not far from the place where Ninus is seated; This Region, of all that we have seen, is most excellent. . . . It is so fruitful in bringing forth Corn, that it yieldeth two hundred fold: the Leaves of Wheat and Barley be-

[22] *Op. cit.*, p. 21.   [23] IV, 264-268.

ing almost four fingers broad: As for the height of Millet and
Sesam, they are even in length like unto Trees, which although
I know to be true, yet I forbear to speak hereof, well knowing,
that those things which are reported of this fruitfulness, will seem
very incredible to those, which never were in the Country of Babylon.[24]

Here palm trees grow of their own accord, and from their
fruits are made "both Meats, and Wine, and Hony." The
palm tree also yields bread and "a kind of fine Flax, of which
People make their Garments." In upper Babylon, "or Region
of *Eden*," these trees are as common as any trees of the field.
"*Sunt etiam* (saith *Strabo*) *passim per omnem regionem
Palmae sua sponte nascentes.* There are of Palms over all the
whole Region, growing of their own accord." To this Raleigh adds the description of Quintus Curtius:

As you travel on the left hand of Arabia (famous for plenty of
sweet Odors) there lieth a Champain Country placed between
Tigris and Euphrates, and so fruitful and fat a Soil, that they are
said to drive their Cattel from the Pasture, lest they should perish
by satiety.

Of the south part of Armenia, which is "the North border of
Eden, or a part thereof," Strabo writes:

Tota enim haec regio frugibus & arboribus abundat mansuetis,
itemque semper virentibus: This Region aboundeth with pleasant
Fruits, and Trees always green.

This, says Raleigh, "witnesseth a perpetual Spring, not found
elsewhere but in the *Indies* only." After much discussion he
concludes:

What other excellencies this Garden of *Paradise* had, before God,
(for mans ingratitude and cruelty) cursed the Earth, we cannot
judge; but I may safely think that by how much *Adam* exceeded
all living Men in perfection, by being the immediate workmanship
of God, by so much did that chosen and particular Garden exceed
all parts of the universal World, in which God had planted (that
is) made to grow the Trees, of Life, of Knowledge; Plants only

[24] *Op. cit.,* p. 31.

proper, and becoming the *Paradise,* and Garden of so great a
Lord. [25]

Probably the richness of Milton's Paradise owes something
to the copious details in Raleigh's full account, which is composed of material drawn from many sources; but Raleigh's extended exposition completely fails to achieve the artistic unity
and the objectivity of Milton's superb word picture.

Not satisfied with a general description of the region, Raleigh labors to determine the precise site of Eden and Paradise.
The following quotations are selected from Raleigh's long discussion of the approximate boundaries of Eden:

But because *Eden* is by *Moses* named by it self, and by the fertility, and the Rivers only described, we must seek it in other Scriptures [than *Genesis*], and where it is by the additions of the
neighbour Nations better described.   In the Prophet *Isaiah* I find
it coupled and accompanied with other adjacent Countries, in these
words spoken in the person of *Senacherib* by *Rabsakeh.   Have the
Gods of the Nations delivered them, which my Fathers have destroyed, as Gosan and Haran and Reseph, and the children of
Eden, which were at Telassar?* and in *Ezekiel,* where he prophe-
sieth against the *Tyrians: They of Haran and Canneh, and Eden,
the Merchants of Sheba, Ashur, and Chilmad, were thy Merchants,* &c.

These passages from *Isaiah* and *Ezekiel,* which associate Eden
with other places, provide the starting point for the determination of its site. Raleigh proceeds:

Now to find out *Eden* . . . we must consider where those other
Countries are found, which the Prophet *Isaiah* and *Ezekiel* joyneth
with it.   For (saith *Isaiah) Gosan, Haran,* and *Reseph, and the
children of Eden, which were at Telassar.* Also *Ezekiel* joyneth
Haran with *Eden,* who together with those of *Sheba, Ashur,* and
Chilmad, were the Merchants that traded with the City of *Tyre,*
which was then (saith *Ezekiel) the Mart of the people for many
Isles.* . . .

Note the association of Haran with Eden and recall Milton's
phrase "From *Auran* Eastward," of which I shall have more to
say. Raleigh continues:

[25] *Op. cit.,* p. 36.

The better to convey these Commodities to that great Mart of *Tyre*, the *Shebans* or *Arabians* entred by the mouth of *Tigris*, and from the City of *Terredon* (. . . now called *Balsara*) thence sent up all these rich Merchandises by Boat to *Babylon*, from whence by the body of *Euphrates*, as far as it bendeth Westward, and afterward by a branch thereof, . . . and then over Land they past to *Tyre*. . . . Now the Merchants of *Canneh*, which *Ezekiel* joyneth with *Eden*, inhabited far up the River, and received this trade from *Arabia* and *India*, . . . S. *Hierome* understandeth by *Canneh*, *Seleucia*, which is seated upon *Euphrates*, where it breaketh into four heads, and which took that name from *Seleucus*, who made thereof a magnificient City. . . .

Observe that Canneh is here identified with Seleucia and recall Milton's lines

> From *Auran* Eastward to the Royal Towrs
> Of Great *Seleucia*, built by *Grecian* Kings,

which are closely related to the passages in the *History*. Let us follow Raleigh:

these people of *Canneh* [that is, Seleucia] . . . inhabited both borders of *Euphrates*, stretching themselves from their own City of *Canneh* in *Shinar* Westward along the banks of *Euphrates*, . . . Therefore those which take *Canneh* for *Charran* do much mistake it. For *Charran*, to which *Abraham* came from *Ur* in *Chaldaea* (called by God) standeth also in *Mesopotamia*, not upon *Euphrates* it self, but upon the River of *Chaboras*, which falleth into *Euphrates*: and the Merchants of *Charran* are distinctly named with those of *Canneh* in *Ezekiel*. . . . Wherefore *Charran* which is sometimes called *Charre*, and *Haran*, and *Aran*, is but the same *Charran* of *Mesopotamia*; and when it is written *Aran*, then it is taken for the Region of *Mesopotamia*: or *Aran fluviorum*, the *Greek* word *(Mesopotamia)* importing a Country between Rivers: . . . And when it is written *Haran* or *Aran*, it is then taken for the City it self, to which *Abraham* came from *Ur*. . . . Thus much of those Countries which border *Eden*, and who altogether traded with the *Tyrians*: of which, the chief were the *Edenites*, inhabiting *Telassar*. . . . For the South part of *Eden*, which stretcheth over *Euphrates*, was after the Floud called *Shiner*, and then, of the

Tower of *Babel*, *Babylonia*, and *Armenia*, which embraceth the banks of *Tygris* between Mount *Taurus*, and *Seleucia*.[26]

Notice that Charran, on the Chaboras, a branch of the Euphrates, is here identified with Haran or Aran, which are similar to Milton's Auran. The spelling varies; Milton, as frequently in other cases, probably chose a form that pleased him. Here Newton's note is of interest: "This province (in which the terrestrial Paradise was planted) extended from *Auran* or Haran or Charran or Charrae a city of Mesopotamia near the river Euphrates, extended, I say, from thence eastward to *Seleucia*, a city built by Seleucus one of the successors of Alexander the great, upon the river Tigris."[27] It has been maintained that Auran is Auranitis or Audanitis, which, says Purchas, is "easily declined from Heden (Eden) mentioned after Moses' time . . ."[28] and that it cannot be Hauran (Vulgate, *Auran*), a region in northeast Palestine, which is separated from Mesopotamia by a desert. Moreover, it is said, "there is no reason to suppose that Milton intended to make Eden of so great extent." On various contemporary maps, however, this region of Auranitis is much too far east to be the western limit of Milton's Eden, the boundaries of which are explained in some detail in Raleigh's *History*, and particularly defined in his "*Chorographical* Description of this terrestrial *Paradise*," which the reader should consult.

Recounting the story of the establishment of the first tyranny on earth, Milton writes that Nimrod, the first tyrant, "Marching from *Eden* towards the West," found a plain where he built the tower of Babel. Mr. Gilbert says that no source has been found for Milton's statement that Nimrod and his crew came from Eden.[29] Perhaps Raleigh is the source. Raleigh explains that Paradise was seated in the lower part of the Region of Eden afterwards called Aram fluviorum or Mesopotamia, of which Shinar is only one division.[30] Shinar is, indeed, only a small part of Eden, as was Paradise. The

---

[26] *Op. cit.*, pp. 26-29.
[27] *Paradise Lost*, I, 242.
[28] Gilbert, *Dictionary*, p. 40.
[29] *Ibid.*, p. 43.
[30] *Op. cit.*, p. 36.

entry into Paradise was from the east. Raleigh insists that Adam, after his expulsion from Paradise, and Cain inhabited toward the east: "*Cain* also in the same Region sought his dwelling-place," where he built the city of Enoch, "the first of the World." The Henochii, who took their name from the city Enoch, "inhabited due East from *Paradise*, and afterwards spred themselves Westward (as all *Noahs* Sons did that came into *Shinar*). . . ."[31] Contrary to most authorities, Raleigh stoutly maintains that the Ark rested, not on a mountain in Armenia, but on a high mountain far in the east.[32] Noah planted himself where he descended from the Ark, from which his sons migrated westward. Raleigh's account is consistent: Adam departed eastward from Paradise and there settled, probably not outside of the bounds of Eden; the Ark, after drifting but a short distance in the Flood, rested in the far east; Noah planted himself there, and thence some of his descendants moved westward, to build in Shinar the tower of Babel. To explain Milton's line, "Marching from *Eden* towards the West," we need merely to extend the bounds of Eden, of which Seleucia may not be considered the extreme eastern limit.

Consider briefly the two famous trees of Paradise. They were not imaginary. Raleigh says:

That these Trees of Life and Knowledge were material Trees (though Figures of the Law and of the Gospel) it is not doubted by the most religious and learned Writers: although the wits of men, which are so volatile, as nothing can fix them, and so slippery, as nothing can fasten them, have in this also delivered to the World an imaginary Doctrine.[33]

For Milton, too, the trees are actual, not allegorical. The fruit of the Tree of Life would have preserved "the growing, sensitive, and rational life of Man," but even if Adam had not sinned, man's life on earth, Raleigh thinks, would have been merely long, not immortal: after a "long, healthful, and ungrieved life," man would have been translated as Enoch was. In *Paradise Lost*, man in Paradise enjoys the prospect

[31] *Ibid.*, pp. 40-41.
[32] *Ibid.*, pp. 64 ff.
[33] *Op. cit.*, p. 37.

of immortality, but the taste of the fruit of the forbidden tree means death. Sir Charles H. Firth thinks that Milton adopted Raleigh's description of the Indian fig tree, which was sometimes identified with the Tree of Knowledge. Raleigh writes in part:

Moses Bar-Cephas in his Treatise of Paradise . . . saith, That the Tree of Knowledge was Ficus Indica, the Indian Fig-tree, . . . This Tree beareth a Fruit of the bigness of a great Pease, or (as Pliny reporteth) somewhat bigger, and that it is a Tree se semper serens, always planting it self; that it spreadeth it self so far abroad, as that a Troop of Horsemen may hide themselves under it.

After various remarks concerning the size and distribution of this tree, Raleigh continues:

when Adam and Eve found themselves naked, they made them Breeches of Fig-leaves; which prooveth (indeed) that either the Tree it self was a Fig-Tree, or that a Fig-Tree grew near it: because Adam being possest with shame, did not run up and down the Garden to seek out Leaves to cover him, but found them in the place it self; and these Leaves of all others were most commodious, by reason of their largeness, which Pliny avoweth in these words; Latitudo foliorum Peltae effigiem Amazoniae habet, The breadth of the Leaves hath the shape of an Amazonian Shield. . . .[34]

Milton's

> Figtree, not that kind for Fruit renown'd,
> But such as at this day to Indians known
> In Malabar or Decan spreds her Armes

probably grew out of Pliny's Natural History, as we shall see.

As Raleigh firmly believed in the reality of Eden and the Fall of man, so he believed that the Flood was God's punishment for man's inordinate sin. Some details here illustrate the striking similarity between the History and Paradise Lost. Before the Flood there were mighty men, which in old time were men of renown. But, Raleigh explains,

these Men of Renown (whom the Scripture afterwards calleth Giants, both for strength of Body and cruelty of Mind) trusted

[34] Ibid., p. 38.

*too much to their own Abilities, . . . for all the imaginations of
their hearts were evil, only evil, and continually evil.*

This wickedness was indeed universal,

when the Children and Sons of God (or of the godly) were corrupted and misled by their idolatrous Wives, the Daughters of
Cain, or of those other Men loving themselves and the World
only.[35]

The Fathers who believed that these Sons of God were angels
were mistaken. In Scripture "good and godly Men" were
frequently called God's children. Besides, it is madness to
suppose that angels, who "behold the face of God, (that is)
always attend his Commandments," should after the Fall of
Lucifer "forsake the glorious presence of their Creator, and
become *Incubi,* or *Succubi,* contrary both to Nature and
Grace."[36] Milton interprets the Biblical phrase "sons of God"
as Raleigh does, making them men, not angels; but characteristically he blames the women:

> After these,
> But on the hether side a different sort
> From the high neighbouring Hills, which was thir Seat,
> Down to the Plain descended: by thir guise
> Just men they seemd, and all thir study bent
> To worship God aright, and know his works
> . . . . they on the Plain
> Long had not walkt, when from the Tents behold
> A Beavie of fair Women, richly gay
> In Gems and wanton dress; to the Harp they sung
> Soft amorous Ditties, and in dance came on:
> The Men though grave, ey'd them, and let thir eyes
> Rove without rein, till in the amorous Net
> Fast caught, they lik'd, and each his liking chose;

To these seeming goddesses, empty of all true womanly honor,
the "sober Race of Men," whose religious lives had justified
that fair title, shall yield up all their virtue, all their fame,

> to the traines and to the smiles
> Of these fair Atheists.[37]

[35] *Ibid.,* p. 45.   [36] *Op. cit.,* p. 45.   [37] XI, 620-621.

Because the wickedness of men was very great, God repented that he had made man. And making known to Noah that an end of all flesh was at hand, that, as Raleigh says, "the Graves of the rebellious and cruel Generations were already fashioned in the Clouds," God instructed him to build the Ark. Milton writes that Noah

> Then from the Mountain hewing Timber tall,
> Began to build a Vessel of huge bulk.[38]

Neither the Bible nor Josephus's *Jewish Antiquities* says anything about the place from which timber for the Ark was obtained. Raleigh writes:

Now in what part of the World *Noah* built the Ark, it doth not appear in the Scriptures, neither do I find any approved Author that hath written thereof: only *Goropius Becanus* in his *Indio-Scythia* conceiveth, that *Noah* built his Ark near the Mountains of *Caucasus*, because on those Hills are found the goodliest Cedars: . . . To this place (saith *Becanus*) *Noah* repaired, both to separate himself from the reprobate Giants, who rebelled against God and Nature, as also because he would not be interrupted in the Building of the Ark; to which also he addeth the conveniency of Rivers, to transport the Timber which he used, without troubling any other Carriages.[39]

Again, Milton writes that the Ark drifted upon the waters:

> He lookd, and saw the Ark hull on the floud,
> Which now abated, for the Clouds were fled.[40]

Here "hull" means "to toss or drive on the water, like the hull of a ship without sails." Believing that the Ark was built near where it rested after the Flood, Raleigh writes:

For *Noah* did not use any Mast or Sail (as in other Ships) and therefore did the *Ark* no otherwise move than the Hulk or Body of a Ship doth in a calm Sea. Also because it is not probable, that during these continual and downright Rains there were any Winds at all, therefore was the *Ark* little moved from the place where it was fashioned and set together.[41]

[38] XI, 724-725.
[40] XI, 836-837.
[39] *Op. cit.*, p. 61.
[41] P. 61.

Because Raleigh was an experienced sailor, his account of the building and the movement of the Ark may have made upon Milton a sharp impression. Note, however, that in *Paradise Lost* the Ark is a vessel "of huge bulk," whereas Raleigh takes pains to show that "so huge a Frame" as was conceived by St. Augustine was not needed to contain all the creatures appointed by God to be preserved.

After the Flood, writes Milton, the people, living in the fear of God and busy with husbandry,

> Shal spend thir dayes in joy unblam'd, and dwell
> Long time in peace by Families and Tribes
> Under paternal rule.

In course of time arose Nimrod, who usurped dominion and quite dispossessed

> Concord and law of Nature from the Earth;
> Hunting (and Men not Beasts shall be his game)
> With Warr and hostile snare such as refuse
> Subjection to his Empire tyrannous:
> A mightie Hunter thence he shall be styl'd
> Before the Lord, as in despite of Heav'n,
> Or from Heav'n claiming second Sovrantie;
> And from Rebellion shall derive his name,
> Though of Rebellion others he accuse.[42]

The tradition that Nimrod was the first tyrant, who began his dominion in Babel, is said to have had its source in Josephus.[43] Mr. Theodore Gaster has shown that all the details in the lines just quoted follow the Rabbinic commentators.[44] For example, the line "And from Rebellion shall derive his name" depends on the derivation of Nimrod from the Hebrew root *m-r-d*, meaning to rebel. Mr. Gaster adds that Milton does not demonstrably depend upon any specific rabbinic source. Mr. Taylor believes that Milton's account of Nimrod and the building of Babel is similar to that in Du Bartas's

[42] XII, 29-37.
[43] *Jewish Antiquities* (London, 1930), I, 113 ff.
[44] *The Times Literary Supplement,* May 9, 1935, p. 301.

Divine Weekes.[45]   Raleigh also records the tradition of Nimrod's tyranny:

The first of all that raigned as Soveraign Lord after the Flood was *Nimrod*, the Son of *Chush*, . . . This Empire of *Nimrod*, both the Fathers and many later Writers call tyrannical: The same beginning in *Babel*, (which is) confusion. . . . *Nimrod* was therefore called *Amarus Dominatur*, *A bitter or severe Governour*, because his form of rule seemed at first far more terrible than Paternal Authority.   And therefore is he in this respect called *a mighty hunter:* because he took and destroyed both Beasts and Thieves.   But S. *Augustine* understands it otherwise, and converts the word [*ante*] by [*contra*] affirming therein, that *Nimrod* was a mighty hunter against God, *Sic ergo intelligendus est Gigas ille, venator contra Dominum.* . . .[46]

In contrast with Milton, Raleigh, who, however much he objected to particular kings, had no quarrel with the monarchical principle, adds that Nimrod had his power rather "by just Authority, than by violence of usurpation." Raleigh develops his theory that the first government was paternal, to which succeeded regal authority, which was then tempered by law. These stages he distinguishes by these terms: Justice Natural, Justice Divine, Justice Civil. The first age after the Flood was the Golden Age, when the law of nature was the rule of life, when men cared not for large territory or magnificent buildings or delicate fare and apparel. Tactfully Raleigh adds that "good and golden Kings make good and golden Ages."

Between the *History* and *Paradise Lost* we have observed fundamental analogies regarding the providence of God and regarding ambition, fortune, and fate. We have studied specific resemblances in the treatment of Eden, the Fall, the Flood, and the government that succeeded. Reserving for later consideration Raleigh's material on the pagan deities, we shall now survey a number of miscellaneous details—first of all Satan, whom Raleigh calls our most industrious and diligent enemy, "now more laborious than ever: the long Day of

[45] *Op. cit.*, pp. 121-122.   [46] *Op. cit.*, p. 105.

Mankind drawing fast towards an Evening, and the Worlds Tragedy and Time near at an end."

According to Raleigh, the Devil, except when he is the minister of God's vengeance, works in one or all of three ways: first, by moving the thoughts and affections of men; second, by his exquisite knowledge of nature; third, by deceit, illusion, and false semblance. These ways are illustrated in *Paradise Lost* and *Paradise Regained*. In the former, Satan accomplishes his purpose by masking his true nature under various disguises, by sophistries, by a shrewd understanding of human nature, and by seducing Eve with the promise of knowledge and power. In the latter he appears in various false shapes; he causes thunder, lightning, and tempests; he makes use of many sophistries—but he fails because Christ penetrates all his disguises and exposes all his juggling.

In the *History* Satan remains purely an abstraction, the embodiment of evil, altogether devoid of the striking features of Milton's superb characterization. But we may notice certain resemblances of detail. Milton compares the perilous flight of Satan through Chaos to the course of the griffin pursuing the one-eyed Arimaspian "ore Hill or moarie Dale."[47] As Sir Charles H. Firth observes, Raleigh tells the story:

Tostatus also gathereth a phantastical opinion out of *Rabanus*, who makes *Ophir* to be a Country, whose Mountains of Gold are kept by *Griffins:* which Mountains *Solinus* affirmeth to be in *Scythia Asiatica*, in these words: . . . For whereas these Countries abound in Gold, and rich Stone, the Griffins defend the one and the other: a kind of Fowls the fiercest of all other; with which Griffins a Nation of people called Arimaspi make war. These Arimaspi are said to have been men with one eye only, like unto the *Cyclopes* of *Sicilia*. . . .[48]

Raleigh proceeds to moralize and rationalize the tale: if men who encounter so many dangers for the sake of gold were not deprived of half their sight or right reason, they would be content with quiet and a moderate estate and would not subject themselves "to Famine, corrupt Air, violent Heat, and

[47] II, 943-950. [48] *Op. cit.*, p. 99.

Cold, and to all sorts of miserable Diseases"; there are, especially in America, many high and impassable mountains rich and full of gold but inhabited only by tigers, lions, and other ravenous and cruel beasts, where "if any man ascend . . . he shall be sure to find the same War, which the *Arimaspi* made against the *Griffins*. . . ."

After Satan had reported to the devils his triumph upon earth, they were sorely punished:

> There stood
> A Grove hard by, sprung up with this thir change,
> His will who reigns above, to aggravate
> Thir penance, laden with fair Fruit, like that
> Which grew in Paradise, the bait of *Eve*
> . . . .
> The Frutage fair to sight, like that which grew
> Neer that bituminous Lake where *Sodom* flam'd;
> This more delusive, not the touch, but taste
> Deceav'd; they fondly thinking to allay
> Thir appetite with gust, instead of Fruit
> Chewd bitter Ashes, which th' offended taste
> With spattering noise rejected.[49]

After describing the Dead Sea, also called the Lake of Asphaltitis because of the bitumen it casts up, Raleigh proceeds:

The Fields not far from this Lake, which were sometime fruitful, and adorned with great Cities, were burnt with Lightning; of which the Ruines remain, the Ground looking with a sad Face, as having lost her Fruitfulness: For whatsoever doth either grow, or is set thereon, be it Fruits or Flowers, when they come to Ripeness, have nothing within them, but moulder into Ashes: Thus far *Tacitus*. And it is found by Experience, that those Pomegranates, and other Apples, or Oranges, which do still grow on the Banks of this cursed Lake, do look fair, and are of good Colour on the Out-side; but being cut, have nothing but Dust within.[50]

Consider also the following illustrations. Milton compares the fallen angels to scattered sedge in the Red Sea,

> whose waves orethrew
> *Busiris* and his *Memphian* Chivalrie,

[49] X, 547-567. [50] *Op. cit.*, p. 220.

While with perfidious hatred they pursu'd
The Sojourners of *Goshen*.[51]

In the *History* may be found the explanation of Milton's use of *Busiris* instead of the Biblical *Pharaoh*. Busiris, Raleigh writes, was "the first oppressor of the Israelites." Most learned writers, he says, believe that Busiris "made the Edict of drowning the *Hebrew* Children." Much addicted to magnificent works, Busiris "wearied the Children of *Israel* in his buildings." From the fame of his cruelty grew the story that he sacrificed strangers. Born five years after the birth of Moses, Busiris was, Raleigh suggests, the viceroy of Sesostris the second, who resigned his kingdom to him. Later Raleigh writes:

But whether *Busiris* did usurp the Kingdom, or protection of the Land by violence: or whether the blind King resigned it, keeping the Title: or whether *Busiris* was only *Regent*, whilst the King lived, and afterwards . . . King himself: it might well be said that Pharaoh's Daughter took up *Moses*, and that *Pharaoh* vexed *Israel*: seeing he both at that time was King in effect, and shortly after King in deed and Title both.[52]

Authorities differ as to the name of the king who perished in the Red Sea; Mercator and Bunting say that it was Amenophis; others say Chencres. Perhaps Raleigh's emphasis upon Busiris as the Pharaoh who oppressed the Israelites led Milton to adopt Busiris as the name of "the wicked *Tyrant*."[53]

Observe one more detail. In the following line Milton indicates the northern limit of Palestine:

From *Paneas* the fount of *Jordans* flood.[54]

Raleigh explains that after Dan became subject to Rome "it

[51] I, 306-309.   [52] *Op. cit.*, pp. 138-139.
[53] To this may be added Vives's note to Chapter 12, Book XVII, of St. Augustine's *City of God* (London, 1620), p. 637: "*Busyris*. King of Egypt; he built Busiris and Nomos in an inhospitable and barren soile, and thence came the fable of his killing his guests: for the heards-men of those parts would rob and spoile the passengers, if they were too weake for them. Another reason of this fable was . . . for that *Typhon* who slew his brother *Osyris*, being red-headed, for pacification of Osyris soule, an order was set downe, that they should sacrifice nothing but red oxen and red-headed men, at his tombe, so that Egypt having few of those red heads, and other countries many, thence came the report that *Busiris* massacred strangers. . . ." Milton may have read this.   [54] III, 535.

had the name of *Paneas*, from a Fountain adjoining so called," and that this city, later called Caesaria Philippi, stood near the junction of those two rivers "which arise from the Springs of *Jor* and *Dan*, the two apparent Fountains of *Jordan*."[55]

Indicative of the fundamental accord between Raleigh and Milton is the fact that both regard pagan mythology as a debased form of Scriptural history, which is superior to all other. For example, according to Raleigh, the Biblical Paradise was the model of Alcinous's Gardens, the Elysian Fields, and the Golden Age. In a chapter entitled "Of Idolatrous Corruptions . . ." Raleigh explains that the Greeks and other ancient nations "by fabulous inventions" tried to conceal the fact that their fables are "borrowed or stoln out of the Books of God."[56] Undeceived by such falsehoods, the lover of God and truth will find "in all the ancient Poets and Philosophers, the story of the first Age . . . amply and lively exprest." On the evidence of learned men, Raleigh goes on to show that Adam was the first Saturn and Cain the first Jupiter; that Jubal, Tubal, and Tubalcain were respectively Mercury, Vulcan, and Apollo; that Noema or Naamath, the sister of Tubalcain, was the first Venus; that the fable of the division of the world among the three sons of Saturn arose from the true story of the dividing of the earth between the three sons of Noah; that the fiction of the golden apples kept by a dragon came from the Scriptural narrative of the Serpent that tempted Eve; that Paradise itself was "transported out of *Asia* into *Africa*, and made the Garden of *Hesperides*"; that the prophecies that Christ would break the Serpent's head and conquer the power of hell were the sources of the fables of Hercules's killing the serpent of Hesperides, descending into hell, and capturing Cerberus. Milton also believes that Scripture is the highest truth and that pagan myths, however beautiful, are corrupt. They are included in Grecian culture, which Christ condemns:

> But these are false, or little else but dreams,
> Conjectures, fancies, built on nothing firm.[57]

[55] *Op. cit.*, pp. 196-197.   [56] *Op. cit.*, pp. 47 ff.
[57] *Paradise Regained*, IV, 291-292.

In *Paradise Lost*, by an old tradition, the fallen angels become the pagan gods; the story of the golden apples of the Hesperides is true only of those that grew in Paradise; it is not true that the three goddesses strove for the golden apple, but the story of Eve is true. The implication of the introduction to Book IX is that the subject-matter of Homer and Virgil is trivial and false. Preoccupied with morality and religion, Milton exalted the truth of Scripture. Trained in the humanistic tradition, his mind was enriched by the secular literature of Greece and Rome, but Biblical events were to him the sacred oracles of God. Characteristically, even his fallen angels excel in prowess all the heroes of classic epic and medieval romance. Inspired by Urania, he soars above the Aonian mount, pursuing "Things unattempted yet in Prose or Rhime."

Besides, in Raleigh's and Milton's conception of law, human and divine, there is a fundamental similarity. Law Raleigh defines as a divine principle and a moral habit that commands our thoughts and actions. Again, *"Lex est omnium divinarum & humanarum rerum Regina; Law is the Queen or Princess of things both humane and Divine."* Fundamental is the eternal or divine law, to which all things are subjected, "as well *Angels* and *Men*, as all other creatures," which directs all things "by the counsel and providence of God," and from which all laws are derived. Natural law is but "an effect of the eternal: as it were a stream from this fountain." Human or temporal law, as it has "the form of right reason," is drawn thence. To love God and to do right to all men "is an effect of the purest reason: in whose highest Turrets, the quiet of conscience hath made her resting place, and habitation." Whosoever is not a law unto himself betrays his own soul and purchases eternal perdition. It is vain to hide our corrupt hearts from the eye of the world; we cannot hide from the eye of the Infinite.

Some Garlands we may gather in this May-game of the World, *Sed flos ille, dum loquimur, arescit; Those flowers wither while we discourse of their colours, or are in gathering them.* . . . Now, as the reasonable mind is the form of Man, so is he aptly moved to those things which his proper form presenteth unto him: to wit, to that which right reason offereth; and the acts of right reason, are the acts of vertue: and in the breach of the rules of this reason, is Man least excusable: as being a reasonable creature.[58]

This would serve as an admirable summary of the religious and moral philosophy underlying *Paradise Lost* and *Paradise Regained*. Obey God and reason. Reason teaches that obedience to God is perfect liberty and the service of Satan complete slavery. In the service of God and right reason lie man's true happiness and final salvation. Raleigh's critical temper, a blend of religion and reason, proves that he was intellectually a brother of Milton, whose spirit, however, was in some respects freer and finer, more consistent, less hampered by practical considerations and the urgency of compromise, more zealously consecrated to a lofty ideal.

These similarities of fact, of thought, and of temper lend some support to the theory that Milton may have been attracted by Raleigh's *History*, which reverently and at times eloquently surveys some of the material from which *Paradise Lost* was created. In the *History* there is, to be sure, interminable discussion; there are many arid stretches. But there are also moving accounts of the power and glory of God, a vivid story of Creation, elaborate discussions of Eden and the Flood, a chorographical description of Palestine, and a history of the Israelites. Interspersed are historical sketches of the Egyptians, the Greeks, the Assyrians, the Trojans, and so on. On the whole, the work presents a body of interesting material, highly regarded by Milton's compatriots. Milton was, of course, widely read in history; but in no other source could he have found that particular blend of material, temper, and style which Raleigh, in spite of collaboration, succeeded in achieving.[59]

Of *Paradise Lost* various evaluations have been offered: it is a theological and historical epic, the substance of which is truth; it deals with an ideal, conventional world but with events

[58] *Op. cit.*, p. 155.
[59] Other references to Raleigh occur in Gilbert's indispensable *Dictionary* under such headings as El Dorado, Guiana, etc.

and personages that were accepted as real and substantial; Satan is the hero, and the theme is the struggle of liberty against authority; the principal merit resides in the style; it is a philosophical fable, not primarily concerned with history or theology but portraying man's struggle against evil and emphasizing the enduring truth of free-will and the possibility of the ultimate triumph of good; it is an allegory embodying an idealistic system of ethics. After a careful survey of the evidence, Mr. H. W. Peck seems justified in concluding that "Milton thought he was dealing with real and historical facts," based upon Scripture.[60] The question is: For Milton, what was the meaning of history? Obviously he accepted Scriptural history as literally and substantially true. In the *Christian Doctrine* he declares, "No passage of Scripture is to be interpreted in more than one sense." On the other hand, Milton's view of secular history seems to have been less strict, more poetic, as is demonstrated by the character of material borrowed from the works of Diodorus Siculus and Pliny, whose histories were indeed not factual in any strict sense.

Living at a time when the Roman power was supreme, when Roman supremacy extended to the bounds of the civilized world, when all mankind was a common society, Diodorus set himself the task—which he left unfinished—of writing a universal history from the Creation to his day.[61] Diodorus's *Library of History*, which is a compilation or convenient summary of events treated in detail elsewhere, surveys such subjects as the myths, kings, and customs of Egypt, the history of Assyria, India, Scythia, Arabia, and Ethiopia, the inhabitants of Atlantis, and the origin of the first gods. It is interesting to observe that Diodorus emphasizes the doctrine of the utility of history. Historians are "ministers of Divine Providence." History provides not only knowledge but moral instruction. The young it endows with wisdom; for the old it multiplies experience. By its divine voice it heralds immortal fame. It

[60] "The Theme of *Paradise Lost*," *PMLA*, XXII, 260.
[61] *Diodorus of Sicily*. With an English Translation by C. H. Oldfather (London and New York, 1933), I, ix. The *History* seems to have been written between 56 and 36 B.C.

urges men to justice, denounces the evil, lauds the good. As Mr. Oldfather puts it, "More often than any extant ancient historian Diodorus stresses the view that history should instruct in the good life."[62] By Raleigh Diodorus is termed "a most approved and diligent Author." According to his translator, Henry Cogan, he was of such high repute among the most learned of all times that he has "justly acquired a prime place amongst the best Historians of former Ages" and he has been followed "by all that have undertaken to write the General History of the world. . . ." Although it has been observed that Milton esteemed and used Diodorus's *Library of History*,[63] it seems desirable to assemble here the relevant material, which falls under the categories of gods and places.

At the outset it may be remarked that Diodorus's account of creation vaguely reminds one of Milton's. In the *History* creation is the process of giving form to a disordered mass, of more solid matter seeking the center and of lighter matter ascending to the upper spaces in "the universal whirl," of the emergence of life from the moist earth under the influence of vital heat. But, according to Diodorus, life at first was bestial; without fire and clothing, man was wretched and often died of cold and hunger; only very gradually were the arts and social life developed. Unlike Milton's, this creation was an entirely natural process, without overruling supernatural powers. Later, in his history of Egypt, Diodorus presents a detailed account of their king-gods, generally worshiped under the form of beasts. Dependent upon various authorities, his accounts of the ancient mythology are inconsistent; he remarks, "But, as a general thing, we find that the ancient myths do not give us a simple and consistent story."[64] His summaries, however, are full and interesting; he writes, "We have expended all the care within our power upon the ancient legends." The two gods who control the world are Osiris and Isis: Osiris, the sun, who surveys all lands and seas; Isis, the moon, horned

[62] *Ibid.*, p. xx.
[63] See especially Mr. Gilbert's *Dictionary* under the names Arabia, Enna, Memphis, Ninevee, Nyseian Ile, Persepolis, Serbonian Bog, and Thebes.
[64] *Diodorus of Sicily*, II, 483.

because the moon is crescent-shaped. Both were founders of civilization. Osiris had two sons, Macedon and Anubis; the latter wore a dog's skin. Osiris was murdered by his brother Typhon and his accomplices, and the dismembered body was scattered. But Isis, the sister and wife of Osiris, avenged his murder with the aid of her son Horus. After slaying Typhon and his confederates, she became Queen of Egypt and recovered all the parts of her husband's body, except one. Both Osiris and Isis were worshiped. To Osiris the sacred bulls, Apis and Mnevis, were consecrated. In the *History* we find the explanation of Milton' statement that fanatic Egypt was abused

> to seek
> Thir wandring Gods disguis'd in brutish forms
> Rather then human.

The Egyptians venerate certain animals, which are sacred in life and death. They are kept in sacred enclosures and cared for by men of distinction. At death they are deeply mourned. Particularly interesting is the account of the worship of the sacred bull Apis. After his death he receives a magnificent funeral. Then the priests seek out a young bull with markings similar to those of the predecessor, and when it is found the people cease their mourning. After various ceremonies, the young bull is put on a state barge "fitted out with a gilded cabin" and conducted as a god to Memphis. The worship of the bull is explained thus: at the death of Osiris his soul passed into this animal and into its successors; when Isis collected the members of Osiris's body, she put them in an ox *(bous)*, which was worshiped.[65] Three reasons why the Egptians worship animals are offered: in the beginning the gods took the forms of animals to escape the savagery and violence of mankind and then out of gratitude made these animals sacred; in war, symbols of these animals portrayed upon standards helped the Egyptians to win victory; in peace, these animals are useful, the cow bearing young and being used to plough the soil, the sheep lambing and providing wool and food, the dog being

[65] *Ibid.*, I, 289-293.

useful in the hunt and for man's protection. This is why "they represent the god whom they call Anubis with a dog's head, showing in this way that he was the bodyguard of Osiris and Isis." The sacred bulls were honored as gods "both because of their use in farming and because the fame of those who discovered the fruits of the earth is handed down by the labours of these animals to succeeding generations for all time."[66] Mingled with ideas from other sources, memories of such material as this in Diodorus's *History* doubtless lingered in Milton's mind when, condemning pagan gods, he wrote of the "brutish gods of *Nile*," Osiris, Isis, Orus, and "their Train."

Besides these, there were other gods: Cronus and Rhea, parents of Osiris and Isis; Zeus, the spirit of life and the father of all things; Hephaestus, fire; Demeter, earth; Oceanus or Nile, water; Athena, air; Hermes, first astronomer and founder of language; Dionysus, discoverer of wine and of all things useful for life. Dionysus or Bacchus is associated with one of Milton's undoubted allusions to Diodorus's *History*. One of the four places with which Paradise is compared is

> that *Nyseian* Ile
> Girt with the River *Triton*, where old *Cham*,
> Whom Gentiles *Ammon* call and *Libyan Jove*,
> Hid *Amalthea* and her Florid Son
> Young *Bacchus* from his Stepdame *Rhea's* eye.[67]

This "Ile" is described in Diodorus's *History*, from Henry Cogan's charming translation of which the following excerpt is quoted:

The *Libians* of *Nysa* say, that there was anciently in their Country a King, named *Ammon*, who took to wife *Rhea*, one of the Daughters of *Coelum*, the Sister of *Saturne* and the other *Tythanes*; and that the said *Ammon* travelling over the *Ceranian* Mountaines became inamoured of a very faire young Maid, named *Amalthea*, by whom he had a Son of excellent beauty and proportion of body, for whose sake he conferred on the said *Amalthea* the Lordship and government of the adjoyning Country, the situation whereof

[66] *Ibid.*, I, 301.   [67] IV, 275-279.

being like unto the horne of an Ox, it was from thence called the
Westerne horne; and because that region was very fertile and
abounding with Vines and all kinde of Fruit-trees, and governed
by a Woman; it was thereupon called the Horne of *Amalthea;*
. . . *Ammon* then, for fear of his Wife *Rhea,* secretly conveyed
away the Child to the City of *Nysa* to be brought up there, in regard it was farre from the place of his residence, where he chose
out an Island, invironed round about with the River *Triton,* which
was precipitous and inaccessible on all parts, except by one avenue
that is called the gates of *Nysa:* The ground of this Island is
exceeding good, distinguished into many pleasant Meadows which
are watered on every side with sweet and delectable streams: it
beares likewise all sorts of Fruites and Vines, growing naturally of
themselves, which for the most part run up on Trees: The aire
there is pure and healthy, insomuch that the Inhabitants thereof are
longer liv'd then otherwhere. The avenue into this Island is in
form like unto a Flute, and so shadowed by the thicknesse of the
Trees growing there, as the Beams of the Sun cannot penetrate
into it: there are also round about it many Springs of cleare and
fresh Water, so that it is a most pleasant place to live in. Neere
unto it likewise is a great and faire Cave or Grot, round about
the which are high Rocks and Precipices, beautified with so many
sorts of colours, and bright shining stones, as more cannot be desired. Before it do naturally grow a number of goodly Trees most
pleasant to behold, for some of them beare Fruit, others are alwaies
green, so that they seeme to be set there to content the sight, and
in them doe a world of Birds nestle, which bring delight to the
Eyes and Eares with their goodly plumes, and sweet singing, so that
the place is delectable, not onely to look upon, but also to heare the
warbling of the Birds, which surpasseth all the Harmony of Musick.
After one is entred into this Grot it appeares to be very spacious,
and light with the rayes of the Sun, imbelished with flowers,
especially with *Cassia,* and other odoriferous things that yield a
sweet smell. In it likewise are seen many dwellings of the *Nymphs*
daintily decked with flowers, not artificial, but naturally perfect in
every kinde of beauty; for in the whole circuit of this Grot there
is not a flower or leaf that ever decayes or withers, so that the
contentment of the Eye and Eare is at no time wanting there.[68]

[68] *The History of Diodorus Siculus* (1653), pp. 159-160. Cf. *Diodorus
of Siculus,* II, 311 ff.

To excel in the description of his own Paradise the natural beauty of this delectable Isle must have been a challenge to Milton's skill. A number of details in Milton's "blissful Paradise"—the lovely landscape, the fertile and well-watered soil, the "goodliest Trees loaden with fairest Fruit," the high crags, the pure air—distinctly remind one of Amalthea's retreat.

In a famous simile Milton contrasts Satan's sensations on his approach to Paradise with those of sailors nearing the coast of Arabia:

> As when to them who saile
> Beyond the *Cape of Hope,* and now are past
> *Mozambic,* off at Sea North-East windes blow
> *Sabean* Odours from the spicie shoare
> Of *Arabie* the blest, with such delay
> Well pleas'd they slack thir course, and many a League
> Cheard with the grateful smell old Ocean smiles.[69]

Doubtless these lines reflect Milton's reading of the following passage in Diodorus:

The next *Arabians* are named *Carbes,* and adjoyning to them are the *Sabeans,* the most populous Nation of all that inhabit *Arabia* the happy, and replenished with all things which we esteeme to be most pretious, . . . In sweete odours, which naturally are produced of their Countrey, they surpasse all other Regions of the World; for *Balsamum* growes in the *Maritime* parts thereof, and *Cassia* likewise; as also another Hearb of a singular vertue, . . . In the *Mediterranean* parts thereof are many goodly Forrests, full of Trees bearing Frankincense, and Myrrhe; therein grow also Palme-trees, Canes, Cinamon, and other such like odoriferous things, whereof it is not possible to recount all the severall sorts in particular, so abundantly hath Nature assembled them there together; so that the odours, which come to our sences from those Trees, seeme to be somewhat that is truly Divine, . . . And certainly such as saile in those Seas (though they be farre from the Continent) partake in the pleasure of those sweet smells; for the winds, which in the Spring time blow from the Land, transport such odours to the *Maritime* parts thereabout; for the vertue of those *Aromaticks* is not weake and faint, but so strong and fresh,

[69] IV, 159-165.

as it pierces through all our senses; so that the winde, in such sort mingled with delicate Savors, blowing upon the Sea, affects the Spirits of passengers with a mervailous sweetnesse, and greatly availes unto health: For this so odoriferous an aire proceeds not from aromaticks brayed in a Morter, but from the very Countrey and Trees themselves, to which it is proper as it were by a certaine Divine nature, so as unto them, who smell such odours, it seems to be that very *Ambrosia*, whereof the Fables speake, and indeed one cannot give a more proper terme to so great an excellency of sweet smells.[70]

When Satan on his way to Paradise stops in the sun, there to consult Uriel about his farther course, Milton describes the splendor of that great luminary whose magnetic beams warm the universe and into every part shoot invisible virtue.

> What wonder then if fields and regions here
> Breathe forth *Elixir* pure, and Rivers run
> Potable Gold, when with one vertuous touch
> Th' Arch-chimic Sun so farr from us remote
> Produces with Terrestrial Humor mixt
> Here in the dark so many precious things
> Of colour glorious and effect so rare?[71]

Discussing Arabia, Diodorus declares that the sun evidently brings great force and virtue for generation to this region, which lies directly under the meridian. There are strange beasts. There is also "a world of pretious stones of different natures as well in colour as splendor; for the stone called cristall, is composed of pure water congealed, not by cold, but by force of a continuall heat, which is the cause that it receives and conserves in its hardnesse many different colours. The Emeralds also and the Berills growing in the Brasse mines, take their form and colour from heaven; and *the heat of the Sunne gives to stones that colour of gold which they have*: . . . The heat of the Sunne likewise makes Carbuncles of divers sorts. . . ." The colors of birds are due to the sun. "Truly it is very apparent, that colours, odors, fruits,

---

[70] *The History of Diodorus Siculus*, pp. 141-142.
[71] III, 606-612.

different savours, greatnesse of creatures, forms of things, and varietie of kindes produced by the earth, are made and procreated by the heat of the Sunne. . . ."[72] The sun, the source of life, aids in the production of each several kind. Nothing made by man equals the work of nature. "Consequently, neither the white marble of Paros nor any other stone which men admire can be compared with the precious stones of Arabia, since their whiteness is most brilliant, their weight the heaviest, and their smoothness leaves no room for other stones to surpass them."[73] This is true not only of Arabia but of all lands, such as Babylonia, India, and Ethiopia, that lie close to the sun. As far as crystals are concerned, the general theory seems to have been that they were produced by cold.[74] This Diodorus denied: *"Crystallum esse lapidem ex aqua pura concretum, non tamen frigore sed divini caloris vi."* Against the opinion of Diodorus, Sir Thomas Browne concluded that the generation of stones and gems, diamonds, beryls, sapphires, and the like, "we cannot with satisfaction confine unto the remote activity of the Sun."[75] It is significant that Milton, here apparently following the idea of Diodorus, was perhaps not in agreement with contemporary scientific thought.

Diodorus's *History* is probably the source of a number of other allusions to or descriptions of places. Milton compares a part of the frozen continent which forms the utmost territory of Hell to

> that *Serbonian* Bog
> Betwixt *Damiata* and mount *Casius* old,
> Where Armies whole have sunk.[76]

This Bog is described by Diodorus:

On the East side the said Land is fortified and defended, as well by the said River of *Nilus* as by certain spacious fields, named *Barathra,* wherein is a very deep Moor, called the *Servonian* Fen, which is between *Siria* & *Egypt,* narrow enough in bredth, and

---

[72] *The History of Diodorus Siculus,* p. 105.
[73] *Diodorus of Siculus,* II, 59.
[74] Sir Thomas Browne, *Pseudodoxia Epidemica* (London, 1650), p. 37.
[75] *Ibid.,* p. 42.   [76] II, 592-594.

above twelve leagues and a half in length, where many unexpected
dangers happen unto them that know not the Country. For it is
strait within, and compassed about with great heaps of sand, which
raised by the Southern wind are carried into the Moor in such great
abundance, as the sand mingled with the water seems to be firm
ground, and it cannot easily be discerned whether it be land or
water; whence it comes to pass, that many, not knowing the nature of the place, nor having a guide, are in holding on their way
swallowed up with their whole Troop; because that when they
are entred into the sand, which seems afar off firm ground, they
slip further in: And sticking so in the bog, it is not possible for
them to go forward, or backward: wherefore being thus sunk in
the mud there is no hope of safety for them. . . .[77]

In *Paradise Lost* Pandemonium and the ease with which
it was created are compared to the greatness of the Pyramids
and the prolonged toil of their building.[78] Diodorus describes
the Pyramids, the three greatest of which "are reckoned
amongst the Wonders of the World." Distant from Memphis
on the Libyan side seven and a half leagues, they are made
of durable stone brought from Arabia. They were built by
mounds of earth, for the builders knew not the use of scaf-
folds. "Certainly it was a marvellous work, especially in a
sandy ground, where there is no sign of any mount, or hewing
of stone, so that this huge fabrick seems to be the work of
Gods, and not of men."[79] To build the first pyramid three
hundred and three score thousand men wrought continually
for the space of twenty years. Pandemonium is also contrasted
with the temple of Bel in Babylon.[80] In *Paradise Regained*
Babylon is part of that fair kingdom which fails to tempt
Christ's unyielding virtue.[81] According to Diodorus, Semir-
amis, the wife of Ninus, employed three million men in con-
structing Babylon. The walls, thick set with many towers,
were twenty-two and a half leagues in circuit and of such
breadth that six chariots might be driven abreast on them. A

[77] *The History of Diodorus Siculus,* pp. 16-17. The Bog is described in
other works, as in Sandys' *Travels.*
[78] I, 692-699.
[79] *Op. cit.,* p. 43.
[80] I, 717-722.
[81] III, 280.

magnificent bridge with a castle at each end connected the parts of the city, which was divided by the Euphrates.

Furthermore, she built a Temple in the midst of the City to the honour of *Jupiter Belus*, the Greatness and magnificence whereof is not found in any Writings, nor in the memory of living men: neverthelesse it is certain, that the wonderful height of this Temple was such, as the *Chaldeans* did by the means thereof, come to the true knowledge and observation of the course of the Stars, . . . and that it was framed of brick and bytumen with excellent Art, and infinite cost: In the highest and most eminent part of this Temple, she caused three huge Statues of Gold to be erected, namely, of *Jupiter*, of *Juno*, and of *Ops*, whereof that of Jupiter is still in being forty foot high, and weighing a thousand *Babylonian* Talents; that of *Ops*, set in a chair, was of like weight, having two Lions standing at her knees, and neer to them two mighty great Serpents of Silver, each of them weighing thirty Talents; the Statue of *Juno* standing upright, was four score Talents in weight, holding in her right hand the head of a Serpent, and in her left a Scepter of stone. . . .[82]

Milton writes that Nimrod and his crew built the Tower of Babel, which was frequently identified with Babylon, of brick and of bitumen which boils out of the ground near by:

Hee with a crew, ...
. . . . shall finde
The Plain, wherein a black bituminous gurge
Boiles out from under ground, the mouth of Hell;
Of Brick, and of that stuff they cast to build
A Citie & Towre, whose top may reach to Heav'n.[83]

According to Diodorus, "the infinite quantity of Asphalta or Bytumen" which grows near Babylon is much to be marveled at. It rises in such abundance that it suffices "not only for the building of those great and sumptuous Edifices, but also the innumerable people which are there, do use it for, and in stead of fuel, after they have dried it; so exceeding much is the quantity of it that comes from the Fountain whence it springs."

[82] *Op. cit.*, pp. 74-75. [83] XII, 38-44.

Near unto it is an overture of the earth, not great, but of a wonderful property, for there issueth out of it an ill smell, as it were
Sulphur, which kills the Creatures that pass by, . . . There is
likewise beyond the River a certain Lake or Moor, of a little circuit,
casting up a fog all round about it, whereunto if any one do unwittingly enter, he is suddenly drawn into the Moor, . . . and . . .
drowned. . . .[84]

In the following passage, in which Milton compares
Raphael to the phoenix,

> as that sole Bird
> When to enshrine his reliques in the Sun's
> Bright Temple, to *Aegyptian Theb's* he flies[85]

the last line is explained by Diodorus. Busiris reigned in
Egypt. He had eight successors, and the last of them, also
named Busiris, "built a great City, which the *Egyptians* called
the City of the Sun, and the *Greeks Thebes*," which was
adorned with great edifices and sumptuous temples to the
gods. Thebes was the "goodliest and richest" city, "not only
of *Egypt*, but of all others in the universal world." Later
Diodorus adds that "*Heliopolis* and *Thebes* are one and the
same City."[86]

Diodorus describes other places mentioned in Milton's
epics: for example, the isle Meroe, one of the largest in Ethiopia, rich in mines of gold, silver, iron, copper, and precious
stones; magnificent Nineveh, built by Ninus, with fifteen hundred towers and with walls upon which three chariots could
drive abreast; the desert land south of Cyrene, almost barren
and inhabited by all manner of snakes, of which the cerastes
has the color of sand and a mortal sting; the arid country beyond the Syrtis, where strange shapes like monstrous animals
gather in the sky and seem to pursue travelers; the Dead Sea;
and fabulously rich India, a land of unusual beauty, well
watered by many rivers, of which the Ganges and the Indus,
with its tributaries Hypanis, Hydaspes, and Acesinus, are the

---

[84] *Op. cit.*, pp. 77-78.
[85] V, 273-275. Commentators say that Milton should have written Heliopolis.   [86] *Op. cit.*, pp. 31, 67.

most notable. These descriptions of strange lands and the naive accounts of foreign customs and pagan gods lend the *History* a distinct charm, which doubtless interested Milton in spite of his expressed dislike of history "obscur'd and blemisht with Fables," to be used by poets judiciously.[87] For secular illustration and decoration, then, Milton seems to have been indebted to Diodorus's *History,* which presented exotic material dealing with the ancient East.

Pliny's *Historia Naturalis,* a "great part" of which was used in the school that Milton conducted,[88] is considered "one of the most precious monuments that have come down to us from ancient times," as the encyclopedia of its age, as a wonderful monument of human industry and a record "of all that was excellent and useful."[89] Always noble and serious in style and marked by a love of justice and virtue, by a detestation of cruelty and baseness, by a contempt for inordinate luxury, it is not merely a natural history but also a survey of astronomy, physics, geography, agriculture, commerce, medicine, and the fine arts, with additional information on metaphysics and the history of nations. A compilation of much that had been written before Pliny's time and astonishingly erudite, the *History* has, nevertheless, delicate perceptions, freedom of thought, and boldness of sentiment. Condemned by Sir Thomas Browne as the repository and propagator of almost every "popular error passant in our daies,"[90] it was lauded by the translator Philemon Holland as appropriate not only to the learned but also to the rude peasant, the painful artisan, and, in fact, to "all sorts of people living in a societie and commonweale." The principal objection to Pliny's *History* was that in attributing so much to Nature it derogated from God. But Holland decided "not to defraud the world of so rich a gem, for one small blemish appearing therein." In the

[87] *History of Britain, The Works of John Milton,* X, 1-3.
[88] Edward Phillips, "The Life of Mr. John Milton," *The Early Lives of Milton,* ed. Helen Darbishire (London, 1932), p. 60.
[89] *The Natural History of Pliny.* Translated by John Bostock and H. T. Riley (London, 1855), I, xix-xxi.
[90] *Pseudodoxia Epidemica* (London, 1650), p. 23.

History Nature is God. Pliny declares that to inquire what is beyond the universe is no concern of man. In certain respects the God of Milton and Pliny is not dissimilar. Like Milton, Pliny does not seek after the shape of God; he does not assign to him a form and image. For God, in truth, is all sight, all hearing, all life, all soul. But, unlike Milton, Pliny conceives of the universe as a deity, eternal, neither created nor subject at any time to destruction; his universe is finite but like what is infinite. Milton's universe is the immediate work of God, who alone is immortal, immutable, and infinite; it is vast but limited; it may be destroyed.

In a somewhat detailed comparison of Pliny's and Milton's universe we may observe instructive differences and analogies. Although various cosmological systems are explained or discussed in *Paradise Lost,* it may be significant that the Ptolemaic system accepted by Pliny is the one generally adopted by Milton for the framework of his universe. Around the earth, which is the center, the sun seems to travel at incredible speed.[91] In Pliny the sun is the ruler, not of times and seasons only and of the earth, but also of the stars and of the heavens themselves. Compare with this Satan's address to the full-blazing sun:

> O thou that with surpassing Glory crownd,
> Look'st from thy sole Dominion like the God
> Of this new World; at whose sight all the Starrs
> Hide thir diminisht heads.[92]

In Pliny the sun is the lord of the world; in *Paradise Lost* Satan compares the sun to a divine ruler. Observe the following excerpt from the *History:*

Now, that these planets are fed doubtlesse with earthly moisture, it is evident by the Moone: which so long as she appeareth by the halfe in sight, never sheweth any spots, because as yet shee hath not her full power of light sufficient, to draw humour unto her. For these spots bee nothing else but the dregs of the earth, caught up with other moisture among the vapors.[93]

[91] I do not forget that Milton leaves this question open. See IV, 589-597, and VIII, 1-178.   [92] IV, 32-35.
[93] *The Historie of the World* (London, 1601), p. 7.

With this compare Raphael's words:

> of Elements
> The grosser feeds the purer, earth the sea,
> Earth and the Sea feed Air, the Air those Fires
> Ethereal, and as lowest first the Moon;
> Whence in her visage round those spots, unpurg'd
> Vapours not yet into her substance turn'd.[94]

With immense velocity and in perfect order the other planets pursue their wandering courses. One of these is Venus, as explained by Pliny:

Below the Sun revolves the great star called Venus, wandering with an alternate motion, and, even in its surnames, rivalling the Sun and the Moon. For when it precedes the day and rises in the morning, it receives the name of Lucifer, as if it were another sun, hastening on the day. On the contrary, when it shines in the west, it is named Vesper, as prolonging the light, and performing the office of the moon. . . . It excels all the other stars in size, and its brilliancy is so considerable, that it is the only star which produces a shadow by its rays. . . . By its influence everything in the earth is generated. For as it rises in either direction, it sprinkles everything with its genial dew, and not only matures the productions of the earth, but stimulates all living things.[95]

This is Milton's star of evening, "whose Office is to bring Twilight upon the earth":

> Fairest of Starrs, last in the train of Night,
> If better thou belong not to the dawn,
> Sure pledge of day, that crownst the smiling Morn
> With thy bright Circlet, praise him in thy Spheare
> While day arises, that sweet hour of Prime.[96]

It is Lucifer, "that bright Starr to *Satan* paragond"; it is Hesperus, "that led The starrie Host" through the glowing firmament, brightest of all until the Moon

> Rising in clouded Majestie, at length
> Apparent Queen unvaild her peerless light,
> And o're the dark her Silver Mantle threw.[97]

[94] V, 415-420.
[95] *The Natural History of Pliny*, I, 29-30.
[96] V, 166-170.   [97] IV, 607-609.

Sprinkling all with its genial dew, Venus, says Pliny, generates, stimulates, and matures. This example illustrates Pliny's belief: "The nature of the celestial bodies is eternal, being interwoven, as it were, with the world, and, by this union, rendering it solid; but they exert their most powerful influence on the earth." With the sun they control the seasons. Each star "has its specific power, which produces its appropriate effects."[98] Plants and animals are individually affected. As we have seen, Adam explains that the kindly heat of the celestial bodies, warming, tempering, and nourishing, imparts to all on earth a stellar virtue. Pliny declares that the Dog-star has the most powerful effects. "When it rises, the seas are troubled, the wines in our cellars ferment, and stagnant waters are set in motion." On the other hand, the death of individuals has no effect upon the stars; we are not so closely connected with the heavens that the shining of the stars is altered by our death. Although Pliny offers a rational explanation of eclipses, he adds, "And with respect to the eclipse of the moon, mortals impute it to witchcraft, and therefore endeavour to aid her by producing discordant sounds."[99] The hell-hounds that dog Sin are, says Milton, far more abhorred than those that follow Hecate, the Night-Hag, when she comes

> Lur'd with the smell of infant blood, to dance
> With *Lapland* Witches, while the labouring Moon
> Eclipses at thir charms.[100]

Stars suddenly formed are, Pliny says, called comets. They are shaggy with bloody locks and have various shapes and motions. "It is generally regarded as a terrific star, and one not easily expiated. . . ." The general dread of comets is suggested in Milton's phrase "fierce as a Comet." Pliny explains: "They [comets] are almost all of them seen towards the north, not indeed in any particular portion of it, but generally in that white part of it which has obtained the name of the Milky Way."[101] Confronting Death, Satan

[98] *The Natural History of Pliny*, I, 66.
[99] *Ibid.*, I, 38.   [100] II, 664-666.
[101] *The Natural History of Pliny*, I, 56-57.

> like a Comet burn'd,
> That fires the length of *Ophiucus* huge
> In th' Artick Sky, and from his horrid hair
> Shakes Pestilence and Warr.[102]

Another portent of calamity:

We have heard, that during the war with the Cimbri, the rattling of arms and the sound of trumpets were heard through the sky, and that the same thing has frequently happened before and since.[103]

In Satan's absence some of the fallen angels indulge in martial games:

> As when to warn proud Cities warr appears
> Wag'd in the troubl'd Skie, and Armies rush
> To Battel in the Clouds, before each Van
> Pric forth the Aerie Knights, and couch thir spears
> Till thickest Legions close; with feats of Arms
> From either end of Heav'n the welkin burns.[104]

Thus, in the order and the portents of Pliny's and Milton's universe are to be observed certain striking resemblances, which, of course, may be due entirely to Milton's acceptance of the conventional cosmology. A further analogy may be noted. Pliny explains that the sun is regarded "as a masculine star, burning up and absorbing everything," and that, on the contrary, the moon is said to be "a feminine and delicate planet."[105] Raphael suggests to Adam:

> and other Suns perhaps
> With thir attendant Moons thou wilt descrie
> Communicating Male and Female Light,
> Which two great Sexes animate the World.[106]

Although, as I point out later, names and descriptions of winds are commonly included in contemporary geographies, Pliny's account of winds may be recalled in connection with Milton's. There are two in or blowing from each of the four

---

[102] II, 708-711.
[103] *The Natural History of Pliny*, I, 88.
[104] II, 533-538.
[105] *The Natural History of Pliny*, I, 129-130.
[106] VIII, 148-151.

quarters: from the east and southeast Subsolanus and Vulturnus (by the Greeks called Apeliotes and Eurus); from the south Notos or Auster and from the west southwest Libs or Africus; from the west Favonius or Zephyrus and from the west northwest Argestes or Corus; from the north Septemtrio or Aparticas and from the north northeast Aquilo or Boreas. The north northwest is Thrascias, the east northeast is Caecias, the south southeast is Euronotus, and the south southwest is Libnotos. The coldest winds, dispelling the clouds, blow from the seven stars. The moist winds are Africus and Auster. Almost all winds blow in their turn. In *Paradise Lost* these names are encountered,[107] but in the first discord of nature, resulting from original sin, the winds war with each other.

From these somewhat general resemblances of the universe of Pliny and Milton we may now, emulating Milton's example, descend to the earth itself, where to prevent duplication the illustrations, which fall under the general categories of places, plants, and animals, may be treated without strict regard for rigid grouping.

When, in *Lycidas*, Milton wrote "And, O ye *Dolphins*, waft the hapless youth," he may have recalled Pliny's stories of the friendship between boys and dolphins. The dolphin, says Pliny, loves not only man but music. He is delighted with the harmony of song and especially with the sound of the water instrument or such kind of pipes. He is not afraid of man but meets his ships, "plaieth and disporteth himselfe, and fetcheth a thousand friskes and gambols before them." Pliny continues:

In the daies of *Augustus Caesar* the Emperour, there was a dolphin entred the gulfe or poole Lucrinus, which loved wonderous well a certain boy, a poore mans sonne: who using to go every day to schoole from Baianum to Puteoli, was wont also about noone tide to stay at the water side, and to call unto the Dolphin, *Simo*, *Simo*, and many times would give him fragments of bread, . . . and by this meane allured the Dolphin to come ordinarily to him at his call. . . . Well, in processe of time, at what houre soever

[107] X, 695 ff.

of the day, this boy lured for him and called *Simo*, were the Dolphin never so close hidden . . . out he would and come abroad, yea and skud amain to this lad: and taking bread and victuals at his hand, would gently offer him his back to mount upon, and then downe went the sharpe pointed prickes of his finnes, which he would put up as it were within a sheath for fear of hurting the boy. Thus when he had him once on his back, he would carrie him over the broad arme of the sea as farre as Puteoli to schoole; and in like manner convey him backe againe home: and thus he continued for many yeeres together, so long as the child lived.[108]

After the boy's death, the dolphin died from grief and sorrow. Other stories of a like nature are recounted, and it is said that there is no end of examples of this kind. Finally, Pliny relates the story of Arion's rescue by the dolphin.

Pliny declares that in India there are huge dragons able to swallow stags and bulls and to destroy elephants, that in Italy there are boas of a vast size, that in the Punic War a serpent one hundred and twenty feet long was taken by the Roman army after having been besieged like a fortress. He explains that in the spring the serpent by the aid of the juices of the fennel throws off its old skin and by rubbing itself on the fennel restores its sight.[109] Milton writes of serpents "Wondrous in length and corpulence," and he has Satan in the Serpent declare that by the odor of the goodly Tree he was more pleased than by the "smell of sweetest Fenel."[110] In the *Natural History* three serpents are briefly described: the Cerastes, often with four small horns, by moving which she amuses the birds and trains them to her; the Amphisbaena, with two heads, "as if shee were not hurtfull ynough to cast her poison at one mouth onely," scaled, spotted, and painted, with most deadly venom; the Aspides, which swell about the neck when they purpose to sting.[111] Later Pliny mentions the serpent Elops, the worm Dipsas, the water snake Hydrus, and the Scorpion. Milton writes:

[108] *The Historie of the World* (1601), I, 238-239.
[109] *The Natural History of Pliny*, II, 292-293; IV, 296.
[110] VII, 482-483; IX, 578-581.
[111] *The Historie of the World*, I, 208.

> dreadful was the din
> Of hissing through the Hall, thick swarming now
> With complicated monsters, head and taile,
> Scorpion and Asp, and *Amphisbaena* dire,
> *Cerastes* hornd, *Hydrus*, and *Ellops* drear,
> And *Dipsas*[112]

In the French ocean, writes Pliny, "is discovered a mightie fish called Physeter, (a Whirlepoole) rising aloft out of the sea in manner of a columne or pillar, higher than the very sailes of the ships: and then he spouteth and casteth forth a mightie deale of water, as it were out of a conduit, ynough to drowne and sinke a ship." The whales called Balenae have in their foreheads mouths or great holes, and as they swim they throw up "a great quantitie of water when they list, like stormes of raine."[113] Seas in contemporary maps were commonly decorated with these huge spouting monsters. One recalls the following passage in the account of the fifth day of creation:

> there Leviathan
> Hugest of living Creatures, on the Deep
> Strecht like a Promontorie sleeps or swimmes,
> And seems a moving Land, and at his Gilles
> Draws in, and at his Trunck spouts out a Sea.[114]

In the borders of the mountains, about the source of the Ganges, Pliny reports, dwell the Pygmies, who, according to Homer, are "much troubled and annoied by cranes." In the spring "they set out all of them in battell array, mounted upon the backe of rammes and goats, armed with bowes and arrowes, and so downe to the sea side they march, where they make foule worke among the egges and young cranelings newly hatched, which they destroy without all pitie. Thus for three moneths this their journey and expedition continueth, and then they make an end of their valiant service. . . ."[115] Describing the hosts of Satan, Milton writes:

[112] X, 521-526. Cf. Taylor, *op. cit.*, p. 109 and note.
[113] *The Historie of the World*, I, 235-237.
[114] VII, 412-416.
[115] *The Historie of the World*, I, 156.

For never since created man,
Met such imbodied force, as nam'd with these
Could merit more then that small infantry
Warr'd on by Cranes.[116]

Later Milton describes the flight of birds:

Part loosly wing the Region, part more wise
In common, rang'd in figure wedge thir way,
Intelligent of seasons, and set forth
Thir Aierie Caravan high over Sea's
Flying, and over Lands with mutual wing
Easing thir flight; so stears the prudent Crane
Her annual Voiage, born on Windes; the Aire
Floats, as they pass, fann'd with unnumber'd plumes.[117]

In similar language, as Verity noted, Pliny describes the migrations of birds:

The nation of the pretie Pigmies enjoy a truce from armes, every yeare (as we have said before) when the Cranes, who use to wage warre with them, be once departed and come into our countries. And verily, if a man consider well how far it is from hence to the Levant sea, it is a mightie great journey that they take, and their flight exceeding long. They put not themselves in their journey, nor set forward without a counsell called before, and a generall consent. They flie aloft, because they would have a better prospect to see before them: and for this purpose a captain they chuse to conduct them, whom the rest follow. In the rereward behind there be certaine of them set and disposed to give signall by their manner of crie, for to raunge orderly in rankes, and keepe close together in array: and this they doe by turnes each one in his course.[118]

Geese and swan make their way forcibly "in a pointed squadron, like as it were the stemme of a foist at sea, armed with a sharpe beakehead (for by this meanes they breake and cut the aire better, than if they drave it before with a streight, even, and square front)." In wedge formation they spread broader and broader, and by this means "they gather more wind to heave them up and set them forward."

[116] I, 573-576. [117] VII, 425-432.
[118] *The Historie of the World*, I, 281.

From the sweet chantress of *Il Penseroso* to the wakeful solemn bird of *Paradise Lost*, Milton's poetry bears witness to his love of the nightingale. One may not doubt that Milton read with appreciation Pliny's interesting analysis of the nightingale's song. For fifteen days and nights together, writes Pliny, the nightingale "never giveth over but chaunteth continually, namely, at that time as the trees begin to put out their leaves thicke." It is passing strange that so loud and clear a voice "should come from so little a bodie."

Moreover, shee alone in her song keepeth time and measure truely; shee riseth and falleth in her note just with the rules of musicke and perfect harmonie: for one while, in one entire breath she draweth out her tune at length treatable; another while shee quavereth, and goeth away as fast in her running points: sometime she maketh stops and short cuts in her notes, another time shee gathereth in her wind and singeth descant between the plaine song: she fetcheth her breath againe, and then you shall have her in her catches and divisions: anon all on a sodaine, before a man would think it, she drowneth her voice, that one can scarce heare her: now and then she seemeth to record to her selfe; and then she breaketh out to sing voluntarie. In summe, she varieth and altereth her voice to all keyes: . . . Thus she altereth from one to another, and singeth all parts. . . .[119]

In the *Natural History* there is an interesting account of the social life of ants, to which Milton may have been indebted. "These silie creatures," Pliny explains, "labour and travell in common, as the Bees doe," with this difference, that bees make their own meat, whereas ants merely store their provision. They have a commonwealth. They do not lack care and foresight. "Looke what seeds or graines they do lay up for provision, sure they will be to gnaw it first, for feare they would sprout and take root again and so grow out of the earth. If a corne or seed be too big for their carriage, they divide it into peeces, that they may goe with it more easily into their house. If their seeds within, chaunce to take wet, they lay them abroad, and so drie them. . . . When they

[119] *Ibid.*, I, 285-286.

are at worke, how painefull are they? how busie, how industrious?" Because they bring their food from divers parts, they
keep certain market days "for a mutuall interview and conference together. And verily, it is a world to see, how then
they will assemble; what running, what greeting, what enter-
course and communication there is betweene them, whiles they
are inquisitive, as they meet one with another, What newes
abroad: even like marchants at a Burse. . . ."[120] Milton
writes:

> First crept
> The Parsimonious Emmet, provident
> Of future, in small room large heart enclos'd,
> Pattern of just equalitie perhaps
> Hereafter, join'd in her popular Tribes
> Of Commonaltie.[121]

But the lines

> swarming next appeer'd
> The Femal Bee that feeds her Husband Drone
> Deliciously, and builds her waxen Cells
> With Honey stor'd:[122]

depend not on Pliny, who tells of the kings and captains of
the bees and who calls the drones servants of the masters, but
probably on Charles Butler's *The Feminine Monarchie* (1634),
which, describing the female government of bees, declares that
the honey bees are the females and that the drones, the male
bees, are idle companions.

With apparent naïveté Pliny describes numerous strange
animals, among which may be mentioned the griffin and the
phoenix. In the northern regions, near the spot from which
the north wind arises, "the Arimaspi are said to exist."

This race is said to carry on a perpetual warfare with the Griffins,
a kind of monster, with wings, as they are commonly represented,
for the gold which they dig out of the mines, and which these wild
beasts retain and keep watch over with a singular degree of cu-

[120] *Ibid.*, I, 328.
[121] VII, 484-489.   [122] VII, 489-492.

pidity, while the Arimaspi are equally desirous to get possession of it.[123]

Recall Milton's comparison of Satan's flight through Chaos to the course of the griffin pursuing the one-eyed Arimaspian. Pliny states that in Ethiopia and India the varied plumage of some birds surpasses description.

In the front rank of these is the phoenix, that famous bird of Arabia; though I am not quite sure that its existence is not all a fable. It is said that there is only one in existence in the whole world, and that that one has not been seen very often. We are told that this bird is of the size of an eagle, and has a brilliant golden plumage around the neck, while the rest of the body is of a purple colour; except the tail, which is azure, with long feathers intermingled of a roseate hue; the throat is adorned with a crest, and the head with a tuft of feathers . . . in Arabia it is looked upon as sacred to the sun . . . it lives five hundred and forty years, . . . Cornelius Valerianus says that the phoenix took its flight from Arabia into Egypt. . . .[124]

This passage in the *Natural History* may have influenced Milton's description of Raphael:

> to all the Fowles he seems
> A *Phoenix*, gaz'd by all, as that sole Bird
> When to enshrine his reliques in the Sun's
> Bright Temple, to *Aegyptian Theb's* he flies.[125]

Even when Raphael resumes his proper shape of a winged seraph, his wings of "downie Gold And colours dipt in Heav'n" and "Skie-tinctur'd grain" resemble the brilliant golden plumage and the azure of the phoenix.

Although the birds exist, there is no truth in the story associated with the last line of the following passage from the *Hymn*:

> The Windes with wonder whist,
> Smoothly the waters kist,
> Whispering new joyes to the milde Ocean,

[123] *The Natural History of Pliny*, II, 123. See the editors' interesting note (no. 35).
[124] *Ibid.*, II, 479-481.   [125] V, 271-274.

> Who now hath quite forgot to rave,
> While Birds of Calm sit brooding on the charmed wave.

Pliny explains that the "seas, and all those who sail upon their surface, well know the days" of the incubation of the halcyon. "They hatch their young at the time of the winter solstice, from which circumstance those days are known as the 'halcyon days': during this period the sea is calm and navigable. . . ." Pliny adds a description of their nests, which "are truly wonderful." Shaped like a ball slightly elongated and strongly resembling a large sponge, they have a very narrow mouth. They cannot be cut with iron but may be shattered with a violent blow, "upon which they separate, just like foam of the sea when dried up." The eggs of the halcyon number five.[126] The ancient notion that the sea is calm when the halcyons brood seems to have been generally accepted. Even Sir Thomas Browne observes that in "the time of their nidulation, and bringing forth their young . . . it hath been observed even unto a proverb, that the Sea is calm, and the windes do cease, till the young ones are excluded, and forsake their nest. . . ."[127]

In the *Natural History* are catalogued and described a large number of trees, shrubs, and curious plants, some of which appear in Milton's poetry. According to Homer moly is a principal and sovereign herb and of singular effect "against the mightiest witchcraft and enchauntments that bee." Some say that this herb, with a black bulbous root and rough leaf, grows about the river Peneus and upon the mountain Cylleum in Arcadia. "The Grecian Simplists describe this Moly with a yellow flower, whereas *Homer* hath written, that it is white. . . ."[128] This may explain the following lines in *Comus:*

> Amongst the rest a small unsightly root,
> But of divine effect, he cull'd me out;
> The leaf was darkish, and had prickles on it,
> But in another Countrey, as he said,

---

[126] *The Natural History of Pliny*, II, 512-513.
[127] *Op. cit.*, p. 105.   [128] II, 213-214.

Bore a bright golden flowre, but not in this soyl:

. . . .

And yet more med'cinal is it then that *Moly*
That *Hermes* once to wise *Ulysses* gave.[129]

Milton's moly, unlike Homer's, has a yellow flower, as does
that described in Pliny's *History*. Note particularly Pliny's
description of nardus, cassia, and myrrh, which grow in parts
of Arabia. Frankincense grows only in the very center of
Arabia, in a district known by the name of Saba.[130] Palms
flourish in Palestine. In Egypt grow most singular herbs and
that "noble Nepenthes" which Polydamnia, wife of King
Thon, gave to Helena and which had the great virtue to
"work oblivion of melancholy . . . and to procure easement
and remission of all sorrows." The fig tree with the leaves
of which Adam and Eve hide their shame is, as editors have
explained, the Indian fig tree described in Pliny's *History:*

First and formost, there is a Fig tree there, which beareth very
small and slender figges. The propertie of this Tree, is to plant
and set it selfe without mans helpe. For it spreadeth out with
mightie armes, and the lowest waterboughes underneath, doe bend
soe downeward to the very earth, that they touch it againe, and
lie upon it: whereby, within one yeares space they will take fast
root in the ground, and put foorth a new Spring round about the
Mother-tree: so as these braunches thus growing, seeme like a traile
or border of arbours most curiously and artificially made. Within
these bowers the sheepheards use to repose and take up their
harbour in Summer time: for shadie and coole it is, and besides
well fenced all about with a set of young trees in manner of a
pallaisado. A most pleasant and delectable sight, whether a man
either come neare, and looke into it, or stand a farre off: so faire
and pleasant an arbour it is, all greene, and framed arch-wise in
just compasse. . . . And the bodie or trunke of the Mother is
so great, that many of them take up in compasse threescore paces:
and as for the foresaid shaddow, it covereth in ground a quarter
of a mile. The leaves of this Tree are very broad, made in forme
of an Amazonian or Turkish Targuet: which is the reason, that
the figges thereof are but small; considering, that the leafe covereth

[129] Ll. 629-637.   [130] *The Natural History*, III, 124.

it, and suffereth it not to grow unto the full. Neither doe they hang thicke upon the Tree, but here and there very thin, and none of them bigger then a beane.[131]

In *Paradise Lost:*

> The Figtree, not that kind for Fruit renown'd,
> But such as at this day to *Indians* known
> In *Malabar* or *Deccan* spreds her Armes
> Braunching so broad and long, that in the ground
> The bended Twigs take root, and Daughters grow
> About the Mother Tree, a Pillard shade
> High overarch't, and echoing Walks between;
> There oft the *Indian* Herdsman shunning heate
> Shelters in coole, and tends his pasturing Herds
> At Loopholes cut through thickest shade.[132]

To maintain that Milton relied greatly upon the geographical information in Pliny's *Natural History* would be as unwise as to assert that there is no connection whatever. We may briefly notice certain undoubted and some probable relationships. Describing embassies that visit Rome from her distant possessions, Milton writes:

> some from farthest South,
> *Syene,* and where the shadow both way falls,
> *Meroe, Nilotic Isle,* . . . .
> From *India* and the golden *Chersoness,*
> And utmost *Indian* Isle *Taprobane,*
> Dusk faces with white silken Turbants wreath'd.[133]

Pliny reports the saying that in Syene, which is about 625 miles above Alexandria, there is at noon in the midst of summer no shadow, because the sun is directly overhead, and that in Meroe, "an island in the Nile and the metropolis of the Aethiopians," there are no shadows twice in the year—in the eighteenth degree of Taurus and in the fourteenth of Leo— when the sun is vertical. Pliny adds, "The Oretes, a people of India, have a mountain named Maleus, near which the

---

[131] *The Historie of the World,* I, 360.
[132] IX, 1101-1110.   [133] *Paradise Regained,* IV, 69-76.

shadows in summer fall towards the south and in winter towards the north."[134] This statement, hitherto not cited in connection with Milton's lines, may be the source of his clause, "where the shadow both way falls." Pliny informs us that after Syene is left behind there are now, according to reports made to Nero by the soldiers sent to discover Ethiopia, only deserts and a vast wilderness where there were formerly various cities and towns. In the days of Augustus Caesar, Publius Petronius, governor of Egypt, penetrated to Meroe with an armed force. Various details regarding the island are reported: the grass and the herbs are fresh and green; the city is within the island seventy miles from the entrance; the Queen was Candace; there was a temple in honor of Jupiter Hammon. As Mr. Gilbert has remarked, "Meroe was the most southern land in Aethiopia known to the Romans."[135]

Pliny describes at length Taprobane, long thought to be a second world but after the time of Alexander the Great discovered to be an island. Taprobane begins "at the Levant sea of Orientall Indians, from which it stretcheth and extendeth between the East and West of India." This we knew from ancient writers. "But wee came to farre better intelligence, and more notable information, by certaine Embassadours comming out of that Island, in the time of *Claudius Caesar*."[136] Pliny's description identifies Taprobane with Ceylon. This location does not agree with the sense of Milton's line or with the preponderant geographical opinion of the seventeenth century, which, as I have shown,[137] identified Taprobane with Sumatra.

In Pliny's *History* other geographical details may have been of interest to Milton: the fountain Arethusa, at Syracuse, which is fed by the river Alpheus from Greece; the rock Scylla and the whirlpool Charybdis, "both of them noted for their perils," in the Strait between Sicily or Trinacria and

[134] *The Natural History*, I, 107-108.
[135] *Op. cit.*, p. 190.
[136] *The Historie of the World*, I, 129-131. Cf. Gilbert, *op. cit.*, pp. 284-285.
[137] "Milton's Taprobane," *The Review of English Studies*, XIII, 209-212.

Italy; Delos, one of the Cyclades, once a floating island, famous for its temple of Apollo; Lixos, in Africa, the subject
of such wonderful fables, thought by some to be the site of
the Gardens of the Hesperides, though others say that these
were on two islands off the west coast of Africa, in the Atlantic
sea, beyond the islands called the Gorgades, the former abodes
of the Gorgons; the Syrtes on the coast of Africa, "rendered
perilous by the shallows of their quicksands and the ebb and
flow of the sea"; in Boeotia, which is the native land of the
two divinities Liber and Hercules, the grove of Helicon, the
birthplace of the Muses; Lake Maeotis, into which flows the
river Tanais, which forms the extreme boundary between
Europe and Asia; in Thessaly a well-wooded valley called
Tempe, between Ossa and Olympus, through which "glides
the Peneus, reflecting the green tints as it rolls along its peb-
bly bed, its banks covered with tufts of verdant herbage, and
enlivened by the melodious warblings of the birds"; in Thrace
Mount Rhodope and the river Hebrus, linked in the tragic
fate of Orpheus. One notes especially Pliny's description of
the land between the Caspian Sea and the country of the
Seres.

The first portion of these shores . . . is totally uninhabitable, ow-
ing to the snow, and the regions adjoining are uncultivated, in
consequence of the savage state of the nations which dwell there.
. . . Hence it is that all around them consists of vast deserts, inhabited by multitudes of wild beasts, which are continually lying
in wait, ready to fall upon human beings just as savage as themselves. After leaving these, we again come to a nation of the Scythians, and then again to desert tracts tenanted by wild beasts, until
we reach a chain of mountains which runs up to the sea. . . .[138]

We recall that Satan, landing upon the waste and wild out-
side of the universe, walked there in a spacious field, as a vulture, flying from Imaus towards the springs "Of *Ganges* or
Hydaspes, Indian streams," lands in search of prey on "the
barren plaines Of *Sericana*."[139] Pliny emphasizes in this region the vast deserts, which Milton seems to have extended

[138] *The Natural History*, II, 36.   [139] III, 418-441.

into the fruitful land of the Seres lying beyond.[140]   At the foot of the mountains Emaus, Emodus, and Caucasus, which are all connected, India, Pliny explains, spreads out in a vast plain, well watered by great rivers, the Ganges, the Indus, "the famous river Hydaspes," and others.

In Pliny we find a detailed account of the Pyramids of Egypt, "so many idle and frivolous pieces of ostentation of their resources, on the part of the monarchs of that country."[141] Three of these pyramids, "the renown of which has filled the whole earth," lie between the city of Memphis and the Delta, four miles from the river and seven miles and a half from Memphis. They are described by many authors.   The largest pyramid is built of stone quarried in Arabia; it required three hundred and sixty thousand men twenty years to build it.   The builders are unknown, "accident having, with very considerable justice, consigned to oblivion the names of those who erected such stupendous memorials to their vanity."   Such are "the marvellous Pyramids," near which there are no vestiges of buildings; only the sand stretches far and wide.   The note of disapprobation is also heard in *Paradise Lost:*

> And here let those
> Who boast in mortal things, and wondring tell
> Of *Babel,* and the works of *Memphian* Kings,
> Learn how thir greatest Monuments of Fame,
> And Strength and Art are easily outdone
> By Spirits reprobate, and in an hour
> What in an age they with incessant toyle
> And hands innumerable scarce perform.[142]

Finally, Pliny's survey of the kingdom of the Persians, "by which we now understand that of Parthia," may have had some influence upon Milton's survey of the same regions in *Paradise Regained.*   Persia lies between two seas, the Persian and the Hyrcanian; it extends from Armenia to the

[140] "The people of Serica, which country with Ptolemy corresponds to the northwestern part of China, and the adjacent portions of Thibet and Chinese Tartary." *The Natural History of Pliny,* II, 36, note 6. Cf. Gilbert, *op. cit.,* pp. 261-263.
[141] *The Natural History,* VI, 335.   [142] I, 692-699.

Scythians. First there is Greater Armenia, then Sophene, then Adiabene, "the most advanced frontier of Assyria." In this region are Nisibis, distant from Artaxata about seven hundred and fifty miles, and Nisus or Nineveh, "a most renowned city." On the other front of Greater Armenia is Atropatene, one boundary of which is the Araxes. Of Atropatene the chief city is Gaza, four hundred and fifty miles from Ecbatana, the capital of Media, which is seven hundred and fifty miles from Great Seleucia. Farther east is Hecatompylos, the capital of Parthia. Persepolis, the former capital of Persia, was destroyed by Alexander. Still farther east, near the Hyrcanian Sea, are Bactra and Margiana, "so remarkable for its sunny climate," and last of all Sogdiana, bounded by the Jaxartes, beyond which are the wild peoples of Scythia.[143] Other sources of the far-flung roll of names in Milton's famous passage will be discussed in the following chapter.

In conclusion, it should be observed that the beneficence of nature and the vanity and wicked perversity of man are themes that recur in Pliny and Milton. The earth, says Pliny, is our mother: she receives us at birth; she nourishes us; she embraces us in her bosom when we are cast out by all others. How kind, mild, and indulgent she is, "ministering to the wants of mortals." What odors and flowers, what forms and colors! What a profusion of medical plants she produces! But man abuses the earth and converts her blessings into curses. The earth is continually tortured for her iron, timber, stone, and corn. Man rifles her bowels, digging out gold, silver, copper, and lead. "We tear out her entrails in order to extract the gems with which we may load our fingers." In our search for treasures we almost invade the infernal regions. But all this wealth ends in crimes, slaughter, and wars, and "while we drench her with our blood, we cover her with unburied bones." Milton condemns man because by sin he violated nature's law and broke the fair harmony of the universe. In *Comus*, the lady denounces Comus's argument which justifies intemperate use of nature's abundance. In Paradise, in-

[143] *The Natural History*, II, 17 ff.

nocent nature was before sin man's friend, but afterwards his foe. Tempted by Satan, men

> with impious hands
> Rifl'd the bowels of their mother Earth
> For Treasures better hid.

Even devils contrive to live at peace among themselves; but men live in hatred and strife,

> and levie cruel warres,
> Wasting the Earth, each other to destroy.

Milton, one feels, must have subscribed to Pliny's opinion that man, whose tenure of life is most frail, is guilty of every luxury and excess, "a prey to ambition and avarice," a victim of frantic and violent passions, and indeed the chief instrument of his own worst misfortunes.

With due allowance for the conventional and the common, it should be admitted that the amount of material linking Milton's poetry, especially *Paradise Lost,* with the histories of Raleigh, Diodorus, and Pliny is impressive. The similarities do not, of course, always indicate indebtedness. But one may confidently assert that there was a definite debt. To insist that Milton was indebted to these histories is not, indeed, to charge that he was lacking in originality or to deny that he was genuinely inspired. Recognition of these relationships considerably extends our knowledge of the area of Milton's purposive reading and tends to weaken the claims that he was heavily influenced by specific sources. Scholars must be prepared to admit that Milton's poetry reflects his rich culture as well as his superb imagination. Of this culture another contemporary element will now be examined.

CHAPTER III

THE USE OF MAPS

IT IS Strabo's opinion that Homer was the founder of the science of geography and that in his care for geographical matter he excels all other poets, including Sophocles and Euripides. Strabo also declares that in adding to fact an element of fiction Homer followed a just poetic tradition.[1] That in his imaginative and accurate use of geography Milton, the English Homer, excels all other English poets competent critics readily admit. One has only to think, for example, of the appeal to the nymphs in *Lycidas,* of the lines describing the worship of Moloch and Chemos, of the passage enumerating the far-flung places mysteriously revealed to Adam in *Paradise Lost,* and of the similar roll of cities and countries in *Paradise Regained* to realize the importance and the beauty of the geographical elements in Milton's poetry. Curiously enough, a specific aspect of Milton's knowledge of geography has never been fully explored: this is the relationship of his poetry to contemporary maps. Certain contemporary maps are, I believe, not only almost indispensable illustrations of the geographical passages in Milton's poetry but also probably important factors in his poetic inspiration.

Milton's interest in geography has, of course, long been recognized. Verity argues that Milton knew George Sandys' *Relation of a Journey* (1615) and that Peter Heylyn's *Cosmography* (1650) was his chief authority for geography and the customs of foreign nations.[2] Having emphasized the widespread interest in geography in the seventeenth century, Mr. E. N. S. Thompson declares that "No scholar in the seven-

---

[1] *The Geography of Strabo* (New York, 1917), I, 5, 73, 169, *passim.*
[2] *Paradise Lost* (1910), II, 383, 440.

teenth century felt a keener interest in geography than did John Milton."[3]   Mr. Allan H. Gilbert reminds us that in his school Milton used Pierre Davity's *Geography;*[4] and in 1919 Mr. Gilbert published his indispensable *Geographical Diction-ary of Milton.* Besides, there is in Milton's prose evidence of his interest in geography.   In the Preface to *A Brief History of Moscovia* (1682) he writes, "The study of Geography is both profitable and delightful. . . ."   In *Of Education* (1644) he includes geography in the course of study, with directions that boys should learn "the use of the Globes, *and all the Maps;*[5] first with the old names, and then with the new . . ." and that they should read the ancient geographers, Mela, Pliny, Solinus.   His special interest in atlases is expressed in a letter to Peter Heimbach, dated Westminster, November 8, 1656, which reads in part:

You have amply fulfilled my request about the Atlas. I did not ask you to buy it for me, but only to find out the lowest price of the book. . . . As far as I am concerned, pictures are, on account of my blindness, of little use to me, whose blind eyes wander in vain over the real world, and I am afraid that any money I spent on that book would only seem to make my deprivation more painful to me.

May I ask you to go to this further trouble on my behalf, to find out and inform me on your return of how many volumes the work consists, and of which of the two editions, that of Blaeu or that of Jansen, is the more complete and accurate.[6]

This important letter, it should be noted, is dated four years after Milton's blindness became complete, and two years be-fore he is thought to have begun the systematic composition of *Paradise Lost.*

Despite the lead offered by this letter, there has been no careful study of Milton's use of contemporary atlases.   There are random notes.   Verity suggests that Milton had used Mer-

---

[3] "Milton's Knowledge of Geography," *Studies in Philology*, XVI, 149.
[4] *The Geographical Review*, VII, 322-338.
[5] Italics mine.
[6] *Milton Private Correspondence.* . . . Translated by Phyllis B. Tillyard (Cambridge, 1932), p. 38.

cator's *Atlas* (1636) in writing parts of *Lycidas,* and he mentions Mercator's map of Tartaria in explanation of the famous Satan-Vulture simile in *Paradise Lost.*[7] Albert S. Cook proves that *Namancos* in the lines

> Where the great vision of the guarded Mount
> Looks toward *Namancos* and *Bayona's* hold

should be spelled *Nemancos,* and that the erroneous spelling was due to Ojea, whose map of Galicia was first published in Ortelius's *Theatrum Orbis Terrarum* in 1606.[8] Laura E. Lockwood shows that the Nyseian isle, girt by the river Triton, is found in the Ortelius of 1624.[9] Thompson refers to Lockwood's evidence and adds that in a few other places Milton must have consulted Ortelius or Mercator. In his *Dictionary,* Gilbert occasionally and incidentally refers to maps. Thus the relationship between Milton's poetry and the maps has been merely suggested rather than systematically studied. But the subject is important. Certain maps and the related explanation are indisputably part of the actual stuff with which Milton's creative imagination worked; they are somewhat crude materials which Milton's magic reshaped into lines of deathless beauty.

Before taking up the maps which are definitely related to Milton's poetry, it may be useful to describe briefly the general character and purpose of some of the old atlases. The original tables in Ptolemy's geographies mark comparatively few rivers and cities; they indicate mountains by a series of small pyramids of uniform size; they do not, of course, include the new world; there are naturally, especially in Africa and Asia, many barren areas.[10] The new tables in Ptolemy's *Geographia* of 1540 are sparingly decorated: monsters of the deep appear; there is a shipwreck in the Mediterranean; there are forests in northern Albion and Germania; in the Caspian

---

[7] *Comus and Lycidas,* p. 153; *Paradise Lost,* II, 683-684.

[8] "Two Notes on Milton," *Modern Language Review,* II, 121-128.

[9] *Modern Language Notes,* XXI, 86.

[10] The first Ptolemy containing tables of the new world was published in 1513.

Sea appears Noah's Ark "que quievit in Montibus Armeniae."
In Ptolemy's *Geographia* of 1605, which has Mercator's maps,[11]
decoration has gone further: huge fish roam the sea; Aetna
Mons erupts with soaring flames; in Africa there is a winged
dragon; in Scythia Extra Imaum men pursue horses, flocks are
being shepherded, near India camels repose. As will be shown
later, Milton used several maps in this Ptolemy of 1605.

In his address "to the Courteous Reader," Abraham Ortelius, author and compiler of the *Theatrum Orbis Terrarum*
(Milton's favorite atlas, as we shall see), makes the following
observations, which, if Milton's poetry is substituted for "Histories," explain the thesis of the following exposition:

For thou shalt meet with many things in the reading of Histories,
(I will not say, almost all) which, except thou have the knowledge
of the countreys and places mentioned in them, cannot onely not
bee well conceived and understood, but also oft times they are
cleane mistaken and otherwise understood then they ought to bee:
. . . But seeing that this is a matter which even experience it
selfe doeth teach to be true, there is no reason why I should stand
long upon the proofe of the same. This so necessary a knowledge
of Geography . . . may very easily be learn'd out of Geographicall
Chartes or Mappes. And when we have acquainted our selves
somewhat with the use of these Tables or Mappes, or have attained
thereby to some reasonable knowledge of Geography, whatsoever
we shall read, these Chartes being placed, as it were certaine glasses
before our eyes, will the longer be kept in memory, and make the
deeper impression in us: by which meanes it commeth to passe, that
now we do seeme to perceive some fruit of that which we have
read. I omit here, that the reading of Histories doeth both seeme
to be much more pleasant, and indeed so it is, when the Mappe
being layed before our eyes, we may behold things done, or places
where they were done, as if they were at this time present and
in doing. For how much we are holpen, when as in the Holy
Scripture, we read of the iourney of the Israelites, which they made
from Egypt, through the Red Sea, and that same huge Wildernesse,
into the Land of promise, when as looking upon the Mappe of
Palestina, we doe almost aswell see it as if we were there, I thinke

[11] Of this Ptolemy the Huntington Library has two copies, in both of
which the maps are hand-colored.

any student in Divinitie, or that History hath oft made triall. Which things being so, how much those which are students and lovers of Histories are combred, hindred and stayd, yea, & many times, even while they are in their race and continued course, drawne backe, it is an easie matter to conceive, when either the description of all countreys cannot be gotten, or if they may be gotten, they are dearer then that every mans money will reach and attaine unto especially those that are but poore, or none of the wealthiest.[12]

After stating the objection to large maps, which could not be opened in small rooms, and explaining the purpose of "this our Theatre," which is to present small models of the best available charts, Ortelius declares that the work has been done "so as nothing, no never so small a thing, is either omitted or altered that was to bee found in the greater: except it be this, which oftentimes thou shalt finde, that the names of places and other things, which in the first Copies could hardly be read, in these our Mappes we have so expressed, that they may perfectly be read of any man. And sometime, where occasion did serve, or need require, and the place would permit, unto the moderne and usuall names of certaine places, wee have added the ancient names mentioned by old writers, but now vulgarly unknowne." Milton must have heartily agreed with Ortelius's opinion that "Geographicall Chartes or Mappes" contribute much to our understanding of history. The legibility of Ortelius's maps and the presence of the old names, especially in the Parergon, were doubtless factors in winning Milton's favor.

The brief descriptions and historical discourses printed on what Ortelius calls the "backsides" of the maps were an especially attractive feature of the *Theatrum*. For example, compare with these lines in *Paradise Lost*

> His Eye might there command wherever stood
> City of old or modern Fame, the Seat
> Of mightiest Empire, from the destind Walls
> Of *Cambalu*, seat of *Cathaian Can*
>
> . . . .
>
> To *Paquin* of *Sinæan* Kings[13]

---

[12] From the English edition of 1606.   [13] XI, 385-390.

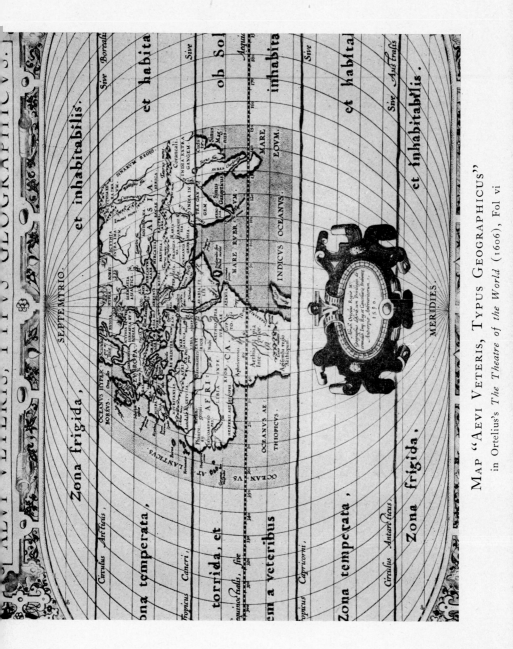

Map "Aevi Veteris, Typus Geographicus"

in Ortelius's *The Theatre of the World* (1606), Fol vi

the following excerpts from the accounts of Tartaria and China in Ortelius:

Heere also is the country of Cataia, whose chiefe city is *Cambalu,* which, as *Nicolaus de Comitibus* writeth, is eighteen Italian miles about, or as M. *Paulus Venetus,* thirty two. But *Quinzai,* a city of the province *Mangi,* which is from hence Eastward, upon the Eastern sea, is thought to be farre bigger than this: For this . . . is in compasse an hundred miles. . . .[14]

Ortelius adds that the Tartars "call their Emperour *Cham,* which signifieth the same that *Princeps,* a Prince: hereupon *Cambalu* is interpreted, The seate or city of the Prince." In Ortelius's map of China, "Paquin" appears instead of "Quinzai," and it is explained that the huge kingdom of China "is the same no doubt with *Sinae* or *Sinarum regio*" and that "*Paquin* [is] a city in the North parts of this kingdome, toward the confines of *Tartaria,* where he ordinarily keepeth his Court. . . ."[15]

Several illustrations may show why Milton was particularly interested in Ortelius's *Theatrum.* In the 1595 and the 1606 *Theatrum,* but not in that of 1570, there is a map entitled "The peaceable or the South Sea, called by the Spaniards Mar del Sur." This Sea, says Ortelius, was unknown to the ancients. It was first seen in 1513 by Vasco Nunnez from the coast of Peru; it was first crossed in 1520 by Magellan, who, "having passed the streight by him found, . . . with an heroick and Herculean courage entred this sea, which uncertaine it is, whether any shippe before his had ever stemmed." His voyage is described:

Departing from *Sivil* with five ships, whereof one being his owne, was called by a name of good presage *Victoria,* he came to the fortunate or *Canary-isles;* then to the *Gorgones* or *Hesperides,* now termed the isles of *Cape Verde;* and thence to the Streight above-named: which when he had found and past thorow, he enters into this sea; where with a fresh and prosperous gale having sailed upon the maine 40. dayes together, and beholding nothing but sea on all sides, and still the sea; when he had crossed the South

[14] Fol. 105.   [15] Fol. 106.

tropick he descried two small barren and unhabited isles: where notwithstanding, because they found good fishing, they staied two dayes. . . . Then he proceeds on his navigation, & in the space of 3. moneths and 20. dayes, having sailed over this vast Ocean 2400. leagues, he attained at length to the Aequinoctiall, and thence to the desired *Moluccos.* . . . But concerning the ship called *La Victoria* learne thus much: it is not sayd amisse: *Bare names oft times things named doe resemble:* Manifest it by this ship, which under this happy name, the first voyage that ever she made, was the only ship that carried away the victory of sailing quite over the maine Ocean, for so many ages before. For departing from Spaine, by the Streight of *Magellan,* to the *Moluccos,* thence having doubled the Cape of *Buona Esperanca,* and returned, whence she first put forth, she was the first of all ships and in all ages, that ever circumpassed the whole earth. The same ship made out of *Spaine* a second voyage as farre as *S. Domingo* and home againe. Thither also she made a third voyage; but in her returne she was quite lost; neither was it ever knowen what became of her. Antiquity would have thought she had been taken up into the skies, and placed among the Constellations, like another *Argo.*

On the map one sees the good ship *Victoria,* with sails set, men at work, winged Victory at the prow, and underneath these verses:

> Prima ego velivolis ambivi cursibus Orbem,
> Magellane novo te duce ducta freto.
> Ambivi, meritoque vocor Victoria; sunt mi
> Vela, alae; precium, gloria; pugna, mare.

With the passage naming the *Gorgones* or *Hesperides* Isles one should compare Ortelius's map "Aevi Veteris, Typus Geographicus," in the Parergon, which shows these islands, so named; and one should recall Raphael's words to Adam:

> the parting Sun
> Beyond the Earths green Cape and verdant Isles
> *Hesperean* sets, my Signal to depart.[16]

In the map "Ulysses Errores,"[17] on the coast of Tyrrhenia is "Aeaea insula, quae Circes domicilium." When Milton wrote in *Comus* that Bacchus

---

[16] VIII, 630-632.   [17] Fol. xxxiv.

> After the *Tuscan* Mariners transform'd
> Coasting the *Tyrrhene* shore, as the winds listed,
> On *Circes* Iland fell

he probably recalled this map in Ortelius. Of the island Lemnos Ortelius writes, "This ile is consecrate to Vulcan: for olde fables do tell, that, being by Jupiter throwen headlong out of heaven, he light in this ile." One recalls the architect of Pandemonium,

> how he fell
> From Heav'n, they fabl'd, thrown by angry *Jove*
> Sheer o're the Chrystal Battlements: from Morn
> To Noon he fell, from Noon to dewy Eve,
> A Summers day; and with the setting Sun
> Dropt from the Zenith like a falling Star,
> On *Lemnos* th' *Ægæan* Ile.[18]

Of Lesbos Ortelius writes, "In the fables we find recorded, that about Antissa, Orphaeus head was buried: and that the nightingals do heere sing much better, than in other places, Antigonus, out of the authority of Myrsilius, borne in this ile, doth affirme for a certaine truth." In *Lycidas,* the poet recalls the death of Orpheus, whose gory visage was sent "Down the swift *Hebrus* to the *Lesbian* shore."

All the evidence indicates that Milton was familiar with the maps in Ortelius, especially with those in the Parergon, and with the related exposition, which must have particularly appealed to all that was poetic in his soul. In *Animadversions upon the Remonstrants Defence,* when he replies to Hall's listing countries without bishops, Milton says, "O do not foile your cause thus, and trouble Ortelius. . . ."[19] This is not an unimportant indication that he was familiar with the *Theatrum.*

Milton certainly knew Camden's *Britannia,* perhaps in the translation by Philemon Holland (1610), which is "Beautified with Mappes of The severall Shires of England." Although he inquired about "Jansen's" atlas, we cannot be sure that he knew Jansson's *Novus Atlas* (1647-1649); but in the ninth volume

[18] *Paradise Lost,* I, 740-746.
[19] *The Works of John Milton* (New York, 1931), III, 138.

of a later edition (1657), doubtless the one concerning which Milton wrote to Peter Heimbach, there is a remarkable chart of the winds which Milton may have used. Thomas Fuller's *A Pisgah-Sight of Palestine* (1650) is limited to a detailed illustration of Biblical story. In one map, for example, Moses with arms outstretched stands on Mount Pisgah, watching the Israelites cross the Jordan; in another, the herd of swine plunges into the Sea of Galilee; in Zion, near David's palace, Bathsheba bathes, and Fuller writes, "Flat was the roof of this palace, whereon David sate, and from whence he beheld *Bathsheba* (hard by is her house) bathing her self. I cannot excuse her action herein."[20] In Mount Libanus we see the goodly cedars, straight and tall, and Solomon's workmen felling and shaping them for the Temple of God. Probably Milton knew Fuller's *Pisgah-Sight*.

From these general considerations turn to the maps that seem to be definitely related to Milton's poetry, first those related to *Comus*. It is important to notice that in the maps of England in Ortelius and Camden *Sabrina* is the name of the Severn river. Ortelius's map of England and Ireland[21] marks the stream twice: "Sabrina flu." and "Sabrina fl." The river flows not far from Ludlow, between which and the stream stands a forest. In Camden's *Britain, Sabrina* is given on the maps of Glocester-Shire, Worcester-Shire, and Montgomery-Shire;[22] and in the description of Montgomery-Shire there is the following:

Five miles hence, the *Hil Plinlimon* whereof I spake, raiseth it selfe up to a wonderfull height, and on that part where it boundeth one side of this shire, it powreth forth *Sabrina*, the greatest river in Britaine next to *Thamis*, which the British tearme *Haffren*, and Englishmen *Severn*. Whence the name was derived I could never read. For, that seemeth to smell of a fable, which *Geffrey* hath devised of the Virgin *Sabrina* therein drowned, and of which a late Poet following his steps hath delivered thus in verse.

. . . .
Into the streame was Abren headlong cast;

[20] *Op. cit.*, p. 334.   [21] Fol. 12.   [22] Pp. 357, 573, 661.

THE USE OF MAPS 103

> The river then taking that Virgins name,
> Hight *Abren,* and thereof *Sabrin* at last,
> Which tearme in speech corrupt implies the same.

The story of Sabrina is, of course, told by Spenser, Drayton, and others, and by Milton in his *History of Britain.* He also alludes to it in *At a Vacation Exercise.* Nevertheless, the presence of the name *Sabrina* on the maps should not be ignored, especially in the light of the following evidence proving that Milton used maps. The reader does not need to be reminded that in *Comus* Sabrina, the gentle nymph "That with moist curb sways the smooth Severn stream," is an important character in the solution of the plot.

In *Lycidas* many lines are intimately associated with the maps and the accompanying explanation. Milton asks where were the nymphs when Edward King was drowned:

> Where were ye Nymphs when the remorseless deep
> Clos'd o're the head of your lov'd *Lycidas?*
> For neither were ye playing on the steep,
> Where your old *Bards,* the famous *Druids* ly,
> Nor on the shaggy top of *Mona* high,
> Nor yet where *Deva* spreads her wisard stream.[23]

Scholars disagree as to the location of "the steep." Masson suggests vaguely that it may be any of the Welsh mountains, and notes Warton's identification of it with "the sepulture of the Druids at Kerig-y-Druidion in South Denbighshire."[24] Verity suggests also Penmaenmawr.[25] But Gilbert explains that Camden, to whom Masson refers, mentions no sepulchres at Kerig-y-Druidion, and "merely makes the name equivalent to Druids' stones."[26] Gilbert suggests Holyhead, called by Holinshed "holie Ile" from the number of holy men buried there. The place Milton refers to is probably the island Bardsey, which in Ortelius's *Theatrum* is described by Humphrey Lhuyd as follows:

[23] Ll. 50-55.
[24] *The Poetical Works of John Milton* (London, 1882), III, 281.
[25] *Comus and Lycidas,* p. 134.   [26] *Dictionary,* p. 24.

Ptolemy the Prince of Geographers, upon the East side of Ireland placeth foure ilands, Monarina . . . , Mona, Adros and Lymnos. The two latter are very well knowen unto us at this day; for that indeed they doe still reteine those auncient names. Adros of our countrey men is called *Ynys ador*, that is, as the words doe signifie, *The Iland of birds*. Lymnos they now call *Enlli*, which the English men call *Bardesey*, that is, as he would faine interpret it, *Insula Bardorum*, The Bardes iland.[27]

Camden's description of Bardsey follows: The island "which the Britains now, name *Enhly*, and *English Berdsey*" is next above Lymen, which the Englishmen today call Ramsey.

As for *Enhly*, it is a name of a later stampe, and came by occasion of a certaine holy and devout man, who heere lived as an Eremite. For, this Island, which toward the East mounteth aloft with an high promontory, but Westward lieth plaine, and is of a fertile mould harboured in old time so many holy men, that . . . ancient histories record there were twenty thousand Saints buried heere. Next unto this lieth *Mona*, that is, *Anglesey*, which the Britains call *Mon*, *Tir-Mon*, and *Ynis Dowyll*, that is *A darke or shady Iland*. . . .[28]

In Ortelius and Camden is the explanation of Milton's line: Ortelius or Lhuyd supplies the "Bards," Camden the "steep" and the holy men, and also associates Bardsey with Mona, which follows in Milton:

Nor on the shaggy top of *Mona* high.

Here, of course, "shaggy" means wooded or covered with forests. In Camden the phrase "A darke or shady Iland" suggests forests. Describing "that most notable *Isle Mona*, the ancient seat of the *Druides*," Camden quotes from Tacitus the story of Suetonius's invasion of Mona, and tells how the Romans after the victory cut down the "groves consecrated to their cruel superstitions. . . ."[29]

[27] From "An Epistle of Humfrey Lhuyd, Written to Abraham Ortel," at the end of the *Theatrum* of 1606. Also in the 1595, Latin, edition. On Lhuyd's work and his connection with Ortelius, see F. J. North, *The Map of Wales* (Cardiff, 1935), pp. 54-57.
[28] P. 203.	[29] *Op. cit.*, p. 671.

Lhuyd quotes the account from Tacitus, and adds: "And that there have beene woods here within these four hundred yeeres or thereabouts, it is very manifest by our histories." Gilbert inquires, "Yet what does Milton mean by calling Mona 'high'?" Ortelius's account of Wales answers this question, and also mentions the forests. Quoting Leland's *Genethliacon of Edward Prince of Wales* in refutation of Polydore Virgil's assertion that Man is Mona, Ortelius writes:

If the name, which yet it retaineth: . . . If the nesse or promontorie Pen-mon, that is, as the word signifieth, The head of Mon: If the huge bodies of trees, and rootes covered over with sand, which daily are digged out of the shore of Tir-mon: If the firre-trees of marvailous length, which in squally grounds are heere and there found within the earth in this Iland, do not sufficiently prove that that was anciently called Mona, which now we call Anglesey, I know not what to say more. . . .[30]

And he proceeds to tell out of Tacitus how the Romans cut down the groves of the Druids on Mona. In Ortelius's map of England and Ireland,[31] as well as in his map of Wales, all these places are marked.

The line

Nor yet where *Deva* spreads her wisard stream

is fully explained in Camden's *Britain*. The Dee, in Latin *Deva*, springs out of two fountains in Wales. "I see not why they should attribute Divinitie to this river *Dwy* above all others . . . unlesse peradventure, because now and then it changeth the channell, and thereby foreshewed a sure token of victorie to the inhabitants upon it, when they were in hostility one with another, according as it inclined to this side or to that, after it had left the channell: . . . Or else, because they observed that contrarie to the wonted maner of other rivers, upon the fall of much raine it arose but little, and so often as the South wind beateth long upon it, it swelleth and extraordinarily overfloweth the grounds adjoining. Peradventure also the *Christian Britains* thought the water of this river

[30] *Theatrum*, fol. 13.   [31] Fol. 12.

to be holy: For, it is written, that when they stood ready to joine battaile with the English Saxons and had kissed the earth, they drank also very devoutly of this river, in memoriall of *Christs* most sacred and pretious bloud."[32]

Consider the following lines:

> Or whether thou to our moist vows deny'd,
> Sleep'st by the fable of *Bellerus* old,
> Where the great vision of the guarded Mount
> Looks toward *Namancos* and *Bayona's* hold.

"Bellerus" is coined from *Bellerium*, the Roman name for Land's End. In the Cambridge manuscript, Milton first wrote "Corineus" and then substituted "Bellerus." Masson thinks the change was made for metrical reasons; but both words may be pronounced as three syllables, with the accent on the penultimate syllable. Milton's desire for geographical consistency probably accounts for the change. In Ortelius's map "Angliae et Hiberniae Accurata Descriptio, Veteribus et Recentioribus Nominibus illustrata,"[33] we read the legend "Antiuestium prom. quod et Belerium prom. vulgo. The Landes end." In Holland's translation of Camden's *Britain*, the map of Cornwall[34] has the legend "Armed knight Landes end Antvesteum Bolerium Sive Velerium Promontorium." In Mercator's *Atlas* (1636), on the other hand, all the maps showing England, as well as the map of the southwest counties, including Cornwall, use the term "The Landes end" and no additional designation.

Verity says that he could not find "Namancos" in Ortelius and concludes that Milton must have used Mercator. But, as Cook proves, the map of Galicia in Ortelius (1606) shows Namancos as well as Bayona. Again, Mercator's *Atlas* does not mark Mount St. Michael. But Ortelius's map of England and Ireland and Camden's of Cornwall show the Mount plainly. Doubtless Milton had read the following account in Holland's translation:

As the shore fetcheth a compasse by little and little from hence Southward, it letteth in a bay or creeke of the Sea, in manner of

[32] P. 602.
[33] Fol. 12.   [34] Between pp. 182-183.

a Crescent, which they call *Mounts-bay:* . . . And in the very angle and corner it selfe *S. Michaels Mount,* which gave its name unto the foresaid Bay; . . . This Rocke is of a good height and craggy, compassed round about with water so oft as it is floud, but at every ebbe joined to the main-land, so that they say of it, It is land and Iland twice a day. . . . In the very top hereof within the Fortresse, there was a Chappell consecrated to *S. Michael* the Archangel, where William Earle of Cornwall and Moriton . . . built a Cell for one or two monks; who avouched that *S. Michael* appeered in that Mount. . . .[35]

Thus the relation between *Lycidas,* on the one hand, and Ortelius and Camden, on the other, seems to be particularly close. The maps and the explanations throw light on several important passages, which for many students are mere lists of names. Moreover, it is likely that in writing, Milton, in fact or in memory, retraced on the maps those sonorous names, Sabrina, Mona, Belerium, and so on, which for all their seeming unreality today were then actual places redolent of the past. Ortelius and Camden are probably the sources of some of the most stirring lines in *Lycidas.*

After *Lycidas* Milton was for many years occupied less with poetry than with religious and political writing, to which finally he sacrificed his sight, becoming completely blind in 1652, after finishing the *First Defence.* When at last he turned to the writing of his masterpiece, his interest in geography survived his calamity. His sure command of geography is an important factor in the artistic triumph of his great epic, with its vast scope. In *Paradise Lost* there is abundant evidence of a phenomenal memory of maps or of skillful assistance in getting at cartographical information; probably memory and visual aid were combined to produce such astonishing results.

In *Paradise Lost* Eden and Paradise naturally occupy first place in a discussion of cartography. As was noted in the preceding chapter, Milton broadly sketched the extent of Eden—

> A Heaven on Earth: for blissful Paradise
> Of God the Garden was, by him in the East

[35] P. 188.

> Of *Eden* planted; *Eden* stretchd her Line
> From *Auran* Eastward to the Royal Towrs
> Of Great *Seleucia*, built by *Grecian* Kings,
> Or where the Sons of *Eden* long before
> Dwelt in *Telassar*.[36]

This is the traditional situation of Eden and Paradise, as is shown by the map in the Bishops' Bible (1568). A similar map is included in several later Bibles.[37] A somewhat more detailed chart of the same territory, corresponding closely to Milton's lines, is found in Raleigh's *History*, with which Milton was probably familiar.

To emphasize the beauty of this Paradise, Milton declares that four other terrestrial paradises are not to be compared with it.

> Not that faire field
> Of *Enna*, where *Proserpin* gathring flours
> Her self a fairer Floure by gloomie *Dis*
> Was gatherd, which cost *Ceres* all that pain
> To seek her through the world; nor that sweet Grove
> Of *Daphne* by *Orontes*, and th' inspired
> *Castalian* Spring might with this Paradise
> Of *Eden* strive; nor that *Nyseian* Ile
> Girt with the River *Triton*, where old *Cham*,
> Whom Gentiles *Ammon* call and *Libyan Jove*,
> Hid *Amalthea* and her Florid Son
> Young *Bacchus* from his Stepdame *Rhea's* eye;
> Nor where *Abassin* Kings thir issue Guard,
> Mount *Amara*, though this by some suppos'd
> True Paradise under the *Ethiop* Line
> By *Nilus* head, enclos'd with shining Rock,
> A whole dayes journey high, but wide remote
> From this Assyrian Garden.[38]

These four places, Enna, the grove of Daphne, the Nyseian isle, and Mount Amara, are all marked in Ortelius's *Theatrum* of 1606. Miss Lockwood finds the Nyseian isle in the Orte-

---

[36] IV, 208-214.
[37] In editions of 1576 (London, Christopher Barker), 1616 (London, Robert Barker), 1644 (Amsterdam, Thomas Stafford).
[38] IV, 268-285.

If there be any kyngdome vnder heauen that is excellent in beautie, in aboundaunce of fruites, in plenteousnes, in delytes and other gyftes: they which haue wrytten of countreys, do prayse aboue all, the same that this figure repreſenteth. Wherfore, with the prayses of thoſe wryters, Moyſes exalteth this paradiſe, as duly belonging vnto it. And it is very well lyke, that the region or kingdome of Eden hath ben ſituated in that countrey, as it appeareth in the .xxvii. Chapter of Eſaias the .xii. vearſe, and in the .xxvii. of Ezechiel the .xiii. vearſe. Moreouer, where as Moyſes ſayde that a flood dyd proceede from that place: I do interprete it, from the courſe of the waters, as yf he ſhoulde haue ſayde that Adam dyd inhabite in the flooddes ſyde, or in the lande which was watered of both ſydes. Howbeit, there is no great matter in that, eyther that Adam hath inhabited vnder the place where both flooddes come together towarde Babylon and Seleucia, or aboue: It is ſufficient þ he hath ben in a place watered of waters. But the thing is not darke nor hard to vnderſtande howe this floodde hath ben deuided in foure heades. for they be two flooddes which be gathered in one, then they ſeperate them ſelues in diuers partes. So in they ioynyng and flowyng together, it is but a floodde, wherof there is two heades into two chanels from aboue, and two towarde the ſea, when it begynneth to ſeperate it ſelfe abrode. But to declare vnto you the diuerſities of the ryuers names, beſydes their vſuall and principall appellations, and howe they be called as they paſſe through eche prouince, with the interpretations of the ſame, I thynke it rather tedious and combreſome, then profitable. Wherfore the ſimple ſenſe of Moyſes is, that the garden wherof Adam was the owner, was watered with waters, becauſe that the courſe of this floodde was there, whiche was deuided into foure heades.

CHART OF GOD'S GARDEN, BISHOPS' BIBLE (1568)

lius of 1624, Africae Propriae Tabula; the same map is in the
Ortelius of 1606. Besides, Ortelius's map "Siciliae Veteris Typus"[39] marks Enna with the legend "Campus Ennensis," and
in this there is a lake bordered with trees, with this legend:
"Pergus Lacus, et umbilicus Siciliae Hic Proserpinam a Plutone
raptam ferunt." The Island and the Lake are described thus
in Sandys' *A Relation of a Journey* (1615):

Sicilia . . . Sacred of old unto *Ceres*, and *Proserpina:* . . . who
are said here first to have inhabited, in regard of the admirable fertility of the soyle: . . . Called by *Cato* the granary and nurse of
the people of *Rome;* . . . Hot bathes, rivers, and lakes replenished
with fish: amongst which there is one called Lago de Goridan;
formerly the navell of *Sicilia*, for that in the midst of the Iland;
but more anciently *Pergus:* famous for the fabulous rape of *Proserpina.* . . .[40]

The northeastern spur of Ortelius's map of Sicily is marked
"Pelorum Prom.," and south of this is "Aetna mons," from
which flames and smoke ascend. Recall Milton's description
of Hell:

> as when the force
> Of subterranean wind transports a Hill
> Torn from *Pelorus,* or the shatter'd side
> Of thundring *Aetna.*[41]

Now turn to Ortelius's description of Sicily:

That this was sometime a *peninsula*, or demy-ile, adioned to *Italy*,
as a part of *Brutium* in *Calabria* . . . and afterward was by violence of tempest severed from the same . . . it is a generall opinion
of all antiquity . . . *Strabo, Pliny* and *Dionysius* do write that
it was caused by an earthquake: *Silius* and *Cassiodorus*, do thinke
it to have been done by the rage and violence of the tide and surges
of the sea. . . .[42]

Scylla and Charybdis, to which Milton often refers, are also
marked on this map of Sicily, as is "Arethusa fons" in an in-

[39] Fol. xxiii.
[40] Pp. 234-235.   [41] I, 230-233.
[42] Under Pelorus, Gilbert refers to Diodorus (*Dictionary*, p. 229).

serted map of Syracuse. Ortelius's map of Sicily must have fascinated Milton, as it does today the student of his poetry.

Returning to Paradise, recall the lines alluding to the grove of Daphne. Ortelius presents a beautiful chart of this famous grove,[43] which he also describes:

Daphne in *Antiochia* in *Syria,* upon the river *Orontes,* that famous and pleasant Suburbs, . . . A delectable and gorgeous place, is distant from the citie about fortie furlongs. It is in compasse fourscore furlongs (or, which is all one, tenne miles) as *Strabo* writeth; who moreover saith, that it is a pretty village, within a huge darke grove, waterd with divers goodly brookes and running waters. But take this larger description of it, out of *Sozomen:* It is a place, sayth he, round beset and shadowed with many Cypresse trees, and those of infinite height, . . . here and there it is bedecked with sundry other sorts of goodly trees: by reason of the thicknesse of whose boughs and leaves, . . . it is all covered over with a shadow as it were with a roofe. Under the trees, the earth, according to the seasons of the yeere, bringeth forth all sorts, most pleasant and sweet-smelling flowers, . . . Here is also a spring, which is supposed to fetch his waters from *Castalius,* a spring by *Parnassus* in *Greece:* wherefore some men have attributed to it the vertue and power of divination, and doe verily perswade themselves, that it was of equal force and nature with that at *Delphos.* . . .

After the Nyseian isle, Milton refers to Mount Amara in Ethiopia. This Mount is marked in Ortelius's map of Africa and in the map "Ethiopia or Alhabas, The country of the Abyssines, or The Empire of Prester Iohn,"[44] with this legend: "Amara Mons, hic Presbiteri Iohannis filii in custodia a praesidiis detinentur." In contemporary maps of this region, this mountain is generally shown. It appears in Mercator's *Atlas;*[45] and in Theodore de Bry's *Vera Descriptio Regni Africani* (1598) buildings are conspicuous on Amara Montes. The place is described by various writers, for example by Davity, Heylyn, and Purchas. Purchas prints "Hondius his Map of the Abisine Empire," which shows this mountain.[46] Purchas stresses the unreality of the place: "I could leade you on in

[43] *Op. cit.,* fol. xxxvii.   [44] Fol. 113.
[45] II, 431.   [46] *Pilgrimage* (1626), p. 738.

CHART OF THE GROVE OF DAPHNE
in Ortelius's *The Theatre of the World* (1606), Fol. xxxvii

a delectable way, but doubtfull, like the Poets writings, and
bring you into *Elisian*, but fabulous fields, fertile in all things
but truth: wherein let the Reader pardon that I have already
been so long, rather then tedious, in this Utopian Aethiopia. . . ."[47]

It should be emphasized that the four places mentioned in
connection with Paradise are found in Ortelius's maps. From
this it is perhaps reasonable to conclude that Milton was familiar with Ortelius and that in his choice of places he was
partly aided by the maps. The maps and the accompanying description gave to the names actuality; Milton endowed them
with immortality.

Turn now to Palestine, which, though not the setting of
Paradise Lost, is the scene of Biblical events often mentioned
in the epic. The ancient name of Palestine, says Ortelius, was
Canaan, until the Israelites, having partly slain and partly subdued all the posterity of Canaan, possessed the territory, from
which time it began to be called the Land of Israel. The higher
country, toward Sidon and Tyre, they called Galilee; the middle, Samaria; the lower, Judea. On the other hand, all the
land of Canaan, as high as the mountains of Thracon near Antioch and the country of Ammon, was called Judea. Ptolemy
and others call it "Palaestina, of the Palaestini, which according
to the propriety of the Hebrew pronunciation in the Holy Scriptures are called Philistim . . . this Nation indeed both for
their great command and warres made with their neighbours
for certaine yeares together, were very famous."[48]

Places directly east of Palestine are mentioned by Milton in
the famous list of devils, which will be discussed more fully
in the chapter on the pagan gods:

> First, *Moloch*, ...
> . . . . Him the *Ammonite*
> Worshipt in *Rabba* and her watry Plain,
> In *Argob* and in *Basan*, to the stream
> Of utmost *Arnon*. . . . .
> . . . .

[47] *Ibid.*, p. 749.   [48] Fol. ii.

> Next *Chemos*, th' obscene dread of *Moabs* Sons,
> From *Aroer* to *Nebo*, and the wild
> Of Southmost *Abarim;* in *Hesebon*
> And *Horonaim*, *Seons* Realm, beyond
> The flowry Dale of *Sibma* clad with Vines,
> And *Eleale* to th' *Asphaltick* Pool.[49]

The geography of this passage is explained in any one of three maps in Ortelius: "The Holy Land," (fol. 111), "Palaestina," (fol. ii), and "Typus Chorographicus, Celebrium Locorum in Regno Iudae et Israhel" (fol. iii). It is remarkable that Milton's spelling as a rule agrees with that of Ortelius's maps. In the map "Iudae et Israhel," for example, we see Argob, Basan, Arnon, Aroer, Nebo, and "Ben Hinnom vallis," near Jerusalem. On this map "Habarim mons" appears, but Milton's form "Abarim" occurs in the other two maps, as does Hesbon, and in the map "Palaestina" is the legend "Lacus Asphaltites, *vel* Mare Mortuum, *aut* Salsum," with which compare Milton's "Asphaltic Pool." However, at this time Asphaltic lake was a common name for the Dead Sea.

Consider also the following lines:

> *Dagon* his Name, Sea Monster, upward Man
> And downward Fish: yet had his Temple high
> Rear'd in *Azotus*, dreaded through the Coast
> Of *Palestine*, in *Gath* and *Ascalon*,
> And *Accaron* and *Gaza's* frontier bounds.[50]

Ortelius's map of Judea and Israel shows Azotus, Gath, Ascalon, and Gaza. Milton's "Accaron" is on this map spelled "Ecron"; but the form "Accaron" appears in the map "Palaestina." Milton's preference for certain forms has been emphasized, in particular his avoiding *sh*, in such words as *Hesebon, Sechem, Sittim, Beersaba.* As a rule, all that Milton needed to do was to take the names from Ortelius's maps, where almost invariably he could find the forms that his ear preferred.

Horonaim is not marked in Ortelius's maps. Gilbert says, "A city of Moab, of unknown site."[51] This place occurs on the

[49] I, 392-411.
[50] I, 462-466.
[51] *Dictionary*, p. 148.

double-page map of Canaan in the first folio edition of the King James Bible. The map, which was begun by John More and finished by John Speed, states:

The citties given to the Levits, are marked with a crosse, and the sixe citties of refuge, with a double crosse, likewise all the bordering countries, upon the land of Canaan, . . . with all the townes, and places which the scripture nameth in them, are exactlie sett downe. So that, ther is not the name of any cittie, towne, countrie, mountaine, river, wildernes or plaine, mentioned in scripture, within the land of Canaan, or in any of their countries above named, but are inserted & in their trew graduations observed. . . .

On this map, Horonaim is east of the Dead Sea and on the Sered river, which flows northwest into the Arnon.[52]

This map in the King James version has a table in which the items are numbered to correspond with the numbers opposite the illustrations "of the chiefest actiones happening in every severall tribe. . . . All tending to this end, to make more plaine unto us, the histories of the holie scriptures, both in ould, and newe testaments." Accordingly, the map shows the Israelites crossing the Red Sea while the waters overwhelm the hosts of Pharaoh; Moses on Mount Sinai receiving from the Lord the tables of the Law; in Edom the serpent on a cross, and this legend "As Moses lifted up the serpent in the wilderness so must the sonne of man bee lifted up"; in the country of the Gergesenes the herd of swine rushing down into the Sea of Galilee; just north of this "Absalon hanged by his heare"; on Mount Tabor Christ transfigured; near Shechem the pit into which Joseph was cast; near Bethel the calf erected by Jeroboam, with which idolatry all the Kings of Israel were stained; Jacob's well, where Christ conferred with the woman of Samaria; Jordan, in which John did baptize; near Askalon the place where Samson slew thirty Philistines; Gaza, whence he carried away the gates, and whither he himself was carried; just east of Jerusalem three small figures, "The wisemen of the east following the starre Christ"; Bethlehem, where Christ,

[52] See also Fuller's *Pisgah-Sight,* map of Midian, Moab, Ammon, and Edom, Book IV, 18-19.

"the glorie of Israel and light of the gentills," was born; near Jerusalem Judas hanging from the tree; Mount Calvary, with its three crosses and the legend "Jesus that he might sanctifie the people with his owne bloud sufred without the gate. Heb. 13. 12." Thus was the geography of the Bible made clear. On this map, however, the spelling of names often differs from Milton's. For example, in the More-Speed map the following forms occur: Mountaines of Yabarim, Elealeth, Heshbon, Shechem, Ashdod, Askalon, Fountaines of Shiloe. All these are spellings that Milton avoided. On the other hand, in Ortelius's maps of the Holy Land occur the forms that Milton preferred.

Ortelius's map of Judea and Israel also illustrates that part of Book XII in which the Archangel Michael points out to Adam the territory to be occupied by Abraham and his seed:

> *Canaan* he now attains, I see his Tents
> Pitcht about *Sechem,* and the neighbouring Plaine
> Of *Moreh;* there by promise he receaves
> Gift to his Progenie of all that Land;
> From *Hamath* Northward to the Desert South
> (Things by thir names I call, though yet unnam'd)
> From *Hermon* East to the great Western Sea,
> Mount *Hermon,* yonder Sea, each place behold
> In prospect, as I point them; on the shoare
> Mount *Carmel;* here the double-founted stream
> *Jordan,* true limit Eastward; but his Sons
> Shall dwell to *Senir,* that long ridge of Hills.[53]

Ortelius's map shows all these places, except Hamath, which is on the More-Speed map: Sechem, which is in the plain of Moreh; Sin desertum, far south; Hermon mons, called also Shenir (Milton's Senir) by the Amorites; Mare Magnum, "the great Western Sea"; Carmelus m. by the Sea; Dan and Jor, the fountains of Jordan. The lines just quoted and the map in Ortelius seem to be intimately associated. Making due allowance for Michael as narrator, one who did not know of Milton's blindness might say that the passage was written immediately after the poet had consulted the map.

[53] XII, 135-146.

The Holy Land is presented in detail in a series of maps illustrating Thomas Fuller's *A Pisgah-Sight of Palestine* (1650). Fuller's charts and commentary abundantly illustrate Biblical story. For example, the map of the tribe of Benjamin[54] shows Jacob and his dream: a ladder set upon the earth, with its top reaching to heaven, and angels ascending and descending. Fuller's commentary is as follows: "*Beth-el*, that is, *Gods house*, was so named by *Iacob* (for formerly it was called *Luz*) who here lying on a stone . . . saw a *Ladder* with God on the top thereof, and Angels ascending and descending thereon. Going down to attend on Gods children according to their commission, and up to give an account of their attendance, and receive farther instruction." One recalls in *Paradise Lost* these lines, which follow the account of Satan's wanderings on the exterior of the dark continent of the universe:

> farr distant hee descries
> Ascending by degrees magnificent
> Up to the wall of Heaven a Structure high,
> At top whereof, but farr more rich appeerd
> The work as of a Kingly Palace Gate
> With Frontispiece of Diamond and Gold
> Imbellisht, thick with sparkling orient Gemmes
> The Portal shon, inimitable on Earth
> By Model, or by shading Pencil drawn.
> The Stairs were such as whereon *Jacob* saw
> Angels ascending and descending, bands
> Of Guardians bright, when he from *Esau* fled
> To *Padan-Aran* in the field of *Luz*,
> Dreaming by night under the open Skie,
> And waking cri'd, This is the Gate of Heav'n.[55]

In the map, below the figure of the dream, there is a pedestal surmounted by a golden calf, and near it a cloven altar with sacrifice burning, which is attended by two figures to whom a third approaches. Fuller writes, "Here Jeroboam set up one of his golden calves: and how busie was he about sacrificing unto it, when a Prophet sent from God denounced the destruction

---

[54] P. 236.   [55] III, 501-515.

of his Altar, which presently clave asunder. . . ." Milton
writes,

> Nor did *Israel* scape
> Th' infection when their borrow'd Gold compos'd
> The Calf in *Oreb:* and the Rebel King
> Doubl'd that sin in *Bethel* and in *Dan,*
> Lik'ning his Maker to the Grazed Ox.[56]

In this map Jericho is surrounded with palms. Fuller writes,
"But Jericho . . . was shaded with trees for pleasure. It is
called *City of Palmes* . . . growing so plentifully round about
it. . . ."[57] Explaining the meaning of the word *Jericho*, Ortelius writes that it comes from "the pleasant and fragrant smell
which partly issued from the gardens and orchyeards of the
rare and soveraigne Balsam, a plant only growing in this place:
and partly from the Palme trees, which here do grow in greater
abundance, than any where else in the world beside. And therefore in the 34. of Deut. it is called the City of Palme trees."[58]
In *Paradise Regained* Jericho is called the "City of Palms."[59]

Another map or chart in *A Pisgah-Sight*, "Terra Moriath,"[60] depicts the holiest of holy ground. Here is Jerusalem,
to the east of which is Mons Scandali with the temples of Moloch and Chemos; here is Mount Olivet, with three summits,
from the middle of which Christ ascended; here is the house of
Simon the Leper, and the grave of Lazarus, and the barren fig
tree that Christ cursed; to the south is Bethlehem, in which
the Prince of Peace was born; hard by is Ramath, where
Herod's soldiers killed the innocent children; northwest of
Jerusalem is Mount Calvary, and at its foot the sepulcher of
the Lord.

It should be added that in *A Pisgah-Sight* Fuller describes
the idols of the Jews. Most of the gods therein mentioned are
found in *Paradise Lost*. Selden's *De Deis Syris*, which is Fuller's avowed authority, describes all of Fuller's gods except
Chemos and Rimmon, both of whom appear in Milton's catalog. In the description of Mount Lebanon, Fuller writes,

[56] I, 482-486.
[57] *Op. cit.*, p. 252.
[58] Fol. iii.
[59] II, 20-21.
[60] P. 288.

Aram of *Damascus* succeeds lying northeast of *Aram-Maachah*, watered with the rivers *Abanah* and *Pharphar*. This *Abanah* in humane writers is called *Chrysoroas* or *golden-streame* from the yellowness of his banks and waters . . . *Abanah* and *Pharphar* were highly beholden to *Naaman*, who preferred them *before all the waters of Israel. . . .*[61]

Of Rimmon Fuller writes, "An Idol of *Syria* whose principall Temple was in *Damascus*." Compare with this Milton's lines:

> Him follow'd *Rimmon*, whose delightful Seat
> Was fair *Damascus*, on the fertil Banks
> Of *Abbana* and *Pharphar*, lucid streams.[62]

Although there is no positive proof that Milton used Fuller's *Pisgah-Sight*, which was published only two years before total blindness overtook him, it is obvious that he might have taken a special interest in the book because of its detailed description and illustration of Biblical history.

To Ortelius's *Theatrum* one should return for the explanation of one of the most magnificent similes in *Paradise Lost*. After his long journey through Chaos, Satan, on his way to earth, alighted on the dark globe of the universe.

> Here walk'd the Fiend at large in spacious field.
> As when a Vultur on *Imaus* bred,
> Whose snowie ridge the roving *Tartar* bounds,
> Dislodging from a Region scarce of prey
> To gorge the flesh of Lambs or yeanling Kids
> On Hills where Flocks are fed, flies toward the Springs
> Of *Ganges* or *Hydaspes*, Indian streams;
> But in his way lights on the barren plaines
> Of *Sericana*, where *Chineses* drive
> With Sails and Wind thir canie Waggons light:
> So on this windie Sea of Land, the Fiend
> Walk'd up and down alone bent on his prey.[63]

In Ortelius the map "Aevi Veteris, Typus Geographicus"[64] illustrates the geography of this figure. "Imaus mons" runs north and south, from the Hyperborean Ocean to the Cau-

---

[61] Book IV, p. 7.
[62] I, 467-469.
[63] III, 430-441.
[64] Fol. vi.

casus, dividing Scythia into two parts. Serica lies slightly south-east of the Imaus mountains, on the vulture's route to the Ganges, which, of course, divides India into two parts. The region marked Serica on this map is approximately the same as that designated "Desertum" in Ortelius's map of China (the desert of Lop or the Gobi desert), on which appear two wa-gons equipped with sails and loaded with passengers. Ortelius's map of India[65] marks the river Hydaspis, which flows into the Indus. This river is very rarely named on contemporary maps. In Ortelius India is described in part as follows:

That there is not a more goodly and famous country in the world, nor larger, comprehended under one and the same name than India, almost all writers jointly with one consent have affirmed. . . . This whole country generally, not only for multitude of nations . . . and for townes and villages almost infinite, but for the great abundance of all commodities . . . is most rich and fortunate. It hath very many rivers, and those very great and faire. These running to and fro in many places crossing and watering the same, do cause it, as in a moist soile, where the sunne is of force to bring forth all things most plentifully. . . .

These maps in Ortelius explain the great Satan-Vulture simile, which is quite meaningless to readers unfamiliar with its geog-raphy. It is not improbable that the maps are also the source of the figure, that directly or indirectly they kindled Milton's imagination.

The map of Ethiopia, to which reference was made in con-nection with Mount Amara, illustrates another simile, that in which Satan's approach to Paradise is compared to the voyage of sailors nearing the coast of Arabia:

> As when to them who saile
> Beyond the *Cape of Hope,* and now are past
> *Mozambic,* off at Sea North-East windes blow
> *Sabean* Odours from the spicie shoare
> Of *Arabie* the blest.[66]

In Ortelius's map "Mozambique" is conspicuous. On Arabia Felix appears this legend, "Ex Arabia Felice Thus ad nos de-

[65] Fol. 108.   [66] IV, 159-163.

fertur; quod hic, & non alibi nascitur. Incolae sua lingua Louvan vocant." It is probable that two external influences were joined in the creation of this sailor simile—the map in Ortelius and, as I have explained, the description of Arabia in Diodorus. Neither source alone accounts for all the details present in the complete figure.

An illustration of Milton's rather precise location of places occurs in the following description of Hell.

> Beyond this flood a frozen Continent
> Lies dark and wilde, beat with perpetual storms
> Of Whirlwind and dire Hail, which on firm land
> Thaws not, but gathers heap, and ruin seems
> Of ancient pile; all else deep snow and ice,
> A gulf profound as that *Serbonian* Bog
> Betwixt *Damiata* and mount *Casius* old,
> Where Armies whole have sunk.[67]

In Ortelius's map Palaestina[68] these three place are marked: on the coast, "Damiata"; eastward, "Casius mons"; between them, "Sirbonis lacus." Neither Diodorus nor Hakluyt locates the Serbonian bog as Milton does; Sandys notes that it is near Mount Casius. Ortelius's map places the bog as Milton does. Besides, it may be significant that in Milton the spelling, "Damiata," is the same as that in Ortelius. Other forms are *Damietta* and *Damiatta*. In this figure also a combination of the influence of map and description (in Diodorus or Sandys) is indicated.

A superb geographical passage is that in which Adam, with the aid of the archangel Michael, from the top of the highest hill in Paradise commands the view of every important city in the world—Cambalu, Samarchand, Paquin, Agra, Lahor, Ecbatana, Hispahan, Byzantium;

> nor could his eye not ken
> Th' Empire of *Negus* to his utmost Port
> *Ercoco* and the less Maritime Kings
> *Mombaza*, and *Quiloa*, and *Melind*,
> And *Sofala* thought *Ophir*, to the Realme
> Of *Congo*, and *Angola* fardest South.[69]

[67] II, 586-593.   [68] Fol. ii.   [69] XI, 396-401.

Ortelius's map of Ethiopia, "Presbiteri Iohannis, sive, Abissinorum Imperii Descriptio," shows the points mentioned in the "Empire of Negus." Here are Ercoco, Mombaza, Quiloa, and Melinde. *Ercoco* rarely appears on contemporary maps. In Mercator's map "Abissinorum sive Pretiosi Iohannis Imperium,"[70] the spelling is *Arquiquo*. In Jansson's *Novus Atlas*, III, 1649, it is spelled *Arquique*. The same spelling occurs in Blaeu's map, X, 1663; and Blaeu explains, "Le port d'Ercocco est aussi nomme d'Arquico, & pris pour l'ancien lieu d'Aduli."[71] Ortelius also explains the term *Negus:* "The same whom we in *Europe* call *Presbyter Iohn*, or *Priest Iohn*, the Moores call Anticlibassi, themselves, that is, the Abyssines or Ethiopians, Acegue and Neguz, that is Emperour and King. . . ." The phrase "the less Maritime Kings" is explained: "These countries now are divided into many smaller provinces, and are called divers and sundrie names, as thou maist see in the Mappe."[72]

In Ortelius's map of Tartaria,[73] the site of Cambalu is marked "Cambalu Cataiae metropolis, habet 28. mill. in circuitu." Just above this legend is a royal tent with a crowned figure before it, and the following explanation: "Magnus Cham, (quod lingua Tartarorum Imperatorem sonat) maximus Asiae princeps." The same map shows far to the west "Samarchand, magni Tamber: quondam sedes." The map of Persia shows Samarchand on a stream that flows into "Abiamu, *olim* Oxus fl." Milton writes:

> from the destind walls
> Of *Cambalu*, seat of *Cathaian Can*
> And *Samarchand* by *Oxus, Temirs* Throne.[74]

It seems clear that Ortelius's maps are definitely behind this long passage, one of the most sublime in the entire epic. Without the maps, it is difficult to imagine how such lines, so astonishingly precise, could have been created. It need scarcely be added that back of the lines lies also a knowledge of history

[70] II, 633.
[71] P. 100.
[73] Fol. 105.
[72] Fol. 113.
[74] XI, 387-389.

Map "Presbiteri Iohannis, Sive, Abissinorum Imperii Descriptio"
in Ortelius's *The Theatre of the World* (1606), Fol. 113

that gives substance to Milton's names. But obviously the maps
were indispensable.

In *Paradise Lost* a vivid but somewhat difficult passage is
that which describes the disastrous effects of sin, especially the
origin of fierce winds, blowing from various quarters of the
universe.

> Now from the North
> Of *Norumbega*, and the *Samoed* shoar
> Bursting thir brazen Dungeon, armd with ice
> And snow and haile and stormie gust and flaw,
> *Boreas* and *Cæcias* and *Argestes* loud
> And *Thrascias* rend the Woods and Seas upturn;
> With adverse blasts up-turns them from the South
> *Notus* and *Afer* black with thundrous Clouds
> From *Serraliona*; thwart of these as fierce
> Forth rush the *Levant* and the *Ponent* Windes
> *Eurus* and *Zephir* with thir lateral noise,
> *Sirocco*, and *Libecchio*. Thus began
> Outrage from liveless things.[75]

This passage is explained much more clearly by maps and
charts showing the territories and the winds mentioned than
by the most elaborate notes. In Ortelius's map "The New
World, commonly called America," Norumbega, a large tract
between Nova Francia and a huge bay and river, includes what
is now New England and New York and a part of Canada. In
the map of Russia, Samoyeda is the extreme northern part.
The winds mentioned in the passage cited are all named in the
"Tabula Anemographica seu Pyxis Nautica ventorum nomina
sex linguis repraesentans" in the ninth volume of Jansson's
Novus Atlas, about which Milton inquired.[76] In this beautiful
chart the names of all thirty-two winds from all points of the
compass are given in six languages, in the following order
reading from the center outward: Greek, Latin, Italian, Span-
ish, French, Dutch. On this chart, Boreas is the north-north-east
wind; Caecias, the east-north-east; Argestes, the north-west;

[75] X, 695-707.
[76] P. 39. The *Atlas* is in eleven volumes, published, apparently, from
1647 to 1662.

Africus (Milton's Afer), the south-west; Thrascias, the north-north-west; Notus, the south; Levant and Ponent, the east and the west, respectively; Eurus, the east-south-east; Zephyrus, the west (the same as Ponent); Sirocco and Libeccio, the south-east and the south-west, respectively. The names of Milton's winds may have been taken from this chart in Jansson's *Atlas*.

Charts of winds are, it is true, common in the old atlases. For example, in Ptolemy's *Geographia* of 1508 there is an excellent full-page chart giving the Greek and the Latin names of twelve winds, from Aparcticas round the circle to Thrascias; and a similar map is printed in the Ptolemies of 1540, 1542, 1562, 1574, 1605, 1621, to mention only a few. In Mercator's *Atlas* (1636),[77] the four principal winds, Eurus, Zephyrus, Boreas, and Notus, are given in a quotation from Ovid, which is translated thus:

> Now straight takes Eurus strength from purple East.
> Now Zephyrus at night is ready prest.
> Now Boysterous Boreas from North doth blow.
> Now Notus in his fore-head wars doth show.

A figure represents these winds and the quarters from which they blow. There are two other tables, one with the Italian names of sixteen winds, the other with the Dutch names of thirty-two winds. In *Le Grand Atlas, ou Cosmographie Blauiane*,[78] chapter nine of the introduction, "Des Plages du Monde & des Vents," has a table giving the names of thirty-two winds, not including the Greek and the Latin.

Some of the names of winds in the passage from *Paradise Lost* are, of course, classical. The others were perhaps derived from the wind-charts, and especially from that in Jansson, which is the only chart giving all the names that Milton used. There can be no question that the proper maps are important in the understanding and enjoyment of *Paradise Lost*. It is safe to conclude that Milton himself found the atlases indispensable, particularly that of Ortelius. Revealing to Adam

[77] I, 36-37.
[78] I, unpaged in the introduction.

the territory to be occupied by Abraham and his descendants, Michael says,

> each place behold
> In prospect, as I point them.

Nearly all Milton's poetry dealing with places has the vivid effect suggested by these lines. The explanation lies not only in Milton's superb imagination but also in his use of maps to achieve precision and actuality. Not otherwise may the geographical passages be satisfactorily explained.

Consider next the relation of the atlases to *Paradise Regained*. As in *Paradise Lost* Michael reveals to Adam future events, so in *Paradise Regained* Satan tempts Christ with the offer of worldly power:

> here thou behold'st
> *Assyria* and her Empires antient bounds,
> *Araxes* and the *Caspian* lake, thence on
> As far as *Indus* East, *Euphrates* West,
> And oft beyond; to South the *Persian* Bay,
> And inaccessible the *Arabian* drouth:
> Here *Ninevee*, of length within her wall
> Several days journey, built by *Ninus* old,
> . . . .
> There *Babylon* the wonder of all tongues,
> . . . .; *Persepolis*
> His City there thou seest, and *Bactra* there;
> *Ecbatana* her structure vast there shews,
> And *Hecatompylos* her hunderd gates,
> There *Susa* by *Choaspes*, amber stream,
> The drink of none but Kings; of later fame
> Built by *Emathian*, or by *Parthian* hands,
> The great *Seleucia*, *Nisibis*, and there
> *Artaxata*, *Teredon*, *Tesiphon*,
> Turning with easie eye thou may'st behold.
> . . . . . . for now the *Parthian* King
> In *Ctesiphon* hath gather'd all his Host
> Against the *Scythian*, whose incursions wild
> Have wasted *Sogdiana*; . . . .

He look't and saw what numbers numberless
The City gates out powr'd, ...
. . . . the flower and choice
Of many Provinces from bound to bound;
From *Arachosia,* from *Candaor* East,
And *Margiana* to the *Hyrcanian* cliffs
Of *Caucasus,* and dark *Iberian* dales,
From *Atropatia* and the neighbouring plains
Of *Adiabene, Media,* and the South
Of *Susiana* to *Balsara's* hav'n.[79]

Many of these names occur in two maps in Ortelius—"Aevi Veteris, Typus Geographicus" and "The Voyage of Alexander the Great," both in the Parergon. The map of the old world shows many of the large divisions and the rivers—Indus, Euphrates, Choaspes, Caucasus, Media, Hircania, Sogdiana, Arachosia. The map of Alexander's empire shows the Araxes flowing into the Caspian Sea, Bactra on the Oxus, "Persepolis regia totius Orientis," Ecbatana, Hecatompylos, Susa on the Choaspes, and others. Several maps in Ptolemy's *Geographia* (1605) show the distinctive names not present on other maps. Table IV of Asia, for example, shows Adiabene and Nisibis. Table V shows Artaxata on the Araxes, Antropatia, Susiana, as well as Babylon, Seleucia, Ctesiphon, Teredon, Hecatompylos, and "Niphates mons" bounding Assyria on the north, where Satan alighted on his way to Paradise. Tables VI and VII in this Ptolemy include other names in Milton's list. Comparison of these maps in the Ptolemy of 1605 with the lines just quoted from *Paradise Regained* will probably convince the most skeptical that the poetry and the maps are intimately associated. From a memory richly stored with historical facts and names Milton may have created these long, comprehensive, detailed geographical passages, without other aid. However, it does not seem likely that he would have denied himself the opportunity of consulting or recalling the maps, which contained in convenient form the place names essential to his purpose.

[79] III, 269-321.

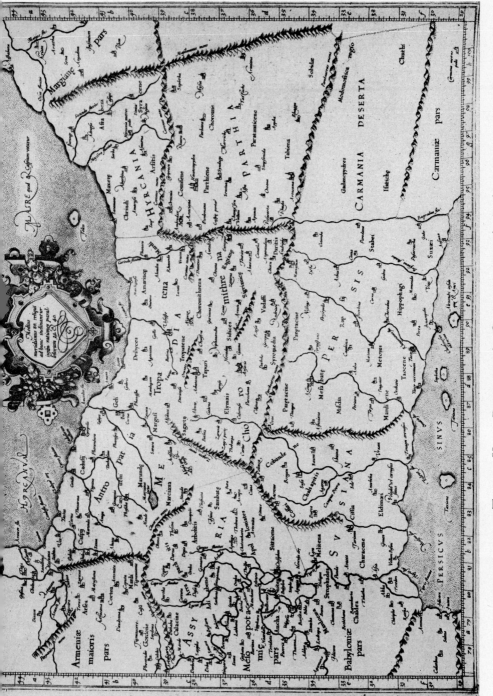

TABLE V IN PTOLEMY'S GEOGRAPHIA (1605)

Christ rejected the offer of the fair Parthian kingdom.
Then Satan, though sorely perplexed and troubled by his ill
success, renewed his assault.

> He brought our Saviour to the western side
> Of that high mountain, whence he might behold
> Another plain, long but in bredth not wide;
> Wash'd by the Southern Sea, and on the North
> To equal length back'd with a ridge of hills
> That screen'd the fruits of the earth and seats of men
> From cold *Septentrion* blasts, thence in the midst
> Divided by a river, of whose banks
> On each side an Imperial City stood,
> With Towers and Temples proudly elevate
> On seven small Hills, with Palaces adorn'd,
> . . . .
> The City which thou seest no other deem
> Then great and glorious *Rome*, Queen of the Earth
> So far renown'd, and with the spoils enricht
> Of Nations; . . . .
> Thence to the gates cast round thine eye, and see
> What conflux issuing forth, or entring in,
> Pretors, Proconsuls to thir Provinces
> . . . .
> Or Embassies from Regions far remote
> In various habits on the *Appian* road,
> Or on the *Æmilian*, some from farthest South,
> *Syene*, and where the shadow both way falls,
> *Meroe*, *Nilotic* Isle, and more to West,
> The Realm of *Bocchus* to the Black-moor Sea;
> From the *Asian* Kings and *Parthian* among these,
> From *India* and the golden *Chersoness*,
> And utmost *Indian* Isle *Taprobane*,
> Dusk faces with white silken Turbants wreath'd:
> From *Gallia*, *Gades*, and the *Brittish* West,
> *Germans* and *Scythians*, and *Sarmatians* North
> Beyond *Danubius* to the *Tauric* Pool.
> All Nations now to *Rome* obedience pay.[80]

[80] IV, 25-80.

Part of this passage is doubtless based upon Milton's visual memory of Rome. Other parts are just as clearly indebted to Ortelius's map of the Roman Empire, "Romani Imperii Imago," in the Parergon. On this map, the configuration of land and sea is just that stated in Milton's verse. Especially prominent are the Apennines, the long "ridge of hills" shielding the coastal plain from northern blasts. On this map are found most of the places mentioned: Siene, on the Nile; Bochi Reg., in northern Africa; Mauritania; "the Black-moor Sea"; Gallia; Gades; Britannicae Insulae; Germania; Danubius; Sarmatiae. *Getae* appears instead of *Scythians;* Meroe and the places mentioned in India are not included. Otherwise the names on the map correspond with Milton's. Especially interesting is Milton's phrase "The Realm of *Bocchus,*" which is obviously a translation of Ortelius's legend "Bochi Reg." Since this name appears on no other contemporary map of northern Africa, we have here another clear proof of Milton's use of Ortelius.[81]

These long and beautiful passages in two books of *Paradise Regained* clearly show the intimate relationship between Milton's poetry and the maps. To this may be added J. S. Smart's proof that in the first Italian sonnet Milton revealed the name of his lady by reference to the district in which Reno is situated—Emilia, a name that Milton may have met with "in many books of Italian geography and history."[82] Milton's allusion to *the flowery vale of Reno,* Smart explains, "has nothing to do with his own Italian travel" but is derived from books. The practice thus early established seems to have persisted throughout his life. His blindness does not seem to have checked his interest in geography or to have impaired his accurate use of maps. Abundant evidence, some of which has been presented in this chapter, leaves no room for skepticism. Appropriate maps were as essential to the creation of the geographical passages as they are now to their full appreciation.

---

[81] The maps in Ortelius's *Theatrum* are, as a rule, not his own, but were drawn and engraved by others. Ortelius always gave credit to the actual makers of the maps that he published. See F. J. North, *The Map of Wales,* p. 55.   [82] *The Sonnets of Milton,* p. 138.

The maps do not, of course, tell the whole story. Milton's choice of names may have been primarily determined by aesthetic and historical considerations, which should not be minimized. The historical implications of Milton's poetry are emphasized in a recent article which deplores the fact that what were once vivid and exciting incidents are now in literature mere allusions over which "the iniquity of oblivion has scattered her poppy," and stresses Milton's interest in the contemporary scene.[83] In *Paradise Lost*, the writer explains, the historical and the political theme which had occupied his mind so long "becomes pervasive; recollected in tranquility, it is now a 'blessed ghost,' gliding whither it would. . . ." After citing illustrations of the poet's intense interest in contemporary affairs, the writer goes on to speak of the sharpness of Milton's mental images.

After his blindness Milton must have had to learn largely from human lips. The clear edges of his mental maps, as well as his pictures, may be due to this mental sharpening, the work of the mind listening for the exact word and framing its image within. There are no such geographical spaces anywhere. . . . Of this historical and political knowledge of his, so incomparably richer than that of all his poetical contemporaries put together, the evidence is hard to set out. It consists in an impressive accumulation of phrases and turns of thought and reference. It did not exist in the Milton who wrote *Comus* and *Lycidas;* it was put aside by the Milton who wrote *Samson Agonistes,* whose mind had withdrawn within to its memories and sense of an epoch closed in ruin. But it is everywhere in *Paradise Lost,* an unsuspected spaciousness of range, and imagination and knowledge that roam the globe.

The clearness, the precision, the range, the richness, and the power of Milton at his best are, of course, the effects of a synthesis of many qualities, some of them intangible, and of a rich culture, inspired and controlled by a remarkable genius. As the preceding quotation indicates and as the following chapters will show, Milton's poetry reflects his multifarious interests, especially those of politics and religion, which are not, however,

[83] *The Times Literary Supplement,* March 30, 1933, pp. 205-206.

permitted to impair the intellectual and artistic unity of his work. Doubtless Milton's passionate sincerity, his devotion to principle, his crusading zeal, which still stir the reader, were also essential factors, quickening his imagination and sustaining his flight. Something of the contribution of the maps, particularly those in Ortelius's *Theatre of the World*, to his artistic triumph is probably by this time obvious. The part played by the atlases was essential and impressive. By their aid alone we cannot pluck out the heart of the poet's secret. With their help, however, we may come nearer to an understanding of what after all analysis must remain a mystery. Critical study seems to indicate that the maps furnished the foundation of many lines, that they supplied the raw material which the poet's touch transmuted into fine gold which far outshines "the wealth of *Ormus* and of *Ind*."[84]

[84] This chapter was finished before the publication of Miss Marjorie Nicolson's very valuable article entitled "Milton's Hell and the Phlegraean Fields," *University of Toronto Quarterly*, VII (July, 1938), 500-513. Miss Nicolson's evidence that in Milton's description of hell there is an imaginative combination of his sense impressions and of literary accounts of the Phlegraean Fields, near Naples, is impressive. With reference to one of the books used, George Sandys' *Relation of a Journey*, the following statement in Humphrey Prideaux's letter to John Ellis is of interest:

He [Sir Richard Willis] showed me among his Italian bookes that out of which Sandys had his travels. I compared both togeather and found the cuts in each to be exactly the same, and therefore I was easyly perswaded to believe what Sir Richard assured me, who had farther compared them, that the matter is the same to, and that Sandys travelled no farther for his observations then into a bookseller's shop in Italy, where he met with this booke, out of which he transcribed them." (*Letters of Humphrey Prideaux*, 1875, p. 20.)

Edward Maunde Thompson, editor of the *Letters*, notes that many of the plates in Sandys' work also appear in Jean Zuallart's *Le Tresdevot Voyage de Jerusalem* (Antwerp, 1608). (*Ibid.*, p. 20.)

CHAPTER IV

A COMPLEXION INCLINED TO MELANCHOLY

IN CONTRAST with the Elizabethan Age, which in spite of a strain of melancholy was on the whole confident and joyous, the seventeenth century, especially the pre-Augustan period, was, broadly speaking, an age of disillusionment, an age when melancholy was not merely a fashionable pose or a literary convention but a prevalent and profound disorder, the effects of which have been traced in the works of Burton, Donne, Herbert, Vaughan, and others. The note of melancholy, however, has not been recognized as one of prime importance in the works of Milton. There is, to be sure, no basis for the theory that Milton was a melancholic and lonely ascetic, dwelling in a kind of moral solitude relieved only by the nocturnal visits of his Muse. Even casual study reveals his intense interest in current problems, which occupied a great share of his attention for almost two decades. We are also assured that he was "extreme pleasant in his conversation" and that in his old age he was often visited by the learned. There is, on the other hand, much evidence that Milton did not escape the prevailing disorder of his time, the "*balneum Diaboli*, the Devil's Bath," to use Burton's striking phrase. By a comparative study of Milton's life and work and of Burton's *Anatomy of Melancholy*, this chapter endeavors to show not only that there is a definite relationship between Burton's and Milton's ideas but also that one may say of Milton, as of Democritus,

> Over his head appears the sky,
> And Saturn Lord of Melancholy.

At the outset, it is important to remember that melancholy assumes a variety of forms. As Burton in his "Abstract" explains, nothing is so sweet as melancholy to one who void of care and sorrow muses all alone, building castles in the air. By the brookside melancholy is the source of a thousand pleasures; but in the dark grove a thousand miseries attend the sour divinity. In one mood sweet music and rare beauties delight the fancy; in another the soul is afflicted by a thousand ugly shapes and doleful cries. A lover's melancholy may be either a paradise or a hell. According to one's character and mood, one finds in the solitary life joy or misery. It has been said that in the *Anatomy* temporary sadness or depression resulting from sickness, death of friends, fear, passion, or other misfortune is distinguished from settled melancholy, which is a chronic malady or a kind of dotage without apparent cause.[1] But Burton, discussing at length the causes of melancholy, insists that divers matters produce a great variety of effects. He declares that the "Tower of *Babel* never yielded such confusion of tongues, as this Chaos of Melancholy doth variety of symptoms,"[2] that no complexion, condition, sex, age is exempted, except fools and stoics. He distinguishes melancholy from madness, fevers, and other maladies to which it may seem nearly allied. In melancholy, the brain, as the seat of reason, and the heart, as the seat of affection, are primarily affected. Broadly interpreted, as it is in this chapter, melancholy is a mental and spiritual condition or disposition which tends to become a habit; in Burton's words, "as it was long increasing, so, now being (pleasant or painful) grown to an habit, it will hardly be removed."[3] The malady is due to certain recognized causes, some of which are illustrated in Milton's life.

Milton, it is well known, was a tireless student. He himself says, "My appetite for knowledge was so voracious, that, from twelve years of age, I hardly ever left my studies, or went to bed before midnight."[4] Commenting upon his uncle's

---

[1] Amy Louise Reed, *The Background of Gray's Elegy* (New York, 1924), pp. 5-6.
[2] *The Anatomy of Melancholy*, ed. A. R. Shilleto (London, 1893), I, 455.   [3] *Op. cit.*, I, 167.
[4] J. H. Hanford, *A Milton Handbook* (New York, 1938), p. 9.

"insuperable industry," John Phillips declares that Milton "generally sat up half the night, as well in voluntary improvements of his own choice, as the exact perfecting of his school exercises."[5] He was, Aubrey says, "a very hard student in the university, and performed all his exercises there with very good applause."[6] In a letter to Alexander Gill, Milton refers with contempt to his associates' smattering of learning and expresses his determination to spend the summer in "literary retirement, and so to speak take cover in the precincts of the Muses."[7] He bitterly complains that just as he was preparing to devote both day and night to the charms of philosophy, he was dragged away to forced participation in official foolery.[8] At Horton five years of leisure were "entirely devoted to the perusal of Greek and Latin authors." In a letter to Charles Diodati, Milton describes his method of study: "My own disposition is such that no delay, no rest, no thought or care for anything else, can divert me from my purpose, until I reach my goal and complete some great cycle of my studies."[9] In spite of distractions and failing sight, the studious habits established in youth persisted. Although we must give due credit to the "strong propensity of nature" and the flame of genius which burned in him so clearly, we should not minimize the importance of that "industrious and select reading," that "labour and intent study" which Milton took to be his portion in this life.

Intensive study has, as Burton explains, its joys and also its dangers. Of the exercises and recreations of the mind within doors none is so "fit and proper to expell Idleness and Melancholy, as that of Study."[10] Most men find in study an extraordinary delight. Burton ecstatically surveys the rich fields of knowledge. "What so sure, what so pleasant?" Wealth is but a child's toy compared with learning, in which, says Burton, he could even live and die, so sweet is its delight. But Burton sagely adds a warning: excessive study is most pernicious. Mel-

[5] *Ibid.*, p. 11.   [6] *Ibid.*, p. 12.
[7] *Milton Private Correspondence and Academic Exercises* (Cambridge, 1932), p. 8.   [8] *Ibid.*, p. 85.
[9] *Ibid.*, p. 11.   [10] *Op. cit.*, II, 100.

ancholy, he declares, is the "common maul" of students and in some measure their inseparable companion. Students are subject to this malady more than others because they live a "sedentary, solitary life" and because their brains and spirits are consumed by vehement industry. Burton lists the diseases that attend excessive study—gouts, catarrhs, bad eyes, winds, consumptions. Neglecting their health and worldly affairs, how many scholars, he exclaims, have lost their wits to gain knowledge, "for which, after all their pains, in the world's esteem they are accounted ridiculous and silly fools."[11] The Muses, Burton explains, have no portion; poverty is their patrimony. On the whole, to behold the "bright countenance of truth in the quiet and still air of delightfull studies" was for Milton a profound satisfaction, which had the richest results but which was not unaccompanied by certain physical disorders and mental strains that are reflected in his work and are the price he paid for intensive study.

Refusing to subscribe slave to the tyranny that had invaded the Church, Milton in early manhood was conscious of unusual ability but had no calling except that of poetry. His situation is comparable to that of the young Wordsworth, who was unwilling to enter the Church and unable to find congenial employment. To Wordsworth his sister Dorothy proved a good angel, renewing his joy in life and stimulating his faith in his poetic mission. Milton, more secure financially, but occasionally subject to self-distrust and assured of no certain future, had to work out his own salvation. The details of Milton's life at Horton are meager, but the letter to his unknown friend and the poem *Ad Patrem* indicate that his not entering into creditable employment was a source of some uneasiness. His friend bluntly told him that he was dreaming away his years "in the arms of studious retirement." Under the circumstances, perhaps his father may have regarded his son's poem as the "barren gratitude of futile words." To unfriendly observers, Milton's life at Horton must have seemed a form of idleness; and idleness, according to Burton, is "the bane of body and

[11] *Op. cit.*, I, 351.

mind, the nurse of naughtiness, stepmother of discipline, the
chief author of mischief, one of the seven deadly sins, and a
sole cause" of melancholy and many other maladies.[12] In early
manhood Milton was at times discontented; he had some sense
of frustration. He said that his life was "yet obscure and un-
serviceable to mankind."[13] In 1637 he wrote to Diodati that
his life at Horton was "obscure and cramped" and that he would
like to take rooms in one of the Inns of Court, where he might
have congenial companions. To one who was conscious of unusual abilities and who thirsted for learning and fame, the
sense of being unprepared and misunderstood, the impression
that his study led to no tangible results, the feeling of obscurity
and frustration must have been particularly galling. In such
conditions there was a soil favorable to the growth of melancholy, which springs from pride, discontent, vexations of the
mind, solitariness, and other causes.

Other biographical evidence is at hand. Among the accidental causes of melancholy, the death of friends is perhaps
first. If parting of friends causes violent grief, "what shall death
do, when they must eternally be separated, never in this world
to meet again?"[14] Sorrow is "an inseparable companion, the
mother and daughter of melancholy," as all the world acknowl-
edges. Milton suffered several bereavements in quick succession. The death of Edward King, who without being an intimate friend inspired the greatest elegy in English, the death
of Milton's mother, the death of his best friend, Charles
Diodati—these losses doubtless moved Milton profoundly and
intensified his feeling of loneliness, of mortality, of frustration.

Add to this his unfortunate first marriage, which had a
decisive influence upon his character and opinions of woman-
kind. Burton includes unhappy marriages as one of the most
important causes of melancholy. It is true that marriage was
appointed by God himself in Paradise and that if the parties
agree it is one of man's greatest felicities; but "if they be unequally matched, or at discord, a greater misery cannot be

[12] *Op. cit.*, I, 278.
[13] Hanford, *op. cit.*, p. 19.   [14] Burton, *op. cit.*, I, 412.

expected."[15] In the *Anatomy* there are few pages more interesting than those in which Burton, the bachelor, reviews the miseries of marriage. While we woo we are in heaven; but when we are once tied and have lost our liberty, marriage is purgatory if not hell itself. When the Devil had taken away Job's goods, friends, and children, he left him his wicked wife "to vex and gall him worse *quam totus infernus,* than all the fiends of hell."[16] Burton exclaims, "In sober sadness, marriage is a bondage, a thraldom, a yoke, an hindrance to all good enterprises." On the other hand, when wife and husband agree, marriage is "full of all contentment and happiness, one of the three things which please God, . . . an honourable and happy estate." Indeed, there is "no joy, no comfort, no sweetness, no pleasure in the world like to that of a good wife." Milton experienced both kinds of marriage. He and his first wife were certainly not happy together. The death of his beloved second wife intensified his loneliness and darkness.

In this survey of the reasons for the development of a melancholy strain in Milton's character, his blindness must occupy an important place. His blindness was not, to be sure, devoid of certain spiritual consolations. As Milton points out in his *Second Defence of the English People,* he had in his blindness no sense of guilt but rather a strong sense of innocence and of important services already rendered to church and state. Miss Eleanor Gertrude Brown has recently suggested that his blindness was not an unmitigated calamity.[17] She justly protests against Tillyard's description of Milton's attitude in the sonnet beginning "When I consider how my light is spent" as that of a beaten dog. In spite of compensations, his blindness was, of course, a grievous affliction. The point need not be labored. For him who loved nature and books the loss of sight was inexpressibly bitter, a death in life.

Besides, we should not forget that political and religious discontent and unrest were common causes of mental depression. Before the Civil War, dissatisfaction was widespread and

---

[15] *Op. cit.,* I, 423.   [16] *Op. cit.,* III, 250.
[17] *Milton's Blindness* (New York, 1934), pp. 52 ff.

profound. To the religious phase of this discontent Milton
gave permanent expression in a famous passage in *Lycidas*.
There followed a period of high hopes for a general reformation, which were very imperfectly realized. Then came reaction, and Milton fallen upon evil days and evil tongues wit-
nessed the blatant triumph of all that he loathed. For him this
disappointment was made more bitter by his financial losses.
We do not need Burton to remind us that loss of temporal
goods, loss of honor, office, and good name "will much torment."[18] Milton suffered no loss of real honor and good
name. But he had many enemies, and his hopes fell flat in
those days when, as Wordsworth says, he uttered odious truth,

> Darkness before, and danger's voice behind.

We may sum up in the words of Mr. E. E. Stoll: "Life was
bitter to him, his outlook upon it was severe, and he died in
his enemies' day."[19]

It may be objected that this sketch of Milton's life presents a distorted picture, one of unrelieved study, sorrow, suffering, and disillusionment. The full story, it is true, is not
altogether so dark. Milton was not always depressed; he was
not the victim of a virulent melancholy. It must be remembered that this disorder assumed a multitude of forms: "The
four and twenty letters make no more variety of words in
divers languages, than melancholy conceits produce diversity
of symptoms in several persons."[20] In an extreme form melancholy is a plague, and of this one may say, with Burton, "if
there be an hell upon earth, it is to be found in a melancholy
man's heart."[21] Since in Milton's habits, experiences, and environment this malady had a fertile soil, we should not be surprised to find important and increasingly prominent evidences
of it in his poetry, to read which is, as Sir H. J. C. Grierson
has said, "to contemplate a tragedy as sublime and poignant as
any in the history of English literature,"[22] a tragedy of the

---

[18] *Op. cit.*, I, 416.
[19] *Poets and Playwrights* (Minneapolis, 1930), p. 241.
[20] Burton, *op. cit.*, I, 469.   [21] *Op. cit.*, I, 497.
[22] *The Poems of John Milton* (London, 1925), I, vi.

idealist, self-confident and confident in humanity, but ill prepared for the disappointments of life, which brought bitter disillusionment on every hand, without, however, destroying his faith in the immutable justice of God.

Although, as scholars have explained, the earlier poets, from Homer, Theocritus, and Virgil to Breton, Sidney, Shakespeare, and Spenser, have had some share in shaping the imagery of *L'Allegro* and *Il Penseroso,* W. J. Courthope is probably right in saying that the "new vein of reflection" in these poems is derived from Burton's *Anatomy,* a book which, from its first appearance in 1621, made a deep impression upon the public and which Milton would have read either while he was at school or at Cambridge. It does not follow, however, that "Burton counted many of l'Allegro's pleasures among what he considered the prime satisfactions of melancholy" and that "in *L'Allegro* no less than *Il Penseroso* . . . Milton courted a melancholy of his own."[23] In the opening lines of *L'Allegro* the dismissal of melancholy is obviously sincere. Milton's companions and his imagined pleasures are those of mirth, not melancholy. In fact, the details of *L'Allegro* correspond remarkably to those cures of melancholy discussed in the *Anatomy* under such headings as "Perturbations of the mind rectified," "Exercise," and so on. Quoting Vives, Burton writes: "Mirth purgeth the blood, confirms health, causeth a fresh, pleasing, and fine colour, prorogues life, whets the wit, makes the body young, lively, and fit for any employment. The merrier heart, the longer life."[24] Pleasant discourse, jests, conceits, merry tales "are that sole *Nepenthes* of *Homer,* . . . to expel grief and care, to cause mirth and gladness of heart." For the man disposed to melancholy travel is recommended: "no better Physick for a melancholy man than change of air and variety of places, to travel abroad and see fashions." We are told that a "good prospect alone will ease melancholy." Varieties of action, objects, air, places "are excellent good in

[23] *John Milton Paradise Regained, The Minor Poems and Samson Agonistes,* ed. Merritt Y. Hughes (Garden City, 1937), pp. xxv, xxvi.
[24] *Op. cit.,* II, 137.

this infirmity." Let there be light; darkness greatly enhances the humour. Idleness and solitariness are to be avoided. Sad and discontented persons are advised to make frequent use of honest sports and recreations. Burton especially recommends rural pleasures: just to be in the country is a joy. One of the chief pleasures of fishing is the "wholesome walk to the Brookside, pleasant shade by the sweet silver streams, . . . good air, and sweet smells of fine fresh meadow flowers, . . . the melodious harmony of Birds."[25] To walk amongst orchards, gardens, fountains, between wood and water, in a fair meadow, by a riverside is, Burton exclaims, a delectable recreation. Various winter sports and pleasures such as dancing, yule games, riddles, merry tales of knights, queens, dwarfs, witches, fairies, and goblins are pleasing diversions. There are also the pleasures of the city—theatres, pageants, games. "What so pleasant as to see some Pageant or Sight go by, as at Coronations, Weddings, and such like Solemnities."[26] Music is particularly valuable: it revives the spirits; it expels the greatest griefs; in a word it ravishes the soul, helps, elevates, and extends it. Recall the tales of Hercules, Orpheus, and Amphion, who could *"saxa movere sono testudinis,* &c. make stocks and stones, as well as beasts, and other animals, dance after their pipes. . . . "[27] There is no mirth without music. To all good students Burton commends the counsel of Marcilius Ficinus: "Live merrily, O my friends, free from cares, perplexity, anguish, grief of mind, live merrily, . . . again and again I request you to be merry. . . ." In this disorder, he concludes, there is nothing better than mirth and merry companions. To compare *L'Allegro* with these and other details of the *Anatomy* is to be convinced that Milton was not courting melancholy but seeking cures. Mirth and her innocent companions and the varied pleasures suggested in immortal verse are welcomed probably as relaxation from over-much study, perhaps as security from occasional periods of despondency, certainly as an expression of a fundamental need in Milton's life. Although in a sense a literary exercise, *L'Allegro* has genuine autobio-

---

[25] *Op. cit.,* II, 85. [26] *Op. cit.,* II, 88. [27] *Op. cit.,* II, 134.

graphical value, as has nearly all Milton's poetry, which is a continual revelation of his character and spirit.

This observation is particularly true of *Il Penseroso*, which is obviously not mere poetic fiction but a sincere expression of sympathy with the pleasing and lighter forms of the mood that with the passing years was to grow more intense and imperious. In *Il Penseroso* Milton deliberately cultivates the thoughts and the situations that according to Burton induce the disorder. He invites leisure and silence; his walks are solitary. Far from all resort of mirth he hears the melancholy song of the nightingale or the bellman's lonely chant; in some remote tower he studies the livelong night; in close covert by some brook he dreams away the day; in studious cloisters he hearkens to the pealing organ. According to Burton, idleness of body or mind is the universal cause of melancholy. Akin to idleness is too much solitariness, which is both cause and symptom. At first voluntary idleness is pleasant. It is most pleasant to walk alone "in some solitary Grove, betwixt wood and water, by a brookside, to meditate upon some delightsome and pleasant subject. . . ."[28] It is an incomparable delight "to melancholize, & build castles in the air, to go smiling to themselves, acting an infinite variety of parts. . . ." Indeed, these toys are so delightful that "they could spend whole days and nights without sleep, even whole years alone in such contemplations, and phantastical meditations, which are like unto dreams, and they will hardly be drawn from them, or willingly interrupt." These pleasures discussed in the *Anatomy* are versified in "The Author's Abstract of Melancholy."

> When to my self I act and smile,
> With pleasing thoughts the time beguile,
> By a brook side or wood so green,
> Unheard, unsought for, or unseen,
> A thousand pleasures do me bless,
> And crown my soul with happiness.
>   All my joys besides are folly,
>   None so sweet as Melancholy.

[28] *Op. cit.*, I, 283.

Just as Burton discusses the pleasures having their source in the earlier and voluntary stage of melancholy before it has become a settled humor, so in *Il Penseroso* we observe the symptoms of the first stage of the disorder. Burton is careful to emphasize the fact that such idle pleasures, such melancholy meditations are treacherous and are likely to deliver their victims into the bonds of fear, sorrow, and despair. In the content and mood of Milton's later work we may discover the verification of Burton's warning. But in *Il Penseroso* the loitering, the meditation, the reading are all unalloyed pleasure. Study, which is sometimes the cure of melancholy, is here its companion. In *Il Penseroso* all the causes of discontent and despondency are excluded. Only the profound satisfactions of the temperate, contemplative, religious humanist remain. Melancholy is not Milton's master but his companion; in imagination he dwells under the benign aspects of Saturn's reign.

Although this interpretation does not definitely fix the date of composition of these two poems, the view that *L'Allegro* represents a sincere search for the cures and *Il Penseroso* a genuine welcome of the pleasing features of melancholy indicates a date later than that urged by some recent critics who, observing certain slight and conventional analogies between these poems, on the one hand, and the First Academic Exercise, Elegies I and VI, and *In Quintum Novembris*, on the other, and regarding the companion poems as merely literary exercises, would date them about 1631. Rejecting Masson's fanciful picture of Milton's ramblings in the lanes of Buckinghamshire and insisting that at Horton Milton undertook a severe and prolonged course of study which apparently was not broken by any delightful interludes, an able scholar has recently concluded that *L'Allegro* and *Il Penseroso* must have been written in the summer of 1631. His argument is based upon certain alleged resemblances between these poems, particularly *L'Allegro*, and Milton's First Academic Exercise or Prolusion, a disputation as to whether day or night is the more excellent.[29]

[29] E. M. W. Tillyard, "Milton: *L'Allegro* and *Il Penseroso*," The English Association, Pamphlet No. 82 (July, 1932); E. M. W. Tillyard, *The Miltonic Setting* (Cambridge, 1938), pp. 1-28.

We are asked to believe that the first lines of *L'Allegro* are burlesque and are derived from the genealogy of the First Prolusion; that in *L'Allegro* the sights of daybreak are from the same work; that *L'Allegro* and *Il Penseroso* are in fact poetic exercises on the theme of day and night; that, indeed, *Il Penseroso*, written in praise of night, corresponds to what "Milton *would have said* had he been called on to take the other side" in the Academic Exercise;[30] that the poems were obviously written for an academic audience at Cambridge; that although they are in the meter of the *Epitaph on the Marchioness of Winchester*, they are less indebted to contemporary literature and more mature in style than the *Epitaph*. One may reply categorically that the opening lines of *L'Allegro* are not burlesque but serious and are organically as much a part of the poem as the opening lines of *Il Penseroso*; that in *L'Allegro* the signs of daybreak which are enumerated, and many others, are probably details inspired by the English countryside, not derived from the First Prolusion; that the severe program of study at Horton did not preclude but in fact demanded some periods of relaxation that would account for the writing of these two poems; that neither poem is restricted to the eulogy of day or night, for Milton pursues the appropriate pleasures, not time; that obviously one cannot base any argument upon what Milton "would have said" about night; that in fact the poems are poetic exercises on the cure and the pleasures of melancholy; that the academic audience is imaginary, the popularity and the "perfect social tone"[31] pointing to a non-academic audience and a more mature style; that the maturity of style in the companion poems is a conclusive argument for a somewhat later date. Very slightly if at all related to the First Prolusion,[32] *L'Allegro* and *Il Penseroso* are much more truly exercises on the theme of melancholy, which has real signifi-

[30] Pamphlet No. 82, p. 15; *The Miltonic Setting*, p. 20. Italics mine.

[31] This is Mr. Tillyard's phrase ("Milton: *L'Allegro* and *Il Penseroso*," p. 9).

[32] Mr. Tillyard's arguments are accepted and slightly augmented by Mr. Merritt Y. Hughes, *op. cit.*, pp. xxiii ff. Mr. Hughes, however, recognizes the fact that Milton's couplets "soon carried him far out of the realm of the prolusion into the bright English landscape. . . ."

cance in Milton's life. It has been said that the two poems record a "sojourn in the realm of purely idyllic beauty" of a mind "free for the moment from temperamental bias of any sort," and that they are studiously objective and "equally Milton."[33] It seems probable that they are equally subjective, the mood of *L'Allegro* being as sincere as that of *Il Penseroso*. But the comprehensive view of Milton's life and poetry indicates that mirth was a desired rather than an actual companion, that *L'Allegro* rather than *Il Penseroso* was a *tour de force,* that in fact the pleasures of *Il Penseroso* were to Milton most congenial. On account of the subject-matter—the treatment of melancholy, a condition that is not so likely to have developed at the University as at Horton, from prolonged study and some sense of frustration—and on account of the style, therefore, I agree with Sir H. J. C. Grierson when he says that "it is with the maturer art of the descriptive passages in *Comus* that *L'Allegro* and *Il Penseroso* associate themselves" and adds that they might have been written after *Comus*.[34]

In view of the stylistic relationship between *L'Allegro* and *Il Penseroso*, on the one hand, and *Comus*, on the other, it is significant that the way of life so vigorously chided and dismissed in the first lines of *Il Penseroso* is that espoused by Comus, whose "cordial Julep" is the alleged cure for toil, pain, and sorrow, and who regards the Lady's defence of temperance and chastity as "meer moral babble" and the "lees And settlings of a melancholy blood. . . ." Comus recommends his drink as follows:

> Not that *Nepenthes* which the wife of *Thone,*
> In *Egypt* gave to *Jove*-born *Helena*
> Is of such power to stir up joy as this,
> To life so friendly, or so cool to thirst. (ll. 675-678)

More than once Burton mentions this Nepenthes. Good counsel and fair promises are "that true *Nepenthes* of *Homer*, which was no *Indian* plant or feigned medicine, which *Polydamna,*

---

[33] J. H. Hanford, "The Youth of Milton," *Studies in Shakespeare, Milton, and Donne* (New York, 1925), pp. 132-133.
[34] *The Poems of John Milton,* I, xix.

Thon's wife, sent *Helen* for a token."[35] Jests and merry tales, as many good authors say, "are that sole *Nepenthes* of *Homer*," which was "so renowned of old to expel grief and care, to cause mirth and gladness of heart."[36] According to Diodorus Siculus, Pliny, Plutarch, and others, bugloss, used in broth, wine, or conserves as a sovereign remedy for melancholy, is "that famous *Nepenthes* of *Homer*, which *Polydamna*, *Thon's* wife, (then King of *Thebes* in *Ægypt*), sent *Helen* for a token, of such rare virtue that, if taken steept in wine, if wife and children, father and mother, brother and sister, and all thy dearest friends, should die before thy face, thou couldst not grieve or shed a tear for them."[37] Finally, Burton declares that a cup of good wine was in fact the true nepenthes of Homer, which removed all grief and care.[38] Prescribing cures for melancholy, Burton frequently identifies them with Homer's nepenthes, to which Comus compares his baneful cup, the pleasing poison of which transforms men into beasts.

Fear, Burton declares, is the constant companion of melancholy. Lost in the dark wood, the Lady exclaims:

> A thousand fantasies
> Begin to throng into my memory
> Of calling shapes, and beckning shadows dire,
> And airy tongues, that syllable mens names
> On Sands, and Shoars, and desert Wildernesses. (ll. 205-209)

Writing of prodigies, Burton mentions "*Ambulones*, that walk about midnight on great heaths and desert places, which . . . draw men out of the way, and lead them all night a by-way, or quite bar them of their way. . . . In the deserts of *Lop* in *Asia*, such illusions of walking spirits are often perceived, as you may read in *Marco Polo* the *Venetian*, his travels. If one lose his company by chance, these devils will call him by his name, and counterfeit voices of his companions to seduce him."[39]

Realizing the dangers that threaten his sister, the Second

---

[35] *Op. cit.*, II, 129.   [36] *Op. cit.*, II, 137.
[37] *Op. cit.*, II, 249.   [38] *Op. cit.*, II, 282.
[39] *Op. cit.*, I, 222-223. This passage from the *Anatomy* is often cited by editors of *Comus*.

Brother is much alarmed.   But the Elder Brother recommends
the charms of solitude and contemplation and urges the invinci-
bility of chastity, asking

> What was that snaky-headed *Gorgon* sheild
> That wise *Minerva* wore, unconquer'd Virgin,
> Wherwith she freez'd her foes to congeal'd stone?
> But rigid looks of Chast austerity,
> And noble grace that dash't brute violence
> With sudden adoration, and blank aw. (ll. 447-452)

It has been truly said that this moral interpretation of the
Gorgon shield is Milton's own.   But it should be recalled that
Burton on the authority of Lucian attributes the same power
to beauty: "And as *Lucian,* in his Images . . . confesseth of
himself, that he was at his Mistress' presence void of all sense,
immoveable, as if he had seen a *Gorgon's* head: which was no
such cruel monster . . . but the very quintessence of beauty,
some fair creature, as without doubt the Poet understood in
the first fiction of it, at which the spectators were amazed."[40]

Before he heard in the hideous wood the familiar din of
Comus and his crew, the Attendant Spirit, playing upon his
pipe, was "Wrapt in a pleasing fit of Melancholy."   Observe
that the Shepherd Lad, who, as Mr. Hanford has argued, may
be Milton himself, was often moved to ecstasy by Thyrsis'
song. From the Shepherd Lad came the magic root that van-
quishes the vile enchanter. *Comus* ends with the triumph of
virtue; but the prevailing tone, in contrast with that of the
masque as a type, is sober and thoughtful.   Life on the earth,
this pin-fold where men "Strive to keep up a frail, and feaver-
ish being," is to be endured rather than enjoyed. The freedom
of the Spirit, who ranges the ocean, the broad fields of the sky,
and the fair gardens where jocund spring and eternal summer
reign, is to be envied. The grave spirit of *Comus,* with its
severe strictures upon vice, clearly reveals Milton's temper and
tendency.

Some critics hold that Milton himself is the subject of
Lycidas and that *Epitaphium Damonis* is a forced perform-

[40] *Op. cit.,* III, 81.

ance.[41] In support of this view of *Lycidas*, the elegiac features are almost ignored and the digressions are treated as central. Strictly speaking, these digressions, in which Milton writes with astonishing force and conviction and which are sanctioned by the pastoral convention, are not more sincere than are the lines of the elegy proper. The use of convention, as John Dewey has explained,[42] is no evidence of insincerity. Accepting the pastoral convention, the sympathetic and informed reader may be convinced that Milton experienced genuine sorrow. In the words of Mr. Hanford, the mood is one "of reflective melancholy and tender pathos rather than of poignant sorrow, though the latter note is not altogether lacking."[43] We hardly need Burton to remind us that sorrow and unrealized ambition are causes of melancholy.[44] Milton's bereavement, his realization of the uncertainty and brevity of life, his indignation against the corruption in the church—here were abundant causes of the development of that somber spirit and character which are the subject of study. If, as has been asserted, Milton in *Lycidas* after a real struggle won "an exalted state of mental calm," this artificial tranquility did not long continue. Exposed to sundry trials and disappointments, it was certainly not his characteristic mood.

When in 1639 Milton returned from his *grand tour*, he had already heard of the death of his friend Charles Diodati. In *Epitaphium Damonis* Milton's intense grief assumes a melancholy cast, as is indicated by the remark of Mopsus:

Thyrsis, what means this? What shameless spleen torments you? Either passion is slaying you, or some star is vexing you with baneful spell. Saturn's star has often rested heavy on shepherds, and with glancing strokes of his leaden shaft has pierced their hearts to the utmost deeps.[45]

This tone is also present in the account of Thyrsis' haunts:

But now, alone, I wander through the fields, alone o'er the meadows, wherever the shadows cast by the branches are close set in

[41] Tillyard, *Milton*, pp. 80-85, 99 ff.; Hughes, *op. cit.*, pp. xlvii ff.
[42] *Art As Experience* (New York, 1934), pp. 78 ff.
[43] "The Youth of Milton," p. 148.   [44] *Op. cit.*, I, 298, 323.
[45] *The Works of John Milton* (New York, 1931), Vol. I, Part I, p. 305.

the vales. There I wait the evening; over my head the rain and
Eurus make mournful sounds, and the rending forests toss in the
evening twilight.

Milton's thoughts naturally dwell upon his loneliness. "But
what of me?" he asks. "To whom shall I entrust my soul?"
Who will help to lighten his consuming cares? Who will be-
guile the long days and nights with sweet converse now that
Damon has taken his way to the stars and his place among
the souls of heroes and gods that live forever? The deification
of Damon emphasizes Thyrsis' lonely sorrow.

Other links in the chain of evidence are found in Milton's
first marriage and in the pamphlets urging more liberal divorce
laws. Although Milton's interest in divorce preceded his experience in marriage, critics generally agree that his unhappy
marriage not only strongly affected his views of woman's character but also profoundly influenced his own character. If it
seem unwise to make this bitter disappointment the central fact
of his life, it is probably true, as Saurat says, that his "highest
ideal, that of love as a harmony between body and spirit, was
[by his first marriage] at once shattered and destroyed."[46] It
is a confirmation of our thesis that Milton regards true marriage
as a cure for loneliness. In *The Doctrine and Discipline of
Divorce* he writes:

And the solitariness of man, which God had namely and principally ordered to prevent by marriage, hath no remedy, but lies
under a worse condition than the loneliest single life, for in single
life the absence and remoteness of a helper might inure him to expect his own comforts out of himself, or to seek with hope; but
here the continual sight of his deluded thoughts, without cure,
must needs be to him, *if especially his complexion incline him to
melancholy*, a daily trouble and pain of loss, in some degree like
that which reprobates feel.[47]

The clause "if especially his complexion incline him to melancholy" reads like a personal confession. A wretched union,

[46] *Milton Man and Thinker* (New York, 1935), p. 55.
[47] *The Student's Milton*, ed. F. A. Patterson (New York, 1930), p. 582.
Italics mine.

Milton declares, does but increase "that same Godforbidden loneliness, which will in time draw on with it a general discomfort and dejection of mind," dangerous to both the individual and the state. Again and again Milton emphasizes loneliness of soul as a reason for marriage, divorce, or remarriage; again and again he declares that "dejection of spirit," grief, and discouragement result from mismated marriages; always he insists that unfitness of mind rather than defect of body is the cause of unhappy wedlock and a true reason for divorce. It is characteristic that by reform of the rigid divorce laws Milton hoped to rescue Christians from "the depth of sadness and distress,"[48] from that dungeon "as irrevocable as the grave." The following passage in *Tetrachordon* is of interest in this connection and also with regard to an earlier argument in this study.

No mortal nature can endure, either in the actions of religion, or the study of wisdom, without sometimes slackening the cords of intense thought and labor, which, lest we should think faulty, God conceals us not his own recreations before the world was built: . . . We cannot, therefore, always be contemplative, or pragmatical abroad, but have need of some delightful intermissions, wherein the enlarged soul may leave off a while her severe schooling, and, like a glad youth in wandering vacancy, may keep her holidays to joy and harmless pastime; which as she cannot well do without company, so in no company so well as where the different sex in most resembling unlikeness, and most unlike resemblance, cannot but please best, and be pleased in the aptitude of that variety. . . . By these instances, and more which might be brought, we may imagine how indulgently God provided against man's loneliness; that he approved it not, as by himself declared not good; that he approved the remedy thereof, as of his own ordaining, consequently good; and as he ordained it, so doubtless proportionably to our fallen estate he gives it; else were his ordinance at least in vain, and we for all his gifts still empty handed. Nay, such an unbounteous giver we should make him, as in the fables Jupiter was to Ixion, giving him a cloud instead of Juno; giving him a monstrous issue by her, the breed of Centaurs, a neglected and unloved race,

[48] *Ibid.*, p. 625.

the fruits of a delusive marriage; and lastly, giving him her with a damnation to that wheel in hell, from a life thrown into the midst of temptations and disorders. But God is no deceitful giver, to bestow that on us for a remedy of loneliness, which if it bring not a sociable mind as well as a conjunctive body, leaves us no less alone than before; and if it bring a mind perpetually averse and disagreeable, betrays us to a worse condition than the most deserted loneliness.[49]

Replying to his opponent, this "pork" who never read philosophy, Milton in *Colasterion* maintains the principle that the natural temperament of mind may scarcely be altered, or if altered, is changed only for the worse. If melancholy is altered, phlegm and choler, instead of sanguine, are apt to succeed.[50] Experience teaches that radical changes in character do not take place. In the long-winded divorce pamphlets Milton's many arguments ultimately rest upon this assumption, that human dispositions are unalterable. Therefore, to prevent certain misery delusive marriages must be dissolved. But Milton was not set free. In the prolongation of his first marriage, although the reunion was, as Edward Phillips says, accompanied by an act of oblivion and league of peace for the future, one may find no remedy for Milton's melancholy complexion.

Faction, says Burton, is a cause of melancholy.[51] From hatred and anger spring contention, bitter taunts, scurrile invectives. Giving up peaceful days and sweet content, we plunge into woes and cares, aggravating our "misery and melancholy." Such was Milton's experience. He faced external as well as domestic difficulties. In *The Reason of Church Government*, writing of learning as a sore burden and of the persecution to which sincere and fearless men are subject, Milton declares that such men following their consciences and sense of duty become "a very sword and fire both in house and city over the whole earth." With Jeremiah he exclaims, "Woe is me, my mother, that thou hast borne me, a man of strife and contention!" It is, says Milton, a hateful thing to displease and molest thousands. But he could not disobey the command of God, whose

---

[49] *Ibid.*, pp. 656-657.   [50] *Ibid.*, p. 717.   [51] *Op. cit.*, I, 307 ff.

"word was in my heart as a burning fire shut up in my bones."
Thus it was that Milton, leaving "a calm and pleasing solitariness," embarked "in a troubled sea of noises and hoarse disputes." Although he is sometimes persuaded in his ecclesiastical
pamphlets that better times will come, Milton's prevailing
mood is one of passionate anger against the enemies of religious
truth and freedom. His disillusionment was increased by his
realization of the worldliness and tyranny of Prelates and Presbyters. With Burton he might have said: Behold our religious
madness—"so many professed Christians, yet so few imitators
of Christ, so much talk of religion . . . so little conscience."[52]
On every hand, Milton, like Burton, saw formalists, flatterers,
time-servers, who in hope of preferment would embrace any
opinion, who like so many vultures watched for a prey of
church goods. More and more Milton the idealist realized
that under the world's vain mask sycophancy, hypocrisy, selfish-
ness abound. By his voluntary service to the cause of true religion he would sustain the drooping church and store up for
himself "the good provision of peaceful hours." And doubtless
from the sense of duty done he won genuine satisfaction. But
the task of reform was difficult and in the end, as he realized,
impossible. The materialism of the clergy excited his righteous
indignation. In *An Apology for Smectymnuus*, in *The Likeliest
Means to Remove Hirelings out of the Church*, in *Lycidas*,
and elsewhere, he denounces those who for the discharge of
a single duty receive that which might satisfy the labors of
many faithful ministers, who let hundreds perish in one diocese
for want of spiritual food, who live as earls and chase away
all the faithful ministers of the flock, whose hands still crave
and are never satisfied, who are sent not from above but from
below "by the instinct of their own hunger, to feed upon the
church." Vainly Milton strove

> to save free Conscience from the paw
> Of hireling wolves whose Gospell is their maw.

The state of religion, so dear to Milton's heart, so fundamental

[52] *Op. cit.*, I, 56.

in individual and national life, did not indeed in Milton's time warrant optimism.

In his political pamphlets, *The Tenure of Kings and Magistrates* and *Eikonoklastes*, Milton's disillusionment is more complete and his mood more bitter. Men are too inconstant, slothful, and enslaved by custom to free the nation from tyranny. The instability and irrationality of the people, their blindness to their own good, their infatuation with the King, the devotion of various factions to their own selfish interests—such factors frustrated the establishment of a just and free commonwealth. The political sonnets strike a somber note, as when in that to Lord Fairfax Milton exclaims

> In vain doth Valour bleed
> While Avarice, & Rapine share the land.

He declares that wisdom and virtue are the foundation of liberty, and adds,

> But from that mark how far they roave we see
> For all this wast of wealth, and loss of blood.

In *The Ready and Easy Way to Establish a Free Commonwealth*, pleading the cause of liberty just before its eclipse, Milton had to say, "If their absolute determination be to enthrall us, before so long a Lent of servitude, they may permit us a little shrove-tide first, wherein to speak freely, and take our leaves of liberty." In those dark days he warned England against creeping back to the thraldom of kingship, against betraying a just and noble cause abused by some bad men but sanctified by "the blood of so many thousand faithful and valiant Englishmen, who left us this liberty, bought with their lives," against ungrateful backsliding from a free commonwealth, approved by the wisest of all ages and commended or rather enjoined by the Savior himself. Milton's last blast against tyranny fell upon deaf ears. His cause was lost.

For the cause of liberty Milton had already sacrificed his sight. His blindness intensified his inclination toward melancholy, as can be seen in the sonnet beginning "When I consider how my light is spent," in which in spite of faith his despondency is evident. Milton, it is true, did not despair. In the second sonnet on his blindness he expressed his undaunted courage. But against this sonnet must be placed that entitled "On His Deceased Wife," the famous passage in Book Three of *Paradise Lost*, and those melancholy lines in which Samson laments his loss of sight:

> Blind among enemies, O worse then chains,
> Dungeon, or beggery, or decrepit age!

There can be no doubt that through Samson Milton speaks.

> O dark, dark, dark, amid the blaze of noon,
> Irrecoverably dark, total Eclipse
> Without all hope of day!

Not unimportant in the history of the development of the melancholy strain in Milton's character and work are the later translations of the Psalms, some of which were made in the year 1653, just after his sight had completely failed. Milton's versions have been considered as mere literary exercises, as translations intended for congregational singing, as means of amusement and consolation after his blindness. Probably the last motive was the strongest. Psalms VI, LXXXVI, and LXXXVIII are especially interesting in relation to the theme of this chapter. Each of these entreats God to have mercy upon a weary and dejected suppliant.

When, near the fall of the Commonwealth, Milton again turned to poetry, the theme of *Paradise Lost*, it is evident, must have been very congenial. The plotting of the story as a drama gave way to a treatment in epic form, which allowed space for full development of the melancholy story with its startling contrasts: the state of the angels before the rebellion and afterwards, the glories of heaven and the horrors of hell, the beauty of Paradise and its destruction, the brief time of innocence and bliss and the long ages of sin and misery. By endowing man with free will Milton attempted to justify the ways of God to man, but his art is lavished upon the contrasts just mentioned. *Paradise Lost* is the supreme expression of that strain in Milton which through the years had grown more dominant. I do not ignore what might be called the orthodox optimism of the epic, which is that of Christian theology. Through Christ man is redeemed and may be regenerated. Through obedience to God, through virtue, patience, temperance, and love man may win a spiritual paradise far better than the terrestrial. But one is impressed with Satan's triumph. One recalls Satan's promise to his dear children, Sin and Death:

> [I] shall soon return,
> And bring ye to the place where Thou and Death
> Shall dwell at ease, and up and down unseen
> Wing silently the buxom Air, imbalm'd
> With odours; there ye shall be fed and fill'd
> Immeasurably, all things shall be your prey. (II, 839-844)

And although Satan is a liar and the father of liars, his promise is kept. One recalls the descent of Sin and Death into the universe, "Spreading their bane." One recalls in Books Eleven and Twelve the story of the future, which is largely the record of their triumph. In short, as regards the thesis of this chapter nothing could be more significant than Milton's choice of the subject of his epic and his elaboration of its theme. It is perhaps equally significant that between *Paradise Lost* and *The Anatomy of Melancholy* there are a number of remarkable and fundamental analogies.

At the outset we may observe two striking illustrations of this similarity. Discussing love, Burton remarks that love is either in the Trinity or for us his creatures, as in the making of the world.[53] God made the world and afterwards redeemed it through his Son. Burton adds, "And this is that *Homer's* golden chain, which reacheth down from Heaven to Earth, by which every creature is annexed, and depends upon his Creator." Recall Satan's first view of the newly created universe. Far off he sees the empyreal Heaven,

[53] *Op. cit.*, III, 17.

> And fast by hanging in a golden Chain
> This pendant world, in bigness as a Starr
> Of smallest Magnitude close by the Moon. (II, 1051-1053)

Verity refers to the *Iliad*, to Plato, Spenser, Bacon, and others, as well as to Milton's academic exercise *De Spherarum Concentu*, in which Milton says that Homer meant the golden chain "as a symbol of the chain of connection and design that runs through the universe."[54]   Mr. Arthur O. Lovejoy has recently said that Milton tends to emphasize the arbitrariness of the deity's action.[55]   But it is certainly true that here in *Paradise Lost*, as in the *Anatomy*, the golden chain is a symbol of divine love.   We know that instead of malign spirits it was God's pleasure to create in their room a better race,

> and thence diffuse
> His good to Worlds and Ages infinite. (VII, 190-191)

Commenting on Adam's sin in eating the forbidden fruit, Burton says, "And this belike is that which our fabulous Poets have shadowed unto us in the tale of *Pandora's* box, which, being opened through her curiosity, filled the world full of all manner of diseases."[56]   Recall Milton's description of Eve:

> More lovely then *Pandora*, whom the Gods
> Endowd with all thir gifts, and O too like
> In sad event, when to the unwiser Son
> Of *Japhet* brought by *Hermes*, she ensnar'd
> Mankind with her faire looks, to be aveng'd
> Of him who had stole *Joves* authentic fire. (IV, 714-719)

These interesting illustrations, which are probably not evidence that Milton was indebted to Burton, may serve as an introduction to a somewhat detailed comparative study of the *Anatomy* and *Paradise Lost*.

The first section of the first member of the first partition of the *Anatomy*, entitled "Man's Excellency, Fall, Miseries, Infirmities; The Causes of them," declares that man, "the most

---

[54] *Paradise Lost* (Cambridge, 1929), II, 428.
[55] *The Great Chain of Being A Study of the History of an Idea* (Cambridge, 1936), p. 160.   [56] *Op. cit.*, I, 150.

excellent and noble creature of the World," the wonder of nature and the "Sovereign Lord of the Earth," was created pure, divine, perfect, happy, and free from all infirmities, and put in Paradise "to know God, to praise and glorify him, to do his will."[57] But, "O pitifull change," this noble creature has fallen and become a castaway, a caitiff, "one of the most miserable creatures of the world." How much he is changed from what he was—"before blessed and happy, now miserable and accursed! He must eat his meat in sorrow, subject to death & all manner of infirmities, all kind of calamities. Great travail is created for all men, and an heavy yoke on the sons of Adam, from the day that they go out of their mother's womb, unto that day they return to the mother of all things. Namely their thoughts, and fear of their hearts, and their imagination of things they wait for, and the day of death." The cause of this fall, the cause of diseases and death, the cause of all temporal and eternal punishments was, of course, the sin of Adam "in eating the forbidden fruit, by the devil's instigation and allurement." For this disobedience the law demands punishment, which is as varied as are our infirmities. The stars, the heavens, the elements, and all creatures are armed against sinners. "For, from the fall of our first parent *Adam*, they have been changed, the earth accursed, the influence of the stars altered, the four elements, beasts, birds, plants, are now ready to offend us. . . . Fire, and hail, and famine, and dearth, all these are created for vengeance. . . . The heavens threaten us with their comets, stars, planets, with their great conjunctions, eclipses, oppositions, quartiles, and such unfriendly aspects; the air with his meteors, thunder and lightning, intemperate heat and cold, mighty winds, tempests, unseasonable weather; from which proceed dearth, famine, plague, and all sorts of epidemical diseases, consuming infinite myriads of men."[58] These ideas appear in the sublime poetry of *Paradise Lost*. After the sin of Adam and Eve,

> The Sun
> Had first his precept so to move, so shine,
> As might affect the Earth with cold and heat

[57] *Op. cit.*, I, 149.   [58] *Op. cit.*, I, 153.

> Scarce tollerable, and from the North to call
> Decrepit Winter, from the South to bring
> Solstitial summers heat. To the blanc Moone
> Her office they prescrib'd, to th' other five
> Thir planetarie motions and aspects
> In *Sextile, Square,* and *Trine,* and *Opposite,*
> Of noxious efficacie, and when to joyne
> In Synod unbenigne, and taught the fixt
> Thir influence malignant when to showre,
> Which of them rising with the Sun, or falling,
> Should prove tempestuous: To the Winds they set
> Thir corners, when with bluster to confound
> Sea, Aire, and Shoar, the Thunder when to rowle
> With terror through the dark Aereal Hall. (X, 651-667)

And so on. Thus began

> Outrage from liveless things; but Discord first
> Daughter of Sin, among th' irrational,
> Death introduc'd through fierce antipathie.

Burton paints a dark picture of discord and calamities in nature: destructive fires, ruinous inundations, fearful earthquakes.

> Whom fire spares, sea doth drown; who sea,
> Pestilent air doth send to clay;
> Who war scapes, sickness takes away.

Living creatures are at deadly feud with men. And the greatest enemy of man is man, "who by the Devil's instigation is still ready to do mischief, his own executioner, a wolf, a Devil to himself and others." We can, says Burton, partly see and avoid diseases, tempests, inundations, dearths; "but the knaveries, impostures, injuries, and villanies of men" no art can avoid, no caution divert. Recall Milton's lamentation:

> O shame to men! Devil with Devil damn'd
> Firm concord holds, men onely disagree
> Of Creatures rational, though under hope
> Of heavenly Grace; and God proclaiming peace,
> Yet live in hatred, enmitie, and strife
> Among themselves, and levie cruel warres,
> Wasting the Earth, each other to destroy. (II, 496-502)

As Burton says, we arm ourselves for our own destruction, and use reason, art, and judgment "as so many instruments to undo us." Thus our sins pull misfortunes upon our own heads, and God uses all his instruments and creatures as executioners of justice.

Burton's subsection entitled "A Digression of the nature of Spirits, bad Angels, or Devils, and how they cause Melancholy" is of particular interest and importance, for it is in fact a summary of learned opinion. Although he admits that the matter is very obscure and beyond the reach of human wit, he ventures to consider it. Dismissing the opinion that there are no devils, he takes his stand upon Scripture, which "informs us Christians, how *Lucifer*, the chief of them, fell from heaven for his pride and ambition; created of God, placed in heaven, and sometimes an Angel of Light, now cast down into the lower aerial sublunary parts, or into Hell, and delivered into chains of darkness (2 Pet. 2.4.) to be kept unto damnation."[59] Psellus, a Christian and a great observer of devils, holds that they are corporeal, that they are mortal, that they feel pain, that their wounds close "with admirable celerity." When Satan was sheared by Michael's sword, he first felt pain;

> but th' Ethereal substance clos'd
> Not long divisible, and from the gash
> A stream of Nectarous humor issuing flow'd
> Sanguin, such as Celestial Spirits may bleed,
> And all his Armour staind ere while so bright. (VI, 330-334)

Augustine, Jerome, Origen, Tertullian, Lactantius, and many other ancient Fathers declare that in their fall the rebel angels "were changed into a more aerial and gross substance." When we first see Satan in Hell, his form has not yet lost all its brightness. Later Zephon reminds him that he is not the same as he was in Heaven:

> That Glorie then, when thou no more wast good,
> Departed from thee, and thou resembl'st now
> Thy sin and place of doom obscure and foule. (IV, 838-840)

[59] *Op. cit.,* I, 206.

Burton explains that demons can assume whatever shape they please, that they can transform bodies of others into any desired shape, that they are very swift and can "pass many miles in an instant," that they can represent castles in the air, prodigies, and other marvels, and produce smells, savors, and sensations to deceive the senses. In *Paradise Lost* Satan assumes various shapes: he is at different times an angel of light, a cormorant, a lion, a toad, a serpent. He journeys extensively, from hell to the universe and round about the earth at pleasure. In *Paradise Regained* he is disguised as an old man. He creates a fearful storm to afflict Christ. Both Burton and Milton adopt the idea of the Fathers of the Church that the gods of the Gentiles were devils.

A recent study of the spirit world in Henry More's *The Immortality of the Soul* and in *Paradise Lost* reaches the conclusion that between them there is a "remarkable correspondence, even in minute details."[60] As proof that Milton knew More's work, it is said that both use the idea that evil spirits assume at will various shapes of beasts, that both More and Milton believe in the corporeality of spirits, and so on. These points are common to the *Anatomy* and Milton's epic. Besides, it must be observed that Burton's demons, like Milton's, are ethereal spirits, not those of human souls translated, as are More's. Relevant parts of the *Anatomy* show that the spirit worlds of More and Milton include a number of conventional ideas.

Not only naming the chief demons, Beelzebub, Belial, Asmodaeus, Satan, Mammon, and some of the terrestrial devils, Dagon among the Philistines, Bel among the Babylonians, Astarte among the Sidonians, Isis and Osiris among the Egyptians, Burton explains the manner of the Devil's working: he "begins first with the phantasy, & moves that so strongly, that no reason is able to resist." In the shape of a toad Satan sat close to the ear of Eve,

[60] Marjorie H. Nicolson, "The Spirit World of Milton and More," *Studies in Philology*, XXII, 433-452.

Assaying by his devilish art to reach
The Organs of her Fancie, and with them forge
Illusions as he list, Phantasms and Dreams. (IV, 801-803)

Thus, says Burton, "the Devil reigns, and in a thousand several shapes"; thus "he rageth while he may to comfort himself, as Lactantius thinks, with other men's fall, he labours all he can to bring them into the same pit of perdition with him." By God's permission he rageth, "hereafter to be confined to hell and darkness, which is prepared for him and his Angels."[61] If we are to judge, not by *De Doctrina Christiana*, which almost ignores the devil, but by *Paradise Lost*, Milton accepted Burton's statement that as the instigator of evil the Devil or Satan is supremely important: "The *primum mobile* therefore, and first mover of all superstition, is the Devil, that great enemy of mankind, the principal agent, who in a thousand several shapes, after divers fashions, with several engines, illusions, and by several names, hath deceived the inhabitants of the earth, in several places and Countries, still rejoicing at their falls."[62]

Among terrestrial devils, says Burton, are fauns, satyrs, wood nymphs, fairies, and Robin Goodfellows, which are most familiar to men. Formerly, fairies were adored with much superstition, "with sweeping houses, and setting of a pail of clean water, good victuals, and the like, and then they should not be pinched, but find money in their shoes, and be fortunate in their enterprises. These are they that dance on heaths and greens. . . . A bigger kind there is of them, called with us *Hobgoblins*, & *Robin Goodfellows*, that would in those superstitious times grind corn for a mess of milk, cut wood, or do any manner of drudgery work."[63] In *L'Allegro* a swain

Tells how the drudging *Goblin* swet,
To ern his Cream-bowle duly set,
When in one night, ere glimps of morn,
His shadowy Flale hath thresh'd the Corn
That ten day-labourers could not end,
Then lies him down the Lubbar Fend. (ll. 105-110)

[61] *Op. cit.*, I, 225.
[62] *Op. cit.*, III, 374. [63] *Op. cit.*, I, 219-220.

In *Paradise Lost* the devils, reduced to a size less than that of smallest dwarfs, are compared to

> Faerie Elves,
> Whose midnight Revels, by a Forrest side
> Or Fountain some belated Peasant sees,
> Or dreams he sees, while over head the Moon
> Sits Arbitress, and neerer to the Earth
> Wheels her pale course, they on thir mirth & dance
> Intent, with jocond Music charm his ear. (I, 781-787)

In addition to the material dealing with the Fall and its consequences and the part played by spirits in human affairs, there are between the epic and the *Anatomy* other analogies, which are in part conventional. According to Burton, the will of man is in its essence free, but it is now much depraved and fallen from its first perfection, although still free in some of its operations.[64] By nature, discipline, and custom, we are now averse from God; and the devil "is still ready at hand with his evil suggestions, to tempt our depraved will" to sin unless we are swayed by divine precepts. "We say," says Burton, "that our will is free in respect of us, and things contingent, howsoever (in respect of God's determinate counsel) they are inevitable and necessary." Milton insists that originally man's will was entirely free.

> I made him just and right,
> Sufficient to have stood, though free to fall.
> . . . .
> . . . They therefore as to right belongd,
> So were created, nor can justly accuse
> Thir maker, or thir making, or thir Fate;
> . . . .
> So without least impulse or shadow of Fate,
> Or aught by me immutablie foreseen,
> They trespass, Authors to themselves in all
> Both what they judge and what they choose; for so
> I formed them free, and free they must remain,
> Till they enthrall themselves. (III, 98-125)

[64] *Op. cit.,* I, 190.

According to *De Doctrina Christiana*, the Fall—a spiritual death, the loss of divine grace and innate righteousness—consists of the obscuring of right reason and "the subjection to sin and the devil, which constitutes, as it were, the death of the will."[65] But some goodness remains: "some remnants of the divine image still exist in us, not wholly extinguished by this spiritual death." By the Fall the liberty of the will is not quite destroyed, but without divine grace the will is impotent.

> Man shall not quite be lost, but sav'd who will,
> Yet not of will in him, but grace in me
> Freely voutsaft; once more I will renew
> His lapsed powers, though forfeit and enthrall'd
> By sin to foul exorbitant desires;
> Upheld by me, yet once more he shall stand
> On even ground against his mortal foe,
> By me upheld, that he may know how frail
> His fall'n condition is, and to me ow
> All his deliv'rance, and to none but me. (III, 173-182)

In the *Anatomy* and the epic, man's will is depraved by the Fall, and only through God's grace and Christ's mediation are his powers renewed and his salvation made possible. Upon the question of sin and regeneration Burton and Milton hold the same orthodox opinion. There is, however, a difference in emphasis: more than Burton, Milton stresses the original freedom of the will and passion as the cause of the Fall.

There is also striking similarity between Burton's and Milton's views of cosmography. Each takes neutral ground, apparently refusing to accept Copernicanism but also ridiculing the attempts of astronomers to salvage the Ptolemaic system. It has recently been declared that in Book Eight of *Paradise Lost* Milton discusses four hypotheses: the theory of the diurnal rotation of the earth, the Ptolemaic, the Copernican, and the doctrine of the plurality of worlds, omitting only the geoheliocentric theory, which was important in his time.[66] The

[65] *The Student's Milton*, p. 999.
[66] Grant McColley, "The Astronomy of *Paradise Lost*," *Studies in Philology*, XXXIV, 209-247.

explanations presented in this very thorough discussion may take the place of the traditional interpretations. But it must be said that Raphael's reply to Adam's enquiry begins by mentioning only two possibilities.

> This to attain, whether Heav'n move or Earth,
> Imports not, if thou reck'n right. (VIII, 70-71)

Raphael then half-heartedly defends the Ptolemaic theory and afterwards explains the Copernican, apparently including the annual rotation of the earth and the plurality of worlds as details of the latter theory. He ends with the admonition that Adam should love and fear God, not dream of other worlds.

In imagination roving about the world and mounting "aloft to those ethereal orbs and celestial spheres," Burton reviews a number of cosmographical ideas familiar to the student of *Paradise Lost*. Burton believes that the matter of the heavens is not hard and impenetrable, but soft as is the air itself, and that the planets move in it as birds in the air and fish in the sea.[67] Similarly, Milton explains that the sun, the moon, and the stars are set in the firmament or heaven which is "liquid, pure, Transparent, elemental air."[68] In *Paradise Lost* there is, says Mr. McColley, no reference to the "physically impossible system of ten solid spheres."[69] There are no solid spheres to obstruct the flight or the sight of Christ, Satan, and the angels.

In detail Burton considers "that main paradox" of the earth's motion, maintained of old by Aristarchus, Pythagoras, Democritus, and many of their disciples and revived by Copernicus, Kepler, Gilbert, Digges, Galileo, and others. If the earth stands still in the center of the world, "as the most received opinion is," and the heavens move, "what fury is that . . . that shall drive the Heavens about with such incomprehensible celerity in 24 hours, when as every point of the Firmament, and in the Equator, must needs move . . .

[67] *Op. cit.*, II, 57.
[68] *Op. cit.*, VII, 264-274.   [69] *Op. cit.*, p. 244.

176,660 miles in one 246th part of an hour: and an arrow out
of a bow must go seven times about the earth whilst a man
can say *Ave Maria*, if it keep the same space, or compass the
earth 1,884 times in an hour, which is *supra humanam cogi-
tationem*, beyond human conceit: . . . A man could not ride
so much ground, going 40 miles a day, in 2,904 years, as the
Firmament goes in 24 hours; or so much in 203 years, as the
said Firmament in one minute; *quod incredibile vide-
tur*. . . ."[70] Here Burton follows Gilbert, termed by Mr.
McColley "the most vigorous English exponent" of the seventeenth-century commonplace that the daily revolution of the
heavens is an unreasonable hypothesis. Computing the magnitude of the universe and her numberless stars that seem "to
roll Spaces incomprehensible," in comparison with which the
earth seems merely a spot, a grain, Adam likewise wonders
how the orbs of the heavens can travel at such incorporeal
speed around the fixed earth.

According to Burton, there are two ways to avoid this im-
possibility. We may ascribe a triple motion to the earth, "the
Sun immovable in the Center of the whole world." With
this we may compare Raphael's words:

> What if the Sun
> Be Center to the World, and other Starrs
> By his attractive vertue and thir own
> Incited, dance about him various rounds?
> . . . .
> The Planet Earth, so stedfast though she seem,
> Insensibly three different Motions move? (VIII, 122-130)

This ascription of a triple motion to the earth was, Mr.
McColley says, in Milton's day an antiquated description, and
he concludes that Milton was indifferent to the study of current astronomy. Burton finds "more probable" than this triple
motion of the earth the theory that assigns to the earth, placed
in the center of the world, only one motion, that is, a daily rotation on its own axis. Either of these hypotheses, Burton

[70] *Op. cit.*, II, 60-61.

declares, will calculate all motions, direct, stationary, retrograde, "without Epicycles, intricate Eccentricks," much more certainly than is possible by the Alphonsine or any tables that depend upon the Ptolemaic theory. To avoid these paradoxes of the earth's motion our mathematicians, says Burton, have invented new hypotheses "out of their own *Daedalean* heads." For example, Fracastorious has coined seventy-two "Homocentricks, to solve all appearances"; according to Ramerus, the earth is in the center but movable, the eighth sphere is immovable, the five upper planets move about the sun, the sun and moon about the earth; according to Tycho Brahe, the earth in the center is immovable, the stars immovable, and the rest is as in Ramerus; Roeslin, who finds fault with all the others, makes the earth the center of the universe and the sun the center of the upper planets, ascribes to the eighth sphere diurnal motion, attributes eccentrics and epicycles to the seven planets, and "so . . . as a tinker stops one hole and makes two, he corrects them, and doth worse himself, reforms some, and mars all."[71]   Milton also ridicules the efforts of astronomers to "save appearances":

> Hereafter when they come to model Heav'n
> And calculate the Starrs, how they will weild
> The mightie frame, how build, unbuild, contrive
> To save appeerances, how gird the Sphear
> With Centric and Eccentric scribl'd o're,
> Cycle and Epicycle, Orb in Orb. (VIII, 79-84)

Like Burton, Milton is interested in the "new astronomy," with which he seems to be fairly familiar. On the whole, Milton, like Burton, seems to prefer the geocentric hypothesis with the diurnal rotation of the earth, but Milton refuses to commit himself. When Satan directed his course towards the sun, Milton cautiously says that it is hard to tell whether he went up or down in the firmament, towards the center or away from it.[72]

[71] *Op. cit.*, II, 65-66.   [72] *Paradise Lost*, III, 573 ff.

Note also the following passages in the *Anatomy:*

. . . if the earth move, it is a Planet, & shines to them in the *Moon*, & to the other Planetary Inhabitants, as the *Moon* and they to us upon the earth: but shine she doth, as *Galileo, Kepler,* and others prove, and then, *per consequens,* the rest of the Planets are inhabited, as well as the *Moon,* . . . & those several Planets have their several *Moons* about them, as the earth hath her's, as *Galileo* hath already evinced by his glasses: four about *Jupiter,* two about *Saturn.* . . . Then (I say) the earth and they be Planets alike, inhabited alike, moved about the Sun, the common center of the World. . . . We may likewise insert with *Campanella* and *Brunus* that which *Pythagoras, Aristarchus Samias, Heraclitus,* . . . maintained in their ages, there be *infinite* Worlds, and infinite earths and systems, *in infinito aethere,* . . . For if the Firmament be of such an incomparable bigness, as these Copernical Giants will have it, *infinitum, aut infinito proximum,* so vast and full of innumerable stars, as being infinite in extent, . . . If our world be small in respect, why may we not suppose a plurality of worlds, those infinite stars visible in the Firmament to be so many Suns, . . . Though they seem close to us, they are infinitely distant, and so, *per consequens,* there are infinite habitable worlds: what hinders? Why should not an infinite cause (as God is) produce infinite effects?[73]

From his consideration of the greatness and variety of the universe Tycho Brahe concludes "that he will never believe those great and huge bodies were made to no other use than this that we perceive, to illuminate the earth, a point insensible in respect of the whole."

Raphael explains that if the sun be the center of the universe, then the earth may be like the other planets, and adds:

What if that light
Sent from her through the wide transpicuous aire,
To the terrestrial Moon be as a Starr
Enlightning her by Day, as she by Night
This Earth? reciprocal, if Land be there,
Feilds and Inhabitants: . . . .
. . . . and other Suns perhaps

[73] *Op. cit.,* II, 62-63.

With thir attendant Moons thou wilt descrie
Communicating Male and Female Light,
Which two great Sexes animate the World,
Stor'd in each Orb perhaps with some that live.
For such vast room in Nature unpossest
By living Soule, desert and desolate,
Onely to shine, yet scarce to contribute
Each Orb a glimps of Light, conveyd so farr
Down to this habitable, which returnes
Light back to them, is obvious to dispute. (VIII, 140-158)

As Satan descends through the universe, he

windes with ease
Through the pure marble Air his oblique way
Amongst innumerable Starrs, that shon
Stars distant, but nigh hand seemd other Worlds,
Or other Worlds they seemd, or happy Isles,
Like those *Hesperian* Gardens fam'd of old,
Fortunate Fields, and Groves and flourie Vales,
Thrice happy Isles, but who dwelt happy there
He stayd not to enquire. (III, 563-571)

Even the casual reader may be impressed by the extraordinary similarity between these passages from the *Anatomy* and *Paradise Lost*.

Less significant is the fact that Burton and Milton agree in condemning the attempt to solve divine mysteries. Burton protests against "absurd and brainsick questions, intricacies, froth of human wit, and excrements of curiosity. . . ." In his own good time, Burton believes, God will reveal his mysteries unto men. To check our impertinent inquiry, God conceals all things in uncertainty, "bars us from long antiquity, and bounds our search within the compass of some few ages." Burton condemns idle curiosity, "an itching humour or a kind of longing to see that which is not to be seen, to do that which ought not to be done, to know that secret which should not be known, to eat of the forbidden fruit." Most of our philosophy, says Burton, is a maze of opinions, idle questions, and metaphysical terms; astrology is merely vain prediction; magic, pernicious foppery; physic, intricate rules and prescriptions; philology, vain criticism; logic, needless sophism; alchemy, a bundle of errors. "Why do we spend so many years in their studies? . . . to what end? *cui bono?* . . ."

> Nescire velle quae Magister maximus
> Docere non vult, erudita inscitia est.
> [It is wise ignorance not to wish to know
>   What our great Master does not wish to teach us.]

In substance this is Raphael's advice to Adam:

> Sollicit not thy thoughts with matters hid,
> Leave them to God above, him serve and feare;
> . . . . Heav'n is for thee too high
> To know what passes there; be lowlie wise:
> Think onely what concerns thee and thy being;
> Dream not of other Worlds. (VIII, 167-175)

After bitter experience Adam is convinced that to obey and fear God, to observe his providence, and to suffer for truth's sake is "the sum Of wisdom."

> . . . hope no higher, though all the Starrs
> Thou knewest by name, and all th' ethereal Powers,
> All secrets of the deep, all Natures works,
> Or works of God in Heav'n, Air, Earth, or Sea,
> And all the riches of this World enjoydst,
> And all the rule, one Empire. (XII, 576-581)

On this principle, in Book Four of *Paradise Regained*, Christ spurns Satan's temptation, bluntly dismissing the art and the learning of Greece:

> But these are false, or little else but dreams,
> Conjectures, fancies, built on nothing firm.
> . . . .
> Alas what can they teach, and not mislead;
> Ignorant of themselves, of God much more. (ll. 291-310)

Both Burton and Milton were devoted students, and they reached the same conclusion—that much of what passes for human learning is futile.

Moderation in intellectual interests suggests the idea of temperance in diet and in all things, a favorite doctrine in the *Anatomy* and *Paradise Lost.* For all, and especially for the melancholy man, Burton commends moderation in food and drink. Eat and drink only to satisfy hunger and thirst. "Nothing pesters the body and mind sooner than to be still fed, to eat and ingurgitate beyond all measure, as many do." Let the diet be moderate and plain. He that loves himself will observe a strict diet "to avoid a greater inconvenience. . . ."[74] Burton quotes Seneca: "Nature is content with bread and water; and he that can rest satisfied with that, may contend with Jupiter himself for happiness." The young must altogether avoid wine, which is a plague if used immoderately. The advice of Euripides is approved: "O my son, mediocrity of means agrees best with men; too much is pernicious." Seeing people buy many things in a fair, Socrates exclaimed, "O ye Gods, what a sight of things I do not want!" Indeed, all happiness resides in a mean estate. Poverty and virtue dwell together. Let others have wealth and honor, which are their misery. Burton insists that he who lives according to nature cannot be poor and he who exceeds can never have enough. But what if we are in the extremity of human misery? What then? Burton's advice is: bear it, and it will be tolerable at last. Be of good courage. Know that "misery is virtue's whetstone." Remember that Job, not the Devil, was the victor. Have faith. You are forsaken by the world but not by God. A good man cannot be overcome. "The gout may hurt his hands, lameness his feet, convulsions may torture his joints, but not *rectam mentem,* his soul is free."[75] You may take away his money, his treasure is in heaven; banish him his country, he is an inhabitant of the heavenly Jerusalem; kill his body, it shall rise again. Have patience and hope. "Wait patiently on the Lord, and hope in him . . . he will comfort thee, and give thee thy heart's desire."

Milton also, as is well known, commends temperance and a stoical-Christian fortitude. In *Comus* one of the sober laws of nature is the "holy dictate of spare Temperance." In *Para-*

[74] *Op. cit.,* II, 34.   [75] *Op. cit.,* II, 191.

dise Lost one of the duties of Adam and Eve is to prune the wanton growth of luxuriant nature. The banquet prepared for Raphael is choice and delicate, with no excess. To avoid disease and misery Michael advises Adam to observe

> The rule of not too much, by temperance taught
> In what thou eatst and drinkst, seeking from thence
> Due nourishment, not gluttonous delight. (XI, 528-530)

Temperance is one of the cardinal virtues emphasized by Michael in parting. In *Paradise Regained* Satan learns that Christ's temperance is invincible. Too late Samson realizes that by temperance in diet he was only half prepared against evil:

> What boots it at one gate to make defence,
> And at another to let in the foe
> Effeminatly vanquish't? (ll. 560-562)

In *Areopagitica* Milton exclaims, "How great a virtue is temperance, how much of moment through the whole life of man!" But temperance alone is inadequate. Miserable beyond all past and future example, faced by the dismal prospect of lasting woes, Adam has recourse to a stoical endurance of evil and to faith in God. Sustained by an abiding faith in God's power, wisdom, and mercy, Milton, like Adam, apparently cared not for long life but sought rather how to be quit

> Fairest and easiest of this combrous charge,
> Which I must keep till my appointed day
> Of rendring up. (XI, 546-548)

In contrast with Burton's conventional faith, there is apparent in Milton a pronounced strain of stoicism.

In addition to agreeing upon the fundamental points of theology, demonology, cosmography, and morality, Burton and Milton condemn war and military glory. What would Democritus have said, Burton exclaims, if he had seen so many bloody battles, so many thousand slain, such vast streams of blood. Pampered statesmen live at home and take their ease while miserable soldiers endure toil, hunger, thirst, wounds, and death. Without remorse, proper men, able in body and

mind, are "led like so many beasts to the slaughter." Through
many ages these massacres and desolations have continued.
What "plague, what fury brought so devilish, so brutish a
thing as war into men's minds?" In spite of reason and humanity, "God's and men's laws are trampled under foot, the
sword alone determines all."[76] Brother fights against brother,
father against son, kingdom against kingdom, Christian against
Christian. Infinite treasures are destroyed, cities consumed,
goodly countries depopulated in war, which is an abominable
thing, the plague of hell, the scourge of God. In spite of all
this, soldiers are highly honored. They alone are brave spirits,
true gallants, with monuments erected to their fame. Although
they are really blood-suckers, desperate villains, inhuman rogues,
and dissolute caitiffs, they are for the most part called courageous and generous spirits, worthy captains, valiant and renowned warriors. To acquire a false name of valor and honor
men run into the cannon's mouth. And what is worse, they are
persuaded that "this hellish course of life" is holy. And so,
says Burton, "they put a note of divinity upon the most cruel,
& pernicious plague of human kind, adorn such men with grand
titles, degrees, statues, images, honour, applaud, & highly reward them for their good service, no greater glory than to die
in the field!"[77] By this means earth wallows in her own blood.
A man is executed for doing privately that for which if done in
public wars he would be honored. For the same deed one is
made a lord, an earl, and another is hanged in chains. "A poor
sheep-stealer is hanged for stealing of victuals, compelled peradventure by necessity of that intolerable cold, hunger, and
thirst, to save himself from starving: but a great man in office
may securely rob whole provinces, undo thousands, pill and
poll, oppress *ad libitum*, . . . tyrannize, enrich himself by the
spoils of the Commons, . . . and, after all, be recompensed
by turgent titles, honored for his good service, and no man
dare to find fault, or mutter at it." Thus Burton pricks the
bubble of military glory.

[76] *Op. cit.*, I, 60.   [77] *Op. cit.*, I, 64-65.

In both his epics Milton exposes the futility of war and the emptiness of military honor. In *Paradise Lost* Adam has a vision of "Concours in Arms, fierce Faces threatning Warr," of theft of herds and flocks, ensuing war, ensanguined field, prolonged siege, oppression, violence, and sword-law, from which there is no refuge. Michael's comment is that in those days military prowess alone shall be called valor and heroic virtue and that military heroes, instead of being

Patrons of Mankind, Gods, and Sons of Gods, (XI, 692)

are in fact destroyers and plagues of men. In *Paradise Regained* Christ rejects the glory of this world and approves the just man. On earth

glory is false glory, attributed
To things not glorious, men not worthy of fame. (III, 69-70)

In words that echo Michael's judgment Christ continues:

They err who count it glorious to subdue
By Conquest far and wide, to over-run
Large Countries, and in field great Battles win,
Great Cities by assault: what do these Worthies,
But rob and spoil, burn, slaughter, and enslave
Peaceable Nations, neighbouring, or remote,
Made Captive, yet deserving freedom more
Then those thir Conquerours, who leave behind
Nothing but ruin wheresoe're they rove,
And all the flourishing works of peace destroy,
Then swell with pride, and must be titl'd Gods,
Great Benefactors of mankind, Deliverers,
Worship't with Temple, Priest and Sacrifice;
One is the Son of *Jove*, of *Mars* the other,
Till Conqueror Death discover them scarce men,
Rowling in brutish vices, and deform'd,
Violent or shameful death thir due reward. (III, 71-87)

Doubtless the sincere expression of Milton's convictions, this denunciation of war and of military heroes, not such a commonplace in the seventeenth century as it is today, reminds one of similar views in the *Anatomy*.

From what has been said it follows that both Burton and Milton scorn the transitory glories of this world. Everything falls to decay. Tombs, cities, provinces "have their periods, and are consumed." Babylon, the greatest of all cities, has now "nothing but walls and rubbish left."[78] Rome, once the queen of all cities, is now in respect hardly more than a village. Greece, once the seat of civilization, is now forlorn and a den of thieves. Ancient families decay. He that stands high today, full of honor, on the top of fortune's wheel, may tomorrow be a beggar. Therefore, the wise man scorns this earthly state and looks up to heaven, which is his home. Imitate Christ. "How many great *Caesars*, mighty Monarchs . . . lived in his days, in what plenty, what delicacy, how bravely attended, what a deal of gold and silver, what treasure, how many sumptuous palaces had they, what Provinces and Cities, ample territories, . . . Yet Christ had none of all this, he would have none of this, he voluntarily rejected all this, he could not be ignorant, he could not err in his choice, he contemned all this, he chose that which was safer, better, and more certain, and less to be repented, a mean estate, even poverty itself; . . . So do thou tread in his divine steps, and thou shalt not err eternally, as too many worldlings do, that run on in their dissolute courses, to their own confusion and ruin. . . ." This is, of course, the central theme of *Paradise Regained*, in which, as Mr. Hanford has said, Christ, protagonist of humanity, faces and overcomes the manifold forms of evil in a developed civilization, and shows all men the vanity of "luxury, wealth, power, fame, the pride of knowledge."[79] Milton's minor epic both illustrates the fundamental principles of Christian ethics and defines more sharply than hitherto Milton's realization

> Of all things transitorie and vain, when Sin
> With vanity had filld the works of men.

In some of the analogies hitherto examined, particularly in those dealing with theology, convention is important. Burton

[78] *Op. cit.*, II, 209.
[79] "*Samson Agonistes* and Milton in Old Age," *Studies in Shakespeare, Milton, and Donne*, p. 170.

and Milton, it is obvious, deal with orthodox material in a fashion that reveals fundamentally sympathetic tastes and tendencies. It is true that in the encyclopedic *Anatomy*, which ranges far over life and literature, there is much greater variety of matter than in Milton's epics. Although I am not primarily interested in proving Milton's indebtedness to the *Anatomy*, it is perhaps significant that in this work a number of details remind one of those in Milton's poems. A few illustrations may suffice. Concerning the devil, Burton, quoting Eusebius, writes, "All the world over before Christ's time he freely domineered, and held the souls of men in most slavish subjection, . . . in divers forms, ceremonies, and sacrifices, till Christ's coming."[80] At Christ's birth, Milton says, in "On the Morning of Christ's Nativity," the oracles at once ceased and the pagan shrines were deserted. Discussing suicide as a release from intolerable misery, Burton writes, "*Cleombrotus Ambraciotes* persuaded I know not how many hundreds of his auditors, by a luculent oration he made of the miseries of this & happiness of that other life, to precipitate themselves: and, having read *Plato's* divine tract *de anima*, for example's sake led the way first."[81] In *Paradise Lost* we read:

> hee who to enjoy
> *Plato's Elysium*, leap'd into the Sea,
> *Cleombrotus*. (III, 471-473)

Melancholy, says Burton, proceeds from fear and sorrow: As Bellerophon in Homer,

> Qui miser in silvis moerens errabat opacis,
> Ipse suum cor edens, hominum vestigis vitans:
> That wandered in the woods sad all alone,
> Forsaking men's society, making great moan;[82]

Milton implores his Muse:

> Return me to my Native Element:
> Least from this flying Steed unrein'd, (as once

[80] *Op. cit.*, III, 374.   [81] *Op. cit.*, I, 503.
[82] *Op. cit.*, I, 455.

Bellerophon, though from a lower Clime)
Dismounted, on th' *Aleian* Field I fall
Erroneous, there to wander and forlorne. (*P.L.* VII, 16-20)

Burton observes that "*Comus* and *Hymen* love masks, and all such merriments above measure,"[83] but, regarding honest objects of love, remarks that in all ages virtue hath been adored, that "No beauty leaves such an impression, strikes so deep, or links the souls of men closer than virtue," that the luster of virtue never fades but is ever fresh and green to all succeeding ages. The quintessence of virtue is God, whose beauty far exceeds the "beauty of Heavens, Sun and Moon, Stars, and Angels," for in Him is "absolute beauty; and where is that beauty, from the same fountain comes all pleasure and happiness."[84] "In this life," says Burton, "we have but a glimpse of this beauty and happiness: we shall hereafter, as *John* saith, see him as he is." To love God is our chiefest good. To that end we were born. But we are carried astray by our vain affections, by our corrupt wills, by our love of this world. "Love not the world, nor the things that are in the world. . . . For all that is in the world, as the lust of the flesh, the lust of the eyes, and pride of life, is not of the Father, but of the world: and the world passeth away and the lust thereof; but he that fulfilleth the will of God abideth forever."[85] These illustrations will suffice to show that in the *Anatomy* Milton could have found an extraordinarily rich body of material drawn from an impressive array of sources, colored by strong religious principles, and controlled by a philosophy entirely congenial.

Finally, observe Milton in old age, which, according to Burton, "being cold and dry, and of the same quality as Melancholy is, must needs cause it, by diminution of spirits and substance, and increasing of adust humours."[86] Certainly Michael paints for Adam no optimistic picture of old age.

This is old age; but then thou must outlive
Thy youth, thy strength, thy beauty, which will change
To withered weak & gray; thy Senses then

[83] *Op. cit.,* III, 205.   [84] *Op. cit.,* III, 362.
[85] *Op. cit.,* III, 363-364.   [86] *Op. cit.,* I, 240.

Obtuse, all taste of pleasure must forgoe,
To what thou hast, and for the Aire of youth
Hopeful and cheerful, in thy blood will reigne
A melancholy damp of cold and dry
To waigh thy spirits down, and last consume
The Balme of Life. (XI, 535-543)

The tone is much more bitter and the personal reference more unmistakable in the following lines from *Samson Agonistes*, in which Samson speaks.

O that torment should not be confin'd
To the bodies wounds and sores
With maladies innumerable
In heart, head, brest, and reins;
But must secret passage find
To th' inmost mind,
There exercise all his fierce accidents,
And on her purest spirits prey,
As on entrails, joints, and limbs,
With answerable pains, but more intense,
Though void of corporal sense.
   My griefs not only pain me
As a lingring disease,
But finding no redress, ferment and rage,
Nor less then wounds immedicable
Ranckle, and fester, and gangrene,
To black mortification.
Thoughts my Tormenters arm'd with deadly stings
Mangle my apprehensive tenderest parts,
Exasperate, exulcerate, and raise
Dire inflammation which no cooling herb
Or medcinal liquor can asswage,
Nor breath of Vernal Air from snowy *Alp*.
Sleep hath forsook and giv'n me o're
To deaths benumming Opium as my only cure. (ll. 606-630)

In the following lines, it is impossible to ignore in the comment of the Chorus the revelation of Milton's own grievance in his challenge of Providence's unreasoning humiliation of good

men who, "solemnly elected" and "With gifts and graces eminently adorn'd," have once reached a height of glory.

> Not only dost degrade them, or remit
> To life obscur'd, which were a fair dismission,
> But throw'st them lower then thou didst exalt them high,
> . . . .
> Oft leav'st them to the hostile sword
> . . . .
> Or to the unjust tribunals, under change of times,
> And condemnation of the ingrateful multitude.
> If these they scape, perhaps in poverty
> With sickness and disease thou bow'st them down,
> Painful diseases and deform'd,
> In crude old age;
> Though not disordinate, yet causeless suffring
> The punishment of dissolute days, in fine,
> Just or unjust, seem alike miserable,
> For oft alike, both come to evil end. (ll. 687-704)

Samson Agonistes is not, of course, a disguised autobiography,
but no student can doubt the occasional identity of Samson's and
Milton's criticism of life. The dominant mood of each is probably the same. For example, Samson's rejoinder to Manoa's
affirmation of faith in the renewal of a happy life with sight
restored is obviously the expression of Milton's mood in his
declining years.

> All otherwise to me my thoughts portend,
> That these dark orbs no more shall treat with light,
> Nor th' other light of life continue long,
> But yield to double darkness nigh at hand:
> So much I feel my genial spirits droop,
> My hopes all flat, nature within me seems
> In all her functions weary of herself;
> My race of glory run, and race of shame,
> And I shall shortly be with them that rest. (ll. 590-598)

Samson is not moved by Manoa's counsel that these suggestions
proceed

From anguish of the mind and *humours black*
That mingle with thy fancy.[87]

His one prayer is for

speedy death,
The close of all my miseries, and the balm.

Without exaggeration one may say that this cry of despair and this prayer are the logical and final utterance of Milton's melancholy, the natural outcome of his character, habits, and untoward circumstances. Thus ends the systematic survey of this important and unaccountably neglected phase of Milton's life and work.

The history just sketched supplies part of the background of that underlying pessimism in *Paradise Lost* which Mr. Tillyard has explored and which Mr. Grierson insists is inherent in Evangelical Christianity.[88] The pessimism, which is present at the outset in Satan's impotence, in the warning at the beginning of Book Four, in the description of Paradise with its "hopeless ache of the unattainable," is strongest in the last four books. "The woes of Adam and Eve are typical of humanity; and they never should have happened: such is, one feels, what Milton thought in the bottom of his heart." The consequences of the Fall are disastrous: discord enters into the animal world; eternal spring is corrupted; the universe is deranged. And these evils are not counterbalanced by the possibility of regeneration in Christ. For Christ does not transform the world. The true elect who are saved through Christ are indeed only a small minority. The crucial passage, Mr. Tillyard thinks, is that in which almost at the end of the epic Michael describes "the state of the world after Christ and the end of all things: . . . [ll. 524-551 of Book XII are quoted] The comfort is nominal, the fundamental pessimism unmistakable. Milton seeks to comfort himself in an imagined new order, but it is not by any such distant possibility that his wound can be healed. For from his youth on Milton had nursed the hope that man-

[87] Italics mine.
[88] Tillyard, *Milton*, pp. 284 ff.; Grierson, *Milton & Wordsworth*, p. 97.

kind would improve out of its own resources. . . . His hopes, elated for a time by political events, were dashed far below their former lowest point, never to recover. Mankind would never in this world be any better; and Milton cannot be comforted."[89] This is admirably stated. The pessimism of *Paradise Lost* is more profound and more poignant than that of Evangelical Christianity; it has a bitter personal note which is the deliberate expression of Milton's character and experience. But this pessimism can be properly appreciated only as the elaborate statement of a mood of which there are many symptoms in Milton's earlier work and of which the black despair of certain passages in *Samson Agonistes* is the culmination. Dismissed in *L'Allegro* and welcomed in *Il Penseroso*, Melancholy in the end became Milton's intimate companion, if not his master, to whom we may owe a debt of gratitude; for as Burton, quoting Aristotle, says, this humour "causeth many times divine ravishment, and a kind of *enthusiasmus,* which stirreth them [learned men] up to be excellent Philosophers, Poets, and Prophets."[90]

[89] Tillyard, *Milton*, p. 287. See, on the other hand, Arthur O. Lovejoy, "Milton and the Paradox of the Fortunate Fall," *ELH*, IV, 161-179, a very valuable sketch of the background of the "happy ending."

[90] *Op. cit.,* I, 461. On the causes of melancholy in the late sixteenth and in the seventeenth centuries see L. C. Knights, "Seventeenth-Century Melancholy," *Drama and Society in the Age of Jonson* (London, 1937), pp. 315-332.

CHAPTER V

PAGAN DEITIES

Not long before the Pythian games two reverend men, Demetrius and Cleombrotus met with others at Delphi, site of the most famous and ancient of all oracles. Presently Cleombrotus, who had visited Ammon's shrine in Egypt, was asked to tell about the oracle there, where the divine influence seemed somewhat enfeebled. When Cleombrotus did not answer, Demetrius declared that there was no need to ask about the shrine in Egypt, for in Greece the oracles had almost completely failed. Some shrines were silent, others were utterly desolate. To illustrate this condition, which is the subject of much discussion, Philip the historian relates a story that he had from his teacher Epitherses. On a voyage to Italy, while they drifted near the island of Paxi, a voice from the island instructed Thamus, the Egyptian pilot, "When you come opposite to Palodes, announce that great Pan is dead." After consideration, the pilot did as commanded, whereupon was heard from the land a great cry of amazement and lamentation.[1] This story is repeated in the May gloss in Spenser's *The Shepheardes Calender*, where it is said that some understand this Pan to be "the great Satanas," whose kingdom Christ then conquered; then "all Oracles surceased, and enchaunted spirits, that were wont to delude the people, thenceforth held theyr peace." In *On the Morning of Christ's Nativity* there is a Christian echo of this tale. At Christ's birth the oracles immediately cease, and the pagan gods forsake their temples. Overshadowed by the power of the mighty Pan (the holy infant of Bethlehem), Apollo, Moloch, Peor, Hammon, Ashtaroth, Osiris, Isis, and

[1] "The Obsolescence of Oracles," Plutarch's *Moralia*. With an English Translation by F. C. Babbitt (London and Cambridge, 1936), V, 401-403.

all the other deities are rendered impotent͏ In *Paradise Lost*
many of these gods reappear as the leaders of Satan's great
host—"Godlike shapes and forms," Powers who once in
Heaven sat on thrones but whose names for their rebellion were
blotted out of the books of life. On earth, where, by God's
sufferance, they corrupted mankind to forsake their Creator
and to transform Him

> Oft to the Image of a Brute, adorn'd
> With gay Religions full of Pomp and Gold,

they were given new names:

> Then were they known to men by various Names,
> And various Idols through the Heathen World.[2]

The catalog of these heathen deities is one of the most impressive and beautiful passages in the epic.

The catalog has been carefully studied by many Milton
scholars. Addison thinks that it "has abundance of learning in
it, and a very agreeable turn of poetry, which rises in a great
measure from its describing the places where they were worshipped, by those beautiful marks of rivers, so frequent among
the ancient poets." He adds that Milton "had doubtless in this
place Homer's catalogue of ships, and Virgil's lists of warriors
in view."[3] Disagreeing with Bentley, who does not consider
this the finest part of the poem, Warburton approves the design
and drawing and praises Milton for thus presenting the origin
of superstition. He insists that Milton's catalog is superior to
those in the works he has imitated in that "the originall of
superstition" is an essential part of a religious epic. In the
course of his elaborate notes, which adequately present the
Scriptural and the classical background, Newton remarks, "We
might inlarge much more upon each of these idols, and produce
a heap of learned authorities and quotations; but we endeavour
to be as short as we can. . . ."[4] This is a judicious statement,
not to be lightly ignored; as is also the concluding sentence in
his elucidation of the idea that spirits can assume either sex at

[2] I, 357 ff.
[3] *Paradise Lost*, ed. Newton, I, 38.   [4] *Ibid.*, I, 41.

will, with reference to Michael Psellus's dialog on demons: "Such an extraordinary scholar was Milton, and such use he made of all sorts of authors."[5] In his full notes Verity explains that Milton's list of devils is a counterpart of Homer's catalog of ships and Virgil's list of warriors, frequently mentions appropriate Scriptural passages, and in particular refers to Sandys' *Relation of a Journey* and Selden's *De Deis Syris*, with both of which Milton was probably acquainted. Mr. Hanford admirably sums up the matter:

Having assembled the infernal host, Milton proceeds to an enumeration, following the precedent of Homer's catalogue of ships and heroes in the second book of the *Iliad*. The names are drawn partly from Scripture, and partly from Egyptian and Greek mythology, on the theory, already adopted in the poem on the nativity, that the divinities worshiped by the idolaters of Palestine and by the Pagans generally were in reality the fallen angels who had subsequently seduced mankind from allegiance to the true God.[6]

Declaring that the standard interpretation, according to which Milton "obtained the plan of his epic catalogue from Homer and the details by a presumably judicious selection from Scripture and mythology," fails to explain the absence of heroes in Milton's list, his "primary objective" of surveying cults and religions, and his resort to a highly dissimilar catalog whose gods he attacked, a scholar has recently argued that Milton used as a guide and followed closely Alexander Ross's *Pansebeia: or, A View of all Religions of the World*,[7] published in 1653 and frequently reprinted, "one of the most widely read books of his age." Like Milton's epic catalog, Ross's *Pansebeia* names the heathen deities, identifies their characteristics, gives the places of their worship, and describes and condemns the practices of their followers. In the treatment of these deities by Milton and Ross, Mr. McColley finds a similarity of characters, ideas, and words, a similar division into geographical groups, and a similar emphasis upon the human character of the Greek

[5] *Ibid.*, I, 44.   [6] *A Milton Handbook*, p. 176.
[7] Grant McColley, "The Epic Catalogue of *Paradise Lost*," *ELH*, IV, 180-191.

gods. He also emphasizes the theory that here as in other places Milton is supposed to have followed his practice of moving backward through his source. Admitting the fact that Milton was well acquainted with the heathen gods, of whom he wrote "briefly" in the poem on the nativity, this interesting study concludes that in writing the epic catalog Milton "had before him and employed *A View of all Religions of the World*."

Examination of three works in Greek, ranging in date from about 700 B.C. to about 30 B.C., one in Latin, composed between 413 and 426 A.D., and three in English, belonging to the seventeenth century, with all but one of which Milton was demonstrably acquainted, shows that from these Milton could have got for his epic catalog not only all the material that has been attributed to Ross's *Pansebeia*, but much more besides. It is a noteworthy fact that all these were available before Ross's work, which appeared in 1653, after Milton was totally blind, and, with one exception, before the Nativity *Hymn*, which as a preliminary catalog of the gods surveyed in *Paradise Lost* is an important document in this discussion and one to which the recent study scarcely gives due weight.

In a preceding chapter, in which Milton's use of Diodorus's *History* was confirmed, Diodorus's full description of the gods of Egypt was briefly noticed—Osiris, the sun, the many-eyed one who surveys lands and seas, the founder of cities and civilization; Isis, the moon, with crescent-shaped horns, the sister and wife of Osiris, and with him ruler and nourisher of the universe. When Osiris had been murdered by his brother Typhon, Isis with her son Horus slew the murderer, became queen, recovered the pieces of her husband's body, and established his worship. Both Osiris and Isis received immortal honors. Consecrated to Osiris were the sacred bulls, Apis of Memphis and Mnevis of Heliopolis, the ceremony of whose worship is vividly described. Diodorus also tells of other gods: Cronus and Rhea, Zeus or Ammon, Anubis, who wore a dog's skin, Dionysus or Bacchus, and many more. Unquestionably Milton was familiar with Diodorus's survey of Egyptian cults.

Another work dealing with Egyptian rites is the "Isis and Osiris" in Plutarch's *Moralia,* parts of which, the "De liberis educandis" and the "De placitis philosophorum," were used in Milton's private school.[8] From "Isis and Osiris" the material that is to the purpose may be briefly surveyed. Osiris and Isis were the children of Cronus and Rhea. At the birth of Osiris a voice declared, "The Lord of All advances to the light," and he was then proclaimed a mighty and a beneficent king. Other gods were born: Arueris or Horus, Typhon, and, on the fourth day, Isis. Another account is that Isis and Osiris were enamoured of each other and "consorted together in the darkness of the womb before their birth." One of the first acts of Osiris was to deliver the Egyptians from barbarism. When he had returned from his civilizing journey, Typhon hatched a treacherous plot against his life. Secretly measuring the body of Osiris, Typhon had made a beautiful and ornamented chest of the same size. At a festivity, where the chest was greatly admired, he offered it to the man whom it would exactly fit. After all others had failed and Osiris had lain down in the chest, the lid was instantly closed and the chest was thrown into the Nile. Learning of this execrable deed, Isis put on mourning and wandered everywhere, asking for the chest. With the help of dogs she found Anubis, Osiris's child, who became her guardian and attendant. When finally at Byblus she found the sacred chest, she wept over it, wrapped it in linen and perfumed it, and then bestowed it in a secret place near her son Horus. But Typhon, hunting by moonlight, found the chest and dismembered the body, the parts of which he scattered widely. In various places Isis recovered all the parts except one, and in those places tombs were erected; or, according to another version, she had effigies made and distributed in several cities, where Osiris received divine honors. Prepared by his father Osiris, who returned from the other world for that purpose, Horus prevailed over Typhon in a great battle. When Isis, to whom Typhon was delivered in chains, released

[8] Edward Phillips, "The Life of Mr. John Milton," *The Early Lives of Milton,* p. 60.

him, Horus wrested from her the royal diadem, but Hermes substituted for it a helmet like a cow's head. In Memphis, "the haven of the good," Plutarch adds, is kept the Apis, which is "the image of the soul of Osiris, whose body also lies there." Of Osiris and other gods, the priests say that their bodies are in the keeping of the priests but that their souls "shine as the stars in the firmament."

Interpreting the myths, Plutarch explains that Osiris is the Nile, Isis the Earth, and Typhon the Sea, which swallows up the Nile. Again, Osiris is water, Typhon the consuming heat. From the lawful union of Osiris and Isis is born Horus, the "seasonable tempering of the surrounding air." Horus is also the terrestrial universe. Another son is Anubis, the horizon, represented as a dog, a deity of the lower world, and a god of Olympus. The diabolical scheming of Typhon is the power of drought, which blazes with parching heat. The story of Osiris having been shut up in his chest means nothing more than the disappearance of water. To break the drought, the priests in impressive rites shroud a cow in black vestments (she is the the image of Isis) and mourn the departure of the goddess. Then they go down to the sea at night and dig up the sacred chest, which is greeted with a great shout because Osiris is found. From the fertile soil and water, mixed with costly spices and incense, is fashioned a crescent-shaped figure, which is clothed and adorned. Typhon is the symbol of everything harmful and destructive. In nature, Plutarch explains, good and evil are mingled: there are two antagonistic principles and forces. Our life and the universe are complex. Nature herself is the source of evil as well as good. There are, as wise men believe, two gods or one god and one demon—"the one the Artificer of good and the other of evil." Osiris is Intelligence, Reason, and the Ruler of all that is good; Typhon is the irrational, the destructive, the diseased.

Plutarch holds the opinion that by worshiping animals the Egyptians made contemptible their sacred offices and encouraged either sheer superstition or atheism. It is a monstrous fable that the gods from fear of Typhon assumed the forms

of animals. It is incredible that the souls of the dead are re-
born in these animals. To account for the worship of animals,
Plutarch reports that, as some say, standards in the forms of
animals were used by Osiris on his great expeditions; that to
terrify their enemies in battle kings wore masks of wild beasts;
that kings encouraged this superstition to keep the people in
subjection. In severe droughts, the priests secretly led away
the sacred animals, which they first threatened and terrified,
and then, if the drought continued, sacrificed to punish the deity.
The Egyptians honored some animals because they were useful
and others because they saw in them "dim likenesses of the
power of the gods." Plutarch insists that we should not worship these images but through them the Divine, who orders all
things. Osiris, in truth, dwells not in the earth but far from
it, "uncontaminated and unpolluted and pure from all matter
that is subject to destruction and death." He is the King of
those free souls who reach the realm of the invisible where
they contemplate "that beauty which is for men unutterable
and indescribable."

Thus Plutarch condemns the Egyptian gods or the vulgar
Egyptian theology. These gods, Plutarch holds, are not the
highest gods; the stories of Osiris, Isis, and Typhon are records
neither of gods nor of men but of demigods. Such, among the
Greeks, are the Giants and the Titans, and also Cronus, Dionysus, and Demeter, who are prompted by jealousy, hostility, revenge, grief, and other passions. Upon hearing certain infamous stories of these gods, Plutarch quotes Aeschylus, "Much
need there is to spit and cleanse the mouth." Like Milton, Plutarch jealously guards the honor of the true gods. He would
preserve the reverence and faith implanted in mankind at birth;
he would not see divine things degraded to the human level.
But Milton's condemnation of Egyptian gods, unlike Plutarch's,
is apparently unaccompanied by any realization of the social
history and the spiritual yearning that found expression in
Egyptian worship. Unlike Plutarch, whose work he most
certainly knew, Milton did not perceive the element of truth
and beauty in heathen theology. He did not understand—in-

deed, in his time few could have understood—that Osiris, child
of sky and earth, was the patron of fertility and civilization,
and not only judge and ruler of the dead but also the pledge
of immortality. He did not understand that Isis was the beneficent goddess and mother "whose influence and love pervaded
all heaven and earth and the abode of the dead," that in her
form "spiritualized by ages of religious evolution" was presented the true wife, the "beneficent queen of nature, encircled
with the nimbus of moral purity, of immemorial and mysterious
sanctity," that her serene figure appeared "like a star in a
stormy sky" and aroused in many people "a rapture of devotion not unlike that which was paid in the middle ages to the
Virgin Mary."[9] Especially in the *Hymn*, where pagan and
Christian elements are strangely blended, Milton with the eye
of the humanist depicts the pagan ceremonies that his Christian
conscience condemned: Apollo quitting the slope of Delphos,
the nymphs mourning in the twilight shade of tangled thickets,
the Tyrian maids lamenting the death of Thammuz, the sable-
garbed sorcerers bearing the ark of Osiris. In *Paradise Lost*
there is more denunciation of idolatry and less yearning for lost
beauty.

Both Diodorus and Plutarch trace the relationship between
the Egyptian and the Greek gods, who, it may be noted, are
separated in Milton's catalog only by Belial. Diodorus ex-
plains that Cronus and Rhea or Zeus and Hera were the parents
of Osiris and Isis, as also of Typhon, Apollo, and Aphrodite.
Osiris translated is Dionysus, and Isis "is more similar to
Demeter than any other goddess." As king and father of the
Egyptians Osiris is by some called Ammon. On his travels
Osiris took with him his brother, whom the Greeks call Apollo.
Conversant with Egyptian gods, Orpheus helped to transfer
their worship to Greece. In fact, Diodorus says that "the
Greeks appropriate to themselves the most renowned of both
Egyptian heroes and gods. . . ."[10] Plutarch insists that the
Greeks identified Osiris with Dionysus. The ceremonies of

[9] J. G. Frazier, *The Golden Bough* (London, 1914), Part IV, Vol. II,
pp. 115 ff.   [10] *Diodorus of Sicily*, I, 75.

their worship are in many respects similar: the priests "fasten skins of fawns about themselves, and carry Bacchic wands and indulge in shoutings and movements exactly as do those who are under the spell of the Dionysiac ecstasies."[11] Osiris is also Pluto. Isis is Athena and also Proserpine. Again, Osiris is Oceanus and Isis Tethys. Armoun or Ammon is the Egyptian name of Zeus. Horus, the power that directs the sun, is the Greek Apollo. The soul of Horus is Orion. In some respects Anubis corresponds to Hecate, both being deities of the lower world. The Greek ceremonies are similar to the Egyptian rites in the shrines of Isis. The Greeks also believe that certain animals are sacred to the deities. The exploits of the Greek gods are compared with those of the Egyptian. When Milton wrote of the Greek gods, however, it is probable that he thought not mainly of Diodorus and Plutarch, but of such Greek writers as Homer, Aeschylus, Sophocles, Euripides, and particularly of the *Theogony* of Hesiod. Edward Phillips reminds us that in Milton's school Hesiod was esteemed "A Poet equal with Homer."[12]

Finishing his roll of deities, Milton writes:

> The rest were long to tell, though far renown'd,
> Th' *Ionian* Gods, of *Javans* Issue held
> Gods, yet confest later then Heav'n and Earth
> Thir boasted Parents.[13]

In the *Theogony*, the Olympian Muses, who "dance on soft feet about the deep-blue spring" and the altar of Zeus, chant of the blessed gods who inhabit Olympus. Uttering their immortal voice, they "celebrate in song first of all the reverend race of the gods from the beginning, those whom Earth and wide Heaven begot, and the gods sprung of these, givers of good things."[14] The gods were born of Earth and starry Heaven and briny Sea. First there was Chaos and then the wide-bosomed Earth, the sure foundation of all things, and Eros,

---

[11] "Isis and Osiris," *Moralia*, p. 85.
[12] *Op. cit.*, p. 60.   [13] I, 507-510.
[14] *Hesiod. The Homeric Hymns and Homerica.* With an English Translation by H. G. Evelyn-White (New York, 1914), p. 81.

"fairest among the deathless gods." From Chaos came forth
Erebus and black Night. One recalls Milton's lines:

> where eldest Night
> And *Chaos*, Ancestors of Nature, hold
> Eternal *Anarchie*, amidst the noise
> Of endless warrs, and by confusion stand.[15]

From Night and Erebus were born Aether and Day. The
Earth bore the starry Heaven, to cover herself on every side
and "to be an ever-sure abiding-place for the blessed gods."
Lying with Heaven, the Earth afterwards bore the Titans,
Oceanus, Hyperion, Rhea, lovely Tethys, and others, and then
Cronus, the youngest and most terrible of her children. But
later, great and presumptuous children, also called Titans, were
born to Earth and Heaven—Cottus and Briareos and Gyes,
each with an hundred arms and fifty heads. Of all the children
born of Heaven and Earth these were the most terrible, and
from the first they were hated by their father, who hid them
away in the earth, which groaned and conspired against the
cruel father. With a jagged sickle provided by Earth, Cronus
dismembered the Titan, from whose blood on the Earth sprang
the Erinyes and the great Giants and from whose immortal
flesh in the Sea sprang the awful and lovely goddess whom
men call Aphrodite and Cytherea. By his own daughter Rhea,
Cronus [Saturn] was the father of splendid children: Hestia,
Demeter, Hera, Hades, and the earth-shaker, wise Zeus, father
of gods and men. To preserve his throne—he had heard that
he would lose it to his own son—he swallowed each child as it
was born. Counseled by Heaven and Earth, Rhea fled to the
rich land of Crete, where Zeus was born and nurtured in safety.
In place of Zeus Cronus swallowed a stone wrapped in swad-
dling clothes. So Zeus was saved.

Aided by the other children, who had been brought to
light from Erebus beneath the Earth, Zeus later assailed the
Titans in a grim battle, which reminds one of Milton's war in
Heaven.

[15] II, 894-897.

These, then, stood against the Titans in grim strife, holding huge rocks in their strong hands. And on the other part the Titans eagerly strengthened their ranks, and both sides at one time showed the work of their hands and their might. The boundless sea rang terribly around, and the earth crashed loudly: wide Heaven was shaken and groaned, and high Olympus reeled from its foundation under the charge of the undying gods, and a heavy quaking reached dim Tartarus and the deep sound of their feet in the fearful onset and of their hard missiles. So, then, they launched their grievous shafts upon one another, and the cry of both armies as they shouted reached to starry heaven; and they met together with a great battle-cry.

Then Zeus no longer held back his might; but straight his heart was filled with fury and he showed forth all his strength. From Heaven and from Olympus he came forthwith, hurling his lightning: the bolts flew thick and fast from his strong hand together with thunder and lightning, whirling an awesome flame. The life-giving earth crashed around in burning, and the vast wood crackled loud with fire all about. All the land seethed, and Ocean's streams and the unfruitful sea. The hot vapour lapped round the earthborn Titans: flame unspeakable rose to the bright upper air: the flashing glare of the thunder stone and lightning blinded their eyes for all that they were strong. Astounding heat seized Chaos: and to see with eyes and to hear the sound with ears it seemed even as if Earth and wide Heaven above came together; for such a mighty crash would have arisen if Earth were being hurled to ruin, and Heaven from on high were hurling her down; so great a crash was there while the gods were meeting together in strife. . . . An horrible uproar of terrible strife arose: mighty deeds were shown and the battle inclined.[16]

Like the rebel angels in *Paradise Lost*, the Titans were overwhelmed and hurled into Tartarus, beyond gloomy Chaos, as far beneath the Earth as Heaven is above it. There in murky night, behind shining gates and bronze thresholds, they were bound to eternity with bitter chains.

In the *Theogony* is described Typhoeus, the youngest child of Earth and Tartarus, to whom Milton refers in the earth-born Typhon "that warr'd on Jove." His hands were strong, his

[16] *Hesiod*, pp. 129-131.

MILTON'S LITERARY MILIEU

feet untiring. "From his shoulders grew an hundred heads of a snake, a fearful dragon, with dark, flickering tongues, and from under the brows of his eyes in his marvelous heads flashed fire, and fire burned from his heads as he glared." And the sound of his voice was unspeakably dreadful. But he was no match for Zeus, who hurled him into Tartarus a maimed wreck.

We are not obliged to conjecture from general or fancied resemblances that these works by Diodorus, Plutarch, and Hesiod are part of the rich literary background of Milton's roll of pagan gods, Egyptian and Greek. From other evidence we know that Milton was acquainted with Diodorus's *History;* from Edward Phillips's *Life* we know that Plutarch and Hesiod were used in Milton's school. There is more than a probability that as a humanist Milton was acquainted with these works; there is clear proof that he knew and used them. Further, Milton's *Commonplace Book* justifies consideration of another important work, a classic of the church, St. Augustine's *De Civitate Dei.* This work may most appropriately be discussed at this point, for it "stands on the confines of two worlds, the classical and the Christian, and it points the way into the Christian."[17] I need hardly remind the reader that St. Augustine was esteemed a devoted servant of Christ, a "great Saint of God," and "one of the worthiest Champions that ever the Church had since the Apostles." He was the author of many works, of which the *De Civitate Dei* was preëminent for its varied learning and its excellent divinity. In the words of Ioannes Lodovicus Vives, St. Augustine was incomparable:

Augustine, (good God) how holy, how learned a man, what a light, what a pillar to the Christian Commonwealth, on whom onely it rested for many rites, many statutes, customes, holy and venerable ceremonies! and not without cause. For in that man was most plentifull study, most exact knowledge of holy writ, a sharpe and cleare iudgement, a wit admirably quicke and piercing. He was a most diligent defender of undefiled piety, of most sweet behaviour,

---

[17] *The City of God by Saint Augustine.* Translated by John Healey, with an Introduction by Ernest Barker (London and Toronto, 1931), p. ix.

composed and conformed to the charity of the Gospell, renowned
and honored for his integrity and holinesse of life. . . .[18]

And the work, says Vives, is no frivolous fiction or practical
handbook, but it is concerned with

both Cities, of the World, and God, wherein Angels, diuels, and
all men are contained, how they were borne, how bred, how
growne, whither they tend, and what they shall doe when they
come to their worke: which to unfold, hee hath omitted no prophane nor sacred learning, which hee doth not both touch and
explane; as the exploites of the Romanes, their gods, and ceremonies,
the Philosophers opinions, the originall of heauen and earth, of Angels, diuels, and men. . . .

After a rapid survey of the contents of the book, which ends,
"Moreouer of the torments of the damned. Lastly of the
ioyes and eternall felicity of Godly men," Vives closes with a
recommendation of his Commentaries.

Of special importance for the present purpose are these
Commentaries, particularly those in which Vives learnedly elu-
cidates the textual allusions to the pagan gods. Dr. Joseph
Mausbach has explained why *De Civitate Dei* is especially rich
in references to these gods:

Die Heiden legten dem Christentum die Schuld an den zalreichen
traurigen Schicksalen bei; die Götter, die Rom gross gemacht,
hätten sich erzürnt abgewandt, weil ihr Kultus, ihre kraftvolle,
weltfreudige Religion durch die christliche Lehre verdrängt worden
sei. So hatte Augustin Gelegenheit, einen Blick auf das Ganze der
antiken Weltherrlichkeit zu werfen und ihren Wert an dem Ideal
des Gottesreichs zu messen.[19]

St. Augustine and Vives perfectly agree as to the transcendental
value of Christianity and as to the wickedness of pagan worship; the only important difference is that Vives was more conversant with the literature of mythology than was the great

[18] *Saint Augustine, Of The Citie Of God.* With The Learned Comments of Io. Lodovicus Vives. Englished first by J. H. And now in this
second Edition compared with the Latine Originall, and in very many
places corrected and amended (London, 1620). Epistle to King Henry
the Eight.
[19] *Die Ethik des Heiligen Augustinus* (Freiburg, 1929), I, 302.

Bishop of Hippo. The fundamental position of both is that
the pagan gods were in fact wicked spirits, who "respected not
how their worshippers lived: nay, their care was to see them
live like diuels." St. Augustine declares that stage plays, licentious spectacles, were first introduced at Rome not by the
wickedness of men but by direct command of the gods. Vives's
note quotes Tertullian to the effect that Socrates, Themistocles,
Tully, and others were better than the gods, and adds, "Many
of the auncient writers neuer denied, that their good men were
better then their gods. . . ."[20] These gods steal; they commit
adultery. "*Ioue* was turned to a Bull, or a Swanne to haue
the company of some wench or other. . . ." Honoring these
deities, people gaze on their guilt and remember their pranks
"as a license for their owne practise!"[21] They are not gods
but devils, "teaching guiltinesse, and ioying in filthinesse. . . ."
Your gods, exclaims St. Augustine, were mortal men. "For
as the earth is the mother, so are they earths children."[22] St.
Augustine condemns the Great Mother of the gods, a monster,
who "exceeded all her sonne-gods, not in greatnesse of deity,
but of obscaenity." She had shamed heaven and polluted
earth "with multitudes of profest and publike *Sodomites*."[23]
"What," exclaims St. Augustine, "is *Mercuries* theft, *Venus*
her lust, the whoredome and the turpitude of the rest . . .
what are they all to this foule euill that the *mother* of the
gods has as her peculiar?" How can anyone who "lies in
bondage to such uncleane filthinesse, and so many damned
diuels" hope for blessedness in the life hereafter? In fact, the
gods of the Gentiles "are most uncleane spirits, desiring . . .
to bee accounted gods, and in their proud impuritie taking
pleasures in those obscaenities as in diuine honours. . . ." These
gods, famous for villany not for virtue, are really wicked fiends
who fell from heaven. From their power we can be saved only
by the mediation of Christ. As Vives says, "So the diuells
haue many waies to draw a man from God, but the Angells
but one to draw him unto him by Christ the mediator."[24] In

[20] *The Citie of God*, p. 43.   [21] *Ibid.*, p. 178.
[22] *Ibid.*, p. 236.   [23] *Ibid.*, p. 272.   [24] *Ibid.*, p. 335.

this contrast between false and true religion, in the condemnation of wicked spirits masquerading as genuine gods, in Vives's
elaborate and learned notes, which provide a serviceable handbook of pagan mythology with abundant references to authorities and with orthodox Christian interpretations, Milton had at
hand most valuable material, embodied in a church classic, between which and *Paradise Lost* there are many fundamental
analogies. The subject of this chapter requires at least a brief
survey of the pagan material in *The City of God*.

In *The City of God* there are frequent references to Egyptian superstition. Citing Cicero's *De Natura Deorum* and Diodorus's *Bibliotheca*, Vives explains that the Egyptians had certain beasts which because of their usefulness they consecrated
as gods—the dog, the cat, the ibis, the ox, the crocodile, the
hawk, etc.[25] St. Augustine declares that the losing of Osiris in
the Egyptian sacrifices and the finding him again, first the
sorrow and then the great joy, "all this is a puppettry and a
fiction. . . ." Vives adds that Osiris was cut into pieces by his
brother Typhon, that Isis and Orus Apollo avenged his death
upon Typhon, that then they went to seek the body of Osiris
"with great lamentation, and to *Isis* her great ioy, found it,
though it were disperst in diuers places: and hereupon a yearly
feast was instituted on the seeking of *Osiris* with tears, and
finding him with ioy."[26] Again, Vives declares that the Egyptians had innumerable things as gods: Apis was adored in the
shape of an ox, Anubis as a dog, Isis as a cow, and so forth.
Their princes being dead, "they ordained them diuine worships
in those shapes."[27] Isis and Osiris are the moon and the sun,
and their secret ceremonies are "most beastly and obscene."[28]
These belong to the infernal deities: the greatest devil, called
Serapis, is, according to Porphyry, Osiris in Egypt and Pluto in
Greece; Isis is Hecate and Proserpina. *Typhus*, Vives explains,
is *Pride*, and the Greeks use Typhon "for the fiery diuell: So
saith *Plutarch* of *Typhon*, *Osiris* his brother, that he was a
diuell that troubled all the world with acts of malice, and

---

[25] *Ibid.*, p. 87.
[27] *Ibid.*, p. 318.
[26] *Ibid.*, pp. 241-242.
[28] *Ibid.*, p. 357.

torment."[29] Augustine writes that Apis, king of Argos, sailed into Egypt and, dying there, "was called *Serapis* the greatest god of Aegypt," from the Greek word for coffin. He adds, "And the *Oxe* which Aegypt (being wonderously and vainely seduced,) nourished in all pleasures and fatnesse unto the honour of *Serapis*; because they did not worship him in a coffin, was not called *Serapis* but *Apis*: which *Oxe* being dead, and they seeking him, and finding another, flecked of colour iust as he was: heere they thought they had gotten a great god by the foote."[30] Vives adds that no man, Greek or Latin, "euer wrote of the Aegyptian affaires, but he had up this *Oxe*,"[31] which he describes:

He was all black, but for a square spot of white in his fore-head, (saith *Herodotus*) on his right side (saith *Pliny*:) his hornes bowed like a Crescent: for he was sacred unto the Moone. *Marcellinus*: He had the shape of an Eagle upon his back, and a lump upon his tongue, like a black-Beetle, and his taile was all growne with forked haires. When he was dead, they sought another with great sorrow, neuer ceasing vntill they had found a new *Apis* like him in all respects. Him did Aegypt adore as the chiefe god, . . . At *Memphis* (saith *Strabo*) was a temple dedicated unto *Apis*, . . . His place where he lay, was called the mysticall bed, and when he went abroad, a multitude of vshers were euer about him: all adored this *Oxe-god*, the boyes followed him in a shole, and he himselfe now and then bellowed forth his prophecies. No man that was a stranger might come into this temple at Memphis, but onely at burials.

These are representative statements regarding Egyptian idolatry.

Vives's commentary is particularly rich in material dealing with Greek and Roman mythology, in the literature of which he seems to have been thoroughly versed. Interpreting St. Augustine's criticism of ancient polytheism, according to which sundry gods ruled in diverse parts of the world, Vives explains that Saturn's three sons shared the government of the world: Jove had heaven, Neptune the sea, Pluto the earth. Juno mar-

---

[29] *Ibid.*, p. 415.   [30] *Ibid.*, p. 623.
[31] *Ibid.*, p. 624. Vives mentions Herodotus, Diodorus, Strabo, Plutarch, Eusebius, Suidas, Varro, Mela, Pliny, Solinus, and Marcellinus.

ried Jove and was made "lady of the ayre." This division is
explained: Jove got the east, "resembling heauen, wherein also
mount *Olympus* stood . . ."; Neptune had the navy; Dis or
Pluto got the west part of the realm "fained to be hell." Saturn was banished into hell "because he fled from the East,
into *Italy*, lying in the West." Neptune was merely a cunning
seaman and was made admiral by Jove, "for which posterity
deified him." Saturn, "a most ungracious fellow," was the son
of Coelus and Terra; he was expelled by his son Jove "as he
had expelled his father, and so made the prouerb true, *Doe as
you would be done unto*."[32] He was called the god of time
and "was faigned by the *Poets* to deuoure his children, because
time deuours all things." Juno is the goddess of the earth, or
Ops, the mother of Jove. Again, Ceres is the earth, "called
Ceres à gerendo, of *bearing corne*, or of *Cereo* to create." The
earth is the mother of all. Her daughter, Proserpina, "had
her name *à proserpendo*, because she crept some while this way
and some while that, being all one with the *Moone* and the
earth." Vives adds that "you may reade of her rape almost
euery where." Ceres was the daughter of Saturn and Ops and
was sister to Vesta and Juno. Vesta is the Greek goddess
Hestia; "her power is ouer fires and altars." Vives explains that
"being a fire, and called a virgin, therefore did virgins attend
it, and all virginity was sacred unto it." Her worship arose in
Egypt and spread far. She is also called Vesta Venus, "not
as barren, but as fruitfull and augmentative, making the Cities
and nations happy in eternall and continuall increase." As
Plato says, there are two Venuses, the one heavenly, the other
earthly; the first daughter of Coelus, the latter daughter of
Jove and Dione. As St. Augustine says, "the one a virgin,
the other a wanton." Doubtless, the "bright-hair'd *Vesta*" who
is the mother of Milton's Melancholy is related to this Vesta
Venus. Vives's commentaries are a mine of information regarding these and other deities—on Minerva, for example,
daughter of Jove and Themis, goddess of wisdom, of whom
Martian writes:

[32] *Ibid.*, p. 158.

Pallas, thou armed Virgin, wisdomes wonder,
Fate iudging faire, fount of Aetheriall light:
Worlds understanding, and arbitresse of thunder,
Arts ardor, spring wherein man cleares his sight,
Discretions arch, which reason reigneth under,
Essence in gods, and men, surmounting bright:
Towering beyond the Spheares, and all in fire,
Thron'd aboue *Ioue, far brighter and far higher.*[33]

This reminds us of the wise Minerva, unconquered Virgin of
Comus. And Diana, the Moon, who had many names—Lu-
cina, Proserpina, Hecate, Diana. "She was fained to be a virgin,
giuen all to hunt much in the woods, and shooting."[34] Of her
Prudentius in the third book against Symmachus writes:

Three times she turnes her shape,
She is the *Moone,* when bright her sphear doth shew:
Latonas daughter when she hunts below.
But thrond in hell, she's *Plutoes* wife, and awes
The furies, giuing sterne *Megaera* lawes.

By this we are reminded of the "Fair silver-shafted Queen for
ever chaste" and of the moon's triform countenance, to use
Uriel's phrase. And there are many more major and minor
gods.

The following brief summaries and transcripts of Vives's
interesting notes on the worship of certain pagan deities will indicate that the tone would have pleased Milton's protestant
sympathies. Observe first the rites of Bacchus. St. Augustine
writes that wine and women, the provokers of lust, are subject
to Liber, who is madly celebrated in Bacchanalian feasts. Vives
explains that satyrs and mad women called Howling Bacchae
followed Bacchus. He quotes Plutarch's description, "First, was
carried a flagon of wine, and a sprig of a vine: then one led
a goate: after a boxe, a pine Apple: and a vine prop: all which
afterward grew out of use, and gaue place to better." The
vine-crop and the pineapple are like the ivy javelins carried by
the Bacchae when Bacchus invaded India. The ivy is used

[33] *Ibid.,* p. 158.   [34] *Ibid.,* p. 162.

because one kind, according to Plutarch, makes men drunk without wine and provokes lust. The Thyrse is a nuptial crown and a lamp born in honor of Dionysius. The Bacchae are "raging bedlem women" who sacrifice to Liber pater; hence they are called Maenades. They were mad, for quiet minds "would not haue committed such fooleries, filthinesse and butcheries. . . ."[35] Later, Vives states that Liber's sacrifices were held on mount Cythaeron every third year; that in these, *Phalli*, that is "huge priuy members," were used; that Priapus and Bacchus have feasts together because they were companions, because without Bacchus Priapus can do nothing; that Bacchus is lord of seed and Priapus the chief instrument and therefore lord of gardens and "hath his feasts kept by the husbandmen with great joy."[36] Ovid's description of Priapus's *fascinum* is quoted. Memories of such bestial celebrations as these, which are described in Ovid's *Metamorphoses*, underlie *Comus* and Milton's reference to

> the barbarous dissonance
> Of *Bacchus* and his Revellers,

from whom he prays to be saved.

Next note "that famous witch Circe," daughter of the Sun and aunt to Medea. She became an excellent herbarist "and could make Philters *(Loue-drinkes:)*." After killing her husband, Scytha, king of Sarmatia, she "was chased into a little desert Ile in the Ocean, or as some say, unto the promontory that beares her name." For information regarding this witch, who "turned Vlysses his consorts into beasts," Vives refers the reader to Homer, Theocritus, Virgil, and many other poets and historians.[37] Regarding Venus, Vives writes in part as follows:

The *Phoenicians* honored *Venus* much for *Adonis* his sake who was their countryman, they kept her feasts with teares, and presented her mourning for him. . . . She had a Statue on *Mount* Libanus, which leaned the head upon the hand, and was of a very sad aspect: so that one would haue thought that true teares had fallen from her eies. That the diuells brought man-kind to this, will be more ap-

---

[35] *Ibid.*, p. 239.   [36] *Ibid.*, p. 268.   [37] *Ibid.*, p. 652.

parent (saith *Eusebius*) if you consider but the adulteries of the *Phoenicians:* at this day in *Heliopolis* and elsewhere they offer those filthy actes as first fruits unto their gods.[38]

This passage is of interest in relation to the worship of Thammuz, to be noticed later. The sacrifice of children to Saturn, who is sometimes identified with Moloch, god of the Ammonites, is of particular interest. Vives quotes Diodorus's account: "They had (saith he) a brazen statue of Saturne, of monstrous bignesse, whose hands hung downe to the earth, so knit one with another, that the children that were put in them, fell into a hole full of fire."[39] In the island Carolina, adds Vives, there have been discovered many statues of devils, "hollow within, brazen all," in which the natives sacrificed their children by burning. Finally, observe Vives's comments on the cult of Ceres, identified with Demeter and Cybele and known also as the Great Mother, St. Augustine's denunciation of whose worship has already been mentioned. Pluto ravished Proserpina, the daughter of Ceres, who "sought her almost all the world ouer." At last she found refuge with King Coelus, at Eleusis, where a solemn yearly sacrifice was celebrated in honor of her and her daughter. Only votaries could witness these sacrifices; and so Virgil wrote, *"Procul, o procul este prophani*, Fly, flye farre hence prophane. . . ." For publishing the mysteries the philosopher Numerius was reprimanded by Ceres. "Which," says Vives, "certainly proued their ceremonies whorish; for had they bin honest, they wold not haue feared divulgation."[40] In Plato Socrates alludes to these ceremonies, commanding that they be kept secret, "and threatning that he would discouer the secrets of *Isis*, which is all one with *Ceres*." The rites are briefly depicted:

Those memorable secrets they beare up unto an hill, and they celebrated the shepheards goad: yes I thinke the shepheards goad, a kinde of rod that the *Bacchanalians* did beare. Further of these secrets I cannot relate: of the basket, the rape, the *Idonerian* gulfe, *Euboleus* his swine, all whom together with the two goddesses, that

[38] *Ibid.*, p. 159.   [39] *Ibid.*, pp. 264-265.   [40] *Ibid.*, p. 266.

one gulfe swallowed up, and thereupon they haue a hogsty in their ceremonies: which the women in the Cities thereabouts obserue in diuers fashions. . . . The women priests carried baskets also couered, one full of flowers, portending the Spring, another with eares of corne, for Autumne. (p. 266)

Such were the rites of the Great Mother, whose ceremonies, St. Augustine says, exceeded those of all other gods in obscenities, and to whom Milton refers in various poems by different names: "mooned *Ashtaroth*," the "Goddesse of Nocturnal sport," and Astoreth,

> whom the *Phoenicians* call'd
> *Astarte*, Queen of Heav'n, with crescent Horns;
> To whose bright Image nightly by the Moon
> *Sidonian* Virgins paid their Vows and Songs.

Familiar as he was with classical literature, Milton did not draw his ideas of ancient polytheism from any single source. In humane learning he may have been a match for Vives himself. The reason for believing that *The City of God* with Vives's learned notes was an important source for Milton is this: that in this famous work (by which, as Vives says, the "great men of this later age have beene much holpen" and which "against Babilon defended that ancient, Christian and better Rome") Milton found an elaborate and standard exposition of true religion linked with a sustained attack upon the pagan gods, a classic "confutation of the peruse contemners of Christ in respect of their idols." As St. Augustine says, there are two sorts of angels, good and evil. The holy angels are ministers of God's justice and mercy; the evil angels are enemies of God and man—"the one inflamed with God's love, the other blowne big with self-loue, . . . the one piously quiet, the other madly turbulent." The devils are wicked angels who kept not their first estate. They are eternally miserable because they are extremely vicious and malicious. If allowed, Vives says, "they would burne, drown, waste, poyson, torture and vtterly destroy man and beast."[41]   Against them

[41] *Ibid.*, p. 416.

man by himself is helpless; they can do more harm than man can repair. The pagan gods were devils: "ancient Paganisme tooke [these spirits] for their gods." From all these false gods and the power of devils man can be saved only by God, the immutable good, and by Christ, whose name "confounds them vtterly" and by whom "wee are purged of sinne, and reconciled unto God."

Observe also some miscellaneous illustrations of the material to be found in *The City of God*. St. Augustine condemns Plotinus's opinion that men's souls have daemons which at death become lares if good and lemures or goblins if evil. In a long note Vives explains that souls separated from the bodies become genii or daemons. According to Proclus, the habitual daemon is a soul practised in divine actions and is a "meane betweene the gods and us." Hesiod's lines are quoted:

> A Daemon or a minde.
> But when set fate call'd hence this glorious kinde,
> Then hight they earthly *Daemones* and pure,
> Mans happy guides from ill, and guards most sure.[42]

We recall that in *Comus* the Attendant Spirit was first called a Daemon. By the ancient Latins, Vives writes, souls freed from the bonds of the body and mortality were called *Lemures;* "and such of these as haue a care of their progeny, and staie quietly about the house, are called *Lares.*" The *Larva* is the evil genius. "If the *Larua* ouerrule a man in this life, then is he damned by it in the life to come, and punished for his folly: if the *Lar* conquer, he is purified, and carried up to blisse, by the said *Lar.*" Vives adds that the "peaceable dead souls are *Lares,* the hurtfull *Larua* or *Lemures.*" According to Porphyry, the Lemures are "Ghosts that affright and hurt men, presaging their death." Flamens, Vives explains, were a sort of priesthood at Rome, who wore upon the tops of their hats tufts of white woolen threads. Therefore they were called "*Flamines quasi Pilamines,* hairy or tufted crownes." At first there were only three, later many, all obedient to the chief

[42] *Ibid.,* p. 331.

priest. They had great authority. The crest was given only
to the greatest, "as now we giue Miters."[43] Recall Milton's
lines:

> In consecrated Earth,
> And on the holy Hearth,
>   The *Lars,* and *Lemures* moan with midnight plaint,
> In Urns, and Altars round,
> A drear, and dying sound
>   Affrights the *Flamins* at their service quaint.

And so on, in chapter after chapter of *The City of God,* where
the essential principles and forces of the Christian religion are
contrasted with those of paganism. For example, when St.
Augustine, discussing the miracles of the pagan gods, writes
that the Epidaurian serpents accompanied Aesculapius to Rome,
Vives declares that the serpent itself was surely Aesculapius,
that "in the shape of a tame Snake . . . he swam ouer into
the Ile of *Tyber,* where his temple was built," and that it was
in truth the great devil, "for the Scriptures call him a Serpent,
and *Phericides* the *Syrian* saith, they all haue serpentine
feete."[44] He adds that Aesculapius was painted with a serpent
wound about a rod and called Ophiucus or Snake-Bearer. Milton compares Satan inclosed in the serpent with those that
changed the god in Epidaurus. St. Augustine insists that many
of the arts practised by the pagans were mere *deceptiones visus*
and flat falsehoods, as the "fetching downe of the Moone."
Vives adds a number of illustrations from Lucan, Virgil, Seneca, Ovid, and Propertius. For example, from Lucan:

> They first disroab'd the spheres,
> Of their cleare greatnesse, and *Phoebe* in her station,
> With blacke enchantments and damn'd inuocation,
> They strike as red, or pale, and make her fade.[45]

And from Ovid:

> She [Medea] workes to fetch swift *Phoebe* from her chaire,
> And wrap the Sunnes bright steeds in darkned ayre.

[43] *Ibid.,* p. 71.
[44] *Ibid.,* pp. 113, 364.   [45] *Ibid.,* p. 365.

And from Seneca:

> So be thy face unshrouded,
> And thy pure hornes unclouded!
> So be thy siluer chaire farre from the reach
> Of all the charmes that the *Thessalians* teach.

Such beliefs are recalled when Milton writes that the Night-Hag came

>   to dance
> With *Lapland* Witches, while the labouring Moon
> Eclipses at thir charms.

Again, writing of certain "fictions" that were spread abroad while the Judges ruled in Israel, St. Augustine mentions Cerberus, the Gorgons, Bellerophon, and many others. Vives explains. Cerberus was begotten by Typhon; his bark was hideous. Seneca's description of the fierce Stygian dog is quoted. The Gorgons are described, and Perseus's victory over them is summarized. The Chimera, overcome by Bellerophon, was, according to Hesiod, "a Lyon in his foreparts, a Dragon in the midst, and a Goate behind." And so on, almost endlessly. If, as Vives says, St. Augustine in *De Civitate Dei* "hath collected (as in a treasury) the best part of those readings, which he hath selected in the ancient authors," Vives proves himself even more learned in his commentaries, which were probably useful to Milton in his comparison of Christianity with paganism.

Important as are the works already reviewed in any study of the comprehensive background of Milton's ideas of demonology, three works of his own century should not be overlooked in a survey of those gods who were adored by the nations adjoining Palestine and who dared abide

> *Jehovah* thundring out of *Sion*, thron'd
> Between the Cherubim; yea, often plac'd
> Within his Sanctuary it self their Shrines,
> Abominations; and with cursed things
> His holy Rites, and solemn Feasts profan'd,
> And with their darkness durst affront his light.[46]

[46] I, 386-391.

The god worshiped by the Ammonites heads Milton's list:

> First *Moloch,* horrid King besmear'd with blood
> Of human sacrifice, and parents tears,
> Though for the noyse of Drums and Timbrels loud
> Their childrens cries unheard, that past through fire
> To his grim Idol.[47]

It is often said that this description was suggested by that in George Sandys' *A Relation of a Iourney* (1615). This may be true. But the worship of Moloch is described in other places, as in Raleigh's *History:*

This *Ahaz* was an Idolater, exceeding all his Predecessors. He made molten Images for *Baalim,* and burnt his Son for Sacrifice before the Idol of *Moloch,* or *Saturn,* which was represented by a Man-like brazen Body, bearing the Head of a Calf, set up not far from *Jerusalem,* in a Valley shadowed with Woods, called *Gehinnom,* or *Tophet,* from whence the word *Gehenna* is used for Hell. The Children offered, were inclosed within the Carkass of this Idol, and as the Fire encreased, so the Sacrificers, with a noise of Cymbals and other Instruments, filled the Air, to the end the pitiful cries of the Children might not be heard: which unnatural, cruel, and devilish Oblation, *Jeremy* the Prophet vehemently reprehendeth, and of which S. *Hierome* upon the tenth of *Matthew* hath written at large.[48]

In Purchas's *Pilgrimage*—an important part of the subject-matter of which is indicated by the following excerpt from the title-page: "Declaring the ancient Religions before the Flovd, the Heathenish, Jewish, and Saracenicall in all Ages since, in those parts professed, with their seuerall Opinions, Idols, Oracles, Temples, Priests, Feasts, Sacrifices, and Rites religious"—we read:

The Ammonites . . . inhabited Northward from Moab; . . . Their chiefe Citie was Rabbath, after called Philadelphia . . . *Moloch,* or *Melchon,* was their Idoll, which is supposed to be *Saturne,* whose bloudie butcherly sacrifices are before spoken of. The word signifieth a king: . . . It was a hollow Image (saith *Lyra*) of Copper, in forme of a man. In the hollow concauitie was made a fire, with

[47] I, 392-396.   [48] P. 333.

which the Idoll being heated, they put a childe into his armes, &
the Priests made such a noyse with their Timbrels, that the cries
of the childe might not moue the parents to compassion, but they
should rather thinke the childes soule receiued of the god into rest
and peace: others adde, That this *Moloch* had seuen Roomes, . . .
if a man would offer sonne or daughter, the seuenth was readie for
that crueltie. . . .

There was a valley neere Hierusalem (sometime possessed by
the sonne of *Hinnom*) where the Hebrewes built a notorious high
place to *Moloch:* it was on the East and South part of the Citie.   It
was also called Topheth, or Tymbrell, of that Tymbrell-Rite, which
those *Corribantes* and bloudie Priests did vse; . . . *Ieremie* prophe-
cieth, That it should be called the Valley of slaughter, because of
the iudgements for the idolatrous high places in it.   Vpon the pol-
lution hereof, by slaughter and burialls, it grew so execrable, that
Hell inherited the same name, called *Gehenna*. . . .[49]

With the last paragraph of this quotation should be compared
Milton's statement that Moloch led Solomon to build

> His Temple right against the Temple of God
> On that opprobrious Hill, and made his Grove
> The pleasant Vally of *Hinnom, Tophet* thence
> And black *Gehenna* call'd, the Type of Hell.

In Fuller's *A Pisgah-Sight of Palestine,* the same rites are described.   Moloch was a monstrous idol, a hollow image of
brass, which embraced children and seared them to death.   The
drums were used to drown the children's crying.[50]   In Fuller's
map of the land of Moriah we see just east of the walls of
Jerusalem "Mons Scandali" with the temples of Moloch and
Chemosh.   According to Adrichomius this place was called the
Rock of Offence.

Consider also the geography of the Moloch passage:

> Him the *Ammonite*
> Worshipt in *Rabba* and her watry Plain,
> In *Argob* and in *Basan,* to the stream
> Of utmost *Arnon.*

[49] P. 99 of the 1617 edition.   [50] Book IV, pp. 133-134.

In his account of "the memorable Places of the Gadites, and the Bordering Places of Ammon," Raleigh writes:

the chief City of the *Ammonites* . . . is called in the Scriptures sometime *Rabbath* as *Deut.* 3.11. but more often *Rabba.* . . . It was conquered by *Og* from the *Ammonites:* . . . the Regal seat of the *Ammonites* . . . as *Sehon* of *Hesbon* had dispossest *Moab*, so had *Og* of *Basan* the *Ammonites.* . . .[51]

A marginal note reads: "*Adrichomius* says it [Rabba] was also called *Urbs aquarum*, because of the river *Jaboc's* winding about it." In Fuller's "Description of Midian, Moab, Ammon, Edom," with the accompanying map, we see that the territory of Ammon extends to the north as well as to the south of the river Jaboc, which flows due west from Rabba to the Jordan. The river Arnon runs due south from Aroar for some distance and then veering westward to the south of Mons Abarim empties into the northeastern part of the Dead Sea. The territory north of the Jaboc, as one sees in the map of the tribe of Gad,[52] is that of Bashan; and the map of the tribe of Manasseh beyond Jordan[53] shows plainly the city Argob and "Terra Argob," to which Milton refers. The land of the tribe of Gad "was of a double nature. For what lay north of the river *Jabbok* was anciently the possession of *Og King of Basan*,"[54] and the land south of the river "was accounted a moity or one half" of the territory of the Ammonites. We read that Bashan was a grazing country "subdivided into severall petty lands: as, first, the *Land of Argob* on the north next Syria." Fuller explains that Rabba, the metropolis of Ammon, was called in Scripture the city of waters "because low and plashy in its situation." Purchas writes that the land of the Ammonites lay northward from Moab and was a valley.

Chemos is next in Milton's catalog:

> Next *Chemos*, th' obscene dread of *Moabs* Sons,
> From *Aroer* to *Nebo*, and the wild
> Of Southmost *Abarim*; in *Hesebon*
> And *Horonaim*, *Seons* Realm, beyond

[51] *Op. cit.*, pp. 223-224.   [52] Fuller, *op. cit.*, Book III, pp. 70-71.
[53] *Ibid.*, III, 88-89.   [54] *Ibid.*, III, 73.

The flowry Dale of *Sibma* clad with Vines,
And *Eleale* to th' *Asphaltick* Pool.

Fuller writes that Chemos was "notoriously known to be the
abomination of *Moab;* yet so that this Idol was held in *Copar-
cenary* betwixt them, and the *Ammonites*."[55]   Fuller explains:
"Thus as *Moab* and *Ammon* once parted the incestuous ex-
traction from the same *Grandfather:* so now they met again at
the Idolatrous adoration of the same God."   Chemosh or
Moloch, he says, was an image of stone, sitting on a throne between two female images, with an altar before him whereon
incense was offered.   According to Purchas, "*Chemosh* was
another Idoll of theirs [the Moabites], to which *Solomon* built
an high place."   Purchas adds: "*Pehor* also, and *Baal-pehor*,
and the rest, whose Rites are now rotten, and the memorie
worne out. This his name it seemes was borrowed of the Hill
Peor, mentioned by *Moses*, where it is likely he had his Altars
and Temple."[56]   Milton identifies Chemos and Peor:

> *Peor* his other Name, when he entic'd
> *Israel* in *Sittim* on their march from *Nile*
> To do him wanton rites, which cost them woe.

As a matter of fact, it is said, Moloch, Chemos, and Baal-Peor
were one deity.

The geography of Milton's lines may be explained by the
following details from Purchas, Raleigh, and Fuller.   Purchas
writes that Moab had the mountains of Horeb on the east, the
Salt Sea and part of Jordan on the west, Arnon on the south,
and the mountains of Pisgah and the Jaboc on the north.   But
Sihon, king of the Amorites, had taken from them the country between the Jaboc and the Arnon.   Raleigh writes that
when Moses had crossed the Arnon he encamped at Abarim,
opposite the City of Nebo.   At that time Moab dwelt on the
south side of the Arnon, having lost "all his ancient and best
Territory" to Sehon the Amorite.   Sibma and Hesbon and
Elhael are the chief cities of the Amorites.   There had been
giants in the land of the Moabites, and their chief city was

[55] *Op. cit.*, IV, 132.   [56] *Op. cit.*, p. 98.

Aroer, near the river Arnon. "*Moab* took the rest of the Coast of the Dead Sea, leaving a part to *Midian*; and passing over *Arnon*, inhabited the Plains between *Jordan*, and the Hills of *Abarim*, or *Arnon*, as far North as *Essebon*, or *Chesbon*. *Ammon* sate down on the North-east side of *Arnon*, and possest the Tract from *Rabba*, afterwards *Philadelphia*, both within the Mountains of *Gilehad*, and without them as far forth as *Aroer*."[57] In Moses' time, Raleigh explains, the Amorites had thrust the Ammonites "over the River of *Jaboc*, as they had done *Moab* over *Arnon*." Later, the land of Canaan extended east of Jordan to include part of this territory. Besides the provinces of Phoenicia and Palaestina, that part east of the Jordan and within the mountains of Hermon, Gilead, and Arnon fell to the possession of Manasseh, Gad, and Reuben, and was accounted a part of Canaan. The easternmost parts are divided into Basan, Gilead, Moab, Midian, Ammon, and so on.[58] It is now, says Raleigh, known by the name of Arabia in general. If one is somewhat puzzled by the boundaries set forth in Milton's lines, one should recall Raleigh's statement that the lands of Midian, Moab, and Ammon are by "our Writers . . . confusedly described, and not easily distinguished."[59] In *A Pisgah-Sight of Palestine* the general map of Palestine places the city Aroer near the headwaters of the Arnon. South of the Arnon the territory is marked "Pars Terrae Moab," and the land between the Arnon and the Jordan is labeled "Campestria Moab." In this division are Nebo and Nebo mons, one of the range named Abarim mons. To the north appear Shibmah, Elealeh, and Heshbon. In the map accompanying the description of Midian, Moab, Ammon, and Edom, in addition to the places already mentioned, we see Horonaim, on or near the Zared river, which flows into the Dead Sea, and Shittim, the last camp in the journey of the Israelites from Egypt to Canaan. On the map of the tribe of Reuben is a vine laden with large bunches of grapes, near Shibmah. Fuller explains that now the Arnon is the northern

[57] *Op. cit.*, pp. 174-219.
[58] *Ibid.*, p. 188.   [59] *Ibid.*, p. 218.

boundary of Moab but that formerly, before Sihon, king of
the Amorites, dispossessed them, the Moabites held much of
the territory north of the river. Aroer, in the northeast on
the river Arnon, is a populous tract. "Let us now request
the Reader, to climbe up the hills of *Abarim, Nebo,* and *Pisgah.*
These are a ledge of mountains rising by degrees from east tc
west. So that some have compared *Abarim* to the Chancell.
Nebo to the Church, and *Pisgah* to the Steeple." From Pisgah
one sees a fair prospect. Southward is the city of Nebo, at the
foot of the mountain of the same name. Both are so called
from Nebo, an idol worshiped there, which some think is the
same with Chemosh and Baal-Peor. Passing northward over
"the pleasant Plains of *Moab,*" we come to "*Sibmah,* so famous for her fruitfull vinyards," and, in the extreme north,
to Heshbon, "the royall Palace of *Sihon* King of the *Amorites.*" Again, Fuller reminds us that "all this land was possessed by the *Moabites,* before *Sihon* [the margin refers to
Numbers 21:26] forcibly expulsed them."[60]

Moloch and Chemos are followed by a group of deities
worshiped among the Sidonians:

> With these came they, who from the bordring flood
> Of old *Euphrates* to the Brook that parts
> *Egypt* from *Syrian* ground, had general Names
> Of *Baalim* and *Ashtaroth,* those male,
> These Feminine . . . .
> . . . . With these in troop
> Came *Astoreth,* whom the *Phoenicians* call'd
> *Astarte,* Queen of Heav'n, with crescent Horns;
> To whose bright Image nightly by the Moon
> Sidonian Virgins paid their Vows and Songs,
> In *Sion* also not unsung, where stood
> Her Temple on th' offensive Mountain, built
> By that uxorious King, whose heart though large,
> Beguil'd by fair Idolatresses, fell
> To Idols foul.

These lines are illustrated by the following excerpts from
Raleigh's section "Of Zidon," in which the detail and the
[60] *Op. cit.,* II, 64-65.

order exactly parallel Milton's. Raleigh writes that the Sidonians

> were in Religion Idolaters, (as the rest of the Canaanites) worshippers of *Baal* and *Astaroth:* Which Idols, tho common to the other of the Issue of *Canaan* . . . yet especially and peculiarly, were accounted the Gods of the *Zidonians;* as appears I *Kings* 11. 5. in the story of *Solomon's* Idolatry, where *Asteroth* is called the God of the *Zidonians:* and I *Reg.* 16. 33. in the story of *Achab,* the chief worshipper of *Baal,* where it is said, that he marrying *Jezebel,* the Daughter of the King of the *Zidonians,* worshipped their *Baal.* Divers *Baals,* and divers *Astaroths,* in their Idolatries they acknowledged; as it appears by the plural Names of *Baalim* and *Astaroth,* I *Sam.* 12. 10. and elsewhere: for even the Name *Astaroth,* as I am informed by a skilful Hebrician, is plural; the singular being *Astoreth:* . . . The occasion of this their multiplying of their *Baals,* and *Astoreths,* may be diversly understood, either in respect of the diversity of the Forms of the Images, or of the Worship in divers places, or of the Stories depending upon them; which (as Fables use to be) were doubtless in divers Cities divers. . . .[61]

One may compare the remarkable similarities between this passage and Milton's lines with the very general analogy indicated in the study previously mentioned,[62] whose author believes that Milton makes Baalim and Ashtaroth deities of the Babylonians.[63] But, as others have pointed out, Milton in the lines

> from the bordring flood
> Of old *Euphrates* to the Brook that parts
> *Egypt* from *Syrian* ground,

defined the limits of Canaan, the Euphrates being properly called a bordering flood because, as Newton said, it was "the utmost limit or border eastward of the promis'd land, according to Gen. XV.18. *Unto thy seed have I given this land from the river of Egypt unto the great river, the river Euphrates.* . . ."[64] As Raleigh writes, Baals and Astaroths were

[61] *Op. cit.,* p. 190.   [62] McColley, *op. cit.,* p. 182.
[63] *Ibid.,* p. 187.   [64] *Paradise Lost,* I, 43.

common idols among the Canaanites but were peculiarly gods
of the Sidonians. Milton does not say that they were Babylonian gods. Purchas declares that *Bel* or *Baal* is a general
name, "agreeing to all the gods of the Gentiles." There were
as many Baals in Syria "as there were Regions, and almost as
many as Cities."[65] As in the western dialect there were many
Joves, so in the eastern dialect there were many Baalim.
Among all the countries of Assyria, Baal or Bel "bare the
bell." Fuller explains that *Baal*, meaning Lord, is "the name
generall for most Idols," that Baal is the chief of the Baals,
that Bel was a Babylonian and Baal a Phoenician deity.[66]

With what Milton writes about Ashtoreth or Astarte the
following may be compared. According to Raleigh, Augustine thinks that Baal and Astarte are Jupiter and Juno. "For
the *Carthaginians* (which were *Tyrians*) call *Juno* by some
such name as *Astarte;* . . . whom he makes to be born of
Tyrus and *Syria,* and to have been the Wife of *Adonis.* . . . And
Hierom, upon *Ezekiel* 8. 44. notes, that *Thammuz* (whom
there the Idolatrous Women are noted to bewail) is the name
of *Adonis* among the *Syrians.*" A marginal note explains that
"*Astoreth* (or *Astarte*)" means sheep. Purchas says that the
"Sydonians also worshipped *Astarte,* in a stately and ancient
Temple" and that "*Astarte* or *Astaroth* was worshipped in the
formes of sheepe" not only by the Sidonians but by the Philistines also. He adds that "wise *Salomon* was brought by doting
on women to a worse dotage of Idolatry with this Sydonian
Idoll among others."[67] Fuller explains that the Septuagint
form of Ashtoreth is Astarte, that she was the goddess of the
Sidonians, that Solomon in his old age, "befooled by his
wives," reintroduced her worship into Jerusalem. "Her image was the statue of a woman, having on her head the *Head
of a Bull,* where the hornes erected resembled the Crescent
Moon. . . ."[68] Fuller's "Pantheon sive Idola Judeorum"
shows such a figure seated before an altar.

Thammuz followed Astoreth:

[65] *Op. cit.,* p. 65.   [66] *Op. cit.,* IV, 130-131.
[67] *Op. cit.,* pp. 89-91.   [68] *Op. cit.,* IV, 129-130.

Thammuz came next behind,
Whose annual wound in *Lebanon* allur'd
The *Syrian* Damsels to lament his fate
In amorous dittyes all a Summers day,
While smooth *Adonis* from his native Rock
Ran purple to the Sea, suppos'd with blood
Of *Thammuz* yearly wounded: the Love-tale
Infected *Sions* daughters with like heat,
Whose wanton passions in the sacred Porch
Ezekiel saw, when by the Vision led
His eye survay'd the dark Idolatries
Of alienated *Judah*.

Raleigh reports that Cicero, in the *De Natura Deorum*, has
divers goddesses of the name of Venus, the fourth of which
was Astarte and wife of Adonis. Macrobius says that Adonis
was commonly worshiped among the Assyrians. Jerome, upon
Ezekiel 8:44, notes that "*Thammuz* (whom there the Idolatrous Women are noted to bewail) is the name of *Adonis*
among the *Syrians*. So that it may seem, that in the Worship of *Astarte*, or *Venus*, they did bewail her Husband
Adonis."[69] Others expound the mourning for Thammuz as
for Osiris, who by the Egyptians is called Ammuz. In his account of the religion of the Phoenicians, Purchas has a full
description of the mourning for Thammuz. At Biblos in the
temple of Venus the yearly rites of Adonis were celebrated
"with beatings and wofull lamentings." Some say that this
lamentation is not for Adonis but for Osiris and that therefore
it is called the mourning for Thammuz, "which *Iunius* interpreteth *Osiris*." Women, it is said, "were the chiefe lament-
ers, if not the onely, as *Ezekiel* testifieth." Plutarch is cited:
"the women kept the Adonia, euery where through the City,
setting forth Images, obseruing exequies and lamentations." In
most cities of the east Adonis is mourned. On a certain night
"they lay an Image in a bed, and number a set bead roll of
lamentations: which being ended, light is brought in, and then
the Priest anointeth the chappes of the Mourners, whispering

[69] *Op. cit.*, p. 191.

these words, *Trust in God, for wee haue saluation*, or deliuer-
ance *from our griefes*." Then the idol is taken out of the
sepulcher. Purchas comments: "Was not this mourning, think
wee, sport to the Deuill?"[70] Note particularly the following
excerpt:

Hereby [Biblos] runneth the Riuer Adonis also, which once a yeere
becommeth red and bloudie: which alteration of the colour of the
water, is the warning to that their *Mourning* for *Adonis*, who at
that time they say is wounded in Libanus.

Purchas's explanation ruins the legend: the redness of the water is due to the red earth, not to the blood of Thammuz. To
the explanation that Thammuz is Adonis Fuller adds: "This
Phenician superstition infected the *Jews; Then he brought me
to the door of the gate of the Lords house, which was towards
the north, and behold there sat women weeping for Tam-
muz. . . .*"[71] Fuller's map of Mount Libanus shows the
river Adonius flowing from the mountains to the sea. One of
the chief rivers of this region, it is "so called from the minion
of Venus worshipped hereabouts."[72] Then came Dagon:

> Next came one
> Who mourn'd in earnest, when the Captive Ark
> Maim'd his brute Image, head and hands lopt off
> In his own Temple, on the grunsel edge,
> Where he fell flat, and sham'd his Worshipers:
> *Dagon* his Name, Sea Monster, upward Man
> And downward Fish: yet had his Temple high
> Rear'd in Azotus, dreaded through the Coast
> Of *Palestine*, in *Gath* and *Ascalon*,
> And *Accaron* and *Gaza's* frontier bounds.

These lines are based mainly on I *Samuel* 5: 1-5, with reminiscences of other passages. Raleigh relates that after a great
victory the Philistines carried the Ark of God to Azotus, where
they set it up in the house of Dagon, their idol; "but that night
the *Idol* fell out of his place, from above to the ground, and

---

[70] *Op. cit.*, p. 90.
[71] *Op. cit.*, IV, 137. Verity refers to Sandys' full account.
[72] *Ibid.*, IV, 1, 17.

lay under the *Ark*. The morning following they took it up,
and set it again in his place. And it fell the second time, and
the Head brake from the Body, and the Hands from the
Arms, shewing that it had nor power nor understanding in the
presence of God." Raleigh goes on to explain that if this idol
could not endure the presence of the true God, it is no marvel
that when Christ was born "all the *Oracles* wherein the Devil
derided and betrayed mortal Men lost power, speech, and op-
eration at the instant. For when that true light which had
never beginning of brightness, brake through the clouds of a
Virgins Body, all these foul and stinking vapours vanished."[73]
We recall in the *Hymn* the "twise-batter'd god of *Palestine*"
and the instant ceasing of the oracles at the birth of Christ.
Raleigh also writes that "*Dagon* had a Mans Face, and a
Fishes Body."[74] In his account of the memorable places of
Dan and Simeon and other regions Raleigh mentions Accaron
or Ekron, sometime one of the five satrapies of the Philis-
tines; Azotus or Asdod, where was dedicated a "sumptuous
Temple" to the idol Dagon; Gaza, the first of the five sa-
trapies of the Philistines and "the South bound of the Land of
Canaan towards *Egypt*"; and Ascalon, "one of the chiefest
and strongest Cities of the *Philistims*."[75] Also mentioned are
Sorek, in the vale of that name, where lived Dalila, "whom
Sampson loved," and Beersheba, "standing on the Border of
the *Arabian Desart*, and in the South bound of *Canaan*." Milton writes that the southern limit of the Promised Land was

> *Beersaba*, where the *Holy Land*
> Borders on *Aegypt* and the *Arabian* shoare.[76]

Purchas states that the Philistines "had fiue principall Cities,
Ascalon, Accaron, Azotus, Gath, Gaza," and that Dagon was
a sea-god: "aboue his bellie hee was of humane shape, beneath
like a fish."[77] Purchas adds this characteristic comment:

Such is Idolatry, diuine it will not be, it cannot content it selfe with
humane, but proueth monstrous, in the vglie and deformed Image,

[73] *Op. cit.*, p. 264.
[74] *Ibid.*, p. 122.
[75] *Ibid.*, pp. 214-215.
[76] *Paradise Lost*, III, 536-537.
[77] *Op. cit.*, p. 92.

exhibiting the character of the true Author of this falshood. . . .
This may wee see and say, when men are giuen ouer to themselues,
then they become beasts, monsters, deuills: yea, worse then such,
for while they worship such, they professe themselues (as Clients
and Votaries) to be worse and baser then their Deities.

After repeating the story of Dagon's overthrow in his own
temple, Purchas exclaims, "Thus true Religion, the more opposed, the more it flourished: the prison-house of her captiuitie
is the throne of her Empire . . ."; with this Milton must have
been well pleased. The shape of Dagon, writes Fuller, "(save
that it was *masculine for sexe*) resembled the Antick laughed
at by the Poet."

> Desinet in piscem, mulier formosa superne.
> Upwards man-like he ascended,
> Downwards like a fish he ended.[78]

"The uglier his shape," Fuller comments, "the handsomer for
an *Idol*; and to keep a *Decorum*, it was fit that he should be
as misshapen in his form, as monstrous in his worship."
    After Dagon came Rimmon:

> Him follow'd *Rimmon*, whose delightful Seat
> Was fair *Damascus*, on the fertil Banks
> Of *Abbana* and *Pharphar*, lucid Streams.[79]

Purchas briefly states that Rimmon was an idol of the Syrians
and that his temple is mentioned in II *Kings* 5:18.[80] In Syria
there were many religions—first, the true religion in the time
of Noah; then, "those superstitions of *Rimmon*" and others
under the Assyrian, Babylonian, Persian, and other govern-
ments. In ancient times Damascus was the city of greatest
fame. In his account of the idols of the Jews, Fuller calls
Rimmon an "Idol of *Syria* whose principal Temple was in
Damascus."[81] There is a marginal reference to II *Kings* 5:18,
which reports the entreaty of Naaman, captain of the host of

---

[78] *Op. cit.*, II, 220.
[79] McColley, *op. cit.*, pp. 181, 187, admits that Rimmon is not in Ross's
list and suggests a resemblance between Rimmon and Mammon, "seducer
of the King in the account of Ross," which vary in only two letters.
[80] *Op. cit.*, p. 81.   [81] *Op. cit.*, IV, 136.

the king of Syria, that the Lord should pardon him when he should go with his master "into the house of Rimmon to worship there." Fuller explains that Aram of Damascus is watered by the rivers "*Abanah* and *Pharphar*," which were highly beholden to Naaman, "who preferred them *before all the waters of Israel*."[82] The map of Mount Libanus shows these rivers flowing through Damascus.

Except for Belial, who will be dealt with in the next chapter, the survey of the pagan gods in Milton's catalog is now complete. But in *Paradise Lost* appear other devils, one of the most interesting of whom is Azazel, bearer of Satan's mighty standard, the Imperial Ensign of the rebel host. As has recently been shown, Azazel is Satan's standard bearer in the apochryphal *Book of Enoch*. Because of its professed antiquity, Purchas summarizes some of the material in this book, which he says is very fabulous. To the sons of men were born fair daughters, and the watchmen (angels) lusted and went astray after them. The names of the rulers are given, among whom is "Azalzel." They took wives and taught them and their children sorceries and enchantment.

Ezael taught first to make swords and weapons for warre, and how to worke in Metals. He taught to make womens ornaments, and how to looke faire, and iewelling. And they beguiled the Saints; and much sinne was committed on the earth.[83]

Then the four great Archangels, Michael, Gabriel, Raphael, and Uriel, looking down "from the holy places of Heauen: and beholding much bloudshed on the earth, and all vngodlinesse and transgression committed therein," appeared before the Lord and said:

Thou art God of Gods and Lord of Lords, &c. Thou seest what *Ezael* hath done, he hath taught mysteries, and reuealed to the World the things in Heauen, &c.

Then the Lord ordered the Archangels to correct these evils, Raphael being commanded to bind Ezael hand and foot and to cast him into darkness in the wilderness until the day of

[82] *Ibid.*, IV, 7.   [83] *Op. cit.*, p. 36.

judgment, when he and the other sinners shall be brought
unto trial and "vnto the prison of the ending of the World."
In *Paradise Lost* there are a number of other false gods, as
Adramelec, Beelzebub, and Nisroch, who are briefly described
in the *Pilgrimage* and in Fuller's "Pantheon." To pursue this
subject further, to discuss what from the Christian point of
view are blind and beastly abominations, to show how idolatry
began with worship of the creature and contempt of the Creator, how it was intended to perpetuate the memory of mortal
men or to praise the immortal lights of heaven, how it was
established by the tyranny of princes, the policies of priests,
the mysteries of philosophers, the fabling of poets, the superstition of the vulgar, and the malice of devils—the phrases
are borrowed from Purchas—would be a task not lightly to
be undertaken and probably not welcomed by the reader.

Finally, a word regarding the nature of devils and, particularly, Satan, the personification and moving spirit of evil. In
The City of God, as in *Paradise Lost,* the Devil himself was
originally innocent, for God created nothing evil. In spite
of Christ's statement that the Devil had been a murderer from
the beginning and that there is no truth in him, St. Augustine
believes that the Devil did not have a wicked nature given him
in creation; he was not created sinful and vicious by nature.
The fact that Lucifer, son of the morning, fell from heaven
proves that he was formerly sinless. Vives quotes Origen:
"The Serpent opposed not the truth, nor was bound to goe
upon his belly, euer from the point of his creation. But as
Adam and Eve were a while sinlesse, so was the Serpent no
Serpent the while of his being in the Paradise of delight. . . ."[84] In creation, the nature of angels, as of man,
was good. Evil came from the will, from pride. In essence,
the difference between the good and the evil angels resides in
their wills. Some, as St. Augustine says, persisted in "God
their common good, and in his truth, loue, and eternity: and
other some delighting more in their owne power, as though
it were from themselues, fell from that common all-blessing

[84] *Op. cit.,* p. 400.

Good, to dote vpon their owne: and taking pride for eternity, vaine deceit for firm truth, and factious enuy for perfect loue, became proud, deceitfull and enuious."[85] Precisely so, it may be parenthetically remarked, was it with man. Endowed with innocence and reason, he might have obeyed his true Creator and "kept his hests," whereby he would have become as one of the angels. But willfully becoming perverse he offended the Lord "by pride of heart" and was justly made the slave of his lusts and without grace the prey of eternal death. In *The City of God* and in *Paradise Lost,* sin for man as for devil resides in the evil will. God's justice, Satan's malice, and man's sin are summed up in the following excerpt from the *Pilgrimage,* which follows a paragraph describing our first parents' perfect innocence, happiness, and blessedness in Paradise:

In this plight did Satan (that old Serpent) see, disdaine and enuie them. It was not enough for him, and the diuelish crue of his damned associates, for their late rebellion, to be banished Heauen, but the inferiour world must bee filled with his venome, working that malice on the creatures here, which hee could not there so easily wrecke on their Creator. And because Man was here Gods Deputie and Lieutenant, as a petty God on the Earth, hee chuseth him as the fittest subiect, in whose ruine to despite his Maker. To this end he vseth not a Lion-like force, which then had beene bootlesse, but a *Serpentine* sleight, vsing that subtill creature as the meetest instrument to his Labyrinthian proiects. Whereas by inward temptation hee could not so easily preuayle, by insinuating himselfe into their minds, hee windes himselfe into this winding Beast, disposing the *Serpents* tongue to *speake to the woman* (the weaker vessell) singled from her husband, and by questioning doth first vndermine her.[86]

Thus with great subtlety the Father of Lies persuaded the woman to lust after new knowledge and to disobey the divine decree. So man sinned and offered almost his first fruits to the Devil. So was he made a slave to the sin within him and to the Devil without.

Such, it seems clear, is part of the broad background of Milton's catalog of pagan gods. In the light of this evidence,

[85] *Ibid.,* p. 419.   [86] P. 25.

it is obviously impossible to attribute with confidence, as in the article mentioned, specific details or the scheme as a whole to any one source. Realizing Milton's thorough familiarity with the Bible, which does not, however, provide a pattern for the epic catalog, and with secular literature, ancient and contemporary; recalling also the fact that in the *Hymn* he made a preliminary survey of idolatry, which, in view of the length of the poem, is very full and which is remarkably like that in *Paradise Lost,* we shall decidedly prefer Mr. Hanford's conservative general summary to the revolutionary and limited one proposed by Mr. McColley. The latter is surely not in complete accord with probability or ascertained fact. Consider especially Belial. In *Paradise Lost* he is a lewd spirit, to whom "no Temple stood Or Altar smoak'd," a personification of lust, violence, and outrage. Mr. McColley, who considers him "Idolatry personified," compares with Milton's description of him Ross's statement that the ancient Persians and Scythians had no altars or temples for their gods and Ross's account of Baal-Zebub and Priapus. He declares that Milton's Belial is not a name drawn from Scripture and believes that he is the Baal-Zebub of *Pansebeia* combined with the idea of gods having neither temples nor altars and with Ross's personification of idolatry. As a matter of fact, Baal-Zebub or Beelzebub, who is Satan's chief lieutenant, was a distinct idol, a sun-god of the Philistines. Fuller calls him God of Ekron or Accaron and Lord of Flies. "*Beelzebub* was the grand Idoll of Ekron, whose name importeth *a Lord of Flies.*"[87] He declares that "in the Testament" he passes for the Prince of Devils. Purchas explains that Bel, the Babylonian deity, was worshiped elsewhere under divers names, as Bel, Baal, Beel-zebub, according to the form in various languages.[88] He adds that Beelzebub was worshiped at Accaron and that by the Hebrews the name was used contemptuously, meaning "dunghill, or dung-Iupiter." On the other hand, Priapus is, of course, a distinct god, who in Greek and Roman religion personified generative power. Diodorus says that the Egyptians deified the

[87] II, 219.   [88] *Op. cit.,* p. 53.

goat as the Greeks honored Priapus and that the ancient myths made Priapus the son of Dionysus and Aphrodite.[89] Although Priapus is in one respect like Belial, it is probable, as the next chapter shows, that Milton fashioned Belial from the Bible and from certain ideas current in contemporary controversy.

[89] *Op. cit.*, II, 357.

CHAPTER VI

BELIAL AND SATAN

LITERARY critics who ignore backgrounds and who insist upon treating poetry as merely an esthetic product have as a rule neglected or condemned Milton's work and interests in the period from 1640 to 1658, which they regard as an unfortunate episode in the life of the poet. Even those who do not deplore his activities in this middle period and who regard his prose as a powerful but unbalanced expression of his genius often fail to observe any relationship between the prose and the later poems. One writer, for example, declares that in these years "Milton was neither writing nor thinking poetry"[1]—a rash statement, for, although we have the prose, a few sonnets, and the *Commonplace Book*, there is no complete record of what then occupied Milton's mind "at home in the spacious circuits of her musings." On the other hand, some scholars recognize in *Paradise Lost* emphatic re-statements of long-cherished convictions. For example, the passage in Book XII[2] denouncing wolves who debauch true religion is a transparent attack upon Episcopacy, which, as every student knows, Milton in his prose polemics violently attacked as a hateful tyranny over religious freedom. Again, without reference to Milton's prose, *Paradise Lost* is explained as "the epic of the English state," and Milton is called a great political philosopher.[3] Recently the relationship between the *Defensio Secunda* and *Paradise Lost* has been emphasized: they were, it has been said, created out of the same mood.[4] In addition, from the Cambridge Manuscript we know that as early as the years 1640 to 1642 Milton's mind was occu-

[1] Mark Pattison, *Milton*, p. 165.   [2] Ll. 507-537.
[3] William Haller, "Order and Progress in *Paradise Lost*," *PMLA*, XXXV, 218-225.
[4] E. M. W. Tillyard, *Milton*, pp. 192 ff.

pied with the theme of *Paradise Lost*, of which, ultimately, his mature judgment, directed by Puritan taste and demanding substantial truth, approved. It is probable that *Paradise Lost*, thus germinated and conditioned, is related more intimately than has been realized not only to Milton's prose but also to the political-religious interests that engrossed the middle period, and in particular to certain concepts and figures in contemporary controversial writing with which Milton was familiar.

It is not necessary here to review that political-religious controversy, which was probably more intense and prolonged than any that England has ever known. Nor is it necessary to discuss in detail the alignment of forces, which found Cavalier arrayed against Roundhead, the largest landholders against the squires and yeomen, the Churchmen against the Puritans, the North and the West against the South and the East. More useful for this study is the distinction between parties drawn by Richard Baxter, whose testimony because of his personal experience is especially valuable. According to Baxter, many adhered to Parliament in the interest of public safety and liberty, "yet was it principally the differences about Religious matters that filled up the Parliaments Armies, and put the Resolution and Valour into their Soldiers, which carried them on in another manner than mercenary Soldiers are carried on." Some who were for good bishops supported the Parliament; but generally the people, "who were then called *Puritans, Precisions, Religious Persons,* that used to talk of God, and Heaven, and Scripture, and Holiness, and to follow Sermons, and read Books of Devotion, and pray in their Families, and spend the Lord's Day in Religious Exercises, and plead for Mortification, and serious Devotion, and strict Obedience to God, and speak against Swearing, Cursing, Drunkennesse, Prophaness, &c. I say, the main Body of this sort of Men, both Preachers and People, adhered to the Parliament." On the other side were the gentry and the people who were not so strict against oaths or gaming or plays or drinking, who did not trouble themselves about the matters of God and the world to come, who were for the King's Book and for dancing and recreation on the Lord's Day, who went to

Church and heard Common Prayer and were glad to hear a sermon "which lasht the *Puritans*" and strictness and preciseness in religion and following sermons and ex tempore praying. There is, Baxter declares, "a universal and radicated Enmity between the *Carnal* and the *Spiritual,* the *Serpent's* and the *Woman's* Seed, the *fleshly Mind,* and the *spiritual Law of God,* through all the World, in all Generations. . . ." So it was in England: "as he that was born after the Flesh did persecute him that was born after the Spirit, even so was it here: The vulgar Rabble of the carnal and prophane, the Fornicators, Drunkards, Swearers, &c. did every where hate them that reproved their Sin, and condemned them by a holy Life. This Difference was universal, and their Enmity implacable. . . ."[5]

The bitter controversies which preceded, accompanied, and followed the Civil War were dominated by a traditional spiritual dualism, in which, as we shall see, Belial and Satan were living forces, dynamic personifications of all that the Puritans particularly detested and abhorred. It is, of course, quite probable, as George Santayana has said, that theology is "not a region of truth or error at all, but rather of poetic and ingenious fancy" and that the symbols here recorded represent a childish state of mind.[6] As far as this study is concerned, Santayana's criticism is hardly relevant. The truth is that in a great number of pamphlets condemnation of malign forces and appeal to Christ's leadership represent an attitude and spirit that pervaded the Puritan party. As a citizen, Milton was inspired by the Puritan spirit. As a poet he almost inevitably reflected this spiritual background. Transferred from a national and controversial to a cosmic and poetic setting, Satan and Belial probably retained for Milton and for some of the first readers of *Paradise Lost* more than a suggestion of their prosaic connotations. Historically speaking, the Satan and the Belial of the Puritan pamphleteers are not negligible sources of *Paradise Lost.* To a partial record of these evil spirits (and their opposites) as they appear in the pamphlet warfare that raged from 1640 to about 1650 this chapter is devoted, in the hope of es-

[5] *Reliquiae Baxterianae,* pp. 31-32.   [6] *Obiter Scripta,* pp. 13-14.

tablishing certain connections with *Paradise Lost,* which for a moment must now be considered.

Of those great devils, "the prime in order and in might," who in Hell answered Satan's call to action, the last was Belial:

> *Belial* came last, then whom a Spirit more lewd
> Fell not from Heaven, or more gross to love
> Vice for it self: To him no Temple stood
> Or Altar smoak'd; yet who more oft then hee
> In Temples and at Altars, when the Priest
> Turns Atheist, as did *Elys* Sons, who fill'd
> With lust and violence the house of God.
> In Courts and Palaces he also Reigns
> And in luxurious Cities, where the noyse
> Of riot ascends above thir loftiest Towrs,
> And injury and outrage: And when Night
> Darkens the Streets, then wander forth the Sons
> Of *Belial,* flown with insolence and wine.
> Witness the Streets of *Sodom,* and that night
> In *Gibeah,* when hospitable Dores
> Yielded thir Matrons to prevent worse rape.[7]

In the great conference in Pandemonium, after fierce Moloch had urged open war, the handsome and fair-spoken Belial, whose thoughts were

> To vice industrious, but to Nobler deeds
> Timorous and slothful,

made his subtle plea for peace, easily demolishing Moloch's rash arguments, urging that the wisest course was acquiescence in their doom, and proffering the hope that ultimately God would relent and that in time

> This horror will grow milde, this darkness light.[8]

His counsel, which excited no applause, was ignored. When, in *Paradise Regained,* Satan again consulted his potentates regarding their campaign against Christ, a new enemy who threatened their final overthrow, it is Belial,

---

[7] I, 490-505.   [8] II, 220.

the dissolutest Spirit that fell
The sensuallest, and after *Asmodai*
The fleshliest Incubus,

who advised

Set women in his eye and in his walk,
Among daughters of men the fairest found.[9]

Admonishing Belial that he weighed all others in his own scale, Satan instantly rejected his counsel.

⌈Such is the character of Belial and his sons: active in vice, slothful in noble deeds, lewd, dissolute, but handsome in figure and eloquent of speech.⌋ Although Belial is an outstanding figure among Milton's demons, no completely satisfactory explanation of his prominence and character has ever been offered. Newton said, "It does not appear that he was ever worshipped; but lewd, profligate fellows, such as regard neither God nor man, are called in Scripture 'the children of Belial,' *Deut.* xiii. 13. See also I. *Sam.* ii. 12, and *Judges* xix, which are the particular instances here given by Milton."[10] Todd refers to Wierus's *Pseudomonarchia Daemonum*, which declares that Belial was created immediately after Lucifer and that he was the father and the seducer of the fallen angels.[11] Verity cites Thomas Heywood's *Hierarchie* (1635), which, he says, made Belial the head of the fourth of the nine orders into which the fallen angels were divided.[12] These references, of course, throw light upon Belial; but the full explanation of Milton's emphasis upon this demon, whose last place in the processional catalog is actually a post of honor, is to be found elsewhere. Milton's lines are doubtless reminiscent of terms that once shed a lurid light upon the pages of controversy. Unquestionably, as has been said, many of the first readers of *Paradise Lost* were keenly aware of the connotations of the terms *Belial* and *Sons of Belial*, which have for modern readers none at all. It is not

[9] II, 150-152.
[10] *The Poetical Works of John Milton*, ed. H. J. Todd (1826), II, 68.
[11] *Ibid.*, II, 68.
[12] *Paradise Lost*, II, 403. Heywood, in fact, makes Belial the leader of the third class. Cf. *The Hierarchie of the blessed Angells* (1635), p. 436.

Milton's verse that is obscure; "it is our minds which have let so much that is noble in the story of our race slide to oblivion!" For the Parliament writers especially, *Belial* and *Sons of Belial* were favorite terms, sanctioned by Scripture and charged with the utmost scorn and detestation. With the Puritans "scandalous misnaming," to use Milton's phrase, was often an effective aid to argument. Only samples of the abundant material may be presented here, but these illustrations from a great variety of sources will suffice to make the point clear. Without apology, examples from sermons, which were often little more than religious-political propaganda, are included.

In *A Sermon Preached before the Honourable House of Commons, now assembled in Parliament, At their publike Fast,* November 17, 1640, upon the text "The Lord is with you, while yee bee with him: and if yee seeke him, he will be found of you: but if yee forsake him, he will forsake you,"[13] Stephen Marshall, who by his enemies was called the trumpet of rebellion, inquiring who are the most desperate traitors and the greatest enemies of God, exclaims:

I pray God there be none such met this day to fast & pray before the Lord. Every son of *Belial*, every one that is a Rebell against God, every one that works wickednesse, is *that wicked Haman*, that sels *Hester*, and all her people to destruction . . . thou art a child of *Belial*, an Idolater, a superstitious person, . . . And hee hath made some of you Noblemen, some Knights, and Gentlemen, and now called you to be the Repairers of our breach, to heale and prevent our ruine. What if you yourselves have a chief hand in these transgressions? What if among you be found swearers, cursers, adulterers, drunkards, haters of Gods wayes, . . . men who goe in your sinfull wayes, and resolve to doe so: and because you are great, will therefore be children of *Belial*, refusing to carry Gods yoak, what if any such should be here? The Lord of heaven forbid.[14]

Synonymous with idolater, adulterer, rebel against God and all his works, the phrase "son of Belial" is conspicuous early in the Puritan plea for reform, for devotion to the cause of righteousness and justice, for the separation of the sheep from the

[13] II *Chronicles* 15:2.   [14] Pp. 17-37.

goats. Marshall was one of the Smectymnuans, who, in *An Answer To A Booke Entituled An Humble Remonstrance* (1641), reply as follows to Bishop Hall's wish that the manifold scandals of the inferior clergy be kept secret:

What? the sinne; alas, that is done already; Doe wee not know, the drunkennesse, profanenesse, Popishnesse of the English Clergie rings at Rome already? yes undoubtedly; and there is no way to vindicate the Honour of our *Nation, Ministry, Parliaments, Soveraigne, Religion, God;* but by causing the punishment to ring as farre as the sinne hath done; that our adversaries that have triumphed in their sinne, may be confounded at their punishments. Doe not your Honours know, that the plaistring or palliating of these rotten members, will be a greater dishonour to the Nation and Church, then their cutting off; and that the personall acts of these *sonnes of Beliall,* being connived at, become Nationall sinnes?[15]

In *Reformation and Desolation: Or, A Sermon tending to the Discovery of the Symptomes of a People to whom God will by no meanes be reconciled* (1642) Marshall interprets the phrase. If you will know the people against whom God hath indignation forever, "the Scripture tells it you in this expression ordinarily, they are the *children of Belial;* so they are usually called in the Old Testament; that is, such as will not beare *God's yoke; . . .* these children of *Belial . . .* are, First, *all unbeleevers . . .* Secondly, the children of disobedience and sonnes of *Belial,* are such, whose lives and conversations are contrary to the rules of the Gospel; who as they will not take *Christ* to be their *portion* by faith, so they will not take Christs *word* in the Gospel to be their *guide;* but they will live indeed without all yoke, doing what is good in their owne eyes; these are the sonnes of Belial."[16] Those who are guilty of idolatry, sensual lusts, contempt of God's ordinances—abominations that fill up the measure of the people's sins—are menaced with God's fierce punishment. Many of the nobility and persons of quality are sons of Belial, "arrand Traytors and Rebells against God." Many ministers are rotten in doctrine, corrupt in their lives, not "fit hog-heards to keepe swine."

[15] Pp. 78-79.   [16] Pp. 14-15.

This denunciation of the sons of Belial, rebels against God, was to be expected of Puritans and Parliament men, who, scandalized by profanity and wickedness, were as a class devout followers of Christ, and who through faith in Him were confident of victory. This assurance is well illustrated in Thomas Temple's *Christ's Government in and over his People*, a sermon delivered before the House of Commons, October 26, 1642. Temple declares:

If Christ bee King of his Church, let Gods people comfort themselves in this, that Christ reignes, that Christ sits as King among us. . . . We that live here in the Isles, have we not a portion in this joy and comfort, that we know Christ is King, and reignes among us; let the earth rejoyce, and the multitude of the Isles be glad Indeed if Gods people consider, they are but a little flock of kids among many lions, a few sheep among many wolves, a single lilly among many thornes: if they consider, what machinations, what pernicious plots are daily contrived against them: if we had not this to support us, to know Christ is King, that he orders all for the best for us, subdues our enemies, protects us from the plots of malignant persons, preserves us in the midst of greatest dangers, it might well cast us into despaire. . . .[17]

The power of Christ, Temple proclaims, "is able to set up his colours and his Scepter there where no earthly King dares set his foot." Christ will crush his enemies with an iron rod; "the Lord at thy right hand shall strike thorow Kings in the day of his wrath, Kings that be his enemies." With the assurance that they were fighting the Lord's battles, the hosts of Parliament proved invincible.

In the illustrations previously cited, "sons of Belial" was applied to wicked rebellious men in general or to profane and popish clergymen in particular. In John Goodwin's *Anti-Cavalierisme, Or, Truth Pleading As well the Necessity, as the Lawfulness of this present War, for the suppression of that Butcherly brood of Cavaliering Incendiaries, who are now hammering England, to make an Ireland Of It* (1642), the phrase includes the entire Royalist party. Against the people of God,

[17] P. 22.

declares Goodwin, have risen the "sons of *Belial*," full of hatred and revenge. Partly in plain words and partly by their insolent behavior, they threaten "to stretch the line of miserable and wofull *Ireland* over you and your City, and whole Nation." In fears, dangers, distractions, loss, expense, and forbearance of their estates, the people of God suffer a kind of martyrdom at the hands of the sons of Belial, who are thorns in their eyes and scourges in their sides "only because we will be that in open or constant profession, which by the grace of God we are inwardly and in the truth of our soules; because we will not prostitute our consciences to the lusts of their Father the Devill. . . ." To his party Goodwin issues this challenge: "stand up like men, and quit our selves with all our might, and all our strength, against those assacinates, and sworne Swordmen of the devill, who have conspired the death and ruine of all that feareth God in the Land."[18]

To make clear the justice of the war against the sons of Belial, *The Late Covenant Asserted* (citing *Judges* 19: 22; 29: 7-13) establishes in detail a parallel between the Cavaliers and the men of Gibeah. A Levite and his wife turn in to lodge in Gibeah of Benjamin where "certaine sonnes of Belial" beset the house and force the woman, who in the morning is found dead upon the threshold. To the tribes the husband gives notice of what lewdness had been committed in Israel. The tribes call a parliament and resolve to execute justice:

So they require their Brother *Benjamin* to deliver-up those children of *Belial*, which are in *Gibeah*, that wee may put them to death (as we have resolved in our Parliament) and put away evill from Israel. *Benjamin* are stout, they will not hearken, they will maintaine the true Religion, according to Covenant, that shall be their prime worke still. And they will maintaine those *Children of Belial* too; All this will agree together (as Christ and *Belial*) so they are resolved.

The tribes make war upon Benjamin, and burn Gibeah with fire. The Benjaminites are trodden down with ease.

[18] Pp. 12, 35-36.

The Case now is Parallel with that, and the Justice of the warre exceeds it: First, Sonnes of *Belial* rise-up then, beset a house round about, and beat at the dores. Here they have done so much and more, they have beset two Kingdomes, beaten downe the house of the Church and State to their Power. They are demanded by the Parliament; 'Deliver us the men the Children of *Belial*, that we may put them to death. . . .'

But, in defence of those sons of Belial, the King, the Queen, and the nobles put forth all their power to destroy the House and the Kingdom. "We have seen the Parallel, how things do now relate to these children of Belial, besetting the House round, and beating at the doores. Now we must see what these *children* did in the streets, and how that relates to the present. . . ." The author proceeds:

these *children of Belial*, who have forced wives and maids too; have wrought villanies, and lewdness in Israel, and defiled two Kingdoms with it, from corner to corner. The Observator hath concluded, That all the Kings Army are Papists. And shall we regard what Papists sweare and vow? . . . And yet I am not assured by what the Observator saies, that all the Kings Army are Papists . . . there are many English monsters there fighting against their countrey; and *Irish* Rogues and Traitors. . . . And the whole Kingdom is assured that it is the most bloodie mischievous most accursed Army, that ever was upon the face of the earth. They have and they will, to their power destroy Religion, that which should be kept pure and undefiled, the Queen hath to her power, (and she hath al in her hands, but God hath put a hook in her Nose, and a bridle in her lips) she hath her loyall Subjects, *children of Beliall*, she hath (I will speak it all in a word) she hath *forced the Spouse of Christ*, I say, *forced her* before the *Lords face*.[19]

But the Lord will drive his enemies as dust before the whirl-wind.

The same Scriptural incident is used in *Great Britains Misery; With The Causes and Cure* (1643), which lists among the instruments of Britain's misery "light, irreligious, prophane,

[19] Pp. 14-15.

broken-fortuned men, Sons of *Belial*," and which thus comments on the cause, including the rebellion in Ireland:

being in it selfe more horrid, and in the consequence much more dangerous to us, than the act of the *Benjaminites in abusing the Levites Concubine*, was to the other *Tribes* of *Israel*. This being every ones case, which we are all bound to vindicate. Me thinkes that Declaration from the Parliament is sent through all *Britaine*, like the divided peeces of the *Concubine*, into all the Coasts of *Israel*, and I cannot but say of it as they said of that, *Consider it*, . . . if we have not more reason, and juster cause then the *Israelites*, to gather together as one man, from all parts of *Britaine*, and resolve never to returne to our owne houses, till those miscreants (those men of *Belial*) be delivered up to the hand of justice. . . .[20]

A searing flame, a call to arms, the phrase runs through Puritan attacks upon the Royalists. With its compelling Scriptural connotations, the term condemned all the Cavaliers, the conduct of some of whom had made the whole party a stench in righteous nostrils. Especially interesting is *Abingtons And Alisburies Present Miseries. Both which Townes being lately lamentably plundered by Prince Robert and his Cavaliers. Expressly related as it was certified to some of the Honourable the High Court of Parliament* (1644?), which has a vivid account of the pillaging of Abington and Alisbury by those "children of *Belial*," by those "insatiate vultures the Cavaliers," whose cruelty had been abundantly testified to throughout England but was especially visited upon these good towns, "sisters in calamity." The entreaties of the men, the tears and prayers of the women could not restrain these "demi-divells," these "violators of all divine and humane Lawes." They stole money, plate, anything of worth portable; they spoiled and made useless the rest; they cut beds in pieces, hewed the tables, pulled down and burned the very wainscot; the cattle in the stalls and yards they "hough'd" or shot to death; in their beastly and libidinous fury they offered violence to honest matrons and beautiful virgins. Thus were these towns spoiled by these sons

[20] P. 61.

of Belial, these "greedy and insatiate Cavaliers," who are the "very scourges of God for our offences."

Meanwhile, Puritan ministers and pamphleteers assure the faithful that Christ is invincible. *A Vindication of the Late Vow and Covenant* (1643) proclaims this truth:

Israel now, as in old time, is marching towards a Promised Land, the Sea is before, the mountaines on each side, a proud Adversary behinde them, . . . The Sea opens now, the waters cleave in sunder, to give *Israel* passage: the Adversary thinkes they open for him, that he may pursue, over-take, divide the spoyle. . . . Now stand still to behold the Salvation of God, for now in the morning . . . now God is looking-out upon the Host of his Enemies; and He will make them as still as a stone.[21]

In *Englands Pressures: Or, The Peoples Complaint* (1645) George Smith is almost equally emphatic. He declares that now God is about no less work than "to set up Jesus Christ on his Throne, and to pull downe Antichrist from his Stage." But Smith warns his readers that as God has his instruments to build, so "the Devill hath his instruments to breake downe; . . . and to that end, sends forth his Agents into the World, uncleane and evill spirits to seduce men, to make them his instruments, who depart from the faith of Christ, and follow after the doctrines of Devills. . . ."[22]

Frequently Christ and Belial are contrasted. In *Brittish Lightning or Suddaine tumults, In England, Scotland and Ireland* (1643), the Bishops are said to have been supported by the Popish lords, "whence men may easily judge what correspondence the Bishops had with the Papists, who ought by the form of their office to have been so far separated from them, as light and darknesse, Christ and Belial." In *A Divine Project to Save A Kingdome,* a sermon preached before the Lord Mayor and the Court of Aldermen, April 22, 1644, Stephen Marshall declares: "Thus, zeale and an unmortified lust, a known sin chosen to be lived in, though never so secret, can no more dwell together in a heart, then *Christ and Belial, Dagon* and the Arke."[23] In *The Noble Cavalier Caracterised, And a*

[21] P. 12.   [22] P. 20.   [23] P. 40.

Rebellious Caviller Cauterised (1644?), John Taylor mentions the Caviller's liking for rebellion, his loathing of loyalty, his hypocritical religion, and then continues: "All which Villanies are so contrary to a *Cavalier,* that a greater disparity is not be-twixt Light and Darknesse, or between *God* and *Belial.*"[24] In *Anapologesiates Antapologias: Or, The inexcusablenesse of that Grand Accusation of the Brethren, called Antapologia* (1646), John Goodwin protests against the inclusion of all in the Church of God. Those who by the Churches of God understand all the inhabitants of the three kingdoms

good and bad, Sonnes of God, and sonnes of Belial &c. one with another, and sweare unto the most High God with their hands lifted up, that they will endeavour to bring these into the nearest con-junction in Religion and forme of Church-Government; what do they (in effect) but sweare . . . that they will endeavour to bring day and night, light and darknesse, . . . Christ and Belial, into the nearest Communion and conjunction they can? Certainly Wolves and Tigers, Beares and Lions, are as capable of politick and civill conjunction with men; as loose, wicked, ungodly and prophane men are. . . .[25]

In *Children of Beliall, Or, The Rebells* (1647), the author attacks the "Jesuiticall, Schismaticall age" and gives the follow-ing account of Belial: sometimes he is called Demon because of his knowledge, sometimes Satan for his malice, sometimes Beelzebub for his filth, sometimes Diabolus for his accusing men, sometimes Belial for his rebellion. Belial signifies "a Masterlesse Imp, and it is not unworthy your remembrance; That wheresoever people are so called, Children of Belial; dis-obedience and rebellion are the ground of it." And the children of Belial are created not by a natural or virtuous generation but by a vicious and sinful imitation. "As Christ told the Jewes, that they were of their Father the Divell, because they sought to kill him, and belye him, and gives the reason of it, for the Divell is a murtherer from the beginning, and the Father of lies: So here the Prophet *Samuel* calls these men the children of Belial, i.e. of the Divell, because they by his

[24] P. 1.   [25] From the preface.

example and tentation sought to shake and cast off the yoke of obedience. . . ."[26] As is shown by the text, "The children of Belial said, How shall this man save us? and they despised him, and brought him no presents,"[27] this pamphlet is an attack upon Parliament.

It seems probable that such passages as these (and there are many more), rather than Wierus's *Pseudomonarchia Daemonum* and Heywood's *Hierarchie,* form the background of Milton's Belial. Scripture is, of course, the source of the figure. But without the definite meanings repeatedly assigned to *Belial* and the *sons of Belial* by Puritan pamphleteers it seems unlikely that Milton would have created such a character. The lewdness, viciousness, and depravity of Belial in *Paradise Lost* and *Paradise Regained* are in keeping with the tradition. His charming and dignified bearing, his persuasive speech, serving merely as a cloak for insincerity, cowardice, and vice, are other aspects that accord with the Puritan notion of the Cavalier. Belial has been called "a son of Epicurus" with "no lax or tenuous fibre."[28] Milton's description, which is more exact, indicates a moral slothfulness offset by an actively vicious nature. This aspect of the character is vividly illustrated by the excerpts quoted in this study. It is on the Puritan conception of the Cavalier that Belial and his sons are modeled. Of the first readers of *Paradise Lost,* those who had lived through the Civil War and who remembered the old battle cries must have immediately understood Milton's innuendo. Doubtless many Puritans relished the idea that the Cavalier disguised as Belial suffered his proper doom in Hell. The character here studied perfectly illustrates the truth that since Milton is peculiarly the product of his age, the full understanding and enjoyment of his work depend upon a reasonably complete reconstruction of his intellectual environment.

There is in *Paradise Lost* one greater than Belial—Satan, who is even more conspicuous in the pages of contemporary controversy. In the pamphlets Satan is naturally the instigator of

[26] Pp. 3-4. [27] I *Samuel* 10:27.
[28] E. E. Stoll, "Belial as an Example," *Modern Language Notes,* XLVIII, 420.

evil and in particular the father of rebellion. As we have seen, the struggle between Court and Parliament was often conceived as a spiritual war and frequently discussed in Scriptural terms. The emphasis upon the Prince of darkness is therefore to be expected. But it is unlikely that Milton's conception of Satan was much influenced by the Satan of controversy. Rather, it seems probable that the current emphasis upon Satan, added to Milton's disillusionment with government and society, served to confirm his earlier interest in the theme of *Paradise Lost*. Milton's life in the middle period not only developed in him the insight and the power to deal with the theme of the epic but also in a sense provided for him the background of the action. The idea that life is a struggle between the forces of good and evil is, of course, fundamental in religion. In the Civil War this strife was dramatized on a vast scale. On every hand, Satan was portrayed as a rebel against God and his Saints.

Some suggestion of this idea has already been presented. There are many illustrations. In Peter Heylyn's *The Rebells Catechisme* (1643) we read the following:

Question. Who was the first Author of Rebellion?
A. The first Author of Rebellion, the root of all Vices & the mother of all mischiefe, (saith the book of Homilies) was Lucifer, first Gods most excellent Creature, and most bounden Subject, who by Rebelling against the Majesty of God, of the brightest and most glorious Angell, became the blackest and most fowlest fiend and Divell, and from the height of Heaven is fallen into the pit and bottom of Hell.[29]

This passage appears in William Ingoldsby's *The Doctrine of the Church of England, Established by Parliament against Disobedience and wilfull Rebellion* (1642), with this addition:

Here you may see the first authour and founder of rebellion, and the reward thereof. Here you may see the grand Captaine and Father of rebels, who perswading the following of his rebellion against God their Creatour, & Lord, unto our first Parents *Adam* and *Eve*, brought them in high displeasure with God, wrought their exile and banishment out of Paradise, a place of all pleasure and

[29] P. 2.

goodnesse, into this wretched earth and vale of misery: procured
unto them sorrowes of minds, mischeifes, sicknes, diseases, death of
their bodies, and which is farre more horrible, then all worldly and
bodily mischeifes; hee had wrought thereby their eternall and everlasting death and damnation; had not God by the obedience of his
Sonne Jesus Christ repaired that, which man by disobedience and
rebellion had destroyed. . . .[30]

Thus, by associating rebellion with Satan, the Royalist writers
endeavoured to weaken the support of Parliament.

On the other hand, in a sermon before the House of Commons, November 17, 1640, Stephen Marshall encourages Parliament to safeguard religion and reformation. He stresses the
necessity of God's help and the active support of God's cause,
which has few friends and many enemies, and now more than
ever. "*Satan* knowes his time is short, hee stirs up all his instruments, as if one spirit possest them all. And is it not a
shame, that the Lords friends should bee more backward in
his cause than the Vassals of Satan are in their Masters?"[31]   It
is significant that Robert Baillie's sermon to the House of Commons, February 28, 1643, is entitled *Satan The Leader in chief
to all who resist the Reparation of Sion.* In all quarrels about
the building or rebuilding of the church, the principal parties,
Baillie declares, "are Christ and the Devill." Men are but the
inferior agents "to these two Princes." Truth, piety, justice
must inevitably triumph. "For it is utterly impossible, that the
Dragon and his Angels, though for a time and long time, they
maintain the fight, should ever prevail over Michael the Arch-
Angel and his followers." This idea is developed throughout
the sermon. "So the Vision of this Chapter, which began with
great trouble and danger, ends with as great peace and joy.
Satan in the entry, with the assistance of *sinne,* vexing the
Church with all the opposition his strength and craft was able
to make: *Christ* in the end by his passion and spirit defeating
Satan and *sin,* closeth the Churches warfare with a happy
peace."[32] Our adversaries, Baillie warns, are restless in their
contrivings, "like the Sea whose motion is perpetuall, . . . like

[30] P. 2.   [31] P. 43.   [32] P. 9.

Satan their leader who cannot sit still, but goes ever to and fro on the earth, seeking whom he may devour, beginning ever some new plot where an old one ends."[33] Baillie lists the enemies of the church: lawless men, a great part of the people, the greatest part of the nobles, sovereignty itself, "and more terrible then all flesh and blood, we have to do with Principalities and Powers, who act and guide, with all the craft and force they are able, our humane adversaries: . . . Our first and main labour would be with Christ, to restrain Satan, for he is the life that vegetates, he is the spirit that stirres up all opposites both in Church and State."

In *Powers to be Resisted: Or A Dialogue Arguing The Parliaments lawfull Resistance of the Powers now in Armes against them* (1643), resistance is justified on the ground that self-will in the King is nothing else "but the *Manager* of the Divels and his Bishops affaires here on earth." The author goes on to say that formerly the devil cast the saints into prison, and so he does still. "It was not the Divell then in person, nor is it now: The Divell did it then by the managers of his wrath, his evill servants, and so he doth the very same now. . . ."[34] The adversary who persecutes the righteous against all the laws of heaven and earth is the devil, not the King, he is careful to say; but the implication is that the King is merely Satan's agent. The author lists the sins of the King, who with all his resources fights against the Almighty. Ferne, the King's apologist, is "the verie *mouth of Satan, that old Adversarie*"; the royalists are rebels because they are in arms against God; the King has chosen devils to be his priests; he does all in his power "to dethrone the Lord Christ, King of Saints."

In *A Medicine for Malignancy* (1644) occurs the following very interesting analogy. His Majesty as he now stands has brought himself out of his place and rule of judicature, and by his corrupt council has become "an utter oppressor and violator of all laws and relation to his subjects." While he fights for an unlimited prerogative, "his popish and prelaticall

<hr />

[33] P. 13.   [34] P. 6.

Counsels have cousened and robbed him of his regall right
. . . and herein those Satanicall seducers doe by his Majesty,
just as their father the Devill, that old deceiver, did by our
first parents, told them they should be as Gods when they had
eate of the forbidden fruit, while indeed they became slaves
to the Serpent . . . or as that old enemy of mankind did
by our Saviour Christ, carried him up into an exceeding high
mountaine, shewed him all the Kingdomes of the earth, and the
glory thereof; saying, All this will I give thee, if thou wilt
fall downe and worship me, . . . even so our Jesuiticall and
Satanicall instruments perswade the King if he will but taste
the fruit of this illegall prerogative tree, he shall be an absolute
monarch, while indeed he becomes a very slave to them and
their devilish devises."[35] In θεομαχια, *Or, the Grand Im-
prudence of men running the hazard of Fighting Against God*
(1644), John Goodwin refers to that war in heaven in which
Michael and his angels fought against the Dragon and his angels, and comments as follows: "the Devill and his Instruments, ignorant and bloud-thirsty men, *fought*, viz. against
Michael and his Angels, against Christ himselfe in those appointed by him to hold forth the way and Gospel of his Kingdome unto the world."[36]

For the royalists, Edward Symmons, in *A Militarie Sermon, Wherein By the Word of God, the nature and disposition
of a Rebell is discovered, and the Kings true Souldier described
and characterized* (1644), declares that Satan is the father of
all rebels, that the devil was the first rebel and the first seducer
of others to rebellion, that when Satan first tempted our parents
to rebel he charged "most wickedly upon the Lord his Soveraigne, his own conditions of falshood and envy." The rebel
is diligent: he digs up evil; he sows strife; he is active in rebellion. Because of his diligence Satan is called Beelzebub, the
god of flies; he is a great fly and the rebels are his flies, "alwaies seeking out sore places and making them worse, nor are
they ever weary in ill doing."[37]

In John Benbrigge's *Gods Fury, Englands Fire. Or A*

[35] Pp. 46-47.   [36] P. 14.   [37] P. 8.

Plaine Discovery of those Spirituall Incendiaries, which have set Church and State on Fire (1646), we see the following significant contrast, which may remind us of that emphasized by Baxter:

Now, whence is it, that the Devill and wicked men (wee may well joyne them together, for they are never asunder) have such an unquenchable fury against goodnesse and good men? What's the matter that nothing will satisfie them, but the ruine and destruction of them that are godly? Is not this the reason? The antipathy that is in their natures against godlinesse; it is so offensive to them, as they cannot endure to see that man or that woman, wherein it appeares never so little. There is a passage in that book of the *Apochrypha*, called, *The Wisdome of Solomon*, that speakes this, even from the very mouths of wicked men themselves; . . . *Let us lie in wait for the righteous, because hee is not for our turne, and hee is clean contrary to our doings; hee upbraideth us with our offending the Law, and objecteth to our infamy the transgressions of our education. He professeth to have the knowledge of God, and calleth himselfe the child of the Lord: He was made to reprove our thoughts, hee is grievous unto us, even to behold; for his life is not like other mens, his wayes are of another fashion, . . .* Is not this the very language of the Cavaliers, Malignants, Papists, Atheists, and carnall Protestants now amongst us? What is the reason that their hearts are set so much against the Parliament, and its friends? Is it not because there is an antipathy in their natures against godlinesse, and the power of it, which that Honourable Court would set up and settle in this Land?[38]

Of those who call sin a trifling matter Benbrigge inquires: "Is it a light matter to affront God to his face? Is it a small one to take his Crowne from his head? Is it a slight thing to set him by, and set thy selfe in his throne? To lay his honour in the dust?" He demands a complete reformation; he pleads for faith. "Our God, is the God Almighty, and can doe more then all the Angels and Saints in heaven, then all the men on earth, and Devills in hell can think."

In *The Burden of England, Scotland, & Ireland: Or, The Watchmans Alarum* (1646), the King and Episcopacy are

[38] P. 40.

joined with Antichrist's kingdom, the damnation of which slumbereth not. The King has been taken "in their pit," and he has been made the head of their army "to war against the Saints." To readers of *Paradise Lost* the following excerpt from this partisan pamphlet should be of interest:

God the Creator of all things, the supreme Lord of heaven and earth, having shewed the severity of his justice on the Angells that 2 *Pet.* 2.4. sinned, whom he spared not at all, but cast them downe to hell, and delivered them into Chaines of darknesse, to be reserved unto the judgement of the great day (in regard they willingly rebelled against him without any others solicitations, and repented not of their wickednesse, . . .) yet in the meane space they have loosenesse and liberty to range abroad in the world, and to goe about seeking whom they I *Pet.* 5.8 may devoure; which liberty, God permitted unto them, to tempt and try our first parents, thereby to declare his justice and mercy, and Satan's malice and cruelty. . . .

In the orthodox fashion, the author goes on to tell of the punishment of man and serpent and of the open war between God's people and the world, the flesh, and the devil. Finally, he points the familiar contrast:

The godly are made light, the wicked *Ephes.* 5.8. are darknesse. Christ dwells in the 2 *Cor.* 13.5. one. Satan *Eph.* 2.3. in the other. The one are made righteous by faith, yea the righteousnesse of 2 *Cor.* 5. 21. God in Christ. The other are unrighteous, yea full of unrighteousnesse, *Rom.* 1. 29. The one are the sonnes of God, *Io.* 1.12. the other children of the Devill, *Joh.* 8. 44. Hence followeth St. Pauls sequell, 2 *Cor.* 6. 14. 15. &c. Be not ye unequally yoked with unbeleevers in friendship, *viz.* nor in marriage, for what fellowship hath righteousnesse with unrighteousnesse? and what communion hath light with darknesse? and what concord hath Christ with Beliall?[39]

This contrast and the emphasis upon Satan as the cause of religious and political strife are met on every hand. In *Englands Remembrancer of Londons Integrity, Or Newes from London* (1647), the Devil is said to be very active and formi-

[39] P. 65.

dable. "Now as the Devil that grand adversary to mans true peace and happinesse never roared more fiercely, nor walked about more furiously, nor sought more cunningly to devour then he doth at this present day; therefore there was never greater cause that this exhortation should be pressed, . . . Be sober, be vigilant: neither was it ever more reasonable to desire the people of God to resist the Devil, . . . then in this backsliding age, wherein the Devil rageth exceedingly. . . ."[40] With this opinion Ethog Grimes, in *England and Scotland United, Disjoyned* (1648), agrees, declaring that the first cause of all these distempers "is the Devil, he suggests evil surmises, suspitions, and jealousies, leads men into errors, and propounds false ends in designs, . . . the Scriptures term him to be an *Adversary, a Tempter,* and a *Murtherer,* . . . the *Old Serpent,* the *Red Dragon,* . . . *The god of this World,* . . . *The spirit that now worketh in the children of disobedience.* . . ."[41] Other examples of this faith might be cited. In fact, among the Puritans, the conviction that Satan was their real foe and the leader of the royalists seems to have been nearly universal.

For some, Satan may have been merely a theological abstraction. For many he was in reality Sir Thomas Browne's "first contriver of Error, and professed opposer of Truth." A popular view of his Satanic Majesty and his associates is illustrated in an incident related by John Vicars in *The Looking-Glasse For Malignants* (1645). About March 10, 1644, some fifteen of "Gorings godlesse Souldiers" were gathered in the "Kathern Wheele," an inn in Salisbury, drinking and carousing, wickedly and profanely blaspheming, drinking healths to the King, the Queen, and the "Prince-Robber." In the height of their "gracelesse guzling" some began to swear that they would drink a health to the Devil if any would pledge. One started up and said that he would not pledge such an oath, for he did not know whether there was God or Devil; but if there were a Devil and he might see him, he would pledge the health. Immediately there was a fearsome, filthy stench, as of brimstone, and a most horrid, ugly monster appeared. All

[40] Pp. 9-10.   [41] P. 17.

rushed out except the man who had spoken so atheistically. When his companions returned, they found the window broken, with stains of blood upon it. The wretch was gone.

In the pamphlets, Satan seldom appears in this grotesque fashion. The tracts represent him less picturesquely. But he and Belial, and the sons of Belial, were names to be reckoned with. They embodied incalculable spiritual forces against which the Puritans perforce girded themselves for battle. As pamphleteer, Milton enlisted in this war, the spiritual forces of which he intimately realized. There is, of course, abundant proof that Milton was conversant with contemporary controversy. He was not, to be sure, solely interested in the religious phase. As he says in the *Second Defence,* he strove also for the restoration of culture and freedom. However, with his profound religious nature Milton could not have been unimpressed by the ideas and terms presented in this study. Here, then, it seems, is part of the background of *Paradise Lost.* Here is one source that has been ignored. It is not strictly a source of detail but rather an indication of the religious setting from which the epic evolved. Here are disclosed the spiritual foes of the Puritans. Here are the unclean spirits that for a space were driven out—and then, at the Restoration, returned, bringing with them seven other spirits more wicked than themselves, so that Milton implored his Muse:

> But drive farr off the barbarous dissonance
> Of *Bacchus* and his Revellers, the Race
> Of that Wilde Rout that tore the *Thracian* Bard
> In *Rhodope,* where Woods and Rocks had Eares
> To rapture, till the savage clamor dround
> Both Harp and Voice.

Such was Milton's mood when in evil days he turned to the composition of his masterpiece. In the inspiring though troubled period of the Civil War, when Milton enjoyed or anticipated the realization of some of his ideals, his conviction was probably that expressed by Alexander Henderson in the conclusion of *A Sermon Preached Before The Honourable House of Lords,* May 28, 1645:

I would upon this ground, give you some comfort for the Cause,
. . . That Christ is our King, and will one way or other van-
quish and subdue all our enemies. . . . His is the power in heaven
and earth, over Angels, over Devils, over Armies of men, and over
all Creatures: . . . The penitent Malefactor on the Crosse, cried out,
Lord remember me when thou commest into thy Kingdom; we
may rather with greater confidence say, Lord remember us, when
now after victory over Satan, the World, and Death, thou dost
possesse thy Kingdome.[42]

Doubtless he shared the opinion of William Sedgwick in *A
second view of the Army Remonstrance* (1649):

The Lord is with you in spirit and truth, eternally, inseparably, in
a *kingdome that never shall be destroyed:* in an *everlasting covenant that cannot be broken.* The kingdome is so with you the
Lords people, as it shall *never be taken from you,* but shall endure
for ever, and all oppressing feares or dark doubts, they are of the
malicious one, your enemy, and the darknesse of hell that *obscures
the glory of God,* which is an everlasting light, a Sun that will not
set: and all attempts of Satan and his instruments, will be as waves
against a rock dash'd in pieces, . . . Tis your *salvation* that is
come, you *shall see evill no more;* let all the world know it, let
the news of it fill the dark and troubled earth, *proclaim* it openly,
he gives you a *reward* of all your paines and sufferings, he brings
all good with him; . . . Tis now cleare what he will doe, *reigne*
over the nations in righteousnesse; set up an *everlasting Kingdome*
for the Saints that shall never be destroyed. . . . God hath *sought
you* out wandring in a wildernesse, and not knowing whither to
goe; . . . though for a *little moment* he left you, *with everlasting
kindnesse hath he gathered you,* and will not forsake you any
more.[43]

Here is the faith that brought assurance of victory. When
it failed of realization, Milton by depicting in *Paradise Lost* the
loss of individual virtue probably sought to show the reason
of that tragic failure to achieve political and religious liberty
and to indicate for the individual the only possible path of
escape. That the relationship here suggested between the epic
and the preceding civic and political background is not a fan-

---

[42] Pp. 30-31.   [43] Pp. 17-34.

cied one is confirmed not only by Milton's vital interest in the issues of that period but also by his use of certain characters as well as by distinct reminiscences of the immediate past. In short, it is important to remember that for Milton the poet as for the Puritan controversialists the War had been a struggle between virtue and vice, and that, in the words of Daniel Tuvil, "There can bee no true fellowship betweene Light and Darknes, between *Christ* and *Belial*, Saint *Michael* and the *Serpent*."[44] Milton being what he was, the Civil War and its controversies not only deferred but also determined the writing of *Paradise Lost*.

[44] *Essaies Politicke, and Morall* (London, 1608), fol. 94.

CHAPTER VII

COMUS AND *ENCOMIUM MORIAE*

QUOTING from *Comus* the lines

> O foolishnes of men! that lend their ears
> To those budge doctors of the *Stoick* Furr,
> And fetch their precepts from the *Cynick* Tub,

and Landor's remark, "It is the first time that Cynic or Stoic ever put on fur," a correspondent in *The Times Literary Supplement*[1] recently remarked that "*Stoick* Furr" suggests the well-known portrait of Erasmus, the very type of "lean and sallow Abstinence," and that in the famous illustrations of *Encomium Moriae* "Milton could have found at least two philosophers in fur." Concluding that Landor seems to have been too hasty, the writer there dropped the subject. By a curious coincidence, I had previously compared *Comus* and *Encomium Moriae*, without having noticed the probable reference to the portrait of Erasmus, which by the way, is reproduced in *The Praise of Folly. Written by Erasmus in 1509 and translated by John Wilson 1668.*[2]

With more or less probability, the plot, the characters, and the ideas of *Comus* have been traced to various sources, particularly to Tasso's *Aminta*, which Mario Praz has recently called "the real model" (*Comus* is termed "a spiritualized *Aminta*"), and to Spenser's *The Faerie Queene*, to which, it has been said, Milton may have been indebted not only for a part of the substance of the Masque but also for the idealism, the purity, and even in a sense for the ability to express his Platonism. Without doubting Milton's use of the sources hitherto explored,

---

[1] May 8, 1937, p. 364.
[2] Ed. Mrs. P. S. Allen (Oxford, 1925). The protrait was painted in May, 1517.

I venture to suggest that for part of the philosophy of Comus, the magician, Milton may have been indebted to Erasmus's *Encomium Moriae*, to which, in a commendation of wit and humor, he refers in his *Sixth Academic Exercise:* "And we are all familiar with that sprightly encomium of Folly composed by an author of no small repute. . . ."[3] That as he matured Milton may have seen in Erasmus's work something more than mere wit is indicated by the following description: "In the 'Praise of Folly' his wit and humour have the fullest play, and the lightness and delicacy of his touch is unequalled: yet all through, his eye is set steadily upon the ills of the world that he wished to see amended."[4] At any rate, it can hardly be denied that the spirit and the argument of Erasmus's goddess—her parentage, her sprightly sophistry, her ridicule of temperance, her attack upon wisdom, her glorification of pleasure, her insistence that those who degenerate nearest unto brutes are happiest—resemble that of Milton's sly enchanter.

Recall the parentage of Folly. Her father was Plutus—not the old and withered Plutus of Aristophanes, but "such as he was in his full strength and pride of youth; and not that onely, but at such a time when he had been well heated with Nectar, of which he had, at one of the Banquets of the Gods, taken a dose extraordinary."[5] Her mother was a nymph. Her birthplace was the Fortunate Isles, where all things grow without toil of husbandry and where there are such fragrant flowers as perfume the Gardens of Adonis. In his "blithe youth" Bacchus, who first from the purple grape "Crusht the sweet poyson of mis-used Wine," was the father of Comus. His mother was the nymph Circe, and his birthplace her island, where potent herbs and baleful drugs grew untended. Folly "was suckled by two jolly Nymphs, to wit, Drunkenness, the daughter of Bacchus, and Ignorance, of Pan."

As Comus is the leader of an antimasque, a rout of monsters who roll with pleasure in a sensual sty, so Folly has a

[3] *Milton Private Correspondence and Academic Exercises,* ed. Tillyard (Cambridge, 1932), p. 91.
[4] P. S. Allen, *Erasmus Lectures and Wayfaring Sketches* (Oxford, 1934), p. 75.   [5] *Op. cit.,* p. 15.

train of attendants or companions—Drunkenness, Ignorance, Self-Love, Flattery, Indolence, Pleasure, Sensuality, Madness, and Intemperance.

Folly, Erasmus declares, is the prime cause of life, than which nothing is more sweet and precious. Without Folly there would be no propagation of mankind. "Nay," exclaims Folly, "even Venus her self, notwithstanding what ever Lucretius has said, would not deny but that all her vertue were lame and fruitless without the help of my Deity." Comus exclaims:

> What hath night to do with sleep?
> Night hath better sweets to prove,
> *Venus* now wakes, and wak'ns Love. (ll. 122-124)

Comus urges the Lady not to be "cosen'd With that same vaunted name Virginity," and declares that nature's coin must not be hoarded but used. Both Folly and Comus hold that youth is the time of pleasure. From Folly comes all the grace of Youth, which in manhood decays; then its briskness fails, its pleasantness grows flat, its beauty fades. Then comes Old Age, hateful not only to others but also to itself. Comus admonishes the Lady:

> If you let slip time, like a neglected rose
> It withers on the stalk with languish't head.

Folly preserves youth:

it is on all sides confessed, that Folly is the best preservative of youth, and the most effectual antidote against age. . . . Well, let fond mortals go now in a needless quest of some Medea, Circe, Venus, or some enchanted fountain, for a restorative of age, whereas the accurate performance of this feat lies only within the ability of my art and skill.

Folly insists:

It is I only who have the receipt of making that liquor wherewith Memnon's daughter lengthened out her grandfather's declining days: it is I that am that Venus, who so far restored the languishing Phaon, as to make Sappho fall deeply in love with his beauty.

Mine are those herbs, mine those charms, that not only lure back swift time, when past and gone, but what is more to be admired, clip its wings, and prevent all farther flight.[6]

One is reminded of Comus's "cordial Julep . . . That flames, and dances in his crystal bounds," one sip of which

> Will bathe the drooping spirits with delight
> Beyond the bliss of dreams.

Comus indorses Folly's doctrine that pleasure is the end of life. Folly inquires, "Can that be call'd life where ye take away pleasure?" Life, she declares, is crabbed, unpleasant, insipid, troublesome, and sad if it be not seasoned with pleasure. Even the Stoics, who severely cried down pleasure and railed against it to the common people, did but dissemble to the end that they might the more amply enjoy themselves. "The next place to the gods," says Folly, "is challenged by the Stoics; but give me one as stoical as ill-nature can make him, and if I do not prevail on him to part with his beard, that bush of wisdom (though no other ornament than what nature in more ample measure has given to goats), yet at least he shall lay by his gravity, smooth up his brow, relinquish his rigid tenets, and in despite of prejudice become sensible of some passion in wanton sport and dallying."[7] Folly insists that the stoical disdain of passion is unnatural, that without passion man is not human:

the Stoics look upon passions no other than as the infection and malady of the soul that disorders the constitution of the whole man, and by putting the spirits into a feverish ferment many times occasion some mortal distemper . . . the stoical Seneca . . . pretends that the only emblem of wisdom is the man without passion; whereas the supposing any person to be so, is perfectly to unman him, or else transform him into some fabulous deity that never was, nor ever will be; nay, to speak more plain, it is but the making him a mere statue. . . .[8]

---

[6] Desiderius Erasmus, *In Praise of Folly.* With Illustrations after Hans Holbein (New York, n.d.), pp. 22-23.

[7] *Ibid.,* p. 13.   [8] *Ibid.,* pp. 56-57.

Much of Comus's "deer Wit, and gay Rhetorick," marshaled against the stoical way of life and pointed against virginity, is an invitation to give free rein to passion. For example:

> Why should you be so cruel to your self,
> And to those dainty limms which nature lent
> For gentle usage, and soft delicacy?

As a matter of course, Folly ridicules wisdom and sobriety. At a feast a formal wise man is a bore: by his "morose silence" he puts the whole table out of humor or by his frivolous questions he tires out all who sit near him. At a dance "he shall move no more nimbly than a camel." At any public performance his very looks "damp the mirth of all spectators." In short, wise men are fools. Folly holds that Gryllus is to be adjudged "wiser than the much-counselling Ulysses, in as much as when by the enchantment of Circe he had been turned into a hog, he would not lay down his swinishness, nor forsake his beloved sty, to run the peril of a hazardous voyage." Discard wisdom, Folly insists, and follow me. This is the philosophy of Comus, who scorns "Strict Age, and sowre Severity" and makes pleasure his occupation. The contrast between wisdom and folly is made explicit in the following excerpt. Is the honor of the name prudence due

To the Wiseman, who partly out of modesty and partly distrust of himself, attempts nothing; or to the Fool, whom neither Modesty which he never had, nor Danger which he never considers, can discourage from anything? The Wiseman has recourse to the Books of the Antients, and from thence picks nothing but subtilties of words. The Fool, in undertaking and venturing on the business of the world, gathers, if I mistake not, the true Prudence, . . . For there are two main obstacles to the knowledge of things, Modesty that casts a mist before the understanding, and Fear that, having fanci'd a danger, disswades us from the attempt. But from these Folly sufficiently frees us, and few there are that rightly understand of what great advantage it is to blush at nothing and attempt every thing.[9]

[9] *The Praise of Folly*, ed. Mrs. P. S. Allen, p. 51.

In *Comus* the Lady, guided by her native innocence and virgin purity, restrained by modesty and fear, spurns the temptation of Comus, who pleads that experience is the source of pleasure and wisdom and who ridicules her objections as mere moral babble.

> List Lady be not coy, and be not cosen'd
> With that same vaunted name Virginity.

As the advocate of lust, Comus contrives to clothe folly in the specious garments of truth. Here, consciously or unconsciously, Milton followed in the steps of Erasmus.

Inevitably Folly attacks philosophers, as in the following:

And next these [lawyers] come our Philosophers, so much reverenc'd for their Fur'd Gowns and Starcht Beards, that they look upon themselves as the onely Wise Men, and all others as Shadows.[10]

In the Latin it runs thus:

Sub hos prodeunt Philosophi, barba pallioque verendi, qui se solos sapere praedicant, reliquos omnes mortales, umbras volitare.[11]

It is obvious that the phrase "Fur'd Gowns and Starcht Beards" resembles Milton's line,

> To those budge doctors of the *Stoick* Furr,

and it should be repeated that in Holbein's two illustrations of the Philosopher the starched beard and furred gown are conspicuous. Wise men, Folly insists, are neglected, unknown, and hated; they have little to do except with poverty, hunger, and chimney-corners. But folly abounds in wealth, commands the state, and flourishes in every way. Whoever intends to "live merry and frolique" must shut his door against wise men. As Horace says, 'tis a pleasant thing to play the fool in season. According to Comus, the Lady's wisdom, which exposes his sophistry, is mere moral babble, directly "Against the canon laws of our foundation." His last words are, "Be wise, and taste." Then the Brothers rush in.

[10] *Ibid.*, p. 112.
[11] *Moriae Enkomion* (Londini, 1777), p. 104.

Observe also in *Encomium Moriae* the Platonic contrast between those who are intent upon eternal things and those who are wholly taken up with the pleasures of this world. Christians and Platonists agree in this, "that the Soul is plung'd and fetter'd in the prison of the body, by the grossenesse of which it is so ty'd up and hinder'd, that it cannot take a view of or enjoy things as they really are. . . ." The common sort "chiefly admire those things that are most corporeal, and almost believe there is nothing beyond 'em." But the devout neglect the body and "are wholly hurry'd away with the contemplation of things invisible." The common sort give first place to riches and to corporal pleasures, "leaving the last place to their soul." The devout rely upon God and the things that come nearest to Him, neglecting the body or meddling with it much against their will. Of the affections of the mind "some have greater commerce with the body than others, as lust, desire of meat and sleep, anger, pride, envy; with which holy men are at irreconcilable enmity, and contrary, the common people think there's no living without 'em." The devout fast "that the Spirit, being less clog'd with its bodily weight, may be the more intent upon heavenly things." The holy man shuns those things "that have any alliance with the body, and is wholly ravisht with things Eternal, Invisible, and Spiritual." In the end, the spirit, as "conqueror and more durable," shall swallow the body, and the good man "shall participate of somewhat ineffable from that chiefest good that draws all things into its self."

And this happiness though 'tis only then perfected when souls being joyn'd to their former bodies shall be made immortal, yet forasmuch as the life of holy men is nothing but a continu'd meditation and, as it were, shadow of that life, it so happens that at length they have some taste or relish of it; which, though it be but as the smallest drop in comparison of that fountain of eternal happiness, yet it far surpasses all worldly delight, though all the pleasures of all mankind were all joyn'd together. So much better are things spiritual than things corporal, and things invisible than things visible; which doubtless is that which the Prophet promiseth: "The eye hath not seen, nor the ear heard, nor has it entred into the heart of man to consider what God has provided for them that love Him."[12]

It is, I think, not improbable that these ideas in *Encomium Moriae* are part of the literary background of the following passage in *Comus*:

> So dear to Heav'n is Saintly chastity,
> That when a soul is found sincerely so,
> A thousand liveried Angels lacky her,
> Driving far off each thing of sin and guilt,
> And in cleer dream, and solemn vision
> Tell her of things that no gross ear can hear,
> Till oft convers with heav'nly habitants
> Begin to cast a beam on th' outward shape,
> The unpolluted temple of the mind,
> And turns it by degrees to the souls essence,
> Till all be made immortal. . . . (ll. 453-463)

But Plato's *Phaedo* is Milton's main source, as it is that of Erasmus.

Folly exclaims, "I run beyond my bounds"; as the Greek proverb has it, "Sometimes a fool may speak a word in season." Resuming her true character, she bids adieu: "Wherefore farewell, clap your hands, live, and drink lustick, my most excellent Disciples of Folly." It is the doctrine of Comus, "this Jugler," who is a somewhat more plausible advocate of sensual pleasure than is Erasmus's sprightly Goddess. Between the two there are, of course, striking differences. Folly is both frank and ironical; Comus is both deceitful and direct. Folly's satire is universal; Comus's sophistry is the servant of his lust. Folly is in fact the friend of virtue; Comus is the foe of chastity. They are, however, in their specious arguments intimately related. And there is one other point that should be mentioned: the lucidity and grace of Erasmus's style, by which Milton was doubtless impressed.

[12] *Op. cit.*, ed. Allen, pp. 185-186.

Erasmus has many claims to fame. Not the least of these, I would suggest, is that his *Encomium Moriae*, "the wittiest and most ironic praise of the passions ever spoken," subserves in Milton's beautiful masque the cause of virtue, the triumph of reason over passion.

CHAPTER VIII

THE HISTORY OF SAMSON

WE HAVE seen that *Paradise Lost*, despite its conventional plot, reflects Milton's interest in the complex issues of the seventeenth century and his knowledge of a varied literary background. So in a more limited way, as befits its smaller scale and purpose, *Samson Agonistes* is probably related to the literary milieu. In 1631, before Milton had left Cambridge University, appeared Francis Quarles's *The Historie of Samson*, an elaborate versification of that "illustrious, and renowned story" in twenty-three sections or scenes, with each section followed by a meditation of almost equal length. It is a somewhat realistic version, which Quarles justifies by the precedent of Solomon's describing a harlot like a harlot: "If my descriptions in the like kinds, offend: I make no question but the validitie of my Warrant will give a reasonable satisfaction. . . ." Insisting that no offense was intended, he adds: "I write to *Bees,* and not to *Spiders:* They will suck pleasing hony from such flowers: These may burst with their owne poyson: But you, whose well-seasoned hearts are not distempered with either of these extremeties, but have the better relish of a Sacred understanding; draw neere, and reade."[1] The evidence presented in this chapter may show that Milton not only accepted Quarles's invitation but also recalled Quarles's *Historie* when, near the end of his life, he wrote *Samson Agonistes.*

It is well known that the subject of Samson had long been present in Milton's mind. It is one of the subjects listed in the Cambridge Manuscript. Besides, in *The Reason of Church-*

---

[1] *The Complete Works in Prose and Verse of Francis Quarles,* ed. A. B. Grosart (1880), II, 136.

Government Milton mentioned "Dramatick constitutions, wherein *Sophocles* and *Euripides* raigne" as one of the forms for poems on which his mind had dwelt.[2] It has been assumed that in the passage just referred to Milton announced a definite program that was to be realized in *Paradise Lost, Paradise Regained*, and *Samson Agonistes*.[3] But it has been argued that such a theory, which ignores the other forms to which Milton refers, does not make due allowance for the evolution of Milton's plans,[4] and that the literary program announced in *The Reason of Church-Government* is part of an anti-Episcopal tract from which it is impossible to infer that Milton "had any of his later compositions in mind."[5] It is, of course, possible that the subject of *Samson Agonistes* was implied. It must also be remembered that in *The Reason of Church-Government* the story of Samson occurs as a political allegory.[6]

These facts and observations, justly interpreted, indicate not that Milton in the 1640's was greatly interested in Samson but that the subject of *Samson Agonistes* had probably long been pondered before the tragedy was written. Not improbably there had been a long period of intermittent incubation, during which Milton read material related to the subject under consideration. Doubtless it is correct to say that for his subject matter Milton relied chiefly upon Scripture.[7] And, of course, classical tragedy was the dominant formative influence. It is impossible, however, to agree with the pronouncement: "There is no convincing evidence that he [Milton] was acquainted with other literary treatments of the theme."[8] Today no one holds a brief for Vondel's *Samson*. Long ago, Verity cleverly exposed Edmundson's absurd claims that Milton was

[2] *The Works of John Milton* (New York, 1931), III, 237.
[3] "*Samson Agonistes* and Milton in Old Age," *Studies in Shakespeare, Milton and Donne* (New York, 1925), p. 168.
[4] E. M. W. Tillyard, *Milton* (New York, 1930), p. 330.
[5] W. R. Parker, "On Milton's Early Literary Program," *Modern Philology*, XXXIII, 52.
[6] E. M. Clark, "Milton's Earlier Samson," *Studies in English*, Number 5, University of Texas Bulletin, 1925, p. 153.
[7] *Milton's Samson Agonistes*, ed. A. W. Verity (Cambridge, 1912), p. xxvii; J. H. Hanford, *A Milton Handbook* (New York, 1938), p. 251.
[8] Hanford, *op. cit.*, p. 251.

greatly indebted to the Dutch play.[9] But Quarles's *The Historie of Samson* cannot be so easily dismissed. Despite the positive assertions that "A plagiarism-quester of the nicest scent would find it hard to show that *Samson Agonistes* owed aught to Quarles' work" and that in *The Historie* "there are no specific parallels with Milton," the facts to be presented seem to indicate that Milton was slightly indebted to his predecessor.

In the first place, it is altogether probable that Milton knew Quarles's *Historie*. Fundamental and pervasive as is Milton's classical culture, his religious character, as every serious student of his life and work is aware, is even more profound. It has recently been shown how completely in one respect Milton was in accord with the tradition of divine as opposed to secular literature.[10] We may assume, therefore, that he read such religious poems as fell into his hands, and among them *The Historie of Samson*. In fact, the burden of proof is on him who would maintain that Milton had not read this poem, which celebrates the life of a character in whom he was deeply interested. In the second place, realizing the different forms of the *Historie* and of *Samson Agonistes* and also being well aware of Milton's eclectic habits, we shall not expect obvious similarities or downright borrowing. We shall look for subtle analogies. We may find some ideas and situations of the *Historie* repeated in *Samson Agonistes*, where, in spite of having undergone a change, they are still recognizable.

The first example is an illustration of a slight verbal parallelism in similar contexts.

> They led him pris'ner, and convai'd him downe
> To strong-wall'd *Azza* (that *Philistian* towne,
> Whose gates his shoulders lately bore away)
> There, in the common Prison, did they lay,
> Distressed *Samson*, who obtain'd no meate,
> But what he purchas'd with his painfull sweate;

[9] *Op. cit.*, pp. 162-168. See George Edmundson, *Milton and Vondel* (London, 1885), pp. 156-192.
[10] Lily B. Campbell, "The Christian Muse," *The Huntington Library Bulletin*, Number 8, pp. 29-70.

For, every day, they urg'd him to fulfill
His twelve howres taske, at the laborious *Mill*.[11]

There I am wont to sit, when any chance
Relieves me from my task of servile toyl,
Daily in the common Prison else enjoyn'd me,
Where I a Prisoner chain'd, scarce freely draw
The air imprison'd also, close and damp.[12]

The passage in the *Historie* illustrates the emphasis upon detail and the blend of realism and solemnity which perhaps foreshadow Milton's treatment; however, in realistic detail Milton is much more severely selective than Quarles. The tone of *Samson Agonistes*, in keeping with the Greek tradition, is serious. It has been said that Milton altered Samson's nature to suit this tone: "the prankish, rather fantastical fellow of the Biblical story never once puts in his appearance."[13] But it should be noted that in Quarles's *Historie* the character of Samson is never intentionally comic. In both passages occurs the phrase "the common Prison," which is not Biblical.

Compare also the following passages, which contrast the present misery of the enslaved Samson with the glorious achievements of his past.

How is our story chang'd?   O, more then strange
Effects of so small time!   O, sudden change!
Is this that holy Nazarite, for whom
Heaven shew'd a Miracle, on the barren wombe?
Is this that holy Thing, againe whose birth,
Angells must quit their thrones, and visit Earth?
Is this that blessed Infant, that began
To grow in favour so, with God and Man?
What, is this hee, who (strengthned by heaven's hand)
Was borne a Champion, to redeeme the Land?
Is this the man, whose courage did contest
With a fierce Lyon, grappling brest to brest;
And in a twinckling, tore him quite in sunder?
Is this that Conquerer whose Arme did thunder

---

[11] Quarles, *op. cit.*, p. 166.   [12] Milton, *op. cit.*, ll. 4-8.
[13] W. R. Parker, "The Greek Spirit in Milton's *Samson Agonistes*," *Essays and Studies* (Oxford, 1935), pp. 26-27.

Upon the men of Askalon? the power
Of whose bent fist, slew thirty in an hower?
Is this that daring Conquerour, whose hand
Thrasht the proud Philistines, in their wasted land?
And was this He, that with the help of none
Destroy'd a thousand with a silly Bone? . . .
Is this the man whose hands unhing'd those Gates,
And bare them thence, with pillers, barres, and Grates?
And is he turn'd a Mill-horse now? and blinde?
Must this great Conquerour be forc'd to grinde
For bread and water?   Must this Heroe spend
His latter times in drudgery?   Must he end
His weary dayes in darknesse?[14]

Chor.   This, this is he; softly a while
Let us not break in upon him;
O change beyond report, thought, or belief!
See how he lies at random, carelessly diffus'd,
With languish't head unpropt,
As one past hope, abandon'd
And by himself given over;
In slavish habit, ill-fitted weeds
O're worn and soild;
Or do my eyes misrepresent?   Can this be hee,
That Heroic, that Renown'd,
Irresistible *Samson?* who unarm'd
No strength of man, or fiercest wild beast could withstand;
Who tore the Lion, as the Lion tears the Kid,
Ran on embattelld Armies clad in Iron,
And weaponless himself,
Made Arms ridiculous, useless the forgery
Of brazen shield and spear, the hammer'd Cuirass,
Chalybean temper'd steel, and frock of mail
Adamantean Proof;
But safest he who stood aloof,
When insupportably his foot advanc't,
In scorn of their proud arms and warlike tools,
Spurn'd them to death by Troops.   The bold *Ascalonite*
Fled from his Lion ramp, old Warriors turn'd

[14] Quarles, *op. cit.*, p. 166.

Thir plated backs under his heel;
Or grovling soild thir crested helmets in the dust.
Then with what trivial weapon came to hand,
The Jaw of a dead Ass, his sword of bone,
A thousand fore-skins fell, the flower of *Palestin*
In *Ramath-lechi* famous to this day:
Then by main force pull'd up, and on his shoulders bore
The Gates of *Azza*, Post, and massie Bar
Up to the Hill of *Hebron*, seat of Giants old,
No journey of a Sabbath day, and loaded so;
Like whom the Gentiles feign to bear up Heav'n.
Which shall I first bewail,
Thy Bondage or lost Sight,
Prison within Prison
Inseparably dark?
Thou art become (O worst imprisonment!)
The Dungeon of thy self. . . .[15]

In method as well as substance the passage from the *Historie* strikingly resembles the Chorus in *Samson Agonistes*. To explain the similarity it may be said that the Chorus of the Danites at its first entrance would inevitably contrast the enslaved and wretched Samson with the free and splendid hero whom they had known. This is true; and yet it must be admitted that in this matter Quarles had clearly anticipated Milton. Perhaps Quarles's insistence upon the lamentable change in Samson's condition is reflected in Milton's line

O change beyond report, thought, or belief!

This is but typical of the similarity that pervades both passages. Although the likeness may be merely the result of independent handling of the same Biblical material, it is useless to deny the presence of a rather startling parallelism of thought—a parallelism that is disguised by the great contrast in style.

Quarles writes concerning the preparations of the Philistines for Samson's marriage to the woman of Timnath:

[15] Milton, *op. cit.*, ll. 115-156.

But now, the crafty *Philistins*, for feare
Lest *Samson's* strength, (which startled every eare
With dread and wonder) under that pretence,
Should gaine the meanes, to offer violence;
And, through the show of nuptiall devotion,
Should take advantages to breed commotion,
Or lest his popular power, by coaction
Or faire entreats, may gather to his faction
Some loose and discontented men of theirs,
And so betray them to suspected feares;
They therefore to prevent ensuing harmes,
Gave strict command, that thirty men of armes,
Under the maske of *Bridemen*, should attend
Untill the nuptiall ceremonies end.[16]

In *Samson Agonistes*, Samson speaks:

Among the Daughters of the *Philistines*
I chose a Wife, which argu'd me no foe;
And in your City held my Nuptial feast:
But your ill-meaning Politician Lords,
Under pretence of Bridal friends and guests,
Appointed to await me thirty spies.[17]

In *Judges* we read, "And it came to pass, when they saw him, that they brought thirty companions to be with him."[18] Compare with this the phrasing in Quarles and Milton: "*crafty Philistins*" and "ill-meaning Politician Lords"; "thirty men of armes Under the maske of *Bridemen*" and "under pretence of Bridal friends and guests, . . . thirty spies." The resemblance is indeed striking.

When Samson retired to the rock Etam, he had, according to the Bible, no definite purpose. Both Quarles and Milton declare that his object was to destroy the Philistines. In the *Historie* Samson speaks:

Brethren; the intention of my coming hither
Was not to wrong you, or deprive you, either
Of lives, or goods, or of your poorest due;
. . . .

[16] *Op. cit.*, p. 147.   [17] Ll. 1192-1197.   [18] 14: 11.

My comming is on a more faire designe,
I come to crush your tyrannous foes, and mine,
I come to free your country, and recall
Your servile shoulders from the slavish thrall
Of the proud Philistines; and, with this hand,
To make you freemen in your promis'd Land.[19]

In *Samson Agonistes* Samson speaks more briefly:

Thir Lords the *Philistines* with gather'd powers
Enterd *Judea* seeking mee, who then
Safe to the rock of *Etham* was retir'd,
Not flying, but fore-casting in what place
To set upon them, what advantag'd best.[20]

To both poets the idea of attributing the same motive for Samson's withdrawal may have occurred independently. But here again Quarles anticipated Milton.

It should also be noticed that as Milton's Samson blames the governors of Israel for their servility and their indifference to his deeds, so Quarles condemns them for their "slavish thoughts," their "servile resolution," their cowardly betrayal of Samson, who was divinely appointed to set them free.

Unkinde *Iudeans,* what have you presented
Before our eyes?   O, what have you attented!
He that was borne on purpose, to release
His life, for yours; to bring your Nation peace;
To turne your mournings into joyfull Songs;
To fight your Battells; To revenge your wrongs;
Even him, alas, your cursed hands have made
This day your prisoner; Him have you betraid
To death.[21]

In *Samson Agonistes* Samson replies as follows to the Chorus's statement that "*Israel* still serves with all his Sons":

That fault I take not on me, but transfer
On *Israel's* Governours, and Heads of Tribes,
Who seeing those great acts which God had done

[19] Quarles, *op. cit.*, p. 158.
[20] Ll. 251-255.   [21] Quarles, *op. cit.*, pp. 158-159.

Singly by me against their Conquerours
Acknowledg'd not, or not at all consider'd
Deliverance offerd: I on th' other side
Us'd no ambition to commend my deeds,
The deeds themselves, though mute, spoke loud the dooer;
But they persisted deaf, and would not seem
To count them things worth notice. . . .[22]

The idea that by surrendering Samson to the Philistines the
Israelites betrayed not only their champion but also their national interests is, of course, implicit in the Biblical narrative.
To introduce into the poems this thought and the others recorded here required no special inspiration. The point is
simply this, that much of the added material, which seems
now to be an integral part of the story, is found first in
Quarles's *Historie*.

As a rule, Quarles's Samson is much less the conscious instrument of God than is Milton's hero. For example, the
Samson of the *Historie* is not aware that his marriage to the
woman of Timnath is divinely directed. On the other hand,
in Meditation 9 Quarles writes of the unutterable and profound decrees of the eternal God and declares:

Behold the progresse, and the royall Gests
Of Heaven's high vengeance; how it never rests,
Till, by appointed courses, it fulfill
The secret pleasure of his sacred will.[23]

With true dramatic insight, Milton consistently develops Samson's awareness of his divine mission. For example:

The first I saw at *Timna*, and she pleas'd
Mee, not my Parents, that I sought to wed,
The daughter of an Infidel: they knew not
That what I motion'd was of God; I knew
From intimate impulse, and therefore urg'd
The Marriage on; that by occasion hence
I might begin *Israel's* Deliverance,
The work to which I was divinely call'd.[24]

[22] Ll. 241-250.
[23] *Op. cit.*, pp. 147-148.   [24] Ll. 219-226.

This sense of God's providence, which is baldly stated in the *Historie*, is the essence of the religious and the didactic tone dramatically presented in *Samson Agonistes*. In Milton's tragedy there is, to be sure, some questioning of Providence, "much brooding over the dark mystery of existence." For example, Samson cannot easily bring himself to acquiesce in his terrible punishment,

> Captive, Poor, and Blind
> Into a Dungeon thrust, to work with Slaves.

But in *Samson Agonistes*, as in the *Historie*, the foundation is the orthodox Christian doctrine: recognition of God's omnipotence and justice, and submission to his punishments.

The real cause of Samson's fall was, of course, his infatuation with Delila, which is thus described in the *Historie*:

> Her name was called *Delila*, the faire;
> Thither, did amorous *Samson*, oft, repaire,
> And, with the piercing flame of her bright eye,
> He toy'd so long; that, like a wanton flye,
> He burnt his lustfull wings, and so became
> The slavish prisner to that conquering flame:
> She askt, and had: There's nothing was too high
> For her, to beg; or *Samson*, to denie:
> Who now, but *Delila?* What name can raise
> And crowne his drooping thoughts, but *Delila's?*
> All time 's misspent, each houre is cast away,
> That 's not imploy'd upon his *Delila:*
> Gifts must be given to *Delila:* No cost,
> If sweetest *Delila* but smile, is lost:
> No joy can please; no happinesse can crowne
> His best desires, if *Delila* but frowne:
> No good can blesse his amorous heart, but this,
> Hee's *Delila's;* and *Delila* is his.[25]

In the following Meditation Quarles condemns Samson's lust, declares that if he had not abused his borrowed power he had still been conqueror, and insists that his punishment, however

[25] P. 162.

dreadful, was just. So Samson interrupts the deadly swarm
of restless thoughts to reflect:

> Yet stay, let me not rashly call in doubt
> Divine Prediction; what if all foretold
> Had been fulfilld but through mine own default,
> Whom have I to complain of but my self?
> Who this high gift of strength committed to me,
> In what part lodg'd, how easily bereft me,
> Under the Seal of silence could not keep,
> But weakly to a woman must reveal it
> O'recome with importunity and tears.[26]

In spite of the bad verse in the *Historie,* Milton probably read
with approval Quarles's emphasis upon Samson's infatuation.

The *Historie* recounts in detail Delila's maneuvers to win
from Samson the secret of his great strength. Caressing Samson, Delila speaks:

> But say, my love, is it some hidden charme,
> Or does thy stocke of youth enrich thy arme
> With power so great, that can overthrow,
> And conquer mighty Kingdomes, at a blow?
> What cause have I to joy! I need not feare
> The greatest danger, now my Samson's here:
> I feare no Rebbels now; me thinks, thy power
> Makes me a Princesse; and my house, a Tower.[27]

Quarles describes Delila's ill-concealed vexation after each of
her three unsuccessful attempts. Then she makes her fourth
plea, a long one ending:

> How canst thou say thou lov'st me? How can I
> Thinke but thou hat'st me, when thy lips deny
> So poore a Suite? Alas, my fond desire
> Had slak'd, had not deniall blowne the fire:
> Grant then at last, and let thy open brest
> Shew that thou lov'st me, and grant my faire request:
> Speake, or speake not, thy Delila shall give ore
> To urge; her lips shall never urge thee more.

[26] *Samson Agonistes,* ll. 43-52.   [27] P. 164.

Compare with these passages the following lines in *Samson Agonistes*:

> Thrice she assay'd with flattering prayers and sighs,
> And amorous reproaches to win from me
> My capital secret, in what part my strength
> Lay stor'd in what part summ'd, that she might know:
> Thrice I deluded her, and turn'd to sport
> Her importunity, each time perceiving
> How openly, and with what impudence
> She purpos'd to betray me, and (which was worse
> Then undissembl'd hate) with what contempt
> She sought to make me Traytor to my self;
> Yet the fourth time, when mustring all her wiles,
> With blandisht parlies, feminine assaults,
> Tongue-batteries, she surceas'd not day nor night
> To storm me over-watch't, and wearied out.
> At times when men seek most repose and rest,
> I yielded, and unlock'd her all my heart.[28]

The passage beginning "each time perceiving . . ." may be reminiscent of Quarles's Delila, who plainly showed her irritation and malice and whose flattery and tongue-batteries were finally successful.

In the Bible, Delilah's only motive in betraying Samson is the earning of the reward of eleven hundred pieces of silver offered to her by the Lords of the Philistines. In the *Historie*, the Philistine lords first urge that it is her patriotic duty to aid in the capture of the dreaded enemy of her country:

> Faire Delila; Thou canst not choose but know
> The miseries of our land: whose ruines show
> The danger, whereinto not we, but all,
> If thou deny thy helpfull hand, must fall:
> Those fruitfull fields, that offer'd, but of late,
> Their plentious favours to our prosprous state;
> See, how they lye a ruinous heape, and void
> Of all their plenty; wasted, and destroyde:
> Our common foe hath sported with our lives;

[28] Ll. 392-407.

Hath slaine our children, and destroy'd our wives:
Alas, our poore distressed land doth grone
Under that mischiefe that his hands have done;
Widowes implore thee, and poore Orphans' tongues
Call to faire Delila, to right their wrongs:
It lies in thee, to help; Thy helpfull hand
May have the Glory to revenge thy land;
For which, our thankefull Nation shall allow
Not onely Honour, but reward.[29]

In *Samson Agonistes*, the Lords appeal to Dalila's sense of duty to state and religion. Dalila speaks:

Since thou determinst weakness for no plea
In man or woman, though to thy own condemning,
Hear what assaults I had, what snares besides,
What sieges girt me round, e're I consented;
Which might have aw'd the best resolv'd of men,
The constantest to have yielded without blame.
It was not gold, as to my charge thou lay'st,
That wrought with me: thou know'st the Magistrates
And Princes of my countrey came in person,
Sollicited, commanded, threatn'd, urg'd,
Adjur'd by all the bonds of civil Duty
And of Religion, press'd how just it was,
How honourable, how glorious to entrap
A common enemy, who had destroy'd
Such numbers of our Nation: . . . . . .
. . . . . . at length that grounded maxim
So rife and celebrated in the mouths
Of wisest men; that to the public good
Private respects must yield; with grave authority
Took full possession of me and prevail'd;
Vertue, as I thought, truth, duty so enjoyning.[30]

In both poems the lady is ostensibly moved by patriotic considerations. Only the critic who ignores such similarities as are pointed out here can declare that in the *Historie* "there are no specific parallels with Milton."

Finally, observe the endings. In spite of Samson's despond-

[29] Pp. 162-163.　　　[30] Ll. 843-870.

ency, *Samson Agonistes* ends on a subdued note of triumph. It
is no time for lamentation, for

> *Samson* hath quit himself
> Like *Samson*, and heroicly hath finish'd
> A life Heroic. . . .

Thus ends the *Historie:*

> Thus dies our *Samson*, whose brave death has won
> More honour, then his honour'd life had done:
> Thus died our *Conquerour;* whose latest breath
> Was crown'd with Conquest; triumph'd over death:

It is only fair to say that the differences between the *Historie* and *Samson Agonistes* are more obvious and more important than are these similarities. The contrasts resulting from
the different forms, narrative and dramatic, are naturally most
striking, although it must be remembered that Quarles introduced a number of speeches. The action of *Samson Agonistes* is
concentrated; that of the *Historie* is episodic and sluggish. Sus-
pense is skillfully handled in *Samson Agonistes;* it is almost
quite lacking in the *Historie*. Milton has real insight into character; Quarles fails to go below the surface. There is in the
Historie none of the spiritual conflict which is the foundation
of Milton's tragedy. Quarles captured little of the pathos and
none of the sublimity which humanize and distinguish *Samson
Agonistes*. Of Milton's style there is, of course, no suggestion
in the *Historie*. In short, as artists Quarles and Milton are
poles apart. In a superficial reading, these differences obscure
the similarities, which are probably not all due to independent
treatment of the Biblical story. It is true that all the points
here compared are implied in the brief Scriptural account. Milton may have been their only begetter, as he was of much besides in his great tragedy. On the other hand, in spite of a
recent declaration that "No matter how much a previous poem
or drama resembled Milton's, we are justified in calling the
similarity pure coincidence,"[31] we may regard some of these
similarities as proof of Milton's indebtedness to Quarles's elaborate, uninspired, and pious *Historie*.

[31] William R. Parker, *Milton's Debt to Greek Tragedy in Samson Agonistes* (Baltimore, 1937), p. 4.

Part II: Prose

CHAPTER IX

BACON AND MILTON

IN ENGLAND the seventeenth century was on the whole an era of transition, but during the first forty years progress was hardly apparent; stagnation and reaction prevailed on the surface, in both church and state, which were closely allied. As Mr. G. M. Trevelyan has said, "Perhaps the period during which the conditions of life underwent least observable change is to be found in the years 1603-40 . . . in society, in economics, in the religious convictions of the people, it is difficult to name any great difference between the England of Shakespeare and the England of Pym."[1] Under the surface, however, a profound change of temper was taking place. Galling political and ecclesiastical restrictions repressed but could not destroy the spirit that demanded change. The world "was moving away from the securities of the Middle Ages and labouring to find new sanctions for the conduct of life. . . . In politics, in thought, in religion, in art there was everywhere a dissolution of accepted things. . . . The story of the epoch is one of disillusion and disbelief, and at the same time of a furious endeavour to reach a new stability."[2] By damning up for years this insistent and growing demand for change, the state and the church merely postponed the hour of reckoning. Finally, in a bloody civil war the barriers were swept aside. Since reasonable evolution was denied, revolution was inevitable. This account applies with particular aptness to religion and especially to the relationship between Bacon's and Milton's views of church reform.

Like other Puritan controversialists, Milton knew Bacon's church tracts, which he cited for his purpose. For example, in

[1] *England under the Stuarts* (London, 1926), p. 3.
[2] John Buchan, *Oliver Cromwell* (Boston, 1934), pp. 4-5.

Of Reformation Touching Church-Discipline in England, arguing that in the early church the authority of the bishops was dependent upon the council, Milton declares that "ev'n in the womb and center of Apostacy *Rome* it selfe, there yet remains a glimps of this truth, for the Pope himselfe, as a learned English writer notes well, performeth all Ecclesiasticall jurisdiction as in Consistory amongst his Cardinals, which were originally but the Parish Priests of *Rome*."[3] Hitherto, this "learned English writer" has been unidentified.[4] He is Francis Bacon, whose *Certaine Considerations Touching the better Pacification and Edification of the Church of England* (first printed, anonymously, in 1604, and reprinted, anonymously, in 1640), in the section "Circumstances in the Government of Bishops" says in part:

Surely, I doe suppose and thinke upon ground, that *ab initio non fuit ita;* and that the Deanes and Chapters were Counsels about the Seas and Chayres of *Byshops* at the first, and were unto them a *Presbyterie,* or *Consistorie* and intermedled not onely in the disposing of their revenues and endowments, but much more in jurisdiction Ecclesiasticall. . . . And wee see that the Byshop of *Rome,* (*fas est & ab hoste doceri,* and no question in that *Church* the first institutions were excellent) performeth all Ecclesiasticall jurisdiction as in *Consistorie.*

And whereof consisteth this *Consistorie,* but of the parish Priests of *Rome.* . . .

Milton's phrasing proves that he refers to *Certaine Considerations,* which is regarded as Bacon's most important utterance on church affairs.

Milton knew also Bacon's first church tract, *An Advertisement Touching the Controversies of the Church of England,* which was written in 1589,[5] but was not published until 1641, under the title *A Wise and Moderate Discourse, Concerning Church-Affaires. As it was written, long since, by the famous Author of those Considerations, which seems to have some*

[3] *The Works of John Milton* (New York, 1931), III, 18.
[4] Mr. W. T. Hale, the editor of *Of Reformation Touching Church-Discipline in England* (New Haven, 1916), says, "It is not known to whom Milton refers" (p. 111).   [5] Spedding, *Life and Letters,* I, 73.

reference to this. Now published for the common good. Replying to Hall's complaint against the swarm of libels, Milton,
in *Animadversions upon the Remonstrants Defence Against
Smectymnuus*, cites Bacon's complaint that the Bishops held an
uneven hand over the pamphlets, allowing those against the
Puritans, but prohibiting those against the Bishops, to the serious damage of religion.[6] It should be added that Bacon was
not in favor of free discussion. In *A Modest Confutation of
a Slanderous and Scurrilous Libell, Entituled Animadversions*
(1642), Hall, in turn, quotes from Bacon's *Advertisement* the
censure of unseemly treatment of religious subjects, and Bacon's
wish that "my Lords the Clergy" should have no dealings with
the libellers. In *An Apology Against a Pamphlet call'd A
Modest Confutation* (1642), Milton justifies his use of satire,
retorts that Hall is a *Mime*, and declares that Bacon's censure
describes Hall's style.[7] Again, Milton ridicules the Confuter's
servile dependence upon Bacon and his "warping and warping"
when he has left Sir Francis's shadow.

Milton's first two references to Bacon's pamphlets on church
reform are introduced independently of any reference to him
by Hall—evidence that at the outset of his writing on the
church and apparently without prompting he was acquainted
with Bacon's opinions. In the light of this fact and because of
the importance of religion in the seventeenth century, a comparative study of the ecclesiastical views of Bacon and Milton
and some consideration of a possible kinship should not be
without interest and value. Although religious matters did not
strictly concern either Bacon's profession or Milton's calling,
both men were keenly interested in the reform of the church.
To state the point more precisely, Bacon sought by proposing
reforms to pacify and strengthen Episcopacy; Milton labored
to destroy Episcopacy and to establish a church government in
harmony with Scripture and his love of freedom. In some

[6] *Op. cit.*, III, 111-112. In his *Common-Place Book* (p. 30) Milton
quotes Bacon's statement regarding the suppression of books, and gives the
reference, "*Sir Fran. Bacon* in a discourse of church affairs." See also
Areopagitica, pp. 326, 332-333 (*The Works of John Milton*, IV [1931]).

[7] *Op. cit.*, III, 295. See also pp. 317, 320.

respects their opinions are widely divergent; in other respects, there is striking agreement. The divergence is explained by the characters of the writers, by the lapse of time, and by changed conditions: Milton published his views roughly a half century after Bacon enunciated his. The agreement is explained by the fact that both men were sincere reformers, though Bacon characteristically did not lead a crusade for the reforms that he proposed.

At the outset, a sharp contrast of mood and purpose impresses the reader. Bacon is dispassionate, impartial, eminently fair. Addressing James I, he says:

I thought it not impossible, but that I, as a looker on, might cast mine eyes upon some things that the actors themselves (especially some being interested, some led and addicted, some declared and engaged) did not or would not see. And that knowing in my conscience (whereto God beareth witness) that these things which I shall speak, spring out of no vein of popularity, ostentation, desire of novelty, partiality to either side, disposition to intermeddle, or any the like leaven; I may conceive hope that what I want in depth of judgment, may be countervailed in simplicity and sincerity of affection.[8]

Although this attitude of the modest, calm, and impartial critic may be in part a pose calculated to disarm the suspicions of the King, it is really characteristic of Bacon's thorough-going moderation, and is in sharp contrast with Milton's zeal and whole-hearted partisanship. In Milton, moreover, the personal and the ethical note is often stressed. Although "led by the genial power of nature to another task," Milton imagines what stories of reproach he would have heard within himself if in the hour of the church's need he had failed to play his part. One may question the truth of the first clause but not the remainder of the following excerpt from *The Reason of Church-Government:*

neither envy nor gall hath enterd me upon this controversy, but the enforcement of conscience only, and a preventive fear least the

---

[8] *The Works of Francis Bacon* (London, 1730), IV, 432.

omitting of this duty should be against me when I would store up to my self the good provision of peacefull hours.[9]

Although Milton certainly considered the welfare of the church and the nation as a whole, the personal note in his anti-prelatical papers is persistent. His denunciation of Episcopacy could hardly be more bitter than it is if he himself had been ejected from his cure or personally humiliated by the Bishops. Without reservations, Milton passionately identified himself with the cause of religious truth and liberty.

This radical difference of temper naturally finds expression in the ecclesiastical views of Bacon and Milton; but it is an interesting fact that at times they occupy common ground in spite of disagreement in detail. Consider their views of truth and its realization in worship. Pleading for unity and commenting upon the confusion among Christians, Bacon writes:

some have sought the truth in the conventicles and conciliables of hereticks and sectaries; others in the external face and representation of the church, and both sorts have been seduced.[10]

Truth is not found in extremes, nor does it reside in forms. Bacon requires some unity of worship; he declares: "*non servatur unitas in credendo, nisi eadem adsit in colendo;* there will be kept no unity in believing, except it be entertained in worshipping." But he adds:

we contend about ceremonies, and things indifferent, about the external policy and government of the church: in which kind, if we would but remember that the ancient and true bonds of unity are one faith, one baptism, and not one ceremony, one policy; if we would but observe the league amongst Christians that is penned by our Saviour, *he that is not against us is with us;* if we could but comprehend that saying, *differentiae rituum commendant unitatem doctrinae;* the diversities of ceremonies do set forth the unity of doctrine; and that *habet religio quae sunt aeternitatis, habet quae sunt temporis;* religion hath parts which belong to eternity, and parts which pertain to time: and if we did but know the virtue of

[9] *Op. cit.*, III, 234.   [10] *Op. cit.*, IV, 418.

silence, and slowness to speak, commended by St. *James* our controversies of themselves would close up and grow together.[11]

Bacon's declaration that faith is more vital than form must have had Milton's approval. Milton desired a unified spiritual church, which the schism of Episcopacy had made impossible. According to him, the real sin of the episcopal hierarchy was that it constituted a materialistic despotism, which monopolized power and profits and by driving away faithful ministers sent "heards of souls starvling to Hell." Milton emphasized the first part of Bacon's formula: religion hath parts which belong to eternity, and parts which pertain to time. Bacon was interested primarily in religious unity; Milton was preoccupied with religious freedom.

Consider their views on the place of ceremony in worship. Bacon does not hold that ceremony is the essence of religion; but he would nevertheless have all things done in order and with decency. He would have the liturgy made agreeable to the Word of God, the example of the primitive church, and that holy decency which St. Paul commends. But Bacon warns against extolling the ritual, which leads to superstition, and in his discussion he tries to steer clear of controversial matters. To Milton ceremonies are the "Paganisme of sensuall Idolatry"; they serve "either as a mist to cover nakednesse where true *grace* is extinguisht; or as an Enterlude to set out the *pompe of Prelatisme.*"[12] It is Milton's conviction that prayer is the gift of the Holy Spirit and that "obedience to the Spirit of God, rather then to the faire seeming pretences of men, is the best and most beautiful order that a Christian can observe." Bacon desires a decent but not arbitrary ritual; Milton rejects all ritual except that dictated by the spirit of God.

Like most Puritans, Milton accepts the Bible as an infallible guide, which directs all conduct, resolves all problems, and determines all controversies. As he says in *Of Prelatical Episcopacy*, the Scripture is "the onely Book left us of *Divine* authority, not in any thing more Divine then in the all-suffi-

---

[11] *Ibid.*, IV, 419.   [12] *Op. cit.*, III, 6.

ciency it hath to furnish us, as with all other spirituall knowledge, so with this in particular, setting out to us a perfect man of *God* accomplish't to all the good workes of his charge." Within the sacred context of the Bible "all wisedome is infolded." Bacon condemns the Puritan custom of seeking "express scripture for every thing," and declares that by ignoring tradition and the authority of the Fathers the Puritans rob the church of special help and support.[13] When Milton advocates the Presbyterian form of church government, he finds for that form Scriptural proof.[14] Bacon frankly confesses that church government is not prescribed in Scripture: "I for my part do confess, that in revolving the scriptures, I could never find any such thing; but that God had left the like liberty to the church government, as he had done to the civil government; to be varied according to time and place and accidents, which nevertheless his high and divine providence doth order and dispose."[15]

In their choice of church government Bacon and Milton stand far apart. Bacon, of course, supports Episcopacy, saying:

First therefore, for the government of bishops, I for my part, not prejudging the precedents of other reformed churches do hold it warranted by the word of God, and by the practice of the ancient church in the better times; and much more convenient for kingdoms than parity of ministers and government by synods. But then farther, it is to be considered, that the church is not now to plant or build; but only to be pruned from corruption, and to be repaired and restored in some decaies.[16]

From this statement it follows, of course, that Bacon opposes in England the adoption of the church government of foreign Protestants, which was admired by many. Their discipline, says Bacon, may be better in theory, "yet many times it is to be sought, *non quod optimum, sed e bonis quid proximum*, not that which is best; but of good things which is the best and readiest to be had. Our church is not now to plant; it is set-

---

[13] *Op. cit.*, IV, 430.
[14] See *The Reason of Church-Government.*
[15] *Op. cit.*, IV, 435.   [16] *Op. cit.*, IV, 436.

tled and established." In fact, Bacon will not admit that the government of foreign Protestants is better than that of the English, "if some abuses were taken away." He suggests that perhaps their fruits "are as torches in the dark, which appear greatest afar off." And he repeats his warning against the parity of ministers and the government by synods, both of which are things "of wonderful great confusion." On the other hand, it is one of Milton's firmest convictions that England must cut away "the noysom, and diseased tumor of Prelacie" and unite with the "Reformed sister Churches," which have long flourished "with the blessings of *peace* and *pure* doctrine."[17] Rejecting Episcopacy, Milton first embraced Presbyterianism, only to abandon it later when bitter experience had convinced him that "*New Presbyter* is but *Old Priest* writ Large." Thereafter, without respect for organization, he steadily supported the cause of freedom, appealing to the state "to defend still the Christian liberty which we enjoy" and to enlarge it "if in aught they yet straiten it."

Bacon's and Milton's opinions diverge so widely at this point that it may seem useless to continue the comparison. But it must be remembered that Bacon advocated a thorough reformation of Episcopacy. E. A. Abbott seems to be justified in declaring that if Bacon's "sensible and statesmanlike" program of reform had been adopted, the House of Commons would have been conciliated and the Civil War of the next generation prevented.[18] It is, therefore, not unimportant to review his proposed reforms and in connection with these Milton's charges against prelacy.

As usual, Bacon goes to the root of the matter. In *An Advertisement Touching the Controversies of the Church of England,* which is a plea to end dissensions in the Church, Bacon declares "that the imperfections in the conversation and government of those which have chief place in the church, have ever been principal causes and motives of schisms and divi-

---

[17] *Op. cit.,* III, 62.
[18] *Francis Bacon An Account of His Life and Works* (London, 1885), p. 110.

sions."[19] Expressing his reverence for the calling and persons of "my lords the bishops" and deploring the detraction of such of them as are men of great virtue, he condemns those churchmen who are inordinately ambitious and those who stiffly maintain that nothing in the present order is to be changed. He insists that change must have place:

leges, novis legibus, non recreatae acescunt; laws not refreshed with new laws, wax soure. *Qui mala non permutat, in bonis non perseverat;* without change of ill, a man cannot continue good. To take away many abuses, supplanteth not good orders, but establisheth them.[20]

The church should be like the good husbandman, who is ever pruning in his field or his vineyard. In *Certain Considerations* Bacon reiterates the point:

who knoweth not that time is truly compared to a stream that carrieth down fresh and pure waters into that salt sea of corruption which environeth all human actions? And therefore if man shall not by his industry, virtue, and policy, as it were with the oar, row against the stream and inclination of time; all institutions and ordinances, be they ever so pure, will corrupt and degenerate.[21]

Why should Parliament purge and restore the civil state with good and wholesome laws, "devising remedies as fast as time breedeth mischief," and, on the contrary, the ecclesiastical state "continue upon the dregs of time, and receive no alteration now for these five and forty years and more?" Those who say that there is a difference between civil and ecclesiastical causes "may as well tell me that churches and chapels need no reparations, though castles and houses do: whereas, commonly to speak truth, dilapidations of the inward and spiritual edifications of the church of God are in all times as great as the outward and material." As part of his program of reform, Bacon suggests the training of sound preachers, the endowment of the bishops with a fervent love and care of the people, the suppression of false accusations, and the avoidance of coercion in matters of faith.

[19] *Op. cit.*, IV, 422.　　[20] *Op. cit.*, IV, 427.　　[21] *Op. cit.*, IV, 433.

Since his first proposals of reform fell upon deaf ears, Bacon in *Certain Considerations Touching the better Pacification and Edification of the Church of England*, published when James I had just ascended the throne, renewed some of his former suggestions and mapped a more detailed plan of reformation. He denies the necessity of one form of discipline in all churches. We must, he declares, "return unto the ancient bonds of unity in the church of God; which was one faith, one baptism; and not one hierarchy, one discipline." In general, Bacon urges that Christ's flock be fed; that there be an orderly succession of bishops and ministers; that the preachers of the gospel live by the gospel; that all things be done in order and with decency; that the government of the church be restored to its primitive simplicity.

But Bacon did not stop with these generalities. He drew up the particulars of reformation. In the first place, he proposes decisive limitations of the bishop's authority. The bishop "giveth orders alone, excommunicateth alone, judgeth alone." This practice has no foundation in good government and seems, therefore, "not unlikely to have crept in, in the degenerate and corrupt times." Bacon also objects to the deputation of the bishop's authority, a practice not warranted by the rules of government. Finally, he demands the reform of episcopal procedure, which also is contrary to the laws and customs of the state. He emphatically condemns the oath *ex officio*, by which men are compelled to accuse themselves and "are sworn to blanks, and not unto accusations and charges declared." By the law of England no man is bound to accuse himself. The practice of examining upon oath "out of accusations secret and undeclared" is contrary to the common law and should be limited.

With regard to ceremony, Bacon takes middle ground. He insists that the liturgy is as high and holy as the sermon, which if too much extolled may degenerate into superstition. He recommends the use of certain set forms and dismisses sundry exceptions as lacking in weight. He thinks absolution improper and unnecessary. He condemns private baptism. He considers the ring ceremony in marriage vulgar. He approves of music in the church, but disapproves of its excess. He opposes the requiring of certain vestments for the practical reason that the silencing of ministers on this account "in this scarcity of good preachers" is injurious to the people as well as to the Puritans. He appreciates the need of an active ministry, but objects to the promiscuous allowance of preachers. "God forbid, that every man that can take unto himself boldness to speak an hour together in a church upon a text, should be admitted a preacher, though he mean never so well." To meet the crying need for preachers, Bacon proposes a threefold plan: the renewing of the old custom of prophesying, under careful regulation; a more exact "probation and examination" of ministers, and solemn ordination, not by the bishop alone; permission for ministers to supply more than one parish, that some churches may not be left destitute. Thus Bacon gives a qualified approval to pluralities. On the other hand, he condemns non-residence as an abuse proceeding from greed and sloth. He even insists that chaplains at Court and in the families of nobles should have no other benefices. He condemns the abuse of excommunication, by which this great judgment is "made an ordinary process, to lackey up and down for fees." He urges that it be restored to its true dignity and that it be exercised only in matters of great importance.

This thorough-going program of reform should have satisfied all but the most radical Puritans. It did not, however, please James I, who was no friend of toleration. He said, "I will have one doctrine, one discipline, one religion, in substance and ceremony"; and he warned the Puritans to speak no more for religious freedom. On that point Bacon spoke no more. His *Certain Considerations* appears to have been called in. Ruthlessly suppressed, Puritanism spread in secret and waited for its opportunity. Finally, Episcopacy itself was brought to the bar; and Milton was one of its most bitter critics.

The bonds of religion, Milton declares, were broken by the tyranny of the Church, which attempted to enforce a rigid conformity even in matters indifferent. Dissension and faction were the result of a corrupt hierarchy; schism and rebellion were the prelates' first-born. Bacon's plea for the curtailment of the bishops' power and jurisdiction is related to Milton's charge that the prelates are a "Tyrannical crew," living in haughty palaces, hoarding up "Lands, Lordships, and Demeanes, to sway and carry all before them in high Courts," haling men to Lambeth and using the oath *ex officio* on them in strappado. For Milton the antiquity of the church was no proof of its worth. Milton, even more than Bacon, believed in the necessity of change. Truth is a stream, and conformity means stagnation and corruption. Milton virtually discarded ceremony, holding that faith needs "not the weak, and fallible office of the Senses, to be either the Ushers, or Interpreters, of heavenly Mysteries, save where our Lord himselfe in his Sacraments ordain'd."[22] Milton, of course, believed in a devout preaching ministry. Preaching is essential to discipline; the minister is the spiritual deputy of God. Under Episcopacy, Milton declares, there was hardly any preaching at all; he outdoes himself in denouncing the wooden, illiterate, lazy, tavern-haunting, mercenary clergy. He denounces the abuse of excommunication, which with the bishops served for nothing "but to prog, and pander for fees, or to display their pride and sharpen their revenge"—the language seems almost an echo of Bacon's.

Milton insisted upon a complete reformation. He would flee as far as possible from a corrupt hierarchy; he would not allow political considerations to impede the establishment of the true church. He has no dread of extremes. It is the "holy reformed Church, and the elect people of God" in whom Milton is primarily interested. Milton is the fervent idealist, who dreams of the perfect church and sees in its opponents not one redeeming quality. Bacon is the practical statesman— granted that his proposed program was practicable. Bacon has no sympathy with those whose scope is to devise merely what is good, not what is possible. Because of the "great and near

[22] *Op. cit.,* III, 1-2.

sympathy between the state civil, and the state ecclesiastical,"
it is dangerous, he holds, radically to alter the church. Bacon
sees clearly the faults of both parties: in the bishops, their imperfection and ambition in conversation and government, their
stubborn refusal to change, their forcing compliance with their
own articles, and so on; in the Puritans, their intemperate censure of the Church, their reckless insistence upon a new discipline, "without consideration of possibility and foresight of
peril," the want of grounded knowledge in their preaching,
their admitting the people to hear controversies, their annihila-
tion of the liturgy, and so forth.

The difference in the opinion and the temper of these two
men is reflected in their style. The modesty, the sanity, the dignity of Bacon's style lift it far above "this immodest and deformed manner of writing lately entertained," which he roundly
condemns. Bacon declares that "to search and rip up wounds
with a laughing countenance, to intermix scripture and scurrility
sometime in one sentence, is a thing far from the reverence of
a Christian, and scant beseeming the honest regard of a sober
man. . . . The Majesty of religion, and the contempt and
deformity of things ridiculous, are things as distant as things
may be." Bacon does not err. He is always courteous, rev-
erent, temperate, impartial. On the other hand, Milton, em-
barking "in a troubl'd sea of noises and hoars disputes," hating
prelacy and loving freedom, has no thought of being impartial.
With passionate intensity and with every resource of language
at his command, he denounces those hirelings who desecrate
the service of God and tyrannize over his church. Hatred of
Episcopacy is one of the ruling passions of Milton's life. In
Lycidas he began his assault upon the corrupt clergy. In his
church pamphlets he renewed the war. In *Paradise Lost* he
did not let slip the opportunity to denounce religious tyranny:

> Wolves shall succeed for teachers, grievous Wolves,
> Who all the sacred mysteries of Heav'n
> To thir own vile advantages shall turne
> Of lucre and ambition, and the truth
> With superstitions and traditions taint,

Left onely in those written Records pure,
Though not but by the Spirit understood.
Then shall they seek to avail themselves of names,
Places and titles, and with these to joine
Secular power, though feigning still to act
By spiritual, to themselves appropriating
The Spirit of God, promised alike and giv'n
To all Beleevers; and from that pretense,
Spiritual Lawes by carnal power shall force
On every conscience; Laws which none shall finde
Left them inrould, or what the Spirit within
Shall on the heart engrave. What will they then
But force the Spirit of Grace it self, and binde
His consort Libertie; what, but unbuild
His living Temples, built by Faith to stand,
Thir own Faith not anothers: for on Earth
Who against Faith and Conscience can be heard
Infallible? yet many will presume:
Whence heavie persecution shall arise
On all who in the worship persevere
Of Spirit and Truth; the rest, farr greater part,
Will deem in outward Rites and specious formes
Religion satisfi'd; Truth shall retire
Bestuck with slandrous darts, and works of Faith
Rarely be found: so shall the World goe on,
To good malignant, to bad men benigne,
Under her own weight groaning, till the day
Appeer of respiration to the just,
And vengeance to the wicked.[23]

Milton's uneven prose, not infrequently informed with a vigor and eloquence that make even Bacon's distinguished style seem flat, is sometimes marred by that "immodest and deformed" manner that Bacon condemns. But Bacon himself has furnished Milton with an adequate defence:

Indeed, bitter and earnest writing must not hastily be condemned; for men cannot contend coldly, and without affection, about things which they hold dear and precious. A politick man may write from

[23] XII, 508-541.

his brain, without touch and sense of his heart; as in a speculation that appertaineth not unto him; but a feeling Christian will express in his words a character of zeal and love.[24]

Here is also clearly stated the contrast between Bacon and Milton: Bacon, the politic observer, with an intelligent interest in the reform of the Church; Milton, the zealous champion, for whom religious truth and liberty were pearls of great price.

It is not the purpose of this comparison of the religious and the ecclesiastical views of Bacon and Milton to suggest that the poet was seriously indebted to the philosopher; for this is not a study of sources. Obviously, there are between their religious tenets great differences in detail. On the other hand, it is not improbable that Milton derived from Bacon's tracts more support, moral if not factual, than is indicated by the connections established at the outset of this chapter. Naturally, in the 1640's Milton could not accept a program of reform proposed forty years previously, before Charles I and Laud had established the tyranny of church and state. In his day Milton could see no hope but in the overthrow of this godless and oppressing government and its punishment in "the darkest and deepest Gulfe of Hell." But as he read Bacon's ecclesiastical pamphlets perhaps he dreamed of what might have been. For a time, we may surmise, the evil present vanished from his sight, and in place of the tyranny of the lordly bishops there rose in his imagination a fair vision of the church, reformed and free, to the service of which by his parents and in his own resolution he had been dedicated.

[21] *Op. cit.,* IV, 420.

CHAPTER X

MILTON AND DIGBY

Having recorded in the preceding chapter Milton's references to Bacon's church papers and having traced the relationship of their ecclesiastical opinions, I come now to the study of a much more direct and immediate connection: that between a part of Milton's *Of Reformation Touching Church-Discipline in England* (1641) and *The Third Speech Of The Lord George Digby, To the House of Commons, Concerning Bishops, and the Citie Petition, the 9th. of Febr: 1640*. The extent and the character of this particular relationship have never been recognized, although it is well known that Milton had some acquaintance with the controversial literature of his day. Besides his allusions to or quotations from Sancta Clara's *Apologia Episcoporum seu Sacri Magistratus*, Hall's *Episcopacie by Divine Right*, Laud's *Relatio contra Fisher*, Sandys' *A Relation of the State of Religion*, and so on, it has been said that in *Of-Reformation* in his answer to the objections brought against the Presbyterian discipline Milton "it seems . . . had before him, at least, Morley's *A Modest Advertisement*, the *Speeches of Sr. Benjamin Rudger* . . . , *The Third Speech of Lord George Digby* . . . , and Lord Falkland's *Speech . . . Concerning Episcopacy. . . .*"[1] This statement (in which Digby's *Speech* is grouped indiscriminately with other contemporary works),

[1] *Of Reformation Touching Church-Discipline in England By John Milton*, ed. Will Taliaferro Hale (New Haven, 1916), p. lviii. In his notes (pp. 180, 186) Mr. Hale cites "Robert Morley, *A Modest Advertisement*" with regard to the reform of ecclesiastical abuses. Morley's first name was not Robert but George. His *A Modest Advertisement Concerning the present Controversie about Church-Government; Wherein the maine Grounds of that Booke, intituled The Unlawfulnesse and Danger of Limited Prelacie. Are calmly examined* (London, 1641) was published in May (*Thomason Tracts*, I, 13), perhaps too late for Milton to have used it in *Of Reformation*.

with five other references,[2] represents modern scholarship's knowledge of the connection between Milton's first church pamphlet and Digby's *Speech*.

As a matter of fact, the refutation in *Of Reformation* is directed chiefly, if not solely, at Digby's *Speech*, the points of which Milton follows in order and the phrases of which he sometimes quotes. The date of this *Speech* and its tone should be particularly noted. The date, February 9, 1641,[3] gives a *terminus a quo* for a part of Milton's first pamphlet.[4] As we shall see, Digby's sarcastic tone in dealing with the London Petition and his unpopular arguments stirred indignation both within and without the Commons. In his *Apologie For Himselfe*, Digby bears witness to his loss of favor after delivering this speech:

> And whosoever remembreth the passages of that time, must call to mind, that the first declination I suffer'd from the interest I seem'd to have, was in the businesse of the Church: in which, having had frequent consultations with the chiefest agents for a reformation, and finding no three men to agree upon what they would have in the place of that they all resolv'd to remove, I agreed not with the prevailing sense, having not hardinesse enough to incline to a mutation, which would evidently have so great an influence upon the peace, prosperity, and interest of the whole Kingdome. And thus, from the first debate of Episcopacy, upon the *London* Petition, all men observ'd the date of my unmerited favour began to expire.[5]

In a reply to this *Apologie* there is further proof of the unpopularity of Digby's *Speech*. The author of *An Answer To The*

---

[2] *Of Reformation* . . . ed. Hale, pp. 139, 157, 184, 186, 187.

[3] In the *Catalogue* of the *Thomason Tracts* this speech is entered under February 8 (I, 7).

[4] The *Speech* is a pamphlet of nineteen pages. In this chapter quotations are from the first edition in the Huntington Library. The *Speech* is included in *Speeches and Passages Of This Great and Happy Parliament: From the third of November, 1640, to this instant June, 1641. Collected into One Volume, and according to the most perfect Originalls, exactly published* (London, Printed for William Cooke, and are to be sold at his shop, at Furnifalls-Inne-gate, in Holbourne, 1641), pp. 65-75.

[5] *The Lord George Digbie's Apologie For Himselfe, Published the fourth of January, Anno Dom. 1642* (Oxford, 1642), p. 3.

Lord George Digbies Apology for Himself (1642) blames
Digby for publishing his speech, calls on him to reflect upon
the censure of at least 15,000 good women of London when
with so keen a knife he dissected the Petition of their husbands,
and would have him "imagine what a report such a clamor
raysed upon you in the City, would have, and I assure you had
in the Country. . . ."[6] Doubtless the notoriety of Digby's
Speech serves to explain why Milton honored him with a categorical reply.

A brief summary of the first part of the *Speech* will help
the reader to appreciate the evidence to be presented later. Beginning with the assertion that he is to speak on a "tender subject" and that "some within these walls are engaged with ear-
nestnesse in contrary opinions to mine," Digby begs the patience of the House. "There is," he declares, "no man within
these walls, more sensible of the heavy grievance of Church
government, then my selfe; nor whose affections are keener to
the clipping of those wings of the Prelates, whereby they have
mounted to such insolencies, nor whose zeale is more ardent to
the searing them, as that they may never spring again." He
freely condemns the notorious faults of Episcopacy: the Bishops have afflicted men of tender conscience; they have introduced innovations, with fresh importations of popery; in their
pride they have trampled in the dirt men of meek and humble
spirit; by their oath they have galled men faithfully addicted
to the Crown; they have set forth books, sermons, and canons
destructive of the property and the liberty of the subject. In
fact, when he considers the outrageous insolencies and the
abominable cruelties of the Bishops, Digby declares he is ready
with the loudest of the 15,000 to cry out "Down with them,
down with them, even to the ground." But as a member, a
"most unworthy and inconsiderable" member, of this great and
wise assembly, he pleads for dispassionate and temperate action; he would divest himself and others "of all those dis-
turbances of Judgement which arise ever from great Provoca-
tions. . . ."

⁶ Pp. 6-7.

From this point of view Digby attacks the London Petition, which in its nature, in the manner of its delivery in the present conjuncture of affairs, both ecclesiastical and civil, he considers "a thing of the highest consequence that any age hath presented to a Parliament. . . ." He professes to look upon it with terror, "as upon a Commet a blazing starre, raised and kindled out of the stench, out of the poysonous exhalation of a corrupted Hierarchy. . . ." He declares that he has not flattered the House, that he could not have flattered the King if fortune had placed him near the King, and that he does not now intend to flatter a multitude. He insists that the Petition abounds in things contemptible, presumptuous, and irrational. He finds very weak arguments in particular articles, and knows not whether it is more preposterous to infer the extirpation of Episcopacy from such slender reasons or to attribute, as they do, all civil grievances to church government: "not a patent, not a Monopoly, not the price of a commodity raised, but these men make Bishops the cause of it." There is no logic, no reason in their demands: "It were want of Logick in mee to expect it from a multitude. . . ." In the Petition there is a multitude of allegations, a multitude of instances of abuses; and it is inferred that because of the abuses the institution should be abolished. "As if they should say, that because Drunkennesse and Adultery are growne so epidemicall, as is alleadged in the Petition, Let there be no more use of Wine, nor of Women in the Land." Digby especially resents what he considers the presumption of the Petitioners: "For the bold part of this Petition, Sir, what can there bee of greater presumption, then for Petitioners, not only to prescribe to a Parliament, what, and how it shall doe; but for a multitude to teach a Parliament, what, and what is not, the government according to Gods word." He is confident that no man of judgment will think it fit for a Parliament under a monarchy "to give countenance to irregular, and tumultuous assemblies, bee it for never so good an end. . . ." We must, declares Digby, uphold the dignity of what former Parliaments have done, "even in those things which in their due time wee may desire, and intend to reverse."

Little wonder that the matter and the tone of this attack deeply offended some of the enemies of Episcopacy. S. R. Gardiner observed that it "was with the sure instinct of a true debater that Nathaniel Fiennes, Lord Saye's second son, replied to Digby and not to Falkland," who also found fault with Episcopacy but urged its retention.[7] That Milton, although no member of Parliament, also had the true debater's gift the following evidence will show. As we shall see, Milton's statement "Here I might have ended, but that some Objections, which I have heard commonly flying about, presse mee to the endevour of an answere" refers unmistakably to Digby's *Speech.* In the following excerpts from the arguments, Milton's rejoinder is in each case cited immediately after each point that Digby makes. For convenience of reference, similar items have the same numbers; they are distinguished by the first letter of the author's name: thus, the first item from Digby is 1 (D); the first from Milton is 1 (M).

The first excerpt deals with the danger of extreme measures:

1 (D). I beseech you gentlemen let us not be led by passion to popular and vulgar Errors, it is naturall (as I tould you before) to the multitude *to fly into Extremes,* that seemes ever the best to them, that is most opposite to the present object of their hate. Wise Councells (M. Speaker) must square their Resolutions by another measure, by what's most just, most honourable, most convenient: Beleeve mee, Sir, great alterations of Government are rarely accompanyed with any of these.

M. Speaker, we all agree upon this; that a Reformation of Church Government is most necessary, . . . but, Sir, to strike at the Roote, to attempt a totall Alteration, before ever I can give my vote unto that, three things must be made manifest unto mee.[8]

[7] *History of England* (London, 1884), IX, 279.
[8] Digby, *op. cit.,* 15-16.

1 (M). We must not run they say into sudden extreams. This is
a fallacious Rule, unlesse understood only of the actions of
Vertue about things indifferent, for if it be found that
those two extreames be Vice and Vertue, Falshood and
Truth, the greater extremity of Vertue and superlative
Truth we run into, the more vertuous, and the more wise
wee become; and hee that flying from degenerate and traditional corruption, feares to shoot himselfe too far into the
meeting imbraces of a Divinely-warranted Reformation,
had better not have run at all. And for the suddenness it
cannot be fear'd. . . . Yet if it were sudden and swift,
provided still it be from worse to better, certainly wee ought
to hie us from evill like a torrent, and rid our selves of
corrupt Discipline, as wee would shake fire out of our
bosomes. Speedy and vehement were the Reformations of
all the good Kings of Juda, though the people had beene
nuzzl'd in Idolatry never so long before; they fear'd not
the bug-bear danger, nor the Lyon in the way that the
sluggish and timorous Politician thinks he sees; . . .[9]

As a true disciple of Bacon, Digby emphasizes the grave dangers of extreme alterations. Idealist that he is, Milton pleads
for a complete reformation, for the destruction of a corrupt
discipline. He foresees no danger at all in change, provided
that it is from worse to better. Milton's phrase "the sluggish
and timorous Politician" obviously refers to Digby.

The next quotation deals with the antiquity of Episcopacy:

2 (D). that Episcopacy a function deduced through all ages of
Christs Church, from the Apostles times and continued by
the most venerable and sacred order Ecclesiasticall; . . .[10]

2 (M). Next they alledge the antiquity of Episcopacy through all
Ages. What it was in the Apostles time, that questionlesse
it must be still, and therein I trust the Ministers will be able
to satisfie the Parliament. But if Episcopacie be taken for
Prelacie, all the Ages they can deduce it through, will make
it no more venerable then Papacie.

Most certaine it is (as all our Stories beare witnesse) that

[9] *The Works of John Milton* (New York, 1931), III, 66. In the following excerpts from *Of Reformation*, references are to this edition.
[10] Digby, *op. cit.*, p. 16.

ever since their comming to the See of Canterbury for neere
twelve hundred yeares, to speake of them in generall, they
have beene in England to our Soules a sad dolefull succession of illiterate and blind guides: to our purses, and goods
a wastfull band of robbers, a perpetuall havock, and rapine:
To our state a continuall Hydra of mischiefe, and molesta-
tion, the forge of discord and Rebellion: This is the Trophey
of their Antiquity, and boasted Succession through so many
Ages.[11]

Milton's repetition of the words "through all ages" and his
violent attack upon the illiterate, avaricious, rebellious clergy—
clearly in reply to the phrase "the most venerable and sacred
order Ecclesiasticall"—point unmistakably to Digby's defence
of Episcopacy.

Martyrs of the Church are discussed in the following excerpts:

3 (D). a function dignified by the learning and Piety of so many
Fathers of the Church, glorified by so many Martyrdomes
in the Primitive times, and some since our owne blessed Reformation. . . .[12]

3 (M). And for those Prelate-Martyrs they glory of, they are to
be judg'd what they were by the Gospel, and not the Gospel
to be tried by them.
And it is to be noted that if they were for Bishopricks and
Ceremonies, it was in their prosperitie, and fulnes of bread,
but in their persecution, which purifi'd them, and neer
their death, which was their garland, they plainely dislik'd
and condemn'd the Ceremonies, and threw away those
Episcopall ornaments wherein they were instal'd, as foolish
and detestable, for so the words of Ridley at his degrad-
ment, and his letter to Hooper expressly shew. Neither doth
the Author of our Church History spare to record sadly the
fall . . . and infirmities of these Martyrs, though we
would deify them.[13]

It is obvious that Milton's expression "those Prelate-Martyrs
they glory of" was suggested by Digby's "glorified by so many
Martyrdomes. . . ."

[11] Milton, *op. cit.*, p. 67.
[12] Digby, *op. cit.*, p. 16.   [13] Milton, *op. cit.*, pp. 67-68.

The next group deals with the approval of Episcopacy by the reformed churches:

4 (D). a government admired (I speake it knowingly) by the learnedest of the Reformed Churches abroad.[14]

4 (M). Lastly, whereas they adde that some the learnedest of the reformed churches abroad admire our Episcopacy, it had been more for the strength of the Argument to tell us that som of the wisest Statesmen admire it, for thereby we might guesse them weary of the present discipline, as offensive to their State, which is the bugge we feare.[15]

Here the similarity of phrasing is so conspicuous that comment is unnecessary.

Corruption of church government is dealt with in the following group:

5 (D). Secondly, such a frame of Government must be layde before us, as no time, no Corruption can make lyable to proportionable inconveniences with that which wee abolish. . . I doe not beleeve there can any other Government bee proposed but will in time be subject to as great or greater inconvenience then Episcopacy, . . . as Divine as our inspection is into things not experimented, if we hearken to those that would quite extirpate Episcopacy, I am confident that in steed of every Bishop wee put downe in a Diocese, wee shall set up a Pope in every Parish.[16]

5 (M). The next objection vanishes of it selfe, propounding a doubt, whether a greater inconvenience would not grow from the corruption of any other discipline, then from that of Episcopacy. This seemes an unseasonable foresight, and out of order to deferre, and put off the most needful constitution of one right discipline, while we stand ballancing the discommodity's of two corrupt ones. First constitute that which is right, and of it selfe it will discover, and rectify that which swervs, and easily remedy the pretended feare of having a Pope in every Parish.[17]

The following excerpts discuss the connection between Episcopacy and the common law of England:

[14] Digby, op. cit., p. 16.
[16] Digby, op. cit., pp. 16-17.
[15] Milton, op. cit., p. 68.
[17] Milton, op. cit., pp. 68-69.

6 (D). Lastly M. Speaker, whether the subversion of Episcopacy, and the introducing of another kind of Government bee practiceable, I leave it to those to judge who have considered the connexion and interweaving of the Church Government with the Common Law, to those who heard the Kings Speech to us the other Day, or who have looked into reason of state.[18]

6 (M). At another doubt of theirs I wonder; whether this discipline which we desire, be such as can be put in practice within this Kingdom, they say it cannot stand with the common Law, nor with the Kings safety; the government of Episcopacy, is now so weav'd into the common Law: In Gods name let it weave out againe; let not humain quillets keep back divine authority. Tis not the common Law, nor the civil, but piety, and justice, that are our foundresses; they stoop not, neither change colour for Aristocracy, democraty, or Monarchy.[19]

Compare Digby's phrase "interweaving of the Church Government with the Common Law" with Milton's "so weav'd into the common Law" and "let it weave out againe."

The last group discusses the relation between monarchy on the one hand and Episcopacy and Presbyterianism on the other:

7 (D). For my part (though no Statesman I will speake my mind freely in this) I do not thinke a King can put downe Bishops totally with safety to Monarchy; not that there is any such Allyance as men talke of 'twixt the Myter and the Crowne, but from this reason; that upon the putting downe of Bishops, the Government of Assemblies is likely to succeed it. That (to bee effectuall) must draw to it selfe the supremacy of Ecclesiastical Jurisdiction that (consequently) the power of Excommunicating Kings as well as any other Brother in Christ, and if a King chance to be delivered over to Sathan, Judge whether men are likely to care much what becomes of him next.[20]

7 (M). Lastly, they are fearfull that the discipline which will succeed cannot stand with the Ks. safety. Wherefore? it is

[18] Digby, op. cit., pp. 17-18.
[19] Milton, op. cit., p. 69.   [20] Digby, op. cit., p. 18.

but Episcopacy reduc't to what it should be, . . . But wherein is this propounded government so shrewd? Because the government of assemblies will succeed. Did not the Apostles govern the Church by assemblies, how should it else be Catholick, how should it have Communion? . . . O but the consequence: Assemblies draw to them the Supremacy of Ecclesiasticall jurisdiction. No surely, they draw no Supremacy, but that authority which Christ, and Saint Paul in his name conferrs upon them. . . . But is this all? No, this Ecclesiasticall Supremacy draws to it the power to excommunicate Kings; and then followes the worst that can be imagin'd. Doe they hope to avoyd this by keeping Prelates that have so often don it? . . . But let us not for feare of a scarrecrow, or else through hatred to be reform'd stand hankering and politizing, when God with spread hands testifies to us, and points out the way to our peace.[21]

It seems unnecessary to present additional evidence; for the passages already quoted and compared demonstrate conclusively the intimate relationship between Milton's refutation and Digby's defence of Episcopacy. There is an obvious similarity of subject matter, and Milton's repetition of Digby's phrasing is particularly noteworthy. There can be no doubt that he worked with a copy of Digby's *Speech* before him. Not otherwise can we account for the striking contrast of arguments and the astonishing similarity of phrasing. One may well wonder why Milton did not mention the name of his antagonist, to whose arguments he replied directly and emphatically. Probably he decided that to suppress Digby's name and to give his refutation the air of answering the entire Episcopal party would be most effective. At any rate, he thought that in refuting Digby he was refuting Episcopacy—an unintentional compliment to the noble Lord. The evidence presented here lends a lively interest to the close of Milton's great pamphlet. In the quiet of his study, this David, we observe, did not attack imaginary antagonists. He aimed point-blank at that uncir-

[21] Milton, *op. cit.*, pp. 70-73.

cumcised Philistine who had dared to defy the armies of the living God. The dramatic quality of this part of Milton's tract helps us to conceive the tense conditions under which he worked. The evidence shows that his first church pamphlet, far from being an academic discussion, was shrewdly planned to have an important part in the great struggle to dethrone Episcopacy. We see Milton in the thick of this combat. Inevitably, looking forward to the poetry, we think also of Abdiel's speech to Satan, which in the light of the facts presented in this chapter may not unreasonably be read as Milton's prophecy of the ruin of Digby and his party:

> O alienate from God, O spirit accurst,
> Forsak'n of all good; I see thy fall
> Determind, and thy hapless crew involv'd
> In this perfidious fraud, contagion spred
> Both of thy crime and punishment: henceforth
> No more be troubl'd how to quit the yoke
> Of Gods *Messiah:* those indulgent Laws
> Will not now be voutsaf't, other Decrees
> Against thee are gon forth without recall;
> That Golden Scepter which thou didst reject
> Is now an Iron Rod to bruise and breake
> Thy disobedience.[22]

[22] V, 874-885.

CHAPTER XI

A REPLY AND A DEBT

In the two preceding chapters I have explored the relationship of Milton's religious and ecclesiastical views to those of certain predecessors. The comparison of the church tracts of Bacon and Milton reveals their deep interest in the reform of the church; it also reveals wide differences, disclosing great contrasts in temperament and character. The direct rebuttal of Digby's *Speech* is an interesting and dramatic phase of Milton's struggle against Episcopacy. In this chapter I turn to the influence of Milton's second church pamphlet.

A Reply to *Of Prelatical Episcopacy*

This hitherto unnoted reply to *Of Prelatical Episcopacy* is doubly interesting and important; for it both helps to fix the date of Milton's first two antiprelatical tracts and also proves that *Of Prelatical Episcopacy* on its merits and not because of personalities was deemed worthy of an answer. The full title of the reply, which is pseudonymous, is *A Compendious Discourse, Proving Episcopacy To Be Of Apostolicall, And Consequently of Divine Institution: By A cleare and weighty testimony of St. Irenaeus a glorious Martyr, and renowned Bishop of Lyons in France, upon the yeere of our Lord, 184. The said Testimony being so declared, pressed, and vindicated from all exceptions, that thereby an intelligent, and conscionable Reader may receive abundant satisfaction in this behalfe. Isaiah 39.8. Let there be peace and truth in my daies.*[1]

First, there is the question of dates. *Of Prelatical Episcopacy* is now generally dated June or July, 1641.[2] Peloni Al-

---

[1] The name assumed by the author is Peloni Almoni. The pamphlet, including the address to the reader, extends to only fourteen pages, which are not numbered.

[2] The *Thomason Catalogue* has July (I, 23); the *D N B*, June-July (XIII, 475); J. H. Hanford, *A Milton Handbook*, June or July (p. 70);

moni dates his address "To the Christian and Judicious Reader" May 31, 1641. Since *A Compendious Discourse* is, as we shall see, a reply to *Of Prelatical Episcopacy*, the dates generally given for the latter must be discarded. Obviously, it was published before the end of May, 1641. Almoni also mentions Milton's *Of Reformation*, which, of course, must also be dated not later than May. On the basis of this new evidence, we can be sure that Milton's first two pamphlets appeared from a month to two months earlier than the dates previously assigned to them.

From the statement in *A Compendious Discourse* that "The late unworthy Author of a booke intituled, *Of Reformation*, &c. hath found some quarrell against" Irenaeus, the casual reader might surmise that *A Compendious Discourse* is a reply to *Of Reformation*. Careful investigation proves this surmise quite unfounded. *A Compendious Discourse* deals almost exclusively with Irenaeus. The author thus limits his subject: ". . . in this latitude of matter, to avoyd longitude of discourse, I have confined my selfe especially to one important Testimony; one instead of many, or of all. . . ." But in *Of Reformation*, although Milton says that there was a threefold corruption in antiquity (the best times were generally infected, the best men of those times were foully tainted, the best writings of those men were dangerously adulterated), there is no special attack upon Irenaeus. In fact, Milton praises Irenaeus for his reproof of Victor, Bishop of Rome; and the name of Irenaeus does not occur in the list of those (Justin Martyr, Clemens, Origen, Tertullian) in whose volumes vanities are "thick sown."[3] On the other hand, in *Of Prelatical Episcopacy* Irenaeus is dealt with at considerable length, and the points made are precisely those controverted in *A Compendious Discourse*.

First, to discredit Irenaeus's testimony that Polycarpus was made Bishop of Smyrna by the Apostles, Milton declares that

---

William Haller, *Tracts on Liberty*, July (I, 17). The Columbia edition of Milton's works remarks that it was "printed anonymously in 1641" (III, 517).

[3] *The Works of John Milton* (New York, 1931), III, 20-21.

Irenaeus was only a boy when he saw and heard Polycarpus, and that a boy cannot be trusted to understand the church constitution or the terms on which Polycarpus received his commission. Almoni exerts himself to the utmost to confirm the testimony of Irenaeus, arguing that his evidence is so clear and weighty that it "may sufficiently determine the whole cause. . . ." He endeavors to answer all possible objections. Without doubt, his insistence upon Irenaeus's antiquity is due to Milton's argument that the evidence of Irenaeus is worthless because he was merely a boy when he saw Polycarpus. Irenaeus, declares Almoni, lived in the time of Eleutherius, the twelfth bishop of Rome. "We have few Authors (grave and certaine) now extant, who lived before his time; except Ignatius," some of whose seven Epistles are "lately cited by the adversaries of Episcopacy under his name." Irenaeus was a holy, learned, and peaceful man, a constant defender of the truth, and finally a patient sufferer for the same. The following seems to be aimed directly at Milton's tract: We are now "upon a point *historical*, viz. Whether this relation of *Irenaeus*, concerning the *Episcopacy* of *Polycarpus*, which he received from the Apostles, be true, or not? Wherein he had information immediately from *Polycarp* himselfe and the whole Church of *Smyrna*, wherein he lived. Who wil, who can, who dareth say that *Irenaeus* hath lyed in this report? He knew *Polycarp* very well, and knew undoubtedly that his *Episcopall* office was derived from the Apostles: why should this relation seem incredible to you?" Inability to understand how anyone could commit the sacrilege of which Milton had been guilty, indignation that one should dare to question the testimony of a Church Father, and loyalty to the Church lend a simple dignity and eloquence to this work of the champion of Episcopacy.

The phrase "the whole Church of *Smyrna*" quoted above reminds us that Milton also discredited the testimony from the Epistle of "those brethren of *Smyrna*," who style Polycarpus a bishop of the Church of Smyrna and a prophet. Polycarpus, says Milton, declared that "hee should die no other death then burning." How then did it come to pass that the fire would not do its work, "but starting off like a full saile from the mast, did but reflect a golden light upon his unviolated limbes exhaling such a sweet odour, as if all the incense of *Arabia* had bin burning, in so much that when the bill-men saw that the fire was overaw'd, and could not doe the deed, one of them steps to him, and stabs him with a sword, at which wound such abundance of blood gusht forth as quencht the fire. . . . Yet these good brethren say he was Bishop of *Smyrna*."[4] In his reply Almoni proceeds, in the seventeenth-century fashion, to multiply authorities: the Scriptures, our best divines, Leontius, Rainolds—all these and more prove that Polycarpus was Bishop of Smyrna. He sums up: "*Irenaeus* hath now related no more touching *Polycarps* Episcopacy, then is warrantable by Scriptures, Fathers, Historians, and our owne Divines."

Having justified Irenaeus's testimony concerning the episcopacy of Polycarpus, *A Compendious Discourse* takes up "some other poore exceptions against the aforesaid testimony." One objection is "that *Irenaeus* was himselfe a Bishop, and so not a competent witnesse in such a case." Milton declares that the "Councels themselves were fouly corrupted with ungodly Prelatisme, and so farre plung'd into worldly ambition, as that it stood them upon long ere this to uphold their now well-tasted Hierarchy by what faire pretext soever they could, in like manner as they had now learnt to defend many other grosse corruptions by as ancient, and suppos'd authentick tradition as Episcopacie."[5] And further: "it is most likely that in the Church they which came after these Apostolick men being lesse in merit, but bigger in ambition, strove to invade those priviledges by intrusion and plea of right, which *Polycarpus*, and others like him possest from the voluntary surrender of men subdu'd by the excellencie of their heavenly gifts, which because their Successors had not, and so could neither have that authority, it was their policy to divulge that the eminence which *Polycarpus* and his equalls enjoy'd, was by right of constitution, not by free wil of condiscending."[6] To this Almoni replies: "Shall then so holy a person

---

[4] *Op. cit.*, III, 95.   [5] *Op. cit.*, III, 84.   [6] *Op. cit.*, III, 92.

be rejected as a lyer? writing otherwise then he saw or heard? This were a desperate evasion, and contemptible; yet followed by the adversaries of Episcopacy, charging the Fathers as partiall in their owne cause. But were they not the principall writers? yet not the onely: for *Tertullian* and *Hierome* were Presbyters only (and not Bishops) whose judgement and testimony I will not decline in this cause. Thus our English Divines are rejected, as being *Bishops,* or affecting Episcopacy, and so their owne Judges. Say what you please; yet I will conclude this passage with the publique protestation of that learned and holy man, D. *Iohn White,* in his Sermon at Pauls Crosse, March 24. 1615. *I protest before God and man: it amazeth me to see such, as can read either Scripture, or Antiquity, to carpe at it (Episcopacy) when the Christian world, for 1400. yeeres after Christ, never saw any other government, &c."* The phrase "the adversaries of Episcopacy, charging the Fathers as partiall in their owne cause" indicates that Milton had adopted a common Puritan argument against Episcopacy and that Almoni was answering the entire party. Nevertheless, it seems clear that *Of Prelatical Episcopacy* is the principal work attacked.

Another exception considered is "that *Polycarp* was no Lord Bishop; he had no civill dignity, no temporall power, &c. and therefore was very different from the Bishops of our Church." Milton admits that Polycarpus may have been "a man of great eminence in the Church, to whom the other *Presbyters* might give way for his *vertue, wisdome,* and the reverence of his age"; but he insists that there is no proof that he belonged to "a distinct, and superior order."[7] If besides his other titles prophetical and apostolical Polycarpus is also styled Bishop of the Church of Smyrna, "it cannot be prov'd . . . that hee was therefore in distinct, and monarchicall order above the other *Presbyters."*[8] Almoni admits that the early church had no civil authority or dignity, but declares that later, beginning with Constantine, temporal power was joined with episcopal offices. He then makes five points: that as for three

[7] *Op. cit.,* III, 91-92.   [8] *Op. cit.,* III, 95-96.

centuries bishops were without temporal power, so they may be bishops without it now; that as the state for good reason gave them temporal power, so the state for good reasons may take it away, but may not lawfully take away Episcopacy; that temporal power may not only adorn but strengthen Episcopacy, for the benefit of church and commonwealth; that the bishops are capable of this dignity and power; and that the adversaries of Episcopacy are not content merely to deprive bishops of civil power, but would cast them wholly out of the church or leave them an empty title without a real office. The last statement describes in part the intention of Milton: he would destroy Episcopacy root and branch.

The final exception is that those "who in the third chapter, are called *Bishops* by *Irenaeus,* are in the second chapter called *Presbyters;* and so *Polycarp,* though called here a *Bishop,* is but a *Presbyter.* . . ." Milton says, "And yet thus farre *Irenaeus* makes against them as in that very place to call *Polycarpus* an Apostolicall *Presbyter.*"[9] Almoni's argument is that although these bishops are called presbyters, it is "with an evident distinction from common Presbyters." The name of bishop once common to all presbyters is now proper to that presbyter placed in rank above all the rest. In antiquity you will sometimes find that a bishop is called a presbyter, but you can never find anywhere that a presbyter is called a bishop. Almoni adds: "I am no stranger in the Councels, Fathers, and Histories, (in which course of studies being now 62-yeeres old, I have spent a moiety of my age) & yet I can remember no such thing. . . ." In defence of his beloved bishops and the Church, to the study of whose annals he had devoted his life, the author concludes: "A Bishop, in the Church of England, doth not unjustly usurpe an office therein by humane institution, but doth justly possesse it by divine right, notwithstanding all malicious scoffes, and unlearned cavils, against so ancient, so venerable, so necessary an Office in the Church of God."

It is true that *A Compendious Discourse* ignores two of

[9] *Op. cit.,* III, 92.

Milton's damaging arguments against Irenaeus: that he had
a Catholic bias, and that he was seduced by the errors of Papias.
Irenaeus was "so negligent in keeping the *faith* . . . as to say
. . . that the obedience of *Mary* was the cause of salvation to
her selfe, and all mankind, and . . . that as *Eve* was seduc't
to fly *God*, so the Virgin *Mary* was perswaded to obey God,
that the Virgin *Mary* might be the Advocate of the Virgin
Eve. Thus if *Irenaeus* for his neerenesse to the *Apostles*, must
be the Patron of *Episcopacy* to us, it is no marvell though he
be the Patron of Idolatry to the Papist, for the same cause."[10]
Again, Milton declares that Irenaeus, with others, was infected
with the errors of Papias, a very ancient writer, but a man of
shallow wit, who "fill'd his writings with many new doctrines,
and fabulous conceits. . . ."[11] Almoni did not reply to these
criticisms. Perhaps the brevity of the *Discourse* led to the
omission. Perhaps the author decided that it would be politic
to ignore these points. Since *A Compendious Discourse* followed close upon the heels of *Of Prelatical Episcopacy*, the
author, it must be observed, had very little time for writing.
The *Discourse* may very easily have been dashed off in one day
or even less.

It is only fair to say that the author of *A Compendious
Discourse* does not mention *Of Prelatical Episcopacy* and that
he does not know Milton by name. To him Milton is only one
of the bitter enemies of the Fathers and of Episcopacy. But,
as we have seen, Almoni does mention *Of Reformation*, the
author of which, he says, had attacked Irenaeus. Milton's first
antiprelatical tracts were, of course, published anonymously;
and Peloni Almoni apparently had no means of discovering the
author of these works, the latter of which he undertook to
answer in part. That Milton's assault upon the Fathers, "that
indigested heap, and frie of Authors," and upon Episcopacy
should provoke a reply was to be expected. Only the general
neglect of the pamphlets contemporary with Milton's (a neglect easily understood by one who is familiar with their dreary

[10] *Op. cit.*, III, 94.   [11] *Op. cit.*, III, 93.

and endless discussion of obsolete ecclesiastical issues) accounts for the previous failure to detect the relation of *A
Compendious Discourse* to Milton's second pamphlet. The discovery here announced calls for some slight revision in the
statement that "Except for the replies of the Halls, Milton's
antiprelatical tracts went unnoticed in the press."[12] The statement just quoted ignores Masson's discovery that in Thomas
Fuller's *The Holy State,* not published until 1642 but in
manuscript nearly a year before that date, there is an angry
allusion to Milton's *Of Reformation,* under the title *Causes
Hindering Reformation in England.*[13] Masson devotes some
pages to the matter, showing that Fuller actually quoted excerpts from Milton's pamphlet. Perhaps a more prolonged
scrutiny of forgotten pamphlets may be rewarded by the discovery of further references to Milton or his work. The following section sheds additional light on the contemporary repute of Milton's second pamphlet.

With regard to the author of *A Compendious Discourse*
nothing more has been discovered than is revealed in the pamphlet itself. The statement of his age and of his devotion to
the writings of the Church has already been quoted. The following excerpt from his address "To the Christian and Judicious Reader" merits reprinting for the light that it throws
both on the distracted state of religion and on the author's sincerity and courage:

. . . if ever there were a season to write, or speake, in defence of
Episcopacy, it is now, or never; wherein men travaile in birth to
bring forth their several conceipts: some doubting whether it be
of divine, or humane institution: some affirming the one, some the
other: some desiring to preserve it, some to destroy it. In such a
time silence is dangerous, wherein liberty is ill given to, or ill taken
by the adversaries of Gods ordinance to publish their raw and un-
digested discourses; fraught with more malice then truth. But canta-
bunt cygni, cum graculi tacuerint.

As for myselfe, I hope that I may make use of this publique

[12] William Haller, *op. cit.,* I, 129.
[13] *The Life of John Milton* (London, 1871), II, 359.

liberty, without offence (which I seeke not) or danger (which I regard not) to speake a word for my Reverend Mother, the Church of England, and my Venerable Fathers, the Bishops thereof: for I may say with S. Hierome, in a cause Ecclesiasticall; Mori possum, tacere non possum. I passe a while under an unknowne name; as some adversaries of Episcopacy do: the person is little to the matter: Res cum re, causa cum causa, ratio cum ratione concertet, as S. Augustine writeth.

Meane while thus much of me unknowne; that I have no dependance upon any Bishop; though there be one, singularly learned and truely religious, in that sacred Order, Cui debeo quicquid possum, & non possum (to use S. Hieromes words) from whom yet, as from the rest, I expect nothing; being rich in my contentment, and private course of life; wherein though I enjoy little, yet I seeke nothing more; but that the truth may have victory, the Church peace, and God the glory; Amen.

With less dependence upon any organized church and a more fervent zeal for the cause of true and untrammeled religion, Milton had previously plunged into the controversy. And, evidently ignoring the slight reply to his second pamphlet, he went straight ahead with his self-imposed task: to aid in the destruction of Episcopacy and in the establishment of a church discipline pure and undefiled. Of those who were united with Milton in the crusade against Episcopacy, one of the most sincere and admirable was Robert Greville, second Lord Brooke.

MILTON AND LORD BROOKE ON THE CHURCH

In *Areopagitica,* pleading with Parliament against the suppression of new and sectarian opinions, Milton cites the exhortation of "one of your own honourable number," who writing of Episcopacy and schism "left Ye his vote, or rather now the last words of his dying charge, which I know will ever be of dear and honour'd regard with Ye, so full of meeknes and breathing charity, that next to his last testament, who bequeath'd love and peace to his Disciples, I cannot call to mind where I have read or heard words more mild and peaceful. He there exhorts us to hear with patience and humility those, however they be miscall'd that desire to live purely, in such a use of Gods Ordinances, as the best guidance of their conscience gives them, and to tolerat them, though in some disconformity to our selves."[14]   The second Lord Brooke, to whom Milton here refers, was killed in an attack on Lichfield Cathedral, March 2, 1643. He is the author of *A Discourse Opening The Nature Of That Episcopacie, Which is Exercised in England,* to which Milton alludes in the excerpt just quoted. It seems probable that for the proof of an important part of his *Discourse* Lord Brooke made use of pertinent material in Milton's *Of Prelatical Episcopacy,* and that Milton in *The Reason of Church-Government Urg'd Against Prelaty* (1642) was, in his turn, indebted to Lord Brooke. If these suggested connections between the work of the man of affairs and the student of politics and religion can be established, we shall have proof of an immediate relationship that is significant and perhaps unique in the annals of seventeenth-century controversy.

First we must consider dates. As has been proved, *Of Prelatical Episcopacy* was in print before the end of May, 1641. Lord Brooke's *Discourse* was, as he said in his address to Parliament, the fruit of "the Retirements of Your Humble Servant in the Last *Recesse,*" which lasted from September 9 to October 20, 1641.[15] Even if we adopt the old dates for *Of Prelatical Episcopacy,* this pamphlet had been published more than a month when Lord Brooke began the composition of his *Discourse.* Thus, the dates do not preclude the relationship suggested.

The *Discourse* is in two sections. The first section shows "how uncompatible *Our Episcopacy* is to Civill Government in *State Policy.*" The second section deals with the antiquity of bishops, referring to that "most Reverend man, famous for learning," who had undertaken the defence of their cause. This was James Ussher, whose *The Iudgement of Doctor Rainoldes touching the Originall of Episcopacy* Milton had answered in

---

[14] *The Works of John Milton* (New York, 1931), IV, 346-347.
[15] *The Cambridge Modern History* (Cambridge, 1906), IV, 294.

Of Prelatical Episcopacy. Brooke declares, "I shall therefore in few words present to Him my thoughts upon those his determinations; Concluding with *Philip of Macedon,* that if I can but win the *chiefe City,* the whole Country is gained. . . ." As the following parallels seem to show, Milton's arguments had a considerable influence in shaping Lord Brooke's thoughts upon the antiquity of Episcopacy.

The first illustration deals with the evidence of Leontius. Bishop of Magnesia:

Of Prelatical Episcopacy

Next to prove a succession of 27. *Bishops* from *Timothy,* he cites one *Leontius Bishop* of *Magnesia,* out of the *Chalcedonian* Councell: this is but an obscure, and single witnesse, and for his faithfull dealing who shall commend him to us, with his Catalogue of *Bishops?* . . . for neither the praise of his wisedome, or his vertue hath left him memorable to posterity, but onely this doubtfull relation, . . .[16]

Discourse

First, He endeavoureth to prove the succession of seaven and twenty Bishops, in the seat of *Timothy:* and this he essayeth by one single (not to say simple) witnesse, a certaine man named *Leontius;* whose writings have not delivered him famous to us for learning, nor his exemplary holinesse (mentioned by others) famous for piety. . . .[17]

The next group also attacks the credibility of Ussher's witness:

Nothing hath been more attempted, nor with more subtility brought about . . . then to falsifie the Editions of the Councels, of which wee have none but from our Adversaries hands, . . . we know that many yeares ere this time which was almost 500. years after *Christ,* the Councels themselves were fouly corrupted with ungodly Prelatisme, . . .[18]

And shall I then give credit to an unknowne Author, in those things that were acted almost five hundred yeares before his birth? . . . Neither is this Author quoted, from witnesse of his owne; but out of a Councell. Now, how Councells have beene abused, those who have ever had place or note in great Assemblies, can too well tell: . . .

Photius's testimony of Timothy's martyrdom is then questioned:

[16] *The Works of John Milton* (New York, 1931), III, 83.
[17] All quotations from the *Discourse* are from pp. 66-68.
[18] Milton, *op. cit.,* III, 83-84.

As for that namelesse Treatise of *Timothy's* martyrdome, only cited by *Photius* that liv'd almost 900. yeares after *Christ*, it hansomely follows in that author, the Martyrdome of the seven Sleepers, . . . This Story of *Timothy's* Ephesian Bishopricke as it follows in order, so it may for truth, if it only subsist upon its own authority, as it doth, for *Photius* only saith he read it; he does not averre it.[19]

That other testimony brought from a fatherlesse Treatise of *Timothy's* Martyrdome, cited only by *Photius* (a learned man, who lived seven or eight centuries after Christ) will be of no weight: for *Photius* doth but say he read it. Hear-say in matter of judicature is no good testimony: . . .

In the next group three witnesses are disqualified:

Those of *Theodoret, Felix,* and *John* of *Antioch* are autorities of later times, and therefore not to be receiv'd for their Antiquities sake to give in evidence concerning an allegation, wherin writers so much their Elders, we see so easily miscarry.[20]

The testimonies of *Faelix, John* of *Antioch,* and *Theodore,* are not of age sufficient to bee registered, among the Ancients, or to be valued, because they are old.

Lord Brooke, it should be observed, raises against Bishop Ussher's witnesses for Episcopacy objections quite similar to those presented in *Of Prelatical Episcopacy.* The detail is often identical, although the phrasing varies slightly. This is true of the following entry, in which the evidence of Ignatius is assailed:

Now come the Epistles of *Ignatius* to shew us first, that *Onesimus* was Bishop of *Ephesus;* . . . a supposititious ofspring of some dozen Epistles, whereof five are rejected as spurious, containing in them Heresies and trifles, . . . those other Epistles lesse question'd are yet so interlarded with Corruptions, as may justly indue us with a wholesome suspition of the rest.[21]

For of *Ignatius* I shall affirme this, that All those who are any whit learned in Antiquity, know that five of his Epistles are spurious; and how unmingled those are which wee allow to be his, wee doe not know, who look upon Antiquity at such a distance.

It seems that Lord Brooke merely paraphrases Milton.

Observe also the following, which deals with the authority of Tertullian:

[19] Milton, *op. cit.,* III, 87.
[20] Milton, *op. cit.,* III, 88.
[21] Milton, *op. cit.,* III, 88-89.

Tertullian accosts us next . . . whose testimony, state but the question right, is of no more force to deduce Episcopacy, then the two former. He saies that the Church of Smirna had Polycarpus plac't there by John, and the Church of Rome Clement or-dain'd by Peter, . . . None of this will be contradicted, . . . it remaines yet to be evinc't out of this and the like places, which will never be, that the word Bishop is otherwise taken, then in the language of Saint Paul, and the Acts, for an order above Presbyters.[22]

The Authority of Tertullian also, is of the same credit: Hee tels us that Polycarpus was placed by St. John at Smyrna; and at Rome Clement by St. Peter. This no body will dispute; (though I am not bound to beleeve it.) but where is the stresse of this Argument?

One who compares Milton's statement "None of this will be contradicted" with Lord Brooke's "This no body will dispute" will scarcely conclude that the identity of these replies to Bishop Ussher's assertion is accidental. The striking agreement between the Discourse and Of Prelatical Episcopacy on this minor point strongly supports the theory that Lord Brooke is indebted to Milton.

The last parallel deals with the authority of Clement of Alexandria:

Lastly . . . that authority of Clemens Alexandrinus is not to be found in all his workes, and wherever it be extant, it is in controversie, whether it be Clements or no; or if it were it sayes onely that Saint John in some places constituted Bishops: questionlesse he did, but where does Clement say he set them above Presbyters? no man will gaine-say the constitution of Bishops, but the raising them to a superiour, and distinct order above Presbyters, see-ing the Gospell makes them one and the same thing, a thousand such al-legations as these will not give Pre-laticall Episcopacy, one Chapell of ease above a Parish Church.[23]

In the last place, that of Clement Alexandrinus, is as much questioned as all the rest. But allow it to bee true, that John did appoint Bishops, they have gained nothing; for I shall allow that Christ also hath instituted Bishops, and that Bishops are Jure divino; yea, I will allow that they are to feed Christs flock, to rule Christs inheritance, in Christs sense; but I shall never allow these Bishops, which are now the subject of our dispute.

[22] Milton, op. cit., III, 96.

[23] Milton, op. cit., III, 98-99.

Again, without restricting himself to Milton's phrasing, Lord Brooke seems to follow closely the subject matter and the method of his predecessor.

The reader is probably convinced that Lord Brooke's arguments against the Fathers are identical with Milton's. Although it is conceivable that in his refutation of Bishop Ussher Lord Brooke independently hit upon precisely the same points that Milton had previously used, such a close agreement of arguments is most satisfactorily accounted for by the hypothesis here maintained—an hypothesis clearly supported by the facts. It is true that the *Discourse* omits most of Milton's detailed proof, including his long discussion of Irenaeus. Here one must bear in mind the different purposes of the two adversaries of Episcopacy. In *Of Prelatical Episcopacy* Milton's special purpose was to recall the people of God from doting upon Antiquity. In the *Discourse* Lord Brooke presented a general discussion of the nature of Episcopacy, with brief consideration of the antiquity of the Church. In his discussion of the latter subject, the evidence seems conclusive that Lord Brooke, who in scholarship was certainly not Milton's equal, made use of *Of Prelatical Episcopacy*, which had but recently appeared and which more than likely had impressed him by its solid learning and its dialectic skill. So much for Lord Brooke's indebtedness to Milton.

On the other hand, it is possible that Milton is indebted to Lord Brooke. In *The Reason of Church-Government Urg'd against Prelaty*, which appeared in 1642, Milton denounced Episcopacy itself as a schism from the true church. Probably he recalled that Lord Brooke, in Section II, Chapter VII, of the *Discourse*, had condemned Episcopacy as "the efficient cause of the most grievous Schismes, and Heresies." Observe the following vehement outburst in the *Discourse:*

They cry out of Schisme, Schisme; Sects and Schismes; and well they may: They make them, and it is strange they should not know them. When they laid such stumbling blocks (Reall Scandals, not only *accepta*, but *data*) in the way of all good men, whose Consciences they have grievously burdened, and wounded with Things (violently pressed on the greatest fines) that are so farre from being indifferent, that many of them were point blank unlawfull: have they not by This even forced their brethren to separate themselves in Judgement and Practice, till they could finde some remote place that might separate their bodies also? Was not This in them the readiest way to produce Divisions, Separations, and (as they call it) *Schismes* in the Church? Rents are bad, I confesse, where ever they be violent; but yet then worst, when most out of the eye. *Schismes* in the *Conscience* are of greatest danger; and to prevent These, if I am forct to That, which they please to call a *Schisme* in the Church, Woe to Him that so forceth me. Scandals, Schismes, and Divisions must come; but woe to him by whom they come. . . . Thus we have, by too too long, great, and sad experience, found it true, That our Prelates have beene so farre from preventing Divisions; that they have been the Parents and Patrons of most Errors, Heresies, Sects and Schismes, that now disturbe This Church and State.

Students of Milton's prose scarcely need to be reminded that he also discusses the same question at length. He declares that schism is to be expected: "Our Saviour and his Apostles did not only forsee, but foretell and forewarne us to looke for schisme . . . it was well knowne what a bold lurker schisme was even in the houshold of Christ . . . early in the Acts of the Apostles the noise of schisme had almost drown'd the proclaiming of the Gospell; yet we reade not in Scripture that any thought was had of making Prelates, no not in those places where dissention was most rife."[24] Episcopacy is no remedy for schism. Under Episcopacy, Milton declares, schism and heresy rage. Episcopacy and faction "with a spousall ring are wedded together, never to be divorc't." Reviewing the history of the church, Milton writes: "So farre was it [Episcopacy] from removing schisme, that if schisme parted the congregations before, now it rent and mangl'd, now it rag'd. Heresie begat heresie with a certaine monstrous haste of pregnancy in her birth, at once borne and bringing forth. Contentions before brotherly were now hostile. Men went to choose their Bishop

[24] Milton, *op. cit.*, III, 210.

as they went to a pitcht field, and the day of his election was like the sacking of a City, sometimes ended with the blood of thousands."[25] Moreover, according to Milton, prelacy and popery are one. It cannot be denied that the Pope arose out of the reason of prelacy. If "Prelaty must still rise and rise till it come to a Primat, why should it stay there?" Episcopacy is, therefore, "the very wombe for a new subantichrist to breed in; if it be not rather the old force and power of the same man of sin counterfeiting protestant." Milton declares: "It was not the prevention of schisme, but it was schisme it selfe, and the hatefull thirst of Lording in the Church that first bestow'd a being upon Prelaty. . . ." With its oppression and leaden doctrine, with its persecution of zealous Christians, Episcopacy would bring upon the people stupidity and blindness; "and by this kind of discipline all *Italy* and *Spaine* is as purely and politickly kept from schisme as *England* hath beene by them." Clearly, Milton prefers schism, which is life, to Episcopacy, which means paralysis and death of the spirit. Hear the poet speak:

With as good a plea might the dead palsie boast to a man, tis I that free you from stitches and paines, and the troublesome feeling of cold & heat, of wounds and strokes; if I were gone, all these would molest you. The Winter might as well vaunt it selfe against the Spring, I destroy all noysome and rank weeds, I keepe downe all pestilent vapours. Yes and all wholesome herbs, and all fresh dews, by your violent & hidebound frost; but when the gentle west winds shall open the fruitfull bosome of the earth thus over-girded by your imprisonment, then the flowers put forth and spring, and then the Sunne shall scatter the mists, and the manuring hand of the Tiller shall root up all that burdens the soile without thank to your bondage. . .[26]

Thus Milton has no fear of the sects, Brownists, Familists, Anabaptists, who condemn the lawless government of Prelacy, its ceremonies, its liturgy, "an extract of the Masse book translated." Looking forward to the unity of the church, he exclaims: "Noise it till ye be hoarse; that a rabble of Sects will

[25] Milton, *op. cit.*, III, 211.   [26] Milton, *op. cit.*, III, 214.

come in, it will be answer'd ye, no rabble sir Priest, but a unanimous multitude of good Protestants will then joyne to the
Church, which now because of you stand separated." This
hope was not to be realized; unity of the church was not to
be gained simply by the suppression of Episcopacy. Milton
underestimated the centrifugal force of dissent. He was on
more solid ground when he declared: "Prelaty is a schisme
it selfe from the most reformed and most flourishing of our
neighbour Churches abroad, and a sad subject of discord and
offence to the whole nation at home."[27]

It is obvious that in opposing Episcopacy Milton and
Lord Brooke agree upon essentials. Especially interesting
is the fact that they condemn not the sects but Episcopacy as
the cause of sects. Milton, however, goes beyond Lord Brooke,
denouncing Prelacy as the cause of discord and as itself a
schism. Neither, it is true, is an advocate of complete toleration in religion; Episcopacy and Popery are both excluded
from their program. Otherwise they are in favor of unre-
stricted toleration. As was said at the outset, Milton recommended to Parliament the policy urged by Lord Brooke at the
conclusion of the *Discourse:*

But when God shall so enlarge his Hand, and unveile his face,
that the poore Creature is brought into Communion and acquaintance with his Creator, steered in all his wayes by His Spirit; and
by it carried up above shame, feare, pleasure, comfort, losses, grave,
and death it selfe; Let us not censure such Tempers, but blesse
God for them. So farre as Christ is in us, we shall love, prise,
honour Christ, and the least particle of his Image in Others: For
we never Prove our selves true members of Christ more then when
we embrace his members with most enlarged, yet straitest Affections.

To this end, God assisting mee, my desire, prayer, indeavour shall
still be, as much as in mee lyes, to follow Peace and holinesse. And
though there may haply be some little dissent betweene my
darke judgement, weak conscience, and other Good men, that are
much more cleare and strong; yet my prayer still shall be, *to keepe
the Unity of the Spirit in the Bond of Peace.* And as many as

[27] Milton, *op. cit.*, III, 219.

walke after This Rule, Peace I hope shall still be on Them, and
the whole Israel of God.

For his purpose Milton could not have cited a better witness.
But the time for toleration was not yet; for more than a century his ideal and that of Lord Brooke remained merely an
aspiration and a dream.

CHAPTER XII

MILTON AND CANNE

FROM the observation of the relationship of Milton's ecclesiastical pamphlets to contemporary writing, we come now to the study of works that are essentially political. Soon after the beheading of Charles I, January 30, 1649, there appeared two remarkable pamphlets: one of these is Milton's famous *The Tenure of Kings and Magistrates*, which in Thomason's *Catalogue* is dated February 13;[1] the other is John Canne's *The Golden Rule, Or, Justice Advanced. Wherein is shewed, That the Representative Kingdom, or Commons assembled in Parliament, have a lawfull power to arraign, and adjudge to death the King, for Tyranny, Treason, Murder, and other high Misdemeanors: And whatsoever is objected to the contrary from Scripture, Law, Reason, or Inconveniences, is satisfactorily answered and refuted. Being, A cleer and full satisfaction to the whole Nation, in justification of the legal proceeding of the High Court of Justice, against Charls Steward, late King of England* . . . (1649), which in Thomason is dated February 16.[2] Canne's work, which, like Milton's, advocates the right of the people to depose and put to death a tyrant, seems to be almost unknown. It is not mentioned in *The Tenure of Kings and Magistrates* edited by William T. Allison,[3] who declares that the ideas set forth in Milton's *Tenure* were there "for the first time applied with astonishing vigor and frankness to a great political crisis in English history" and that in making his first plea for civil liberty Milton anticipated "modern thought in the statement and defence of great and generous principles."[4] The statement is true but incomplete. As a mat-

[1] I, 723. This was four days after the publication of *Eikon Basilike* (*ibid.*, I, 723).   [2] I, 724.
[3] (New York, 1911).   [4] Pp. xiv-xv.

ter of fact, the opinions expressed in the *Tenure* are essentially the same as those in Canne's *Golden Rule*. Between two works having the same purpose a certain community of ideas is to be expected, but the close correspondence between Milton's and Canne's pamphlets is indeed surprising. To demonstrate this similarity is the purpose of this comparative study. Generous quotations from the *Golden Rule*, which is inaccessible to most readers, are introduced.

One of the most striking parallels is that which includes a reference to Seneca. To show what the people may lawfully do against a tyrant, as "against a common pest, and destroyer of mankinde," Milton refers briefly to the practice of the Greeks and the Romans:

The *Greeks* and *Romans*, as their prime Authors witness, held it not onely lawfull, but a glorious and Heroic deed, rewarded publicly with Statues and Garlands, to kill an infamous Tyrant at any time without tryal: and but reason, that he who trod down all Law, should not be voutsaf'd the benefit of Law. Insomuch that Seneca the Tragedian brings in *Hercules* the grand suppressor of Tyrants, thus speaking,

> . . . . *Victima haud ulla amplior*
> *Potest, magisque opima mactari Jovi*
> *Quam Rex iniquus* . . . .
> . . . . There can be slaine
> No sacrifice to God more acceptable
> Then an unjust and wicked King. . . .[5]

This should be compared with the following quotation from *The Golden Rule:*

The putting to death of Tyrants in former times hath been held so lawful and honorable, as large rewards have been propounded to the undertakers and authors thereof, and to the living they have given the goods of the Tyrant as to the deliverer of their Country, and honored the deed with *Epitaphs, and Statues of brasse,* as in *Athens, Harmodius,* and *Aristogiton,* together with *Brutus,* and *Cassius;* in Greece *Aratus* the *Sycienian,* and . . . those monuments of *Tyrant-killers* by antiquity were so honored and highly

[5] *The Works of John Milton* (New York, 1932), V, 19.

esteemed of, as they placed them in their Temples on sacred ban-
queting beds: . . . And what the Poet wrote was the opinion then,
and common saying of the people.

> . . . . . Victima haud ulla amplior
> Potest, magisve opima mactari Jovi
> Quam Rex iniquus.
> To God no better offering can men bring,
> Nor fatter, than a wicked Tyrant King.[6]

These passages are closely related. The fact that the one from
Milton occurs not far from the opening of the *Tenure* and that
the one from Canne is near the end of *The Golden Rule* suggests the theory that Canne may have rounded out his pamphlet
after reading Milton's. It is also possible that the following
similarities are due to Canne's direct borrowing from Milton,
but more probably they are the result of common opinions and
common efforts to disarm the followers of royalty.

Opposing the Royalist dogma that subjects owe unconditional obedience and complete submission to the king, both Milton and Canne distinguish between just rulers, who are to be
obeyed, and tyrants, who are to be resisted; and both make this
distinction with reference to *Romans* 13: 1, 2, which was the
Royalist authority in Scripture. Canne argues that there is
nothing in the Apostle's words against the arraignment of tyrants:

For 1. The *Higher Powers* must be submitted to: and why? Because *they are ordained of God, and are Gods ordinances*. vers. 1, 2.
That is so far as they govern according to reason and just laws,
preserve the peoples liberties, persons, and estates. But where is it
said, When they prove traitors to the Kingdom, and are the Devil's
agents, they may not be severely punished for it. 2. Because those
who resist lawful authority, and just commands, receive to themselves condemnation, is not this, *a non sequitur*, that the Parliament
whose jurisdiction and power is above the King, may not call him
to an account for tyranny and mis-government. 3. Rulers must
be obeyed, Because *they are not a terror to good works, but to evil*.
verse 3. Is not this a good consequence, when they are profest ene-

[6] Pp. 35-36.

mies to all good works, and do evil and continually evil with both hands, that same power which hath set them up, cannot take them down again. 4. Obey him saith the Apostle, why? *because he is the minister of God to thee for good.* v. 4. But can this be applied to a Tyrant, who hath destroy'd the people in body & goods; doth it not rather plainly imply, that those who are the devils ministers to us for evil, rather than Gods for good, by a lawful power above them, should be thrust out of their place.

Canne sums up this point as follows:

Howsoever the lawfull power of Princes be of God, yet the tyranny it self, and abuse of this power is of Satan, and therefore though the power it self which is good and profitable, be to be honored and continued, yet the tyrant justly may be condemned to death, as not within the compasse of this text.[7]

Similarly, Milton argues that obedience is due only to lawful and just power:

It must also be understood of lawfull and just power, els we read of great power in the affaires and Kingdoms of the World per-mitted to the Devil: . . . Therefore Saint *Paul* in the forecited Chapter tells us that such Magistrates he meanes, as are, not a ter-ror to the good but to the evil; . . . So that if the power be not such, or the persons execute not such power, neither the one nor the other is of God, but of the Devil, and by consequence to bee resisted. . . . So that we see the title and just right of raigning or deposing, in reference to God, is found in the Scripture to be all one; visible onely in the people, and depending meerly upon justice and demerit.[8]

Both Canne and Milton declare that David's sparing Saul is no argument for unconditional obedience. Canne writes:

The difference was but private and personal between *Saul & David, David* being *Sauls* private subject, servant and son-in-law; not pub-lick between *Saul* and his Parliament or Kingdom. Now many things are unlawful in private quarrels, which are just and honour-able in publick differences.[9]

[7] Pp. 21-24.
[8] *Op. cit.*, pp. 16-18.   [9] *Op. cit.*, p. 7.

Milton writes:

And if *David* refus'd to lift his hand against the Lords anointed, the matter between them was not tyranny, but private enmity, and *David* as a private person had bin his own revenger, not so much the peoples.[10]

As proof of their doctrine that the king is responsible only to God, Royalists cited David's cry: "Against thee, thee only, have I sinned, and done this evil in thy sight. . . ."[11] Canne explains that by murder and adultery David had sinned not only against God but also against Uriah, his wife, children, and kindred; that kings are subject to the laws of God, of nature, and of nations; that David simply meant that his sin was not concealed from God and that he had sinned against God principally.[12] According to Milton, David meant that the depth of his guilt was known to God only or that the sin against God was incomparably greater than that against Uriah. In Canne, however, there is nothing to match Milton's contemptuous remark: "Whatever his meaning were, any wise man will see that the patheticall words of a Psalme can be no certaine decision to a poynt that hath abundantly more certain rules to goe by."[13]

In much the same way Milton and Canne dispose of the Royalist doctrine that the king's power is unlimited. Milton declares:

For if they may refuse to give account, then all cov'nants made with them at Coronation; all Oathes are in vaine, and meer mockeries, all Lawes which they sweare to keep, made to no purpose; for if the King feare not God, as how many of them doe not? we hold then our lives and estates, by the tenure of his meer grace and mercy, as from a God, not a mortal Magistrate, a position that none but Court Parasites or men besotted would maintain.[14]

Canne declares:

Royallists and *Court-flatterers* do allow such an absolute prerogative to Kings, that if they would make use of their plenitude and

[10] *Op. cit.,* p. 22.
[11] *Psalms,* 51.
[13] *Op. cit.,* p. 13.
[12] *Op. cit.,* p. 15.
[14] *Op. cit.,* p. 12.

unlimited power, there is no such wickednesse but they may doe. viz. violently ravish matrons, deflower virgins, unnaturally abuse youth, cut all their Subjects throats, fire their houses, sack their cities, subvert their Liberties, and (as *Bellarmin* puts the case of the Popes absolute irresistible authority) send millions of souls to hel; yet no man under pain of damnation, may or ought demand of him, *Domine, cur ita facis?* Sir, what do you? such a slavery those vermine have sought to bring all Subjects into.[15]

Against the Royalist dogma that the king's power is unlimited and that his subjects owe him unconditional obedience the arguments of Milton and Canne are strikingly similar. If this agreement is not proof merely of the unanimity of opinion and argument among the Independents, it may be an indication that Canne was influenced by Milton's views.

Milton and Canne support unreservedly the principle that all political power resides in the people, who, as Milton says, may either choose their ruler or reject him, retain or depose him, "meerly by the liberty and right of free born Men, to be govern'd as seems to them best." The power of kings is derivative, "transferr'd and committed to them in trust from the People, to the Common good of them all, in whom the power yet remains fundamentally, and cannot be tak'n from them, without a violence of thir natural birthright." Canne likewise insists that "the people are above and more excellent then the King, and the King in dignity inferior to the people and the whole Kingdom. . . ." He labors to establish this fundamental point. He declares that the king is the shepherd of his people, the minister of God for their good; that the king is but part of the kingdom, and that the part is less than the whole; that the king is temporary and mortal, but the people as a species eternal; that the people were before the king and may exist without him. In proof that the people are superior, Canne appeals to reason, law, and experience. He affirms that every "efficient and constituent cause is more excellent then the effect: every mean is inferior in power to the end. But the people are the efficient cause, the King is the effect; . . . Com-

[15] *Op. cit.*, p. 8.

mon reason, Law, and experience, manifests that the whole, or greater part in all politick or natural bodies is of greater power and jurisdiction, then any one particular member. Thus in all corporations the Court of Aldermen is of greater power then the Major alone, though the chief officer: so the whole Bench, then the Lord chief Justice, and the whole Councel then the President. And it is Aristotles expresse determination, *Majorum rerum potestas jure populo tribuitur.*"

Milton and Canne argue that the king is accountable to the people and that his power is revocable. Milton explains that kings and magistrates were bound by conditions and oaths to do impartial justice, often with express warning that if they proved unfaithful "the people would be disingag'd."[16] With Aristotle, he declares that "monarchy unaccountable, is the worst sort of Tyranny," and by free men is not to be endured. Canne ridicules the notion that the people have resigned their power to the king and cannot recall it: "It is a thing neither probable nor credible that any free people when they voluntarily incorporated themselves into Kingdoms, and of their own accord set up an elective King over them, that there was such a stupidity and madness in them, as absolutely to make away their whole power to the King and his heirs forever, and to give him an entire, full, and incontroulable Supremacy over them, and so to make the Creature superior to the Creator, the derivative greater than the primative, the servant more potent than themselves, and so of free-men to make themselves slaves and for their more safety to be more enslav'd."[17]

Since kings are subject to the people, they should not be exempt from punishment for their crimes. Canne declares that kings may be unkinged and that for treason and murder they may lawfully be put to death. He ridicules the doctrine that the king can do no wrong, that only his wicked counselors must be punished. The Lord, says Canne, decreed that the soul that sins shall die, and "in all ages hath punished the author of sin, and persons commanding such and such wickednesse, more severely and extreamly, then the agent. . . ." In

[16] Pp. 9-10.   [17] *Op. cit.,* pp. 26-27.

answer to the plea that the person of the king is sacred, Canne, with grim humor that reminds one of Milton, relates this incident: "I have read in *Plutarch*, that *Alexander Magnus* published he was the son of *Jupiter Hammon;* yet when he saw the humor running down from his wounds, was constrained to say, this is . . . *the blood of man not of God:* and smelling the stench of his own flesh, asked his flatterers, *if the gods yeelded such a stench.* Princes (specially of late) have deem'd themselves to be *None-such,* and altogether unlike other men, but when they shall see themselves as prisoners stand at the bar, and justice don upon them, they will think otherwise of their condition."[18] In some places Canne is more outspoken than Milton. For example, he writes as follows: "*Charles Steuart* in a hostile and publick way hath murdered many thousands of his best subjects, by giving Warrants and Commissions under his own hand to Atheists, and Papists, personally appeared in many battles to destroy the people, caused sundry villages, towns, and cities to be ruinated by fire, plunder, and rapine, authorised villanous Pirates of other nations, (not to mention his own Son, nor *Rupert* that monster of mankind) to rob and kill his own subjects at sea; gave *Ormond* commission, and the bloody Irish, to kill and massacre, not so few as two hundred thousand, men, women, and children, of the Protestant religion in *Ireland;* not to speak of fifteen hundred widowes which he made in one morning, as Mr. *Henderson* told him; nor the loss of *Rochel* in *France,* by his lending *ships* to the *French* King; and this was his trade and constant practice many yeeres together, and doubtlesse would have continued so to this day, had not the Lord of Hosts by a powerfull hand (using our Army as instrumental means) supprest him: and for all this his heart never smote him as it could be perceived, but he remain'd impenitent and incorrigeble in his sins."[19] Although Milton nowhere mentions the King by name and leaves the particular charges and proofs to others, he has Charles I in mind throughout the *Tenure.*

In reply to those who insisted that there was neither prece-

[18] *Op. cit.*, p. 24.　　　　[19] *Op. cit.*, pp. 16-17.

dent nor law for the trial and execution of the King, both Milton and Canne declare that the Council of State should act without precedent if necessary. Milton writes: "And if the Parlament and Military Councel doe what they doe without precedent, if it appeare thir duty, it argues the more wisdom, vertue, and magnanimity, that they know themselves able to be a precedent to others. Who perhaps in future ages, if they prove not too degenerate, will look up with honour, and aspire toward these exemplary, and matchlesse deeds of thir Ancestors, as to the highest top of thir civill glory and emulation. . . ."[20] Canne insists that the Commons have "a Soveraign power to judge him [the King] to death, if his crimes deserve the same."[21] Canne appeals to reason: "If a King commit murder, adultery, theft, and be a traitor, a waster, and destroyer of his people, their goods, lives, Laws, Liberties, contrary to his oath and Coronation-Covenant, in this case I confidently affirm, there is no law (that hath reason, equity, or justice for its bottom and ground) against the putting of such a King to death by the great Councel of State. . . . And the reason is cleer, for the people have no power to make a law, that the King shall not die by the hand of Justice what wickedness soever he should commit." The Royalists and Presbyterians who declared that for the trial of the King there was no example in Scripture or history are informed that all things that are lawful are not written in Scripture; that states merely opposing the tyranny of princes without cutting them off "have brought upon themselves and the whol Realm the more mischief and misery afterward"; that former examples are no binding rules otherwise than as men have acted according to reason, religion, and law; that if "Kings formerly have not judicially been put to death for murder, treason, and other capital crimes, it is the more needful and useful that such a thing should now be done, that all other Nations far and neer may hence know and learn, what their duty is, and what they may lawfully do, in point of Law and conscience, and not stand still as if they were beasts in a base and sencelesse slavery any

[20] *Op. cit.*, p. 41.   [21] *Op. cit.*, p. 32.

longer."[22] Certainly Canne is as bold as Milton and at times almost as vigorous and trenchant.

On the other hand, precedent and authority are not ignored. Canne, for example, says that he would gladly be informed by any jurist or statist, if a tyrant without a title may be killed, even by a private man, "why a Tyrant that hath lost his right and title to the Crown, by the highest Judicature in the Kingdom, may not lawfully be put to death." The first, he says, is allowed by law, "and it is so generally held by *Vasquez, Barclay*, and others. And for the latter, observe what *Royalists* themselves acknowledge, *Winzetus* against *Buchan*, saith of *Nero*, that he seeking to destroy the Senate and People of *Rome*, and seeking to make new laws for himself, *excidit jure Regni*, lost all right to the kingdom. And *Barclay* saith, a Tyrant such as *Caligula, spoliare se jure Regni*, spoileth himself of the right of the Crown. So *Grotius, Si Rex hostili animo in totius populi exitium feratur emittit regnum*, If he turn enemy to the kingdom for their destruction he loseth the kingdom: because (saith he) *Voluntas imperandi, & voluntas perdendi, simul consistere non possunt*. A wil or mind to govern or destroy, cannot consist together in one."[23] Canne gives a number of examples of tyrants who were put to death: Andronicus, apprehended, deposed, and slain by the people; Julianus, deposed and by authority slain in his palace; Heliogabalus, executed with the approbation of the senate and the people; Dardan, King of Scotland, beheaded with the unanimous consent of the nobles and the people; and a number of others. For Milton reason alone is a sufficient guide; but for others he fills many pages with examples of tyrants punished and with opinions of tyrant-quellers.

These are some of the most important analogies between Milton's *Tenure* and Canne's *Golden Rule*. Although there are differences in detail, the essential ideas are the same. But in *The Golden Rule* there is nothing corresponding to Milton's denunciation of "the ignorance or the notorious hypocrisie and self-repugnance of our dancing Divines" and there is no criti-

[22] *Op. cit.*, p. 34.   [23] *Op. cit.*, p. 33.

cism of the Presbyterians. Canne does not condemn any religious party. His spirit and purpose are revealed in his epistle dedicatory to the Commons and Fairfax:

I have made the more hast to publish the First Part, because I perceive not only Royalists and Cavileers accuse you of high injustice against the Person of the King, and that the action hath been formerly carried forth meerly by power, without Law, reason or conscience: But also, the lawfulnesse of the thing, is by some better minded, and persons more honest, doubted, and are not cleerly satisfied therein: And for these latter, I say, specially for their sake, I have taken in hand, not your cause so much, as the cause of the whole Nation, and have not only given a satisfactory answer to what may be objected against the act, but justified what hath been done by your authority in point of Law and conscience, to all rational and indifferent men.

Canne ignores the Presbyterian case based upon the clause in the Covenant guaranteeing the preservation of the King's person, crown, and dignity, a point that Milton discusses at some length. However, in *The Snare is Broken,* the dedication of which is dated April 21, 1649, Canne dealt in detail with this matter. With better judgment, Milton considered all points in one pamphlet.

It may be that Canne was not seriously indebted to Milton. Canne's thirty-six-page pamphlet may have been finished before Milton's *Tenure* appeared. The similarity of ideas may be explained by the fact that the authors were the unofficial spokesmen of one party and were influenced by that party's opinions. One may, for example, compare Milton's and Canne's pamphlets with Lord President Bradshaw's Speech before he passed sentence upon the King.[24] Bradshaw admonished the King that as the law is his superior so the people of England as the authors of law are his superiors and have the right to alter laws

[24] *King Charls His Tryal: or A perfect Narrative of the whole Proceedings of the High Court of Justice In The Tryal of the King in Westminster Hall. Begun Saturday January 20. and ended on Saturday January 27. 1648. With the several Speeches of the King, Lord President, and Solicitor General. Together with that Eloquent and Learned Speech of the Lord President before he gave Sentence, not before published. Corrected & enlarged by a more perfect copy . . . 1649.*

as they see fit; that the end of having kings or any other governors is the enjoying of justice; that the king is but an officer in trust upon oath, and that if he offends he should be called to account by Parliament; that the people of almost all nations and especially of Scotland and England have called tyrants to account; that the bond between the king and his people is reciprocal, requiring protection from the sovereign and subjection from the people, and "if this bond be once broken farewell Soveraignty"; that by God's law whoso sheddeth man's blood, by man shall his blood be shed. Here are the fundamental ideas in both Milton's and Canne's pamphlets. Consider the following excerpt from Bradshaw's Speech:

Sir, we know very well that it is a question much on your side prest, by what President we shall proceed; truly Sir, for Presidents, I shall not upon these occasions institute any long discourse, but it is no new thing to cite presidents almost of all nations, where the people (when power hath been in their hands) have made bold to call their Kings to account; and where the change of government hath bin upon occasion of the tyranny and misgovernment of those that have been placed over them; I will not spend time to mention either France, or Spaine, or the Empire, or other countries, volumes may be written of it; . . .[25]

Canne and especially Milton elaborate this point, which Bradshaw had time only to mention. So it is with many other ideas.

As was said at the outset, in works having a common purpose some likeness of ideas is inevitable. Besides, there were some commonplaces in the political theories and arguments of the first half of the seventeenth century. Indeed, the specific purpose of this chapter is to show that none of the fundamental ideas voiced so vigorously and eloquently in the *Tenure* is peculiarly Milton's. They are the ideas of a party, of which Milton was not the only self-appointed spokesman. John Canne, divine and printer, who had recently returned from Amsterdam, earnestly advocated the same principles and almost as promptly vindicated the High Court of Justice. Be-

[25] P. 36.

cause of its kinship with Milton's famous work and also in its own right, *The Golden Rule* merits resurrection from its long oblivion. But it is only fair to say that it is on the whole quite undistinguished in style. It has nothing of the sustained eloquence and force of Milton's *Tenure*, which doubtless attracted the attention of prominent Independents and won for Milton the post of Latin Secretary to the Council of State.

CHAPTER XIII

THE WRITING OF *EIKONOKLASTES*

ALTHOUGH *Eikonoklastes* was an assigned work, which seems to have had little influence upon contemporary opinion, it is highly regarded by discriminating critics, who rank it second only to *Areopagitica*. Inspired by a genuine hatred of autocracy and of Charles I, by a lofty scorn for the casuistry of *Eikon Basilike*, and by an intense desire to thwart the machinations of the enemies of liberty, Milton wrote with unaccustomed directness, astonishing power, and unwavering insight. To the student of Milton and of English history *Eikonoklastes* is of unusual interest. But to some modern critics it is a rather hurried work and in large part indebted to predecessors. Some years ago Mr. Warren H. Lowenhaupt undertook to show the circumstances under which *Eikonoklastes* was written.[1] He makes it clear that Milton's work was not the first but the fourth pamphlet in the *Eikon Basilike* controversy and declares that Milton was strongly influenced by recent writers on this subject. In particular, Mr. Lowenhaupt states that for "certain definite references, arguments, and intellectual twists" Milton was indebted to *Eikon Alethine*,[2] a reply to *Eikon Basilike*. Admitting that evidence of borrowing must be spectacular or cumulative to be convincing, he presents a list of thirty-six alleged parallels between *Eikon Alethine* and *Eikon-*

---

[1] "The Writing of Milton's *Eikonoklastes*," *Studies in Philology*, XX (January, 1923), pp. 29-51.

[2] *Eikon Alethine The Pourtraiture Of Truths most sacred Majesty truly suffering, though not solely. Wherein the false colours are washed off, wherewith the Painter-steiner had bedawbed Truth, the late King and the Parliament, in his counterfeit Piece entituled Eikon Basilike, Published to undeceive the World.* . . . In Thomason's *Catalogue*, I, 765, this pamphlet is dated August 26, 1649. *Eikonoklastes* was published by October 6, 1649.

oklastes. Admitting also that some of the parallels may have been due to chance or common knowledge or a common source, he suggests that such a large number of similarities could not be accidental, declaring that Milton answered twenty-four of Charles's arguments "in language or references strikingly similar to expressions occurring under like circumstances in *Eikon Alethine.*" Indeed, Mr. Lowenhaupt discovers such a strong Miltonic strain in *Eikon Alethine* as to be convinced that Milton touched it up or contributed to it phrases and passages. He also thinks it fair to assume that Milton took the form of *Eikonoklastes* from the preceding work. Moreover, Mr. Lowenhaupt believes that Milton knew and profited by *Eikon Episte,* a Royalist answer to *Eikon Alethine,* but admits that here the evidence is not very strong. He concludes that in this borrowing "we have new knowledge of Milton's sources and of his methods of composition."

At first accepting Mr. Lowenhaupt's conclusions, Mr. Hanford writes of Milton's indebtedness "for many of his arguments, allusions, and turns of phrase" to *Eikon Alethine* and declares that Milton must have composed *Eikonoklastes* "very rapidly between August 26, the date of *Eikon Alethine,* and October 6, when his own pamphlet was on sale." Later, he ignores Mr. Lowenhaupt's arguments.[3] Thus, in this case, Milton's methods of composition and indebtedness appear to be open questions.

As a matter of fact, Mr. Lowenhaupt's conclusions are decidedly dubious. Most of the parallels cited in his article have little weight when one examines the language of other books and documents which seem to be Milton's real sources or authorities. In this chapter some of these authorities are examined and Mr. Lowenhaupt's evidence is closely scrutinized. A careful survey of the field reveals much evidence that in writing *Eikonoklastes* Milton relied not upon the hasty work of partisan pamphleteers (some of which he may have known) but upon a dignified history of recent events and upon state papers

[3] *A Milton Handbook* (New York, 1933), pp. 96-97; revised edition (New York, 1938), p. 96.

and declarations—in short, upon authorities that he considered unimpeachable.

Milton cites some of his sources, but he does not mention one to which his debt is considerable: Thomas May's *History of the Parliament of England* (1647). At the outset, one should observe that Thomas May was a valued writer in the cause of Parliament; that he was rather intimately acquainted with Court life, of which in his early writings he had revealed the follies and vices; that he took up his work for Parliament not from hope of reward but from a sense of duty; that he was appointed a Secretary of Parliament before July, 1645; and that his *History* was written by the order of the Houses of Parliament.[4] It can scarcely be doubted that Milton found in May not only a kindred spirit but also a valued historical guide.

In the following pages I give samples of Milton's use of May's *History*, illustrating a specific point by a quotation from the source, immediately followed by an excerpt from *Eikonoklastes*. The quotations from May's *History* are from the first edition, which is in three books: Book I, pages 1-119; Book II, pages 1-128; Book III, pages 1-115; the quotations from *Eikonoklastes* are from the Columbia University edition of *The Works of John Milton*, V (1932). For convenience of reference the quotations are numbered continuously, in each case the number before the source being repeated before the excerpt from *Eikonoklastes*. A brief heading indicates the thought of each illustration.

The courtiers and the clergy support the King:

1. The Courtiers would begin to dispute against Parliaments in their ordinary discourse, That they were cruell to those whom the King favoured, and too injurious to his Prerogative; . . . and that they hoped the King should never need any more Parliaments. . . . The Clergy, whose dependence was meerely upon the King, were wholly taken up in admiration of his happy Government, which they never concealed from him-

⁴ Allan G. Chester, *Thomas May: Man of Letters, 1595-1650* (Philadelphia, 1932), pp. 53, 63, 66. Mr. Chester discovers no relation between May and Milton except in their devotion to liberty and in the influence of their classical studies upon the development of this ideal.

selfe, as often as the Pulpit gave them accesse to his eare; and not only there, but at all meetings, they discoursed with joy upon that Theam; . . . (May, I, 18, 22)

1. Those neerest to this King and most his Favorites, were Courtiers and Prelates; men whose chief study was to finde out which way the King inclin'd, and to imitate him exactly. How these men stood affected to Parlaments, cannot be forgott'n. No man but may remember it was thir continuall exercise to dispute and preach against them; and in their common discourse nothing was more frequent, then that *they hoped the King should now have no need of Parlaments any more*. (*Eikonoklastes*, p. 75)

Obviously May's *History* is the source, from which the italcized clause in *Eikonoklastes* is quoted.

The King is an enemy of Parliament:

2. the King . . . grew extremely dis-affected to Parliaments, calling them for nothing but to supply his expences, dissolving them when they began to meddle with State Affaires, . . . After the breaking off the Parliament . . . the people of *England* for many years never looked back to their ancient liberty. A Declaration was published by the King, wherein aspertions were laid upon some Members; but indeed the Court of Parliament it selfe was declared against. . . . The people of *England* from that time were deprived of the hope of Parliaments; . . . (May, I, 6, 14)

2. who never call'd a Parlament but to supply his necessities; and having supply'd those, as suddenly and ignominiously dissolv'd it, . . . And still the latter breaking was with more affront and indignity put upon the House and her worthiest Members, then the former: Insomuch that in the fifth year of his Raign, in a Proclamation he seems offended at the very rumor of a Parlament divulg'd among the people: . . . By which feirce Edict, the people, forbidd'n to complain, as well as forc'd to suffer, began from thenceforth to despaire of Parlaments. (*Eikon.*, pp. 75-76)

The King oppresses the people:

3. To begin with the faults of the higher powers, and their illegal oppression of the people, . . . multitudes of Monopo-

lies were granted by the King, . . . Large sums of Money were exacted thorow the whole Kingdome for default of Knighthood, . . . Tonnage and Poundage were received . . . that great Tax of Ship-money was set on foot. . . . These things were accompanied with an enlargement of Forrests, . . . the forcing of Coat and Conduct-Money, . . . New illegal Oathes were enforced upon the Subjects, and new Judicatories erected without Law; and when Commissions were granted for excesse of Fees, and great exactions discovered, the Delinquents were compounded with, not onely for the time past, but immunity to offend for the time to come; . . . By this time, all thoughts of ever having a Parliament againe, were quite banished; so many oppressions had been set on foot, so many illegal actions done, that the onely way to justifie the mischiefes already done, was to do that one greater, To take away the meanes which was ordained to redresse them, the lawfull Government of *England* by Parliaments. (May, I, 16-17)

3. Whereupon such illegal actions, and especially to get vast summs of Money, were put in practise by the King and his new Officers, as Monopolies, compulsive Knight-hoods, Cote, Conduct and Ship money, the seizing not of one *Naboths* Vineyard, but of whole Inheritances under the pretence of Forrests, or Crown-Lands, corruption and Bribery compounded for, with impunities granted for the future, as gave evident proof that the King never meant, nor could it stand with the reason of his affaires, ever to recall Parlaments; having brought by these irregular courses the peoples interest and his own to so direct an opposition, that he might foresee plainly, if nothing but a Parlament could save the people, it must necessarily be his undoing. (*Eikon.*, pp. 76-77)

Milton's order here is more nearly that of May than of *A Remonstrance of the State of the Kingdom*, . . . 15 Decemb. 1642.[5] It seems clear that Milton summarized May's account, adopting also his conclusion that by these illegal exactions the King had in effect made the meeting of Parliament impossible.

The King summons a Parliament for his war against Scotland; he dissolves the Parliament:

[5] See *An Exact Collection* . . . (1643), pp. 6-7.

4. Upon the thirteenth of *Aprill* the Parliament began; when
the King produced that forenamed writing of his Scottish Subjects . . . as an apparent token of their disloyalty, . . .
Twelve Subsidies were demanded by the King, . . . to
which demand answer was made. . . . That redresse of
grievances was the chiefe end of assembling Parliaments, and
ought to precede granting of Subsidies. . . . The King promised that grievances should be afterwards redressed, but required the Money first, . . . To which it was answered by
many, That the people had no reason to pay for that which
was never caused nor desired by them, nor could any way
prove to their good, but quite contrary to the danger and detri-
ment of the whole Kingdome; . . . But whilest the busi-
nesse was in debate; whether they were not quick enough in
granting, or the conditions were too much feared by the
King, . . . The King in person came into the House upon
the fifth of *May*, and dissolved the Parliament, . . . (May,
I, 59-61)

4. hee calls a Parlament . . . where his first demand was but
twelve Subsidies, to maintain a Scotch Warr, condemn'd and
abominated by the whole Kingdom; promising thir greevances
would be consider'd afterward. Which when the Parlament,
who judg'd that Warr it self one of thir main greevances,
made no hast to grant, not enduring the delay of his impa-
tient will, or els fearing the conditions of thir grant, he breaks
off the whole Session, and dismisses them and thir greevances
with scorn and frustration. (*Eikon.*, p. 77)

Milton's phrasing, "promising thir greevances would be consider'd afterward" and "fearing the conditions of thir grant,"
is obviously based upon May's.

The King favors papists at court:

5. But the Queenes power did by degrees give priviledge to Papists; and among them, the most witty, and Jesuited, to converse, . . . not only with inferiour Courtiers, but the King
himselfe, and to sowe their seed in what ground they thought
best; and by degrees, as in complement to the Queene, Nuntio's from the Pope were received in the Court of *England*,
Panzani, Con, and Rossetti; . . . (May, I, 21) the Queene

Mother of *France* had long been entertained by the King, . . . during her abode here, the two Kingdomes of *England* and *Scotland* were imbroyled in great troubles; which the people were apt to impute in some measure to her counsels, knowing what power the Queene her Daughter had with the King. (May, I, 107-198)

5. his permitting . . . the Popes *Nuntio*, and her Jesuited Mother here, . . . it is op'nly known that her Religion wrought more upon him, then his Religion upon her, and his op'n favouring of Papists, . . . made most men suspect she had quite perverted him. (*Eikon.*, pp. 140-141)

Mr. Lowenhaupt (p. 35) quotes the following passage from *Eikon Alethine:* "Thirdly, for her loyalty as a subject, it appears in entertaining a *Nuncio* from the Pope. . . ." This supplies only one fact, whereas May supplies all that Milton used and more.

The King and the bishops countenance looseness and irreligion:

6. The example of the Court, where Playes were usually presented on Sundaies, did . . . reflect with disadvantage upon the Court it selfe, . . . The countenancing of loosenesse and irreligion, was, no doubt, a good preparative to the introducing of another Religion: And the power of godlinesse being beaten downe, Popery might more easily by degrees enter; . . . (May, I, 24)

6. the licentious remissness of his Sundays Theater; . . . whose unsincere and levenous Doctrine corrupting the people, first taught them loosness, then bondage; loosning them from all sound knowledge and strictness of life, the more to fit them for the bondage of Tyranny and superstition. (*Eikon.*, pp. 81, 154)

No doubt, familiar facts are stated in these quotations. But it is important to notice that Milton and May are in complete accord.

The King invades the Commons:

7. For upon that day the King came to the Parliament in Person, attended with a great number of Gentlemen, Souldiers,

and others armed with Swords and Pistols to the number of about three hundred, who came up to the very door of the House of Commons, and placed themselves there, and in all passages neer unto it: The King in Person entered the House of Commons, and demanded five Members of that House to be delivered to him. (May, II, 21)

7. that violation and dishonor put upon the whole House, whose very dore forcibly kept op'n, and all the passages neer it he besett with Swords and Pistols cockt and menac'd in the hands of about three hunderd Swaggerers and Ruffians, who but expected, nay audibly call'd for the word of onset to beginn a slaughter. (*Eikon.*, p. 99)

In writing this account of the King's invasion of the Commons, Milton, I believe, used not only May's *History* but also *A Declaration of the House of Commons, touching a late Breach of their Priviledges . . . ,*[6] which in part runs as follows:

many Souldiers, Papists, and others . . . came with His Majesty . . . to the said House of Commons; . . . and divers of them pressed to the doore of the said House . . . holding up their Swords, some and holding up their Pistols ready cock'd neer the said doore; . . .

Note in Milton the phrase "and Pistols cockt," which does not occur in May's *History* or in *Eikon Alethine*. It is characteristic of Milton to catch up such expressions. On the other hand, May is the only source that gives three hundred as the number of the King's guard, and this is the number that Milton uses.

The King has the chambers of the five members searched:

8. For the day before the third of *January,* . . . the Chambers, Studies, and Trunks of those five Members by a Warrant from the King were sealed up; . . . (May, II, 24)

8. But yet he mist, though thir Chambers, Trunks, and Studies were seal'd up and search'd; . . . (*Eikon.*, p. 101)

Lowenhaupt (p. 33) quotes from *Eikon Alethine:* "Then how could he have missed . . . such writings, having sealed up their Chambers, Studies, and Trunks." This is parallel num-

[6] *An Exact Collection* (1643), pp. 38-41.

ber 6 in Lowenhaupt's article, and his comment is that "No. 6 is an instance of verbal similarity, as well as of identity of argument. . . ." Obviously, verbal parallels that are common to a number of works have little weight as proof unless other evidence supports the relationship.

A conspiracy in Scotland; malignants in London:

9. Letters came from the English Committee in *Scotland*, . . . importing the discovery of a Treasonable plot against the lives of Marquesse Hamilton, and others, the greatest Peeres of *Scotland*; . . . The malignancy, which at that time began to appear in people, . . . and was not only expressed in usual discourse amongst their companions, but vented in scurrilous and bitter Libels against those Lords and Commons, who were generally reputed the most Sedulous for the common-wealth, . . . (May, II, 3-4)

9. The Parlament moreover had intelligence, and the people could not but discover, that there was a bitter & malignant party grown up now to such boldness, as to give out insolent and threatning speeches against the Parlament it self . . . a conspiracy in *Scotland* had bin made, while the King was there, against some chief Members of that Parlament; . . . (*Eikon.*, p. 105)

The citizens of London demonstrate their loyalty to Parliament:

10. For people about that time in great numbers used to present Petitions to the Parliament, and make Protestations of their fidelity to them, in these times of fears and jealousies, which grew now so great, that the House of Commons, . . . Petitioned him [the King] to allow them a Guard for security of their Persons while they sate: . . . commanded by the Earl of Essex, Lord Chamberlain of his Majesties Houshold, . . . Which Petition was denied by the King; . . . his Majesty . . . had lately fortified White-hall with men and munition in an unusuall manner: Some of which men had abused with provoking language, and with drawn swords wounded divers unarmed Citizens passing by. (May, II, 20, 26)

10. The people therefore, lest thir worthiest and most faithfull Patriots . . . should want aide, or be deserted in the midst of

these dangers, came in multitudes, though unarm'd, to witness thir fidelitie and readiness in case of any violence offer'd to
the Parlament . . . The Parlament . . . conceaving themselves to be still in danger where they sat, sent a most reasonable and just Petition to the King, that a Guard might be
allow'd them out of the City, whereof the Kings own *Cham-*
berlaine, the Earl of *Essex* might have command; . . . This
the King refus'd to doe, . . . He had . . . begun to fortifie
his Court, and entertained armed Men not a few; who standing at his Palace Gate, revil'd, and with drawn Swords
wounded many of the People, as they went by unarm'd, and
in a peaceable manner, whereof some dy'd. (*Eikon.,* pp.
106-107)

It is evident that Milton closely follows his authority, which is
May or perhaps various petitions of Parliament, some of which
are quoted in the *History*.

The next five illustrations relate to Section II, "Upon the
Earle of Straffords Death," in *Eikonoklastes*.

The Earl of Strafford is accused of high treason:

11. The Charge against him consisted of nine Articles, which afterwards upon a further impeachment, were extended to eight
and twenty. . . . The first and second being much alike, concerning his ruling of *Ireland,* and those parts of *England,*
where his Authority lay, in an Arbitrary way, against the
fundamentall Lawes of the Kingdome, . . . That he ma-
liciously had indeavoured to stir up Hostility betweene *England*
and *Scotland.* . . . That to preserve himselfe from questioning, he had laboured to subvert Parliaments, and incense the
King against them. . . . After all this long Triall, the House
of Commons . . . voted him guilty of high Treason in
divers particulars of that Accusation, . . . and in more particular he was voted guilty of High Treason, for his opinion
given before the King, at a secret Councell, which was discovered by some notes of Sir Henry Vane, who was also a
Privy Councellor, and present at that time; in which notes
it was found that the Earle of *Strafford* had said to the King,
That he had an Army in Ireland, which his Majesty might
employ to reduce this Kingdome to obedience. (May, I, 89,
92-93)

11. He had rul'd *Ireland*, and some parts of *England* in an Arbitrary manner, had indeavour'd to subvert Fundamental
Lawes, to subvert Parlaments, and to incense the King against
them; he had also endeavour'd to make Hostility between
England and *Scotland:* He had counceld the King to call
over that Irish Army of Papists, which he had cunningly
rais'd, as appear'd by good Testimony then present at the
Consultation. For which, and many other crimes alledg'd
and prov'd against him in 28. Articles, he was condemnd of
high Treason by the Parlament. (*Eikon.*, pp. 91-92)

Mr. Lowenhaupt (p. 33) cites from *Eikon Alethine* only the
last charge—that Strafford advised the King to conquer England with an Irish army—and compares this with Milton's
statement. *Eikon Alethine* does not mention the secret consultation, the total number of articles in the charge against
Strafford, the charges listed by Milton. Of the parallel, which
is number 4 in his list, Mr. Lowenhaupt writes: "No. 4 is an
example of the use of the same historical reference under similar stimulus." It is apparent that this parallel is worthless.
May's *History* is Milton's source.

The clergy, the courtiers, and the court ladies support the
Earl:

12. The Clergy in generall were so much fallen into love and
admiration of this Earle, that the Archbishop of *Canterbury*
was almost quite forgotten by them. The Courtiers cryed
him up, and the Ladies, whose voices will carry much with
some parts of the State, were exceedingly on his side. It
seemed a very pleasant object, to see so many Semproniaes
(all the chiefe Court Ladies filling the Galleries at the Tryall)
with penne, inke, and paper in their hands, noting the passages, and discoursing upon the grounds of Law and State.
They were all on his side; whether moved by pitty, proper
to their Sex, or by ambition of being thought able to judge
of the parts of the Prisoner. (May, I, 92)

12. None were his Friends but Courtiers, and Clergimen, the
worst at that time, and most corrupted sort of men; and Court
Ladies, not the best of Women; who when they grow to
that insolence as to appeare active in State affaires, are the

certain sign of a dissolute, degenerat, and pusillanimous Com-mon-wealth. (*Eikon.*, p. 92)

May gives a rather full and graphic account of the pomp and circumstance of this great trial. An interesting item is the fact that the King, who attended the trial every day, sat, not in public, but with the Queen and other ladies in a close gallery purposely made for him. The King "tooke notes himselfe in writing" of the proceedings.

The King's conscience is not satisfied:

13. But the King was not satisfied in conscience, as he declared to both Houses two daies after, to condemne him of High Treason; and he told them, No feares or respects whatsoever should make him alter that resolution, founded upon his con-science: . . . (May, I, 94)

13. Last of all the King . . . was not satisfi'd in conscience to condemn him of High Treason; and declar'd to both Houses, *That no fears or respects* whatsoever should make him alter that resolution founded upon his conscience. (*Eikon.*, p. 92)

A more perfect parallelism of fact and phrase it would be diffi-cult to find. Who can deny that Milton wrote with May's *History* at his elbow?

After taking counsel, the King consents to the execution of the Earl:

14. The King at last, wearied with these complaints, called a Privy Councell at *White-Hall,* where he spent a great part of the day, calling also the Judges to deliver their opinions before him, concerning the Earle of *Strafford;* and sent for foure Bishops, to resolve him upon scruple of conscience. After which he granted a Commission . . . to signe that Bill for the execution of the Earle of *Strafford* . . . (May, I, 95)

14. For within a few dayes after, when the Judges at a privie Counsel, and four of his elected Bishops had pick'd the thorn out of his conscience, he was at length perswaded to signe the Bill for *Straffords* Execution. (*Eikon.*, pp. 92-93)

Milton's account, which represents the King as meeting the judges and the bishops at a session of the Privy Council, is not quite accurate; but there can be no doubt that it is based upon May's *History*.

The King is privy to a plot to free the Earl of Strafford from the Tower:

15. For to prevent the Earle of *Straffords* death, an escape for him out of the Tower was contrived. To further which, and to curbe the Parliament in other things by force of Armes, a great conspiracy was entred into by many Gentlemen of ranke and quality. . . . The persons of chiefest note in it, were Master *Henry Percy*, . . . Master *Henry Jermin*, . . . Master *Goring*, eldest Sonne to the Lord *Goring*, Master *Wilmot*, . . . Colonell *Ashburnham*, . . . But that which grieved the hearts of honest men, and made them almost despaire of that happinesse which was before hoped for by this Parliament, was, That they discovered the King himself to be privy to this conspiracy against them; which was plainly testified by Colonell *Gorings* examination; as likewise by a Letter written by Master *Percy* to his Brother the Earle of *Northumberland;* where he names the Kings discourses with him, and the desire which the King had to joyne such as he thought fit with them . . . The Report made in Parliament . . . discovered many branches of their designe. One was concerning the Tower of *London,* That Souldiers should have been put into it. For Sir *John Suckling,* and some others of the Conspirators, under pretence of raising Forces for the *Portugall,* had gathered men in *London,* who were to possesse themselves of the Tower. . . . Another branch, and that the chiefe of this designe, was to bring up the English Army, which was in the North, as yet undisbanded, and to engage it against Parliament, . . . To joyne with these Forces, and strengthen the Plot, a French Army was to be landed at *Portsmouth,* . . . The Irish Army, consisting of eight thousand, almost all Papists, when the Earle of *Strafford* had escaped out of the Tower, was to be brought over under his conduct, . . . The Parliament were most grieved to finde the King so farre in it; and then re-called to minde, how His Majesty . . . had told the Houses, That he could not allow of the disbanding of the Irish Army for divers reasons best knowne to himselfe. (May, I, 97-99)

15. The King being soon after found to have the chief hand in a most detested conspiracy against the Parlament and Kingdom, as by Letters and examinations of *Percy, Goring,* and other Conspirators came to light; that his intention was to rescue the Earle of *Strafford,* by seizing on the Towre of *London;* to bring up the English Army out of the North, joyn'd with eight thousand Irish Papists rais'd by *Strafford,* And a French Army to be landed at *Portsmouth* against the Parlament and thir friends. For which purpose, the King, though requested by both Houses to disband those Irish Papists, refus'd to do it, and kept them still in Armes to his own purposes. (*Eikon.,* p. 94)

In his brief summary of May's account Milton characteristically puts the chief blame upon the King. It will be admitted that these passages relating to Strafford clearly demonstrate Milton's use of the *History.* To establish this indebtedness no other evidence is needed; but several other illustrations are introduced mainly to dispose of some of Mr. Lowenhaupt's parallels.

The King's expeditions fail:

16. the King with great expence of Treasure, raised an Army and Fleet to assault *Cales,* the Duke of Buckingham bearing the Title both of Admirall and Generall, . . . but the matter was so ordered, that the expedition proved altogether successlesse, and as dishonourable as expensive. They complained likewise of another designe . . . about that time put in practice, a thing destructive to the highest interest of the Nation, the maintenance of the Protestant Religion; a Fleet of English Ships were set forth, and delivered over to the French, by whose strength all the Sea forces of *Rochell* were scattered and destroyed, a losse to them irrecoverable, and the first step to their ruine . . . immediately upon it, the King, by what advice the people understood not, made a breach with *France,* by taking their Ships, to a great value, without making any recompence to the English, whose Goods were therupon imbarr'd, and confiscate in that Kingdome. In revenge of this, a brave Army was raised in *England,* and commanded by the Duke of Buckingham in person, who landing at the Isle

of *Rhea*, was at the first encounter victorious against the
French; but after a few Moneths stay there, the matter was
so unhappily carried, the Generall being inexperienced in Warlike affaires, that the French prevailed, and gave a great defeat, where many gallant Gentlemen lost their lives, and the
nation much of their ancient Honour. (May, I, 8-9)

16. what peace was that which drew out the English to a needless
and dishonourable voyage against the *Spaniard* at *Cales*? Or
that which lent our shipping to a treacherous and Antichristian
Warr against the poore Protestants of Rochell our suppliants?
What peace was there which fell to rob the *French* by Sea,
to the imbarring of all our Merchants in that Kingdom?
which brought forth that unblest expedition to the Ile of
Rhee, doubtfull whether more calamitous in the success or in
the designe, betraying all the flowre of our military youth,
and best Commanders to a shamefull surprisal and execution.
(*Eikon.*, p. 153)

Mr. Lowenhaupt presents two parallels from *Eikon Alethine*:

16. Indeed the murdering of so many of the most warlick and
expert *English* Gentry at *Cales* and *Re* . . . might make our
peace admired, and envied.

17. . . . and lent his ships to destroy the Navy of the poore Protestants in *Rochel*, whom he promised to aid.

And he comments as follows: "Nos. 16 and 17 are more significant in that they reveal both men seizing on a chance line
in *Eikon Basilike*: . . . It will be noticed that in reply the
same historical events are cited, and other examples are excluded." The *Eikon Alethine* confuses the order, mentioning
"*Cales* and *Re*" and then "*Rochel, Cales, Re*"; it does not
mention the loss to the English merchants. The *Remonstrance*
of 15 December 1642 refers to the loss at Rochelle and Cales,
but says nothing about the expedition against Re. The *Declaration* of 1648, which Milton followed in several other places,
mentions only the betrayal of Rochelle. Again, it is perfectly
clear that Milton followed May's *History*.

The Queen carries off the Crown jewels:

17. But the Queen carried with her all or the greatest part of the Crown-Jewels of *England*, which immediately she pawned in *Holland*, and with that money bought Arms and Ammunition for that sad War which ensued not long after, . . . advertisement by Letters was given to the Parliament, that the Crown-Jewels were pawned at Amsteldam [*sic*], and other places of the Netherlands; upon which money was taken up, and Warlike Ammunition provided in those Parts, as Battering-pieces, Culverins, Field-pieces, Morter-pieces, Granadoes, with great store of powder, pistols, carabines, great saddles, and such like. (May, II, 84)

17. the Queen into Holland, where she pawn'd and set to sale the Crown-Jewels . . . and to what intent these summs were rais'd, the Parlament was not ignorant. . . . Were Praiers and Teares at so high a rate in *Holland* that nothing could purchase them but the Crown Jewels? Yet they in *Holland* . . . sold them for Gunns, Carabins, Morter-peeces, Canons, and other deadly Instruments of Warr, . . . (*Eikon.*, p. 169)

This is number 18 in Mr. Lowenhaupt's list, and his comment is that it "is noteworthy for the resemblances in actual phrasing." The similar phrasing is common to the *History* and *Eikonoklastes* and is no proof of Milton's debt to *Eikon Alethine*.

The forces of Prince Rupert are speedily augmented:

18. Prince Rupert, the elder brother, and most furious of the two, within a fortnight after his arrivall, commanded a small party of those Forces which the King had at that time gathered together, which were not of so great a body as to be tearmed an Army, with which he marched into divers Counties, to roll himselfe like a snow ball, into a larger bulke, by the accession of Forces in every place: Through divers parts of *Warwickshire, Nottingham-shire, Leicester-shire, Worcester-shire,* and *Cheshire,* did this young Prince fly with those Troops which he had, not inviting the people so much by faire demeanour . . . as compelling them by extreme rigour to follow that side which he had taken. (May, III, 3)

18. Those numbers which he grew to *from small beginnings,* were not such as out of love came to protect him, . . . but were such as fled to be protected by him from the fear of that Reformation which the pravity of thir lives would not bear. Such a Snowball he might easily gather by rowling through those cold and dark provinces of ignorance and leudness, where on a sudden he became so numerous. (*Eikon.,* p. 241)

The remarkable similarities in the examples cited seem to demonstrate Milton's heavy indebtedness to May's *History* for many facts and occasionally for phrasing. Milton did not follow May slavishly: he selected; he rearranged; he skillfully condensed. He is often emphatic and ironical where May is mild. Invariably he stresses the King's faults and crimes. But there can be no doubt that he freely used the *History.* I have pointed out the bearing of this fact on Mr. Lowenhaupt's evidence, much of which has been proved worthless. Other fallacies in his argument will be exposed in connection with what follows. It is obvious that the *History* was not Milton's sole guide. Having evidently decided that on some topics May was not sufficiently detailed, Milton relied upon state papers, especially upon *Declarations* of Parliament, to complete his case. His use of some of these documents will now be illustrated.

Milton says that Charles broke off his first Parliament to protect the Duke of Buckingham

19. against them who had accus'd him, besides other hainous crimes, of no less then poysoning the deceased King his Father; concerning which matter the Declaration of *No more addresses,* hath sufficiently inform'd us. (*Eikon.,* p. 76)

The *Declaration* to which Miltons refers, entitled *A Declaration Of The Commons Of England In Parliament assembled; Expressing Their Reasons and Grounds of passing the late Resolutions touching No farther Addresses or Applications to be made to the King,* gives a detailed account of the charge that Buckingham poisoned James I.[7] In spite of Milton's refer-

[7] Pp. 12-17.

ence to his source, Lowenhaupt, in parallel 33, traces his statement to *Eikon Alethine,* omitting from his quotation Milton's
citation of his source.

To this *Declaration* Milton refers in two other places: with
regard to the King's attempt to destroy Parliament by means
of the English army, and in proof that the King was responsible for the rebellion in Ireland.[8] It seems that Milton also
uses this Declaration in the following instances:

The King and the Pope:

20. And besides the Kings Letters to the Pope, when hee was in
Spaine, and others long since his return, . . . It is clear, that
some Moneths before the Irish Rebellion, the King had an
Agent in Rome, as by divers of his owne Secretaries papers
appeareth. (*Declaration,* p. 28)

20. his Letter of compliance to the Pope, his permitting Agents at
Rome . . . (*Eikon.,* p. 140)

This example may be compared with number 5 in this chapter.

The King and Denmark:

21. And before that time, the King had dispatched an Agent into
Denmark, complaining against the Parliament . . . and there-
fore desired Ayde . . . the King was assured of Horses and
Money from *Denmark.* . . . There were also comming from
Denmarke Ships with ten thousand Armes for Foot, and
Fifteen hundred Horse for the Kings use, . . . (*Declaration,*
p. 31)

21. The King sends an Agent with Letters to the King of *Denmark,* requiring aid against the parlament; and that aid was
comming, . . . (*Eikon.,* p. 166)

The King refuses to disband the Irish army:

22. It hath formerly been declared, how wee desired and pressed
the King to disband that Irish Army, . . . But sometimes hee
would give no answer at all, and sometimes did plainly tell
us, Hee could not disband it for Reasons best known to himself: Sometimes the *Scots* must first disband; and then there
was a new pretence of divers Regiments promised to *Spaine,*
. . . there were Regiments raising and listing in *London,*

[8] Pp. 105, 192-193.

. . . under pretence of souldiers for *Portugal* . . . some of
these came to seize & possesse . . . the Tower, . . . (*Declaration*, pp. 21-25)

22. there were 8000 *Irish* Papists which he refus'd to disband,
though intreated by both Houses, first for reasons best known
to himself, next under pretence of lending them to the *Spaniard*; . . . He was also raising Forces in London, pretendedly
to serve the *Portugall*, but with intent to seise the Tower.
(*Eikon.*, p. 166)

The King wounds his mother's honor:

23. And in *Cockrans* latter Instructions. . . . The King saith. . .
That in pursuance of their great design of extirpating the
Royall Blood and Monarchy of England, they have endevored likewise to lay a great blemish upon his Royall Family, endevoring to Illegitimate all derived from his Sister, at
once to cut off the Interest and pretentions of the whole
Race; which their most detestable and scandalous Design
they have pursued, . . . and which, as His sacred Majesty
of England in the true sense of Honor of his Mother doth
abhor, and will punish; . . . (*Declaration*, pp. 32-33)

23. Was it not more dishonourable in himself to faine suspicions
and jealousies, which we first found among those Letters,
touching the chastitie of his Mother, thereby to gaine assistance
from the King of *Denmark*, as in vindication of his Sister?
(*Eikon.*, p. 253)

This is number 21 in Mr. Lowenhaupt's list. His comment
is: "No. 21, it seems to me, is too out of the way to occur independently to two writers. The king had maintained that
the publication of the Naseby letters was dishonorable. Both
answers reply, Wasn't your letter about your mother more
dishonorable? Surely the laws of chance would have led one
Parliamentarian to cite other questionable epistles."[9] It is obvious that Mr. Lowenhaupt did not understand contemporary
conditions. The King's letter regarding his mother's honor
was the one letter to cite at this point. And Milton was familiar with the *Declaration* of 1648, in which this letter is reprinted—a very good reason why he should cite it.

[9] *Op. cit.*, p. 43.

In the section on the King's retirement from Westminster, Milton quotes Digby's remark to his guard:

24. That the principal cause of his Majesties going thence, was to save them from being trodd in the dirt. (*Eikon.*, p. 125)

This statement, which is not found in May's *History* or in *Eikon Alethine*, occurs in *The Declaration or Remonstrance of the Lords and Commons* . . . May 19, 1642:[10]

24. The Listing of so many Officers, Souldiers, and others, . . . the carrying them out of Towne, after which they were told by the Lord *Digby* That the King removed on purpose, that they might not be trampled in the dirt: . . .

This should be compared with the very slight similarity of Mr. Lowenhaupt's number 12.

In Section VIII, "Upon His repulse at Hull, and the fate of the Hothams," Milton turned to *The Declaration, Votes and Order of assistance of both Houses of Parliament, Concerning the Magazin at Hull, and Sir Iohn Hotham, Governour there,*[11] as the following excerpts show.

Parliament appoints Sir John Hotham governor of Hull:

25. one of the members of the House of Commons, being a Gentleman of the same County, . . . to take upon him the Government of that Town, and to draw thither some of the Trained Band for the Guard thereof: . . . (*Declaration . . . of both Houses*, p. 160)

25. sir *John Hotham* a member of the House, and Knight of that county, to take *Hull* into his custody, and some of the Train'd bands to his assistance. (*Eikon.*, p. 142)

The King maneuvers to get possession of Hull:

26. About which time Captain *Leg* (a man formerly imployed in the practice of bringing up the Army against the Parliament) had direction by Warrant . . . under the Kings hand and signe Manuall, to enter Kingston upon Hull, and to draw thither such of the Trained Bands as he should think fit: And that the Earl of *Newcastle* came thither in a suspicious

---

[10] *An Exact Collection*, p. 212.   [11] *An Exact Collection*, pp. 160-162.

way, and under a feigned name, and did endeavour to possesse himself of the said Town, by vertue of the like Warrant
and Authority. (*Declaration . . . of both Houses*, p. 161)

26. Parlament had . . . notice giv'n them of his privat Commissions to the Earl of *Newcastle*, and to Colonel *Legg*, one of
those imploid to bring the Army up against the Parlament;
who had already made som attempts, & the latter of them
under a disguise, to surprise that place for the Kings party.
(*Eikon.*, p. 142)

It should be noticed that Milton erroneously attributes the
disguise to Colonel Legg, not to the Earl of Newcastle.

The number of the King's horse:

27. The King was attended with about four hundred Horse, . . .
(*Declaration . . . of both Houses*, p. 160)

27. attended with about 400. Horse (*Eikon.*, p. 143)

May's *History* does not give the number of the King's cavalry.

Hotham refuses to admit the King into Hull:

28. Which Answer His Majestie was not pleased to accept of;
but presently caused him and his Officers to be proclaimed
Traitors before the wals of the Towne, . . . (*Declaration
. . . of both Houses*, p. 161)

28. the Governour besought humbly to be excus'd, till he could
send notice to the Parlament . . . whereat the King much
incens'd proclaims him Traitor before the Town Walls; . . .
(*Eikon.*, p. 143)

In the substantial first paragraph of the section on Hull
there is proof that Milton used two other state papers. The
first of these is the *Declaration* of 1648.

Digby's advice and service:

29. What his Errand was beyond Sea, we may well conclude
from the List of Arms and Ammunition . . . taken amongst
his Papers, and printed with his Letters to the Queen, . . .
What advice he gave for the Kings retiring to some safe place,
and declare himself; and how the King followed it, is known
well enough . . . wee had certain intelligence from the Low-
Countreys of Forraign Forces from *Denmark*, to come in

about *Hull,* whither also came with the Lord *Digby,* divers Commanders, with much Ammunition and Arms from other Forraign parts. (*Declaration,* pp. 30-31)

29. And letters of the Lord *Digby* were intercepted, wherin was wisht that the K. would declare himself, and retire to some safe place; other information came from abroad, that *Hull* was the place design'd for some new enterprise. And accordingly *Digby* himself not long after, with many other Commanders, and much forrain Ammunition landed in those parts. (*Eikon.,* p. 142)

The other state paper used here is *His Majesties Message sent to the Parliament the eighth of Aprill, 1642. Concerning His Resolution to go into Ireland for suppressing the Rebels there.*[12] The King desired that his guard on the proposed expedition should be equipped from Hull:

30. His Majestie being grieved at the very soule, for the Calamities of his good Subjects of *Ireland* . . . Hath firmly resolved with all convenient speed to goe into *Ireland,* to chastise those wicked and detestable Rebels (odious to God and all good men) thereby so to settle the Peace of that Kingdom, and the Security of this . . . (*His Majesties Message . . .*)

30. [The King] sends a message to them [Parliament] that he had firmly resolv'd to go in person into *Ireland;* to chastise those wicked Rebels (for these and wors words he then gave them) . . . (*Eikon.,* p. 142)

Milton's reference to the King's message and the phrase "to chastise those wicked Rebels" point clearly to his source. In the light of these illustrations, one is not surprised to read Milton's statement: "This relation, being most true, proves that which is affirm'd here [in *Eikon Basilike*] to be most fals." He had taken unusual care to make his account accurate and convincing. The paragraph just examined is an excellent illustration of the pains that Milton exercised in assembling his proof.

Section XII, "Upon the Rebellion in Ireland," is also based upon a number of Declarations. For proof of his point

[12] *An Exact Collection,* pp. 133-135.

that Charles had dispatched to Ireland a commission under the great seal of Scotland commanding all the Irish to rise in rebellion, Milton refers to *The Mysterie of Iniquity* (1643) and to the "Declaration of *no more addresses*," which has the following:

31. we have a copy thereof [the Commission] attested by Oath, with depositions also of those who have seen it under the Seal. (p. 24)

31. they have one copy of that Commission in thir own hands, attested by the Oathes of some that were ey-witnesses, and had seen it under the Seale. (*Eikon.*, pp. 192-193)

To prove that the King was friendly with the Irish papists, and therefore responsible for the Irish rebellion, Milton made use of *A Declaration Of the Commons assembled in Parliament. Concerning the Rise and Progress of The Grand Rebellion in Ireland. Together with a multitude of Examinations of Persons of quality, whereby it may easily appear to all the World, who were, and still are the Promoters of that cruell and unheard of Rebellion . . . July 1643.*[13] This mentions the sale of indulgences to the Irish, tells of certain active papists who were consulted and caressed at Whitehall, and who "had divers private conferences with the King in the Queenes presence," and

32. what Clandestine agreement was made with those Rebels may easily be imagined, when upon their private mediation His Majesty was induced to give away these five whole Counties, with a great part of the Counties of *Limerick* and *Tipperary;* after so great an endeavour had bin used for divers yeers together, to entitle His Majesty to the same; and all for a rent of 2000 £. or therabouts. (*Declaration* . . . 1643, pp. 7-8)

32. The Summer before that dismal *October,* a Committy of most active Papists, all since in the head of that Rebellion, were in great favour at *White-Hall;* and admitted to many private consultations with the King and Queen. And to make it evident that no mean matters were the subject of those

[13] On p. 193 Milton refers to this *Declaration.*

Conferences, at their request he gave away his peculiar right to more then five Irish Counties, for the payment of an inconsiderable Rent. (*Eikon.*, pp. 190-191)

To show that Charles I was a friend of the Irish rebels, Milton declares that the King, without the advice of Parliament, made a "Cessation" of the war in Ireland in the interest of the Papists; and he adds that "the plot of this Irish Truce is in good part discovered in that Declaration of *September* 30th. 1643."[14] The following quotations show that in one paragraph Milton made an excellent summary of *A Declaration of the Lords and Commons Assembled in Parliament, shewing the present Designe now on foot (by vertue of a pretended Commission from his Majestie) for a Cessation of Armes, or a Treaty of Peace with the Rebels in Ireland:*[15]

33. The rebels are so farre brought low in some parts of *Ireland,* that if they can be deprived of the benefit of this Harvest, they are not likely to see the next summer . . . being in want of most things necessary, . . . not onely for the maintaining of a warre, but even of life, . . . the famine amongst many of them, hath made them unnaturally and Caniball-like eat and feed upon one another: . . . by warrant of his Majesties ample Commission sent to that effect; . . . this designe of a Cessation is a deepe Plot layd by the Rebells, and really invented for their owne safety, and falsely pretended to be for the benefit of our Armies . . . their wicked counsels have had that influence, as to procure the intercepting of much provisions which were sent for *Ireland,* so that ships going for *Ireland* with Victuals, and other comming from thence with Commodities to exchange for Victuals have been taken, . . . by English Ships commanded by Sir *John Pennington* under His Majestie. And moreover, the Parliament Messengers sent into severall Counties . . . for Loanes and Contributions, have been taken and imprisoned, their Money taken from them, and not one peny either Loane or Contribution hath beene suffered to be sent in for *Ireland,* from those Counties which were under the power of the Kings Army, . . . (p. 341)

[14] *Op. cit.*, p. 199.
[15] *A Collection of all the publicke Orders Ordinances and Declarations, Of both Houses of Parliament,* . . . (1646), pp. 340-342.

33. after that the Parlament had brought them every where either
to Famin, or a low condition, he, to give them all the respit
and advantages they could desire, without advice of Parlament,
. . . makes a Cessation; in pretence to releive the Protestants,
. . . but as the event prov'd, to support the Papists, by divert-
ing and drawing over the English Army there, to his own
service heer against the Parlament. For that the Protestants
were then on the winning hand, it must needs be plaine; . . .
And if the Protestants were but *handfuls* there, as he calls
them, why did he stop and waylay both by Land and Sea,
to his utmost power, those Provisions and Supplies which were
sent by the Parlament? (*Eikon.*, p. 199)

Section XVIII, "Upon the Uxbridge Treaty, &c.," includes
some details found in *His Majesties Answer to the aforesaid
Petition* of Parliament requesting a treaty:[16]

34. We take God to witnesse. . . . We have shewed Our readi-
nesse of Composing all things in a fair way by Our severall
offers of Treaty, . . . The same tendernesse to avoid the
Destruction of Our Subjects . . . shall make Us willingly
hearken to such Proposition whereby these bloudy distempers
may be stopped . . . And to that end shall reside at Our
own Castle at *Windsore* . . . till Committees may have time
to attend Us with the same . . . (*His Majesties Answer*)

34. For after he had tak'n God to witnes of his continual readi-
nesse to Treat, or to offer Treaties to the avoiding of blood-
shed, had nam'd *Windsor* the place of Treaty, . . . till Commissioners by such a time were speeded towards him . . .
(*Eikon.*, pp. 235-236)

On the other hand, Milton's statement that the King's forces
moved under cover "of a thick Mist, which fell that evening"[17] possibly depends upon May, who says that the

35. Kings Artillery . . . advanced forwards with divers Troops
of Horse, . . . and taking advantage of a great mist which
happened that Friday night, they marched to *Brainford*, and
fell upon the Parliament Forces which were there quartered
. . . (*History*, III, 32-33)

[16] *An Exact Collection*, pp. 747-748.   [17] *Op. cit.*, p. 236.

A true and perfect relation of the barbarous and cruell passages of the Kings Army at old Braintford[18] does not mention the weather. Here, then, in brief compass, is further proof of Milton's careful work: the reconstruction of an episode on the basis of two, and perhaps three, sources, one of which is the King's own *Answer*, the relevant details of which Milton includes.

There can be no doubt that Milton used *The Kings Cabinet* (1654). The following parallel is representative.

36. I being now as well freed from the place of base and mutinous motions (that is to say, our Mungrell Parliament here) . . . for whom I may justly expect to be chidden by thee, for having suffered thee to be vexed by them, . . . (*The Kings Cabinet*, pp. 12-13)

36. by him nicknam'd, and casheer'd for a *Mungrill Parlament that vext his Queen with thir base and mutinous motions*, as his Cabinet letter tells us? (*Eikon.*, p. 115)

Obviously, Milton quotes from the letter. Mr. Lowenhaupt cites two parallels here, numbers 9 and 10; of these, only 9 is close, but even this passage in *Eikon Alethine* omits the word *vexed*, which occurs in the *Cabinet* and in *Eikonoklastes*. Mr. Lowenhaupt's comment is: "And out of the whole volume they both use the same trivial reference and draw an almost verbally similar conclusion."[19] He is twice mistaken. The reference is not trivial. According to *Eikon Basilike*, the King was sometimes prone to think that his last Parliament would have been more loyal if it had met in any other place than London. It was a telling point to reply that the King was highly dissatisfied with his own Parliament at Oxford. Moreover, verbal parallelism links *Eikonoklastes* with the *Cabinet*. Consider one more example.

37. As for gaining particular persons besides security, I [the King] give you power to promise them rewards for performed services, not sparing to engage for places; . . . (*The Kings Cabinet*, p. 25)

[18] *An Exact Collection*, pp. 758-761.   [19] *Op. cit.*, p. 42.

37. his instructions to bribe our Commissioners with the promise of *Security, rewards,* and *places;* . . . (*Eikon.,* p. 238)

Other illustrations might easily be added, but it is scarcely necessary to multiply examples. Since Milton's use of the sources mentioned in this chapter cannot be questioned, many of Mr. Lowenhaupt's parallels must be discarded. In *Eikon Alethine* the passages which he so highly values as sources of Milton's ideas and style are in fact not such sources at all. This fact renders suspect all his other examples, some of which may now be mentioned.

From the introductory letter to *Eikon Alethine,* Mr. Lowenhaupt quotes as part of his parallel number 27 this sentence:

Bee not cheated out of your innocency by this subtill Serpent with an Apple of Sodom, which at the touch of truth will fall to ashes.

And with it he compares Milton's sentence:

Thus these pious flourishes and colours examin'd throughly, are like the Apples of *Asphaltis,* appearing goodly to the sudden eye, but look well upon them, or at least but touch them, and they turne into Cinders. (*Eikon.,* p. 263)

This simile was probably a familiar one. As I pointed out in Chapter II, Milton was familiar with Raleigh's *History of the World,* which describes the "Lake of *Asphaltitis*" and the desolate bordering fields on which whatsoever grows "be it Fruits or Flowers, when they come to Ripeness, have nothing within them, but moulder into Ashes."[20]

Mr. Lowenhaupt describes item number 29 as "a spectacular parallel." It is as follows:

Nero could not seale a malefactors death without teares, and sighing out an *Oh that he could not write* . . . (*Eikon Alethine*)

The Tyrant *Nero,* though not yet deserving that name, sett his hand so unwillingly to the execution of a condemned Person, as to wish *He had not known letters.* (*Eikonoklastes,* p. 155)

In Chapter X it has been shown that in *Of Reformation* Milton replied to the Speech of Lord Digby, which was printed

[20] P. 220.

February 9, 1641. On the same date was published *A Speech to the House of Commons Concerning Episcopacy*, by the Lord Viscount Faulkeland, which Milton probably read. In this speech occurs the following passage regarding the bishops and the Service Book which they attempted to force upon Scotland:

Wee shall find of them to have both kindled & blowne the common fire of both nations, to have both sent and maintained that booke, of which the authour no doubt hath long since wish'd with *Nero; Utinam nescissem literas*, and of which more then one Kingdome hath cause to wish, that when hee writ that, hee had rather burnd a library, though of the value of Ptolomie's. (p. 9)

The expression attributed to Nero is not uncommon in the seventeenth century.

Consider now Mr. Lowenhaupt's parallel number 26.

The Presbyter and Independent in this cause are like Hypocrates twins, they must live and die together. *(Eikon Alethine)*

Milton wrote:

He would work the people to a perswasion, *that if he be miserable they cannot be happy*. What should hinder them? Were they all born Twins of *Hippocrates* with him and his fortune, one birth one burial? *(Eikon.*, 253-254)

Mr. Lowenhaupt comments: "No. 26, for instance, is a very recondite allusion. It is found in the *Euphues* (ed. Croll, p. 194), and Milton might have remembered it, but it is so rare that its appearance in two successive books is almost certain evidence that Milton's memory was refreshed by seeing it in *Eikon Alethine*."[21] Reading seventeenth-century pamphlets, I have noted casually several instances of the use of this simile. The following is from Henry Parker's *The Contra-Replicant, His Complaint To His Majestie* (1644):

This sitting of the Lords and Commons in severall Houses, does not prove them severall Courts, nor does the observance of particular Priviledges in either House, and not laying all things common between both, prove any independance of either: doubtlesse they are

[21] *Op. cit.,* p. 43.

like the twines of *Hippocrates,* they both must live and die together. (p. 17)

Another example occurs in William Beech's *More Sulphure For Basing* (1645):

If the Common-wealth faile, farewell Religion; and if Religion be corrupted, cursed is the Common-wealth: Experience tells us, that the decay or flourishing estate of the Church depends upon the well or ill being of a Common-wealth: the Church and State (like *Hippocrates* Twins) live and dye together: . . . (p. 27)

Fair discussion of Milton's prose depends upon a broad knowledge of his intellectual and literary background. Mr. Lowenhaupt's fatal mistake is that he ignored all contemporary writing except that which he regards as the immediate source of *Eikonoklastes.* His conclusions, based on such a limited survey, are obviously unsound.

Other parallels in his list may be challenged on different grounds. For example, Milton's statement that he undertook his task, not to descant upon the dead, but to defend liberty; his use of the simile of the gnat and the camel; his references to the Queen's anger, the King's coronation oath, Pharaoh's divinity and Joseph's piety, Cham's revealing Noah's nakedness, Ahab's penitence, and the dissension at the building of Jerusalem; his remark that the King admitted his responsibility for the war—all these are easily accounted for by suggestions in *Eikon Basilike* and by Milton's character and his undisputed familiarity with Scripture and recent English history. Similarly, Milton may be given credit for having independently thought of Turkish tyranny and the riddle of the Sphinx. It is unnecessary, it is even ridiculous, to assume that Milton needed prompting in using such common ideas. The inescapable conclusion is that in writing *Eikonoklastes* Milton was not indebted to *Eikon Alethine.* All the evidence points to his use of the authorities surveyed in this chapter.

The evidence seems to justify two conclusions. It is now, of course, unnecessary to assume that *Eikonoklastes* was written after *Eikon Alethine* appeared. Mr. Lowenhaupt's conclusion that the "actual writing of *Eikonoklastes* was probably done in the first three weeks of September, 1649," after *Eikon Alethine* was published, may now be discarded. Although Milton says that he began *Eikonoklastes* late, the length of the work and the evidence of unusual care exercised in collecting information render the theory of hasty writing untenable. Milton's statement that it was finished "leisurely, in the midst of other imployments and diversions" is much more in accord with the facts revealed in this investigation.

The second conclusion is perhaps more important. Milton now stands out, not as a plagiarist (that is, of course, what Mr. Lowenhaupt's theory implies), but in his true character: a diligent, though partisan, controversialist, using a formidable array of reputable parliamentary authorities to establish facts which, winged by his invective, might damage the King's reputation and thus deal the Royalists a heavy blow. The crisis was grave. The Cavaliers were planning revenge. The people were clearly hostile to the party in power. Although the writing of *Eikonoklastes* was "a work assign'd," Milton made no scruple "to take up this Gauntlet, though a Kings, in the behalf of Libertie, and the Commonwealth." Under the circumstances, for him to have borrowed freely from a predecessor, as charged, would have been particularly reprehensible. It would have been proof of Milton's lax moral character and of his utter failure to respond worthily to the trust of the state. Strangely enough, the recent demonstration of alleged plagiarism seems to have convinced and not to have shocked Milton scholars. This study of the real authorities used in writing *Eikonoklastes*, proving the Lowenhaupt theory untenable, completely exonerates Milton, who obviously told the plain truth when he said that he wrote "with industrie and judicious paines." If the reader is convinced of Milton's industry and integrity, the purpose of this study has been achieved.

CHAPTER XIV

CONCLUSION

THE LITERARY background of Milton's work is much more extensive and complex than the restricted phases here studied. He was a lifelong and devoted student of Scripture, which he terms "the onely Book left us of *Divine* authority"; he was steeped in classical literature, moving in the main stream of the Christian Renaissance and knowing Homer and Ovid and Horace and Virgil almost by heart; he was, as Smart observed, among English poets the most complete and accomplished Italian scholar; he knew English poetry and his debt to Spenser is acknowledged. The number of works mentioned in his prose and listed in his *Commonplace Book* is most impressive. The field stretching before the student who would survey all the sources of Milton's culture is a vast one, extending far into antiquity and embracing almost all subjects except perhaps experimental science, in the technical details of which he was apparently not interested. Science, indeed, attracted a considerable and growing interest in the seventeenth century, when determined and sustained efforts were made "to arrive at a 'true' world-view along scientific lines," when Bacon and the Baconian method exerted an increasing influence,[1] and when the truth of poetry had to face the challenge of fact. In the world of science, of rational religion, of real philosophy, there was little place for the world of fancy or traditional feeling, the world of beauty and glory of the poetic imagination, or the unreal inhabitants of a "false" world. All fantastical forms, all classical mythology, all the "Wit of the Fables and Religions of the Antient World" were to be vanquished by reason, to be banished into the limbo of vanities, to disappear in the

[1] Richard F. Jones, *Ancients and Moderns* (St. Louis, 1936).

bright light of common day. Perhaps Milton's freedom was restricted by this scientific tendency. Mr. Willey has sagely remarked that Milton's dismissal of fabled knights, battles feigned, and all the tinsel trappings of romance, "a rejection of 'fiction' by the protestant consciousness," is, in part, evidence of the power of the scientific movement.[2] Whatever may be the strength of this influence, Milton was probably directed by the strong bent of his own nature, by his profound interest in moral, political, and religious questions, as well as by the intellectual climate of the age. And so for his great poems Milton, "too old, too disillusioned, and too noble to spend his stored resources on anything but the highest truth," turned for his fable to Scripture, which was not only poetic but true and which would furnish him with subjects joining "the Glory of God Almighty . . . with the singular utility and noblest delight of Mankind." At any rate, since his culture is so rich, the material with which he deals so frequently traditional, and his style invariably so individual, the study of his sources is a difficult and, indeed, a hazardous occupation. It is unfortunate that some scholars, who in theory recognize Milton's rich culture, are in the zeal of research sometimes persuaded to attribute his ideas, in large part, to specific sources, to Spenser, to the Zohar, to rabbinical commentaries, and so on. The method that leads to such definite but sometimes contradictory conclusions is obviously imperfect. Obviously also in the present state of uncertainty as to Milton's real sources it is a rash enterprise to discuss his methods of source adaptation. To obtain a true perspective of the relation of Milton's work to that of his age, limited and specific studies must be corrected by a comprehensive survey of his entire literary background. This volume presents a part of that background. Primarily not a study of sources but of literary relations, it should serve as a supplement to those studies devoted mainly to Milton's work and to those devoted to the discovery of his specific sources. Although incomplete, it may enable the student to

[2] *The Seventeenth Century Background* (London, 1934), p. 227.

understand more clearly than hitherto the general background
of Milton's work or, so to speak, the soil out of which it grew.
It may also help, in Mr. Tillyard's words, to set Milton "as
a poet firmly in his own age," to show that the Milton "who
lived and moved and had his being in the seventeenth century"[3]
was not, as some have said, "a superb and monstrous alien."

In retrospect, we observe interesting analogies and more
striking contrasts between Bacon's and Milton's ecclesiastical
views, which are characteristic both of the men and of the
time when they wrote. Both were Puritans, but their tempers
and characters differed radically. Bacon would reform Episcopacy; Milton would destroy it. Bacon was conservative, practical; Milton was radical, idealistic. Bacon's interests were
chiefly those of the statesman: he would preserve but improve
existing institutions, fearing that in sweeping changes much
established good would be endangered if not destroyed. Milton was primarily interested in religion, in the reform of which
he would destroy what seemed to him a godless and tyrannical
hierarchy and then build anew on some more spiritual, just,
and democratic foundation. Despite these differences, there can
be little doubt that the reputation of the great Chancellor as
a church reformer was a real aid to Milton, as to other Puritans, in the campaign against Episcopacy.

Lord Digby's *Speech,* which Milton answered in the conclusion of *Of Reformation,* was essentially Baconian in its moderation, though severe in its attack on the bishops: Digby
wished to retain a limited and reformed Episcopacy. But he
made no proposals for reform, and he bitterly assailed the
London citizens who had petitioned against the Church. Milton's answer betrayed his contempt for half-measures. He
would tolerate no compromise in matters of right and wrong.
Impatiently he dismissed Digby's argument that the destruction of Episcopacy would jeopardize the State. Bishops, Milton
declared, were the real enemies of monarchy. From a thoroughly reformed church the just state would have nothing to

[3] "Milton and the English Epic Tradition," *Seventeenth Century Studies,*
pp. 211, 234.

fear. At first Milton failed to see that the possession of power tends to corrupt any organization. By events he was soon convinced that presbyters were every whit as intolerant as bishops, that change of organization was no guarantee of freedom. It may be added that in attacking Digby's *Speech* Milton enjoyed a tactical advantage, for after this *Speech* Digby was a notorious and somewhat discredited apologist for Episcopacy.

The pseudonymous reply to *Of Prelatical Episcopacy* and Lord Brooke's probable borrowing from this pamphlet are chiefly interesting as evidence of the influence of Milton's ecclesiastical pamphlet. In writing a categorical reply to *Of Prelatical Episcopacy*, the author of *A Compendious Discourse* unwittingly paid a tribute to Milton. The statement that "Except for the replies of the Halls, Milton's antiprelatical tracts went unanswered in the press"[4] must be qualified. In avoiding Masson's hero-worship of Milton, it is perhaps possible to swing too far to the opposite extreme. For example, in the discussion of Robert Baillie's reference to Milton in his *A Dissuasive from the Errours of the Time*, it is said: "Enumerating the tenets of the Independents, Baillie mentions 'a large treatise' in which 'Mr. Milton' 'hath pleaded for a full liberty for any man to put away his wife, whenever he pleaseth,' a statement which may be no more than an echo of Prynne's 'divorce at pleasure.' "[5] Later one reads: "Little or nothing was known of him to the pamphleteers and the general public, save as the author of a scandalous book which was widely condemned, but not widely read."[6] The implication that Baillie had not read Milton's first divorce tract runs counter to Masson's statement that in his notes Baillie "quotes sentences to the amount of a page" from Milton's tract.[7] If one consults Baillie's *Dissuasive*, he will see not only that Masson is right but also that Baillie quoted passages from the following pages of *The Doctrine and Discipline of Divorce*: 6, 15, 16, 63, 76—evidence that he had at least scanned Milton's pam-

---

[4] *Tracts on Liberty*, I, 129. [5] *Ibid.*, I, 132.
[6] *Ibid.*, I, 139. [7] *The Life of John Milton*, III, 467.

phlet.   Milton's actual reputation should not be damaged in the laudable effort to correct Masson's exaggeration.   Lord Brooke's borrowing from *Of Prelatical Episcopacy* proves that the pamphlet was immediately serviceable to and probably esteemed by a Parliament leader eminent and active in the cause of reform.   It is not implied that Milton was personally known to the reformers.   It is simply urged that his antiprelatical tracts were not "Unknown, and like esteem'd."

Another bit of precious evidence, hitherto unnoticed, should be recorded.   In the "Annotations" to *Clement, The blessed Paul's Fellow-labourer in the Gospel, His First Epistle to the Corinthians* (1647), William Burton, the author, refers to Milton, William Perkins, and others, unnamed, as "very learned men" who have objected to a passage in one of Ignatius's Epistles.   The passage from Burton is as follows: With the reader's leave and patience, Burton says that he will

doe *Ignatius* a piece of right, . . . There is a passage in one of his Epistles, at which very learned men have taken offence, and very deservedly. It is that to the Church of Smyrna, . . . *My son,* saith he, *honour God and the King: But, I say; Honour God indeed as the Author and Lord of all: and the Bishop, as the High-Priest: and after him we ought to honour the King.* This they say, and truly, doth in plain terms *contradict the Spirit of God in Salomon:* From which presumptuous gain-saying to excuse *Ignatius,* we may take notice that this is but an adulterate piece, . . .[8]

The margin opposite the phrase "very learned men" carries the reference: "Guil. Perkins in Probl. Jo. Milton, &c."   Although in this there is no mention of Milton's work, Burton refers to *Of Prelatical Episcopacy,* from which he quotes, as the following excerpt shows:

Now come the Epistles of *Ignatius* . . . a supposititious ofspring of some dozen Epistles, whereof five are rejected as spurious, . . . a little further he plainly falls to contradict the Spirit of *God* in *Salomon,* Judge by the words themselves. My Son, saith he, honour *God* & the King; but I say, honour *God* and the Bishop as High-priest, . . . and after him honour the King.[9]

[8] P. 79.   [9] *The Works of John Milton,* III, 88-90.

That Burton followed Milton rather than Perkins the following excerpt from Perkins's work shows:

Besides, in his epistle *ad Smirenses* he takes upon him to correct (or rather contradict) *Salomon: My sonne* (saith he, Prov. 24.8.) *Honour God and the king:* but I say (quoth this counterfeit *Ignatius*) *Honour God as the Authour of all things, and the Bishop as the highest of Priests, and after him wee must honour the King.*[10]

Burton's phrasing, *"contradict the Spirit of God in Salomon,"* shows that Milton is quoted. Latinist and noted philologist, Burton was, says Anthony à Wood, an excellent critic and antiquary and was beloved of all learned men of his time. Famous as a Puritan preacher and teacher at Cambridge, Perkins was throughout the seventeenth century regarded as an authority second only to Hooker and Calvin. To be bracketed with Perkins was indeed high honor for Milton. This recognition from Burton is a signal tribute to Milton's contemporary reputation.

The comparison of Milton's and Canne's views on the tenure of kings reveals, not definite proof of indebtedness, but a striking similarity of ideas, the ideas of a party of which Bradshaw was the official spokesman. Between *The Tenure of Kings and Magistrates* and *The Golden Rule* there is the most complete concord of theory and argument. But a man's utterance is conditioned by his character and discipline. Canne wrote without distinction and power—and his work was forgotten. Milton's words, obeying his genius and disclosing a passionate hatred of tyranny, made his a name not to be ignored—and the state soon found work for him to do.

The new light on the composition of *Eikonoklastes* shows that it is based on a thorough investigation of sound authorities, that it is not a patchwork of phrases and ideas borrowed from *Eikon Alethine*. The fact merits emphasis. In truth, Milton appears as a diligent and conscientious workman, unremitting in his efforts to establish the cause of Parliament and

[10] *The Workes Of That Famous And Worthy Minister Of Christ, In The Universitie of Cambridge M. William Perkins* (London, 1613), pp. 490-491.

to destroy the sophistries of the "martyr" king. Scholars do not seem to have realized the import of the Lowenhaupt theory, which presented Milton in a distinctly discreditable light. If it had been sustained, this hypothesis would have made not merely one breach in Milton's reputation. It could have been cogently argued that in other work Milton followed approximately the same method, drawing directly and verbally from a comparatively few sources. In short, Mr. Lowenhaupt's theory is the fundamental one of all narrow studies of Milton's sources. That is why the proving of the Lowenhaupt position untenable seems especially significant. This study, which shows that *Eikonoklastes* was carefully written and solidly documented, has far-reaching implications.

If Milton labored thus diligently for the cause of religion and country, he spared no pains in the service of his art, for which few have prepared themselves more faithfully. As has been said, the wisdom of a learned man cometh by opportunity of leisure. Milton, in whose incomparably rich poetic nature learning was only one important element, seems to have used his leisure to good effect.

The evidence of the sources of the rich culture embodied in his poetry cannot easily or certainly be defined. For example, in *Paradise Lost* the story of creation, a curious blend of Christian and Neoplatonic elements, is sometimes attributed to specific sources but seems to have none that may be confidently proclaimed. There are analogies with Spenser and with Du Bartas; certain details, especially those regarding Adam and Eve, agree with those in More's *Conjectura Cabbalistica;* the description of light and of the creation of the sun reminds one of similar material in Raleigh and Purchas. Frequently, in the emphasis upon chaos, the vitality of nature, the scale of life, and the immanence of God, Milton agrees with the story of creation in Mercator's *Atlas.* In its emphasis upon the Divine his account is profoundly religious; in its conformity with Scripture it is apparently orthodox. But it incorporates much unorthodox material, the sources of which Milton alone, and perhaps not even he, could tell.

Although some details in Milton's poetry, mainly in *Paradise Lost,* had been traced to the histories of Raleigh, Diodorous Siculus, and Pliny, it seemed desirable to collect in one study all analogous material. After due allowance has been made for other sources, it seems clear that Milton drew rather freely upon these histories for a variety of detail. Apparently he consulted or recalled Pliny and Diodorus Siculus for information regarding nature and out-of-the-way lands and customs. Raleigh seems to have been used more frequently, particularly as a guide to the geography of Eden and the history of the Holy Land. Raleigh's eulogy of history, as stated in the following excerpt, indicates the spirit in which Milton wrote *Paradise Lost.* Raleigh declares that by the aid of history

we plainely behould living now, as if we had lived then, that great World, Magni Dei sapiens opus, the wise worke (saith Hermes) of a great God, as it was then, when but new to it selfe. By it I say it is, that we live in the very time when it was created: we behold how it was governed: how it was covered with waters, and againe repeopled: How Kings and Kingdomes have florished and fallen; and for what vertue and piety God made prosperous; and for what vice and deformity he made wretched, both the one and the other. . . .[11]

Milton's choice of place names has often been admired, sometimes with the implication that they were selected at random merely for the sound.[12] It was not fully realized how carefully the names were chosen or how large a part contemporary maps, particularly those in Ortelius's *Theatre of the World,* may have played in the choice and perhaps in the spelling of these names. To compare the maps in Ortelius's "Parergon" with relevant passages in Milton's poetry is to be

[11] "The Preface" of the first edition (1614), Sigs. A 2-3.

[12] Mr. T. S. Eliot, who believes that Milton's poetry is for the most part mere verbal music, obviously holds to this interpretation ("A Note on the Verse of John Milton," *Essays and Studies* [Oxford, 1936], pp. 32-40). In the essay entitled "Milton and Poussin" Mario Praz has, I think, effectively disposed of Mr. Eliot's strictures on Milton's style (*Seventeenth Century Studies,* pp. 192-210). See also E. M. W. Tillyard, "A Note on Milton's Style," *The Miltonic Setting,* pp. 105-140.

convinced not only that Milton was familiar with this Atlas but that the maps were probably a not unimportant aid to his imagination. Back of those clear mental maps, those far-flung geographical spaces, the imagination and knowledge that roam the globe are, among other things, those charts that Ortelius recommended as indispensable aids in the study of history, by which "we may behold things done, or places where they were done, as if they were at this time present and in doing." It is even so. Let the skeptic follow Ortelius's advice. When he reads Milton, let him place before his eyes Ortelius's maps as "certaine glasses." Of the verdict I have no doubt.

A systematic survey shows that Milton was profoundly influenced by melancholy, the prevailing disorder of his age. In fact, it appears that the mood and a fairly large part of the subject matter of Burton's *Anatomy of Melancholy* are paralleled in Milton's work. The conditions and the experiences of his life perfectly illustrate many of the causes of melancholy discussed in the *Anatomy*. In his work, from *L'Allegro*, in which the cures of melancholy are surveyed, to *Samson Agonistes*, in which the blindness, the disillusionment, and the misery of Samson constantly remind the reader of the somber mood and the despair of Milton in old age, we may trace the progress of the theme, which is, indeed, much more prominent than is commonly recognized. Incidentally, if this interpretation is accepted, the two companion poems, *L'Allegro* and *Il Penseroso*, will be understood not as mere academic exercises but as richly autobiographic utterances, written not at the University or in some vacation period but probably at Horton, where circumstances of intensive study and comparative isolation favored the composition of such work. In the development of this mood, an important factor is Milton's disillusionment with his country, a statement of which, as Mr. Tillyard has recently pointed out, occurs in the *History of Britain*:

For Britain, to speak a truth not often spoken, as it is a land fruitful enough of men stout and courageous in war, so it is naturally not over-fertile of men able to govern justly and prudently in peace, trusting only to their motherwit; who consider not justly, that civility, prudence, love of the public good more than of money and vain honour, are to this soil in a manner outlandish. . . . Valiant indeed and prosperous to win a field; but to know the end and reason of winning unjudicious and unwise; in good and bad success alike unteachable. . . .[13]

Induced by this disillusionment to abandon a patriotic subject for his epic, Milton chose in *Paradise Lost* a theme which permitted the most elaborate expression of his prolonged pessimism, a fundamental element in his character.

In the *Hymn* and in *Paradise Lost* the impressive catalog of pagan deities may be taken as a test case of the breadth of Milton's culture. According to the conventional interpretation, the catalog in the epic followed the precedent of Homer's catalog of ships and heroes and was elaborated by names drawn from Scripture and from Greek and Roman mythology. On the other hand, Mr. McColley's recent study maintains that in the catalog Milton merely employed the pattern and the material found in Ross's widely read *Pansebeia: or, A View of all Religions in the World* (1653), which apparently he consulted directly for this purpose. Here is clearly illustrated the contrast between two types of critics: one credits Milton with a retentive memory and a broad knowledge of relevant material; the other insists upon his literal and direct borrowing from a specific source. A rapid survey of several works with which Milton was demonstrably acquainted conclusively shows that in the catalog of deities he made use of a rich literary background and that the attribution of pattern and material to Ross's *Pansebeia* is untenable. In fact, to accept the recent interpretation one must do more than ignore the *Hymn* and the other works in which these pagan deities appear. One must assume that when Milton composed the catalog his mind was practically a blank except for the material derived directly from Ross. Inherent probability and knowledge of Milton's mind and culture decidedly favor the traditional interpretation.

[13] "Milton and the English Epic Tradition," *op. cit.*, pp. 230-231.

Likewise in *Paradise Lost* are presented convictions and images that had engaged Milton's attention during the Commonwealth and the Civil Wars. This period has often been considered a blank as far as his poetry is concerned, and it was not fruitful in the actual composition of poetry. Milton's preoccupation with urgently practical affairs evidently left little time for his cultivation of the Muse. But the vivid images and the vital issues of the period between 1640 and 1658 were not forgotten in the following years. Aside from his choice of the theme of *Paradise Lost,* perhaps the best proof of this fact is found in the treatment of Satan and Belial, in their moral, religious, and political implications. These evil spirits had haunted the pages of Puritan controversy. They were the despised but dreaded leaders of the Royalists, the Cavaliers, men leagued against God and his Son. The idea that in the Civil Wars the Saints were fighting the enemies of God is not, of course, a novel one. What seems to have been only partially realized is the fact that in contemporary Puritan pamphlets the Civil War was often dramatized as a struggle between Satan and God, between Belial and Christ. It can hardly be doubted that the Satan and the Belial of the Puritans found an apotheosis in Milton's sublime epic and that for many of the first readers of *Paradise Lost* Satan, Belial, and their like were familiar demons, not theological abstractions but symbols of loathed enemies who had plunged the land into civil war and had finally been defeated, only to triumph at the Restoration. To read *Paradise Lost* without being aware of these connotations is to miss what must have been for Milton a vital though subordinate part of its significance. The background is a factor in the interpretation as it was in the creation of such figures. As an artist, Milton made Satan a dynamic and fascinating leader, but a leader of wickedness, even as his prototype in the pamphlets. In the light of these facts, Milton would have been astounded by the critics who insist that Satan is the hero of the epic.

In *Comus* the composition of varied elements, ancient and modern, illustrates, it is said, Milton's assimilative mind and the highly individual quality of his genius. Various details come from the Circe episode in the *Odyssey*, from Jonson's *Pleasure Reconciled to Virtue*, and from Peele's *Old Wives Tale*; but the paramount influence is, Mr. Hanford thinks, certain episodes in *The Faerie Queene*, or, according to Mario Praz, Tasso's *Aminta*, which is Milton's real model "transformed almost beyond recognition into a morality in antique garb." In addition to these, which are doubtless the important sources of *Comus*, I suggest that the plausible arguments of the magician in the masque may have been colored by Milton's memory of Erasmus's *Encomium Moriae*, a work praised in his *Sixth Academic Exercise*. At any rate, the parentage of Folly, her sprightly sophistry, her ridicule of temperance and wisdom, her glorification of sensual pleasure—all find a parallel in Milton's grave masque, so different in spirit from Erasmus's rollicking satire.

Finally, *Samson Agonistes* seems to embody reminiscences of Quarles's *Historie of Samson*, which appeared when Milton was a student at Cambridge. Although it may be that Milton deliberately turned back to the poem, it seems more probable that the influence of the *Historie* on *Samson Agonistes* was remote, that Milton drew from the well of his memory ideas and suggestions the actual source of which he may have forgotten. The nature of the resemblances supports this interpretation. There is almost no verbal reminiscence. To be sure, the style of Quarles's poem is not one by which Milton is likely to have been influenced. But, as Mr. John Livingston Lowes has remarked in another connection, "Coincidence alone, in the case of so many correspondences, is too improbable for credence."[14] The analogies between the *Historie* and *Samson Agonistes* indicate a probable but not an intimate relationship.

One is tempted to declare that Milton's relation to his sources is almost never intimate, but such a generalization may be misleading. The truth of the matter is that in most cases we do not absolutely know. Generally, as Mr. Douglas Bush

[14] "Moneta's Temple," *PMLA*, LI, 1102.

has said, Milton's supremely individual style disguises or obliterates the source: "Spenser, Marlowe, Shakespeare, have highly individual styles, yet at times they reflect the tone of a particular source, such as Ovid. Milton knew Ovid better than any of these, but almost from the beginning he wrote in such a consistently personal idiom than any one can very rarely say, 'This is like Ovid,' or 'This is like Homer.' Wherever Milton gets his material the result, except in a few early pieces, is simply John Milton."[15] To safeguard the study of specific sources, which in Milton's case is so frequently futile, the well-advised student will endeavor to know Milton's broad cultural background. He will also recall the ways in which poets work. In spite of all that has been written about Milton's bookishness, he, like Goethe and many others, was not unvisited by impressions of a hundred kinds, "sensuous, lively, lovely, many-hued," which, with others derived from his rich knowledge of literature, from his intense concern with vital moral issues, and from his superb imagination, he moulded into imperishable forms of truth and beauty.

Finally, full appreciation of Milton depends upon adequate realization of the profound religious spirit that pervaded his life and work, over which may stand as a motto his own prayer:

O perfect and accomplish thy glorious acts; for men may leave their works unfinisht, but thou art a God, thy nature is perfection; . . . the times and seasons passe along under thy feet, to goe and come at thy bidding, and as thou didst dignifie our fathers dayes with many revelations above all the foregoing ages, since thou tookst the flesh; so thou canst vouchsafe to us (though unworthy) as large a portion of thy spirit as thou pleasest; for who shall prejudice thy all-governing will? seeing the power of thy grace is not past away with the primitive times, as fond and faithless men imagine, but thy Kingdome is now at hand, and thou standing at the dore. Come forth out of thy Royall Chambers, O Prince of all the Kings of the earth, put on the visible roabes of thy imperiall Majesty, take up that unlimited Scepter which thy Almighty

[15] *Mythology and the Renaissance Tradition in English Poetry* (Minneapolis, 1932), p. 249.

Father hath bequeath'd thee; for now the voice of thy Bride calls thee, and all creatures sigh to bee renew'd.

We know, of course, that Milton's sanguine hopes were disappointed—and we know that hope deferred maketh the heart sick. But the Milton who wrote this prayer also wrote near the end, amid the gathering shadows:

> All is best, though we oft doubt,
> What th' unsearchable dispose
> Of highest wisdom brings about,
> And ever best found in the close.

In this spirit, turning directly to Milton's work, which in all investigation of the literary milieu is the center of interest, the student will pay homage to that artistic achievement which both expresses and transcends the age and to the great poet who was neither a mere student buried in his library nor an austere fanatic always at war with nature, who gives

> Authentic tidings of invisible things;
> Of ebb and flow, and ever-during power;
> And central peace, subsisting at the heart
> Of endless agitation,

in whose noble speech is enshrined much of the courage, the ideals, and the faith of protestant humanity. In his life and work, nourished by a richer culture than we know, dedicated to high aims, and touched to profound issues, there are qualities infinitely rare and precious: the charm of old gardens under sunshine or gentle rain, the solemnity of temples planted round with shade "Of laurel ever green, and branching palm," the sublimity of cloud castles built by the sun upon the summer seas, the spiritual wind that sweeps away the clouds and mists from this dim spot called earth and admits by "Cleer Spring, or shadie Grove, or Sunnie Hill" gleams of that radiant light which is the essence of divinity.

APPENDIX

"THE GRIM WOOLF"

In the decade before the Civil War, English Catholics enjoyed extraordinary privileges. As Mr. Godfrey Davies has recently remarked, Charles I, listening to his wife's entreaties, spared her co-religionists. The laws against them were not strictly enforced; letters of grace protected favorite Catholics; the chapels of the Queen and foreign ambassadors were thronged; Catholic works were imported into England and even published there. "There would seem to have been a distinct Catholic revival in the 1630's, with some notable conversions."[1] This is the background for the well-known lines in *Lycidas*, which follow the famous passage denouncing the corruption of the Church:

> Besides what the grim Woolf with privy paw
> Daily devours apace, and nothing sed.

Mr. Patterson thinks these lines "probably" refer to the activities of the Catholics but notes that in *Paradise Lost* Satan is compared to a wolf.[2] Mr. Hughes believes that there may also be a reference to the partisans of Archbishop Laud.[3] Browne states that the wolf may refer to the legendary origin of Rome.[4] Masson declares that the grim wolf is undoubtedly the Church of Rome, "the numerous private secessions to which in England in Laud's time were a subject of alarm and complaint among the Puritans."[5]

[1] *The Early Stuarts 1603-1660* (Oxford, 1937), p. 207.
[2] *The Student's Milton* (New York, 1936), p. 60 of the notes.
[3] *Paradise Regained, The Minor Poems, and Samson Agonistes* (New York, 1937), p. 292.
[4] *English Poems by John Milton* (Oxford, 1906), I, 302.
[5] *The Poetical Works of John Milton* (London, 1882), III, 284.

Curiously enough, Bishop Hall, the famous apologist for
Episcopacy and Milton's formidable foe in the pamphlet skir-
mishing of the 1640's, clearly shows the alleged menace of
the Wolf, which is the Church of Rome. In *No Peace with
Rome,* first written in Latin and then "Englished," and devoted to the thesis that the Reformed religion cannot be reconciled with the Romish, Bishop Hall attacks the heresy, the
idolatry, and the tyranny of Rome, which has thrust the Protestants out of doors and "spet upon, railed at," and slandered
them. "What heresie," exclaims Hall, "is there in all times,
which that *Romulean* Wolfe, and her bawling Clients are not
wont to cast upon us?"[6] Whoever infringes the power of the
Pope and of Rome, which is now a "Citie of bloud," is a heretic
to be converted or destroyed. Ironically Hall exclaims: "Oh
happy Chaire of *Peter,* firme, eternall, full of prodigious vertue!" And he adds: "Christ said indeed, *Thou art Peter:* but,
Thou art *Paul* the Fift, he never said: He said, *I have prayed
for thee, that thy faith faile not:* so he said too, *Goe behinde
me, Satan, thou savourest not the things of God."*[7] He cites
other popish opinions, pernicious to the Church and commonwealth: the power of both swords, the deposition of princes,
the disposing of kingdoms, the absolving of subjects, the frustration of oaths—arrogant principles "palpably opposite to the
libertie of Christian Government." These gross heresies and
venomous opinions have bred much trouble and danger to the
church of God. After pointing out many other damnable errors of popish doctrine, Hall declares that no wise man could
ever suspect that "wee will ever grow to that height of mad-
nesse, as to runne perfidiously from the standard of God, to
the Tents of that Roman Antichrist."[8] Since there is no possibility of reconciliation and since Rome will not change, Hall
demands a war against heresy and prays that the true Church
may have victory.

In the "Fift Decade" of the third volume of his *Epistles,*
dedicated to the Prince of Wales, the first epistle discourses of

[6] *The Works of Joseph Hall B. of Exceter* (London, 1634), p. 608.
[7] *Ibid.,* p. 612.   [8] *Ibid.,* p. 631.

the causes and means of the increase of popery. The zeal of the Jesuits, seconded by Satan, has established for the world of popery a new support in hell. The Jesuits make use of all agencies: they lie shamelessly; they appeal to superstition and ignorance; they misinterpret antiquity; they amaze and besot the people with gaudy altars, magnificent places, triumphant festivals; disguised, they thrust themselves into all companies and courts; they have "their painted Ladies (not dead, but living) both for objects, and instruments," the stales "of their spirituall fornications." Besides, they have a great organization which encourages zeal, prevents friction, and bestows rewards upon students. By their fair outside, pretended miracles, bloody inquisitions, and unscrupulous zeal they overcome English characteristic indifference, slackness, tolerance, and downright sincerity.[9] However, trusting in the King (who may dare "to grapple with that great infallible Vicar, for his triple Crowne,")[10] the able bishops, the learned doctors, the flourishing universities, and God's favor, Hall hopes for success in spite of the gates of hell. The fourth epistle of the "Sixt Decade" argues that popery, by substituting a new rule of faith and a new head of the church (not Christ, but a Man of Sin) razes the foundation of morality and religion.[11]

In *Quo Vadis? A Just Censure of Travell, As It Is Commonly Undertaken by the Gentlemen of our Nation,* Hall deplores the English practice of sending sons abroad to countries where they will be infected by impiety or superstition. He asks:

If we desired to have sons poysoned with misbeleefe, what could we doe otherwise? Or what else doe those Parents, which have bequeathed their children to Antichristianisme? Our late journey into *France* informed me of some ordinary factors of *Rome,* whose trade is the transporting and placing of our Popish novices beyond the seas; one whereof (whose name I noted) hath bin observed to

[9] *Ibid.,* pp. 327-330.
[10] Cf. Milton's "The triple Tyrant" in "On the Late Massacre in Piemont."
[11] *The Works of Joseph Hall,* pp. 351-353.

carry over six severall charges in one yeare. . . . Doe we send our
sons to learne to be chaste in the midst of *Sodome?* [12]

There are displayed most temptingly the gaudy magnificence
of pompous ceremonies, "wherewith the hearts of children and
fooles are easily taken"; there are colors, perfumes, wanton
dresses; there are rich shrines, stately processions, a thousand
sensual temptations.   There the complete traveler suffers a
double danger: corruption of religion and depravation of man-
ners. Gradually the poison works; long acquaintance makes
vice familiar; in time the "politike position, and practices of
the Romanists" seem plausible; in the end popery seems no
ill religion. Gazing on this Diana, men lose their spiritual
chastity, the Church, and themselves.

How many have wee knowne strocken with these Aspes, which
have died sleeping?   And in truth, whosoever shall consider this
open freedome of the meanes of seducement, must needs wonder
that wee have lost no more; especially, if he be acquainted with
those two maine helps of our Adversaries, importunity, and plausi-
bility.   Never any Pharisee was so eager to make a Proselyte, as our
late factors of Rome: . . . No man setteth foot upon their coast,
which may not presently sing with the Psalmist, *They come about
mee like Bees.* . . . But in the meane time, there is nothing
wherein I wish we would emulate them, but in this heat of diligence
and violent ambition of winning. . . . The world could not stand
before us, if our truth might be but as hotly followed as their falshood.   Oh that our God, whose cause wee maintaine, would en-
kindle our hearts with the fire of holy zeale, but so much as Sathan
hath inflamed theirs with the fire of fury and faction.   Oh that he
would shake us out of this dull ease, and quicken our slacke spirits
unto his owne worke.   Arise O North, and come O South, and
blow upon our garden, that the spices thereof may flow forth. [13]

Hall's phrases "dull ease" and "slacke spirits" are mild by contrast with Milton's tremendous denunciation of the corrupt
clergy, but the bishop's realization of the menace of Romanism
is as keen as the poet's.

[12] *Ibid.*, p. 641. *Quo Vadis?* was first published in 1617.
[13] *Ibid.*, p. 649.

These sutors will take no deniall, but are ready (as the fashion was to doe with rich matches) to carry away mens soules whether they will or no. Wee see the proofe of their importunitie at home: No bulwarke of lawes nor barres of Justice (though made of three trees) can keepe our rebanished fugitives from returning, from intermedling. How have their actions said in the hearing of the world, that since heaven will not heare them, they will try what hel can doe? And if they dare bee so busie in our owne homes, where they would seeme somewhat awed with the danger of Justice; what (thinke wee) will they not dare to doe in their owne territories. . . .

No place, Hall declares, is free from these spies: "What State is not haunted with these ill spirits? yea what house? yea what soule? Not a Princes Councell-Table, not a Ladies Chamber can be free from their shameless insinuations?"[14]

Appealing to the King and his ministers for a strict enforcement of the laws, Bishop Hall concludes:

Since then wee have no more wit, or care, then to bee willingly guilty of our owne shame; oh that the hands of supreme Authoritie would be pleased to locke us within our owne doores, and to keepe the keyes at their owne girdle! And (to speake truth) to what purpose are those strait and capitall inhibitions of the returne of our factious fugitives into this Kingdome, if whiles the wicket is shut upon them, that they should not come to us, the Posterne bee open to us, that wee may goe to them? As all intercourse is perilous, so that is most, which is by our owne provocation. Here yet they dare but lurke in secret, and take only some sudden snatches at a weake prey, like unto evening-wolves, that never walke forth but under the cloak of night; but in their owne territories, they can shew the Sunne their spoiles, and thinke this act worthy of garlands and trophees. Here wee have mastives to secure our flockes: there the prey goes stragling alone to the mouth of their dennes, without protection, without assistance, and offers to be devoured. Yee whom the choice of God hath made the great Shepheards of his people, . . . suffer not their simplicitie to betray their lives unto the fangs of these cruel beasts; but chase them home rather, from the willfull search of their owne perdition, and shut them up together in your

[14] *Ibid.*, p. 650.

strong and spacious folds, that they may be at once safe, and yee glorious.[15]

Although Milton certainly sympathized with Hall's plea that the laws against the Catholics should be strictly enforced, he ventured to ignore the Bishop's warning against traveling in popish territories.   When he visited Italy, his age and his firm protestantism preserved him from the poison of Romanism. In fact, as he says, he openly defended the reformed religion in "the very metropolis of popery."   Later, engaging the Bishop in heated controversy, he revived the issue in *Lycidas* and contemptuously characterized the work of Hall and his fellows thus:

a swashbuckler against the Pope, and a dormouse against the Devil, while the whole Diocese be sown with tares, and none to resist the enemy, but such as let him in at the posterne, a rare superintendent at *Rome,* and a cipher at home.   Hypocrites, the Gospell faithfully preach'd to the poore, the desolate parishes visited and duely fed, loyterers throwne out, wolves driven from the fold, had beene a better confutation of the Pope and Masse, than whole Hecatontomes of controversies, . . .[16]

Did Milton, one wonders, ever feel a secret pity for the Bishop, who at heart leaned to low church and puritanism, whose references to Antichrist in *Episcopacy by Divine Right* had been expunged by Laud's orders, and who, from the Tower, to which he had been committed December 31, 1641, protested to a friend that he had not exercised his jurisdiction tyrannically, that he had not suppressed "painfull and peaceable Preachers," that he hated all illegal impositions and innovations, that in many pulpits and presses he had cried down both popery and Arminianism, that he had zealously cared for the spiritual needs of his flock, and that he was glad to have defended with his pen his calling, which is no other than "the most holy Fathers of the Church and the Primitive and suc-

[15] *Ibid.,* p. 657.   Characteristically, Milton's "two-handed engine" seems to refer, not to the King and his ministers, but to Parliament.

[16] *Animadversions upon The Remonstrants Defence, Against Smectymnuus, The Works of John Milton* (New York, 1931), III, 174-175.

ceeding Ages . . . have been guilty of"? Full of scorn for
the whole Hierarchy, Milton may have mocked at the Bishop's
assurance that in his own good time God would give him
"beauty for bonds, and for a light and momentary affliction, an
eternall weight of glory." In Milton's view the Bishop's impressive crusade against popery could not atone for the fact
that he was a member of the hated crew who had deformed
and ruined religion and had left the hungry sheep shepherd-
less, a prey to wolves.

SATAN AND THE SERPENT

In his note on *Paradise Lost* IX, 553-566—lines expressing
Eve's natural surprise upon hearing the "Proem" of the Serpent—Verity quotes from Sir Thomas Browne's *Vulgar Errors,*
I, 1, a passage the sense of which is that some are puzzled not
only because Eve was deluded by a serpent but also because
"without fear or doubt" she discoursed with this creature and
"without suspicion of imposture" heard him speak. We may
be sure, Verity adds, that Milton was acquainted with the first
two chapters of *Vulgar Errors,* which discuss the causes of errors, and particularly with what Pater calls "the intellectual
and moral by-play of the situation of the first man and woman
in Paradise, with strange queries about it."[1]

Curiously enough, no commentator, it seems, has detected
the relation of a later chapter *of Pseudodoxia Epidemica* to
Milton's description of the demon-possessed Serpent. In Book
V, Chapter iv, entitled "Of the Picture of the Serpent tempt-
ing Eve," Browne writes:

In the Picture of Paradise, and delusion of our first Parents, the
Serpent is often described with human visage; not unlike Cadmus,
or his wife, in the act of their Metamorphosis. Which is not meerly
a pictoriall contrivance or invention of the Picturer, but an ancient
tradition and conceived reality, as it stands delivered by Beda and
Authors of some antiquity; that is, that Sathan appeared not unto

[1] *Paradise Lost,* II, 578-579.

Eve in the naked form of a Serpent, but with a Virgins head, that thereby he might become more acceptable, and his temptation finde the easier entertainment. Which neverthelesse is a conceit not to be admitted, and the plain and received figure, is with better reason embraced.[2]

Attempting to explode the tradition that the Serpent had a virgin's head, Browne declares that "the assumption of humane shape, had proved a disadvantage unto Sathan; affording not only a suspicious amazement in Eve, before the fact, in beholding a third humanity beside her self and Adam; but leaving some excuse unto the woman, which afterward the man took up with lesser reason; that is, to have been deceived by another like her self." Browne's argument proceeds as follows:

There was no inconvenience in the shape assumed, or any considerable impediment that might disturb that performance in the common form of a Serpent. For whereas it is conceived the woman must needs be afraid thereof, and rather flie then approach it; it was not agreeable unto the condition of Paradise and state of innocence therein; if in that place as most determine, no creature was hurtfull or terrible unto man, and those destructive effects they now discover succeeded the curse, and came in with thorns and briars.[3]

Taking pains to show, as a marginal note runs, why "Eve wondered not at the Serpents speaking," Browne says that she "might not yet be certain that only man was priviledged with speech, and being in the novity of the Creation, and inexperience of all things, might not be affrighted to hear a Serpent speak."

However gorgeous, Milton's Serpent does not admit the "conceit" of a Virgin's head. Except for his upright carriage, he is merely serpent in appearance, having, like Browne's, no human quality except the power of speech:

---

[2] *Pseudodoxia Epidemica: or, Enquiries into Very many Received Tenents, And commonly Presumed Truths.* The Second Edition, Corrected and much Enlarged by the Author (London, 1650), p. 200.

[3] *Ibid.,* p. 201.

> So spake the Enemie of Mankind, enclos'd
> In Serpent, Inmate bad, and toward *Eve*
> Address'd his way, not with indented wave,
> Prone on the ground, as since, but on his reare,
> Circular base of rising foulds, that tour'd
> Fould above fould a surging Maze, his Head
> Crested aloft, and Carbuncle his Eyes;
> With burnisht Neck of verdant Gold, erect
> Amidst his circling Spires, that on the grass
> Floted redundant: pleasing was his shape,
> And lovely, . . .[4]

Like Browne's Serpent, Milton's has no human shape that might have excited in Eve "a suspicious amazement." So beautiful is the appearance of Milton's Serpent-Satan and so ingratiating are his movements that Eve is attracted rather than repelled. With a surer sense of drama than Browne had, Milton writes that Eve was "Not unamaz'd" by the words of the Serpent, which as mere serpent was, like all other animals before the Fall, quite innocent and harmless. In Milton's words:

> shee busied heard the sound
> Of rusling Leaves, but minded not, as us'd
> To such disport before her through the Field,
> From every Beast, more duteous at her call,
> Then at *Circean* call the Herd disguis'd.

Besides this similarity, there are in *Paradise Lost* and *Pseudodoxia Epidemica* other analogies in the treatment of the temptation and the Fall: in Browne, as in Milton, "the inservient and brutall faculties" overpowered reason; Eve was overcome by art and fallacy but Adam by a "naked offer"; Adam, "the wisest of all men since," was not ignorant of the fall of the angels and had their example and punishment to deter him. With respect to *Paradise Lost*, the following statement in Browne is particularly striking: "Pleasure and profit already overswaying the instructions of honesty, and sensuality perturbing the reasonable commands of vertue." Thus were our

[4] IX, 494-504.

"Grand Parents" deluded, there being "nothing infallible but God, who cannot possibly erre." In short, it is not improbable that Milton was acquainted with *Pseudodoxia Epidemica*, not the least value of which to him may have been that in this work, "of such concernment unto Truth," Browne was, in his own words, "often constrained to stand alone against the strength of opinion."

A SELECTED BIBLIOGRAPHY

Abbott, Edwin A. *Francis Bacon An Account of his Life and Works.* London, 1885.

Abingtons and Alisburies Miseries. Both which Townes being lately lamentably plundered by Prince Robert and his Cavaliers. Expressly related as it was certified to some of the Honourable the High Court of Parliament. . . . London, [1644?].

[Adrichomius, Christianus]. *A Briefe Description of Hierusalem and of the Suburbs thereof, as it florished in the time of Christ. Whereto is annexed a short Commentarie concerning those places which were made famous by the Passion of Christ, and by the Actes of holye men, confirmed by certeine principall Histories of Antiquity. Verie profitable for all Christians to read,* . . . Translated out of Latin into English by Thomas Tymme Minister. London, 1595.

Allen, P. S. *Erasmus Lectures and Wayfaring Sketches.* Oxford, 1934.

Anglicanism The Thought and Practice of the Church of England, Illustrated from the Religious Literature of the Seventeenth Century. Compiled and edited by Paul Elmer More and Frank Leslie Cross. Milwaukee, 1935.

An Answer to the Lord George Digbies Apology for Himself; Published Jan. 4. Anno Dom. 1642 . . . London, 1642.

Augustine, Saint. *Of The Citie of God: With The Learned Comments of Io. Lodovicus Vives.* Englished first by J. H. and now in this second Edition compared with the Latine Originall, and in very many places corrected and amended. London, 1620.

————. *The City of God.* Translated by John Healy With an Introduction by Ernest Barker. London and Toronto, 1931.

[Bacon, Francis]. *Certaine Considerations touching the better Pacification and Edification of the Church of England:* . . . London, 1604.

————. *A Wise and Moderate Discourse, Concerning Church-Affaires. As it was written long since, by the famous Author of those Considerations, which seems to have some reference to this . . . 1641.*

————. *The Works of Francis Bacon . . .* London, 1710.

————. *The Works of Francis Bacon.* Ed. by Spedding, Ellis, Heath. London, 1868.

Bagehot, Walter. *Literary Studies.* London, 1910.

Baillie, Robert. *A Dissuasive From The Errours of the Time: Wherein the Tenets of the principall Sects, especially of the Independents, are drawn together in One Map, for the most part, in the words of their own Authors, and their maine principles are examined by the Touch-Stone of the Holy Scriptures.* By Robert Baylie Minister at Glasgow . . . London, 1645.

————. *Satan the Leader in chief to all who resist the Reparation of Sion.* A Sermon Preached to the House of Commons, Feb. 28, 1643. London, 1643.

Baker, J. N. L. "England in the Seventeenth Century," *An Historical Geography of England Before A.D. 1800.* Cambridge, 1936.

Baxter, Richard. *Reliquiae Baxterianae: Or, Richard Baxter's Narrative of the Most Memorable Passages of His Life and Times. Faithfully Publish'd from his own Original Manuscripts.* By Matthew Sylvester . . . London, 1696.

Benbrigge, John. *Gods Fury, Englands Fire. Or A Plaine Discovery of those spirituall Incendiaries, which have set Church and State on Fire. With a serious Exhortation to all Persons to joyne together in seeking to quench it . . .* London, 1646.

The Holy Bible, Conteyning the Old Testament, and the New: Newly Translated out of the Original Tongues: and with the former Translations diligently compared and revised, by his Majesties speciall Commandement . . . London, 1611.

Brown, Eleanor Gertrude. *Milton's Blindness.* New York, 1934.

Browne, Sir Thomas. *Pseudodoxia Epidemica: Or, Enquiries Into Very many Received Tenents, And commonly Presumed Truths.* London, 1650.

Buchan, John. *Oliver Cromwell.* Boston, 1934.

Bullough, Geoffrey. "Bacon and the Defence of Learning," *Seventeenth Century Studies* (Oxford, 1938), pp. 1-20.

The Burden of England, Scotland, and Ireland: Or, The Watchmans Alarum. In a plain Declaration to the Kings most Excellent Majesty, pointing out the chiefe sins, and causes of this Civill War, and of all those judgements under which the three Kingdomes now groane, plainely proved by Gods Word, and our practice . . . London, 1646.

Burton, Robert. *The Anatomy of Melancholy.* London, 1893.

Bush, Douglas. *Mythology and the Renaissance Tradition in English Poetry.* Minneapolis, 1932.

Camden, William. *Britain, Or A Chorographicall Description Of The Most flourishing Kingdomes, England, Scotland, and Ireland, and the Ilands adioning, out of the depth of Antiquitie: Beautified with Mappes of the severall Shires of England Written first in Latine by William Camden* . . . Translated newly into English by Philemon Holland . . . Finally, revised, amended, and enlarged with sundry Additions by the said Author. Londini, 1610.

Campbell, Lily B. "The Christian Muse," *The Huntington Library Bulletin*, Number 8. Cambridge, 1935.

Canne, John. *The Golden Rule, Or, Justice Advanced. Wherein is shewed, That the Representative Kingdom, or Commons assembled in Parliament, have a lawfull power to arraign, and adjudge to death the King, for Tyranny, Treason, Murder, and other Misdemeanors* . . . London, 1649.

Carpenter, John. *Geography Delineated Forth in Two Bookes. Containing the Sphaericall and Topicall Parts Thereof* . . . Oxford, 1625.

Chester, Allan G. *Thomas May: Man of Letters, 1595-1650.* Philadelphia, 1932.

Clark, E. M. "Milton's Earlier Samson," *Studies in English*, Number 5. The University of Texas Bulletin, 1925. Pp. 144-154.

A Collection of all the publicke Orders Ordinances and Declarations, of both Houses of Parliament, from the Ninth of March 1642. Untill December 1646. Together with severall of his Majesties Proclamations and other Papers Printed at Oxford. Also a convenient Table for the finding the severall Date and Title of the Particulars herein mentioned . . . London, 1646.

Collier, Katharine Brownell. *Cosmogonies of our Fathers Some Theories of the Seventeenth and the Eighteenth Centuries.* New York, 1934.

A Compendious Discourse, Proving Episcopacy To Be Of Apostolicall, And Consequently Of Divine Institution . . . London, 1641.

Cook, John. *King Charls his Case: Or, An Appeal to all Rational Men, Concerning His Tryall at the High Court of Justice* . . . London, 1649.

Cooper, Thomas. *Thesaurus Linguae Romanae et Britannicae* . . . London, 1565.

Danaeus, Lambertus. *The Wonderfull Woorkmanship Of The World: wherein is conteined an excellent discourse of Christian naturall Philosophie, concernyng the fourme, knowledge, and use of all things created: specially gathered out of the Fountaines of holy Scripture,* by Lambertus Danaeus: and now Englished, by T. T. London, 1578.

De Bry, Theodore. *Indiae Orientalis Pars IX. Historicam Descriptionem Navigationis ab Hollandis et Selandis in Indiam Orientalem* . . . Francofurti, 1612.

————. *Vera Descriptio Regni Africani, Quod Tam ab Incolis Quam Lusitanis Congus Appelatur.* 1598.

A Declaration Of The Commons Of England In Parliament assembled; Expressing Their Reasons and Grounds of passing the late Resolutions touching No farther Addresses or Applications to be made to the King . . . London, 1647.

De Filippis, Michele. "Milton and Manso: Cups or Books," *PMLA*, LI, 745-756.

Digby, George. *The Lord George Digbie's Apologie For Himselfe,* . . . Oxford, 1642.

————. *The Third Speech Of The Lord George Digby, To the House of Commons, Concerning Bishops, and the Citie Petition,* the 9th. of Febr: 1640 [1641].

Diodorus Siculus. *The History of Diodorus Siculus. Containing all that is Most Memorable and of the greatest Antiquity in the first Ages of the World Until the War of Troy.* Done into English by H. C. Gent. London, 1653.

————. *Diodorus of Sicily* With an English Translation by C. H. Oldfather. London, 1933-1935.

Du Bartas His Devine Weekes and Workes. Translated: and Dedicated to the Kings most excellent Maiestie by Joshua Sylvester. Now thirdly corrected & augm. London, [1611].

Edmundson, George. *Milton and Vondel A Curiosity of Literature*. London, 1885.

Eikon Alethine The Pourtraiture Of Truths most sacred Majesty truly suffering, though not solely. Wherein the false colours are washed off, wherewith the Painter-steiner had bedawbed Truth, the late King and the Parliament, in his counterfeit Piece entituled Eikon Basilike, . . . London, 1649.

Eliot, T. S. "A Note on the Verse of John Milton," *Essays and Studies*. Oxford, 1936. Pp. 32-40.

Erasmus, Desiderius. *In Praise of Folly*. With Illustrations after Hans Holbein. New York, n.d.

———. *The Praise of Folly*. Written by Erasmus in 1509 and translated by John Wilson 1669. Ed. with an Introduction by Mrs. P. S. Allen. Oxford, 1925.

An Exact Collection of all Remonstrances, Declarations, Votes, Orders, Ordinances, Proclamations, Petitions, Messages, Answers, and other Remarkable Passages betweene the Kings most Excellent Majesty, and his High Court of Parliament beginning at his Majesties return from Scotland, being in December 1641, and continued untill March the 21, 1643 . . . London, 1643.

Figgis, John Neville. *The Divine Right of Kings*. Second Edition. Cambridge, 1922.

Firth, Sir Charles H. "Sir Walter Raleigh's History of the World," *Proceedings of the British Academy 1917-1918*. London, n.d. Pp. 427-446.

———. *Essays Historical & Literary*. Oxford, 1938.

Fletcher, Harris F. *Milton's Rabbinical Readings*. Urbana, 1930.

Frazier, J. G. *The Golden Bough*. London, 1914. Part IV, Vol. II.

French, J. Milton. "The Autographs of John Milton," *ELH*, IV, 301-330.

———. "Milton, Needham, and Mercurius Politicus," *Studies in Philology*, XXXIII, 236-252.

———. "Milton's Annotated Copy of Gildas," *Harvard Studies and Notes in Philology and Literature*, XX, 75-80.

Fuller, Thomas. *The Holy State*. Cambridge, 1642.

———. *A Pisgah-Sight of Palestine And The Confines Thereof, With The History of the Old and New Testament acted thereon* . . . London, 1650.

Gardiner, S. G. *History of England From the Accession of James I to the Outbreak of the Civil War 1603-1642.* London, 1883-1884.

Gilbert, Allan H. *A Geographical Dictionary of Milton.* New Haven, 1919.

———. "Pierre Davity: His 'Geography' and its Use by Milton," *The Geographical Review,* VII, 322-338.

———. "Milton and the 'Aminta,'" *Modern Philology,* XXV, 95-99.

Goodwin, John. *Anapologesiates Antapologias: Or, The inexcusablenesse of that Grand Accusation of the Brethren, called Antapologia.* London, 1644.

———. *Anti-Cavaliersme, Or, Truth Pleading As well the Necessity, as the Lawfulnesse of this present War, for the suppression of that Butcherly brood of Cavaliering Incendiaries,* . . . London, 1642.

Gottfried, Rudolph. "Milton, Lactantius, Claudian, and Tasso," *Studies in Philology,* XXX, 497-504.

Le Grand Atlas, ou Cosmographie Blauiane, En Laquelle est Exactement Descritte La Terre, La Mer, et Le Ciel . . . Amsterdam, 1663.

Green, C. C. "The Paradox of the Fall in 'Paradise Lost,'" *MLN,* LIII, 557-571.

Greenlaw, Edwin. "A Better Teacher than Aquinas," *Studies in Philology,* XIV, 196-217.

———. "Spenser's Influence on *Paradise Lost,*" *Studies in Philology,* XVII, 320-359.

Grierson, H. J. C. *Cross Currents in English Literature of the XVIIth Century* . . . London, 1929.

———. *Milton & Wordsworth Poets and Prophets A Study of their Reactions to Political Events.* New York, 1937.

Hanford, James H. "The Chronology of Milton's Private Studies," *PMLA,* XXVI, 251-314.

———. *A Milton Handbook.* New York, 1938.

———. "The Pastoral Elegy and Milton's *Lycidas,*" *PMLA,* XXV, 403-447.

———. "*Samson Agonistes* and Milton in Old Age," *Studies in Shakespeare, Milton, and Donne.* New York, 1925. Pp. 167-189.

————. "The Youth of Milton," *Studies in Shakespeare, Milton, and Donne.* Pp. 89-163.

Hartwell, K. E. *Lactantius and Milton.* Cambridge, 1929. Pp. 149-157.

Henderson, Alexander. *A Sermon Preached before the Honourable House of Lords,* May 28, 1645 . . . London, 1645.

Hesiod. *The Homeric Hymns and Homerica.* With an English Translation by Hugh G. Evelyn-White. London and New York, 1914.

Heylyn, Peter. *Cosmographie in foure Bookes Contayning the Chorographie and Historie of the whole World, and all the Principal Kingdomes, Provinces, Seas, and Isles Thereof . . .* London, 1652.

Heywood, Thomas. *The Hierarchie of the Blessed Angells. Their Names, Orders and Officers The Fall of Lucifer with his Angells.* London, 1635.

James I. *The Political Works of James I Reprinted from the Edition of 1616.* With an Introduction by Charles H. McIlwain. Cambridge, 1918.

James, Margaret. *Social Problems and Policy During the Puritan Revolution 1640-1660.* London, 1930.

Jones, Richard F. *Ancients and Moderns.* St. Louis, 1936.

Josephus, Flavius. *The Famous and Memorable Workes of Iosephus, A Man of much Honour and Learning among the Iewes.* Faithfully translated out of the Latin, and French, by Tho. Lodge . . . London, 1602.

————. *Jewish Antiquities,* with an English translation by H. St. J. Thackeray. London and New York, 1930.

Keightley, Thomas. *An Account of the Life, Opinions, and Writings of John Milton.* London, 1859.

Kelley, Maurice. "Milton's Debt to Wolleb's *Compendium Theologiae Christianae,*" *PMLA,* L, 156-165.

King Charls His Tryal, Or A perfect Narrative of the whole Proceedings of the High Court of Justice In The Tryal of the King in Westminister Hall. With the several Speeches of the King, Lord President, and Solicitor General . . . London, 1649.

Knights, L. C. "Seventeenth-Century Melancholy," *Drama and Society in the Age of Jonson.* London, 1937. Pp. 315-332.

Larson, Martin A. "Milton and Servetus," *PMLA*, XLI, 891 ff.

[Lauder, William]. *An Essay on Milton's Use and Imitation of the Moderns in his Paradise Lost.* London, 1750.

Leach, A. F. "Milton as Schoolboy and Schoolmaster," *Proceedings of the British Academy 1907-1908.* London, n.d. Pp. 295-318.

Lemmi, Charles W. *The Classic Deities in Bacon A Study in Mythological Symbolism.* Baltimore, 1933.

Lovejoy, Arthur O. *The Great Chain of Being A Study of the History of an Idea.* Cambridge, 1936.

———. "Milton and the Paradox of the Fortunate Fall," *ELH*, IV, 161-179.

Lowenhaupt, Warren H. "The Writing of Milton's *Eikonoklastes*," *Studies in Philology*, XX, 29-51.

McColley, Grant. "The Astronomy of *Paradise Lost*," *Studies in Philology*, XXXIV, 209-247.

———. "The Epic Catalogue of *Paradise Lost*," *ELH*, IV, 180-191.

———. "Milton's Dialogue on Astronomy: The Principal Immediate Sources," *PMLA*, LII, 728-762.

———. "Milton's Technique of Source Adaptation," *Studies in Philology*, XXXV, 61-110.

Marshall, Stephen. *A Divine Project to Save a Kingdome*, a Sermon Preached before the Lord Mayor and the Court of Aldermen, April 22, 1644. London, 1644.

———. *Reformation and Desolation: Or, A Sermon tending to the Discovery of the Symptomes of a People to whom God will by no meanes be reconciled.* London, 1642.

———. *A Sermon Preached before the Honourable House of Commons, now assembled in Parliament, at their publike Fast,* November 17, 1640. London, 1640.

Masson, David. *The Life of John Milton.* Cambridge, 1859-1894.

Mausbach, Joseph. *Die Ethik des Heiligen Augustinus.* Freiburg, 1929.

May, Thomas. *The History of the Parliament of England: . . .* London, 1647.

Mercator, Gerhard. *Atlas Sive Cosmographicae Meditationes De Fabrica Mundi et Fabricati Figura.* Amsterodami, 1623.

――――. *Gerardi Mercatoris et I. Hondü. Atlas or A Geographiche Description of the Regions, Countries and Kingdomes of the World, through Europe, Asia, Africa, and America, represented by new & exact Maps.* Translated by Henry Hexham. Amsterdam, 1636.

――――. *Historia Mundi: Or Mercator's Atlas . . . Lately rectified in divers places, as also beautified and enlarged with new Mappes and Tables.* Englished by W. S. London, 1635.

Metz, Rudolf. "Bacon's Part in the Intellectual Movement of his Time," *Seventeenth Century Studies.* Oxford, 1938. Pp. 21-32.

Milton, John. *A Common-Place Book of John Milton.* Ed. by A. J. Horwood. Revised Edition, 1877.

――――. *Paradise Lost . . .* With Notes of Various Authors, By Thomas Newton. London, 1749.

――――. *Paradise Lost.* Ed. by A. W. Verity. Cambridge, 1929.

――――. *The Poetical Works of John Milton.* Ed. by the Rev. H. C. Beeching. Oxford, 1900.

――――. *The Poetical Works of John Milton.* With Notes of Various Authors. The Third Edition. By the Rev. H. J. Todd. London, 1826.

――――. *Private Correspondence and Academic Exercises.* Translated by Phyllis B. Tillyard. Cambridge, 1932.

――――. *Of Reformation Touching Church-Discipline in England.* Ed. by W. T. Hale. New Haven, 1916.

――――. *The Sonnets of Milton.* With Introduction and Notes by J. S. Smart. Glasgow, 1921.

――――. *The Tenure of Kings and Magistrates.* Ed. by W. T. Allison. New York, 1911.

――――. *The Works of John Milton.* New York, 1931 ――――.

Milton Memorial Lectures 1908. Ed., with an Introduction, by P. W. Ames. London, 1909.

More, Henry. *Conjectura Cabbalistica. Or A Conjectural Essay of Interpreting the minde of Moses, according to a Threefold Cabbala . . .* London, 1653.

Nicolson, Marjorie H. "Milton and the *Conjectura Cabbalistica,*" *Philological Quarterly,* VI, 1-18.

――――. "Milton and the Telescope," *ELH,* II, 1-32.

———. "Milton's Hell and the Phlegraean Fields," *University of Toronto Quarterly*, VII, 500-513.

———. "The Spirit World of Milton and More," *Studies in Philology*, XXII, 433-452.

Nordenskiöld, A. E. *Facsimile-Atlas to the Early History of Cartography with Reproductions of the most important Maps Printed in the XV and XVI Centuries.* Translated by Johan A. Ekelöf and Clements R. Markham. Stockholm, 1899.

North, F. J. *The Map of Wales.* Cardiff, 1935.

Novus Atlas. Das ist Welt-beschreibung mit schönen aussführlichen Taffeln Inhaltende Die Königreiche und Lände der gantzen Erdtreiches. Amstelodami, 1647-1662.

Ortelius, Abraham. *Theatrum Orbis Terrarum. The Theatre of the whole World: Set forth by That Excellent Geographer Abraham Ortelius.* London, 1606.

Parker, William R. "The Greek Spirit in Milton's *Samson Agonistes*," *Essays and Studies.* Oxford, 1935. XX, 21-44.

———. *Milton's Debt to Greek Tragedy in Samson Agonistes.* Baltimore, 1937.

Peck, H. W. "The Theme of *Paradise Lost*," *PMLA*, XXII, 256-269.

Perkins, William. *The Workes of that Famous and Worthy Minister of Christ, In the Universitie of Cambridge.* London, 1613.

Phillips, Edward. *The New World of Words: Or, a Generall English Dictionary* . . . London, 1671.

Phillips, Philip Lee. *A List of Geographical Atlases in the Library of Congress with Bibliographical Notes.* Washington, 1909.

Pliny. *The Historie of the World. Commonly called, The Naturall Historie of C. Plinius Secundus.* Translated into English by Philemon Holland. London, 1601.

———. *The Natural History of Pliny.* Translated, with Copious Notes and Illustrations, by John Bostock and H. T. Riley. London, 1855-1857.

Plutarch's Moralia With an English Translation by F. C. Babbitt. London, 1936.

Polo, Marco. *The Most Noble and Famous Travels of Marco Polo together with the Travels of Nicolo de Conti.* Ed. from the Elizabethan Translation of John Frampton with Introduction, Notes and Appendixes. By M. M. Penger. London, 1929.

Powers to be Resisted: Or A Dialogue Arguing The Parliaments lawfull Resistance of the Powers now in Armes against them; And that Archbishops, Bishops, Curates, Neuters, all these are to be cut off by the Law of God; . . . London, 1643.

Praz, Mario. "Milton and Poussin," *Seventeenth Century Studies.* Pp. 192-210.

Pritchard, John P. "The Fathers of the Church in the Works of John Milton," *Classical Journal,* XXXII, 79-87.

Ptolemy. *Claudii Ptolemaei Alexandrini Geographiae Libri Octo Graeco-Latini* . . . *cum tabulis geographicis ad mentem auctoris restitutis per Gerardum Mercatorem.* Amsterodami, 1605.

————. *Geography of Claudius Ptolemy.* Translated into English and Edited by Edward Luther Stevenson . . . With an Introduction by Professor Joseph Fischer. New York, 1932.

Purchas, Samuel. *Purchas his Pilgrimage. Or Relations of the World and the Religions Obserued in all Ages and Places Discouered, from the Creation unto this Present* . . . London, 1626.

Quarles, Francis. *The Complete Works in Prose and Verse of Francis Quarles.* Ed. by the Rev. A. B. Grosart. 1880.

Quiller-Couch, Sir Arthur. *Studies in Literature. Second Series.* Cambridge, 1922.

Raleigh, Sir Walter. *The Cabinet Council: containing the Cheif Arts of Empire and Mysteries of State;* . . . *By the ever-renowned Knight, Sir Walter Raleigh,* published by John Milton, London, 1658.

————. *The Discoverie of the large and bewtiful Empire of Guiana by Sir Walter Ralegh.* Ed. from the Original Text, with Introductions, Notes and Appendixes . . . By V. T. Harlow. London, 1928.

————. *The History of the World, in Five Books.* London, 1614.

Raleigh, Walter. *Milton.* London, 1900.

Robbins, Frank E. *The Hexaemeral Literature A Study of the Greek and Latin Commentaries on Genesis.* Chicago, 1912.

Sandys, George. *A Relation of a Iourney begun An: Dom: 1610. Foure Bookes. Containing a description of the Turkish Empire, of Aegypt, of the Holy Land, of the Remote Parts of Italy, and Ilands adioyning.* London, 1615.

Saurat, Denis. *Milton Man and Thinker.* New York, 1925.

Seventeenth Century Studies Presented to Sir Herbert Grierson. Oxford, 1938.

Stebbing, William. *Sir Walter Ralegh A Biography.* Oxford, 1891.

Stern, Alfred. *Milton und seine Zeit.* Leipzig, 1877.

Stoll, Elmer E. *Poets and Playwrights.* Minneapolis, 1930.

Strabo. *The Geography of Strabo* with an English Translation by Horace L. Jones. London and New York, 1917.

Symons, Edward. *A Militarie Sermon, Wherein by the Word of God, the nature and disposition of a Rebell is discovered, and the Kings true Souldier described and characterized.* 1644.

Taylor, George C. *Milton's Use of Du Bartas.* Cambridge, 1934.

Temple, Thomas. *Christ's Government in and over his People,* a sermon delivered before the House of Commons, October 26, 1642. London, 1642.

Thaler, Alwin. "The Shakesperian Element in Milton," *Shakespere's Silences.* Cambridge, 1929. Pp. 139-208.

Thompson, Edward. *Sir Walter Ralegh The Last of the Elizabethans.* London, 1935.

Thompson, Elbert N. S. "Milton's Knowledge of Geography," *Studies in Philology,* XVI, 148-171.

Tillyard, E. M. W. *Milton.* New York, 1930.

———. *Milton L'Allegro and Il Penseroso.* The English Association Pamphlet No. 82.

———. *The Miltonic Setting Past & Present.* Cambridge, 1938.

———. "Milton and the English Epic Tradition," *Seventeenth Century Studies.* Oxford, 1938. Pp. 211-234.

Tracts on Liberty in the Puritan Revolution 1638-1647. Ed., with a Commentary, by William Haller. New York, 1934.

Trevelyan, George M. *England under the Stuarts.* London, 1926.

Willey, Basil. *The Seventeenth Century Background Studies in the Thought of the Age in Relation to Poetry and Religion.* London, 1934.

Williams, Arnold. "Commentaries on Genesis as a Basis for the Hexaemeral Material in the Literature of the Late Renaissance," *Studies in Philology,* XXXIV, 191-208.

Wood, George A. "The Miltonic Ideal," *Historical Essays by Members of the Owens College, Manchester . . .* Ed. by F. F. Trout and James Tait. London, 1902. Pp. 357-376.

INDEX

ABARIM, the mountains, 36, 108, 112, 203-204.
Abbana, 117, 212-213.
Abbott, Edwin A., 274, 378.
Abdiel, 292.
Abraham, 49, 114.
Abyssines, 108, 119-120.
Accaron, 112, 210-211.
Adam, 12-13, 30, 34, 43, 44, 47, 51, 87-88, 152, 167, 175, 232.
Addison, Joseph, 178.
Adiabene, 92, 124.
Adonis, 39, 195-196, 209-210, 243.
Adrichomius, Christianus, 202, 203, 378.
Aeaea, 100-101.
Aemilian Road, 125.
Aesculapius, 199.
Afer, 79, 121-122.
Age, infirmities of, 172-174, 244.
Ahaz, 201.
Alcinous, gardens of, 46, 60.
Alimoni Peloni, 293-294, 299-300.
Allen, P. S., 242, 243, 378.
Allison, W. T., 311, 386.
Amalthea, 66-67, 108.
Ambition, 41-42.
Ambrosia, 69.
Ambulones, 142.
Aminta. See Tasso.
Ammon, 66, 108.
Ammonites, 201, 202-203, 205.
Amorites, 204-205.
Angels, when created, 14; good and evil, 197-198, 214-215.
Anglesey, 104.
Angola, 119-120.
Ants, 83-84.
Anubis, 65, 191.
Aparticas, 79.
Apis, 191, 192.
Appian Road, 125.
Arabia, 38, 46, 49, 68-69, 87, 118, 123, 205.
Arachosia, 124.

Aram, 50.
Araxes, river, 92, 123, 124.
Arethusa, 89, 109-110.
Argestes, 79, 121.
Argob, 111, 112, 202-203.
Arimaspi, 39, 57, 84-85.
Arion, 80.
Ark, 54-55.
Armenia, 47.
Arnon, river, 36, 111, 112, 202-204, 205.
Aroer, 112, 203-204.
Artaxata, 92, 123, 124.
Ascalon, 112, 210-211.
Ashtaroth, 197, 206-207.
Asphalt, 72-73.
Asphaltic Lake or Pool, 58, 112.
Assyrian Garden, 108.
Assyrian Mount, 38.
Astarte, 36, 197, 206-208.
Astoreth, 197, 206-208.
Atlases, Milton's interest in, 95. *See also* Maps.
Atropatia, 124.
Aubrey, John, 131.
Augustine, Saint, 8, 55, 59, 155; *City of God*, 188-200; unique importance of, 188-189; Vives's Commentary, 189-200; Milton interested in, 197-198.
Auran, 45, 48, 49, 50.
Auranitis, 49, 50.
Azazel, 213.
Azotus, 112.

BAAL, 204, 207, 208.
Baalim, 201, 206-208.
Babel, 50, 55-56, 72, 91, 130.
Babylon, 46, 47, 50, 71, 123, 197.
Bacchanalians, 196, 197.
Bacchus, 66, 108, 194-195, 239.
Bacon, Sir Francis, 9-10; creation a natural process, 9-11; Milton's knowledge of his church tracts, 267-269; *Certaine Considerations*,

268, 275, 277; *An Advertisement*, 268-269, 274-275, 277; his and Milton's interest in reform, 269-270; his attitude, 270, 279; on ceremony, 272; on church government, 273-274; against dissension, 274-275; for change, 275; program of church reform, 276-277; contrast with Milton, 279.

Bactra, 92, 123, 124.
Bagehot, Walter, 379.
Baillie, Robert, 233-234, 357, 379.
Baker, J. N. L., 379.
Balsara, 49, 124.
Bards, 103.
Bardsey, 103-104.
Barker, Ernest, 188.
Basan, 111, 112, 202-203.
Baxter, Richard, 219-220, 379.
Beech, William, 352.
Beelzebub, 216.
Beersaba, 211.
Bees, 84.
Bel, 72, 216.
Belerium, 106.
Belial, 184, 213, 216-217, 218-231; character in *P. L.*, 221-222; contemporary significance, 223-231; Christ and Belial, 229-230, 364.
Bellerophon, 171-172, 200.
Benbrigge, John, 235-236, 379.
Benjamin, 226.
Bethel, 116.
Bible, 4, 11-13, 21, 60, 63; maps in, 108; More-Speed map, 113-114; and Fuller's *Pisgah-Sight*, 115-117; and Milton, 216; main source of *S. A.*, 252; an infallible guide, 272-273.
Birds, 22, 82-83.
Bitumen, 72.
Blaeu, *Le Grand Atlas*, 120, 122.
Bocchus, realm of, 125-126.
Boreas, 79, 121.
Bradshaw, Lord President, 321-322.
Brahe, Tycho, 162-163.
Britannia. See William Camden.
British Academy, *Proceedings* of, 10, 39.
Brooke, Lord, 301-302; his *Discourse* and Milton's *Of Prelatical Episcopacy*, 302-306; Milton's debt to, 306-309; his tolerance, 309-310.

Brown, Eleanor G., 134, 379.
Browne, Sir Thomas, *Pseudodoxia Epidemica*, 70, 74, 238, 374-377, 379.
Buchan, John, 267, 379.
Buckingham, Duke of, 340-341.
Bullough, Geoffrey, 11, 379.
Burton, Robert, *The Anatomy of Melancholy*, xi, 129-176; "Abstract," 129-130, 138; intensive study, 131-132; marriage, 133-134; *L'Allegro*, 136-138; *Il Penseroso*, 138-139; *Comus*, 141-143; the *Anatomy* and *P. L.*, 150-173; the Fall, 152-153; devils, 155-156; the will, 158-159; cosmography, 159-164; divine mysteries, 164-165; temperance, 166; war condemned, 167-168, 362, 380.
Burton, William, 358-359.
Bush, Douglas, 365-367, 380.
Busiris, 58-59.
Butler, Charles, 84.
Byzantium, 119.

Cabbala, 11, 13, 24.
Cabinet-Council. See Sir Walter Raleigh.
Caecias, 121.
Cambalu, 98-99, 119, 120.
Camden, William, *Britannia*, 101, 102, 104, 105-106, 107, 380.
Campbell, Lily B., 21, 253, 380.
Candaor, 124.
Canne, John, *The Golden Rule*, date of, 311; and Milton's *Tenure*, 312-320; Seneca quoted, 312; tyrants to be resisted, 313-314; king's power limited, 315-316; political power rests in people, 316-317; kings subject to punishment, 317-320; and Milton, 359, 380.
Canneh, 49.
Cape Verde, 99-100.
Caspian Lake, 90, 123.
Cassia, 67, 68.
Castalian Spring, 108, 110.
Cataia, 99.
Catalog of devils, source of in *P. L.*, 178-217; conventional interpretation, 178-179; relation to Ross's

Pansebeia, 179-180; other sources, 180-215; conclusions, 215-216.

Caucasus, 124.

Ceremony, 272, 276-277.

Ceres, 108-109, 193, 196.

Ceylon, 89.

Cham, 66, 108.

Chaos, 6, 8; and Cupid, 9-10; in *P. L.*, 15, 19; in Raleigh's *History*, 16-17; in Mercator's *Atlas*, 17-18, 23, 29, 31; in Hesiod's *Theogony*, 185-187.

Charran, 49, 50.

Charybdis, 89, 109-110.

Chastity, 143, 244, 246, 249.

Chemos, 112, 201-202, 203-204, 206.

Chersoness, 88, 125.

Chester, Allan G., 326, 380.

Chimera, 200.

China, 99, 117.

Choaspes, river, 123-124.

Christ, as Creator, 3, 6, 7, 14, 23, 35; and Hercules, 60; and Satan, 57, 214, 233, 235; places associated with, 113-114; temptation of, 123-126, 156, 165, 167; and redemption, 159, 175-176, 235; and worldly glory, 169-170; and oracles, 177; and Belial, 221-222, 229-230.

Circe, 100-101, 195, 243.

City of God. See Saint Augustine.

Clark, E. M., 252, 380.

Clark, G. N., viii.

Clemens, Alexandrinus, 305.

Cleombrotus, 171, 177.

Cogan, Henry, 64.

Collier, Katharine B., 4, 380.

Comets, 77-78.

Compendious Discourse, reply to *Of Prelatical Episcopacy*, 293-294; date of, 294; defends Irenaeus, 294-296; defends bishops, 296-298.

Congo, 119-120.

Conjectura Cabbalistica, 11-13, 29.

Conti, Natali, *Mythologiae*, 10.

Cook, A. S., 96.

Cooper, Thomas, 381.

Copernican System, 159, 160, 162, 163, 164.

Cosmography, 159-164.

Courthope, W. J., 136.

Cowley, Abraham, *Davideis*, 36-37.

Cranes, 81-82.

Creation of the world, 3-35; Milton's account, 3; Milton and the Mosaic account, 4; Lambertus Danaeus on, 4-5, 6-8; Purchas on, 5; Plato on, 5, 7; and the Word, 6; and Hesiod, 8; Bacon on, 9-11; Henry More on, 11-13; order, 14; plan of, 19-20; initial act, 22-23; natural process, 23-24; details of, 24-32; of man, 32-34.

Cromwell, Oliver, 39.

Cronus, 184, 186-187.

Crystalline Ocean, 29-30.

Cupid, 9-10.

Curiosity, idle, 164-165.

DAGON, 112, 210-211.

Dalila, 211, 261-263.

Damascus, 117, 212-213.

Damiata, 119.

Damon, 145.

Danaeus, Lambertus, *The Wonderfull Woorkmanship of the World*, 4, 5, 6-8, 35.

Danubius, 125, 126.

Daphne, grove of, 108, 110

Davenant, Sir William, 37-38.

Davies, Godfrey, viii, 368.

Davity, Pierre, 95.

Dead Sea, 58.

Death, 133, 151, 173-174.

De Bry, Theodore, 110, 381.

De Civitate Dei. See The City of God.

Declarations of Parliament, 340-348.

De Filippis, Michele, 381.

Demogorgon, 16-17.

Descartes, 13.

Deserts, 90-91, 114, 118, 142, 211.

Destiny, 42-43.

Deva, river, 103, 105-106.

Devils. *See* Satan.

Dewey, John, 144.

Digby, Lord, *Speech*, 282-283; summary of, 284-286; Milton refutes, 286-291; 356; 381.

Diodati, Charles, 131, 133.

Diodorus Siculus, 36, 38; his *History* and *P. L.*, 64-74; purpose of his-

tory, 63-64; Egyptian worship, 64-66; Nyseian Isle, 66-67; Sabean odors, 68-69; sun's force, 69-70; Servonian Fen, 70-71; pyramids, 71; Babylon, 71-72; asphalt, 72-73; Thebes, 73; Meroe, 73; rivers in India, 73-74; 381.
A Discourse Opening the Nature of that Episcopacie. See Lord Brooke.
Disease, 130, 132.
Dolphins, 79-80.
Druids, 103-105.
Du Bartas, Guillaume de Salluste, *Devine Weekes and Workes,* ix-x, 8-9, 21-22, 35, 381.

EARTH, center of universe, 24-25; her bounty, 92; wronged by man, 92.
Ecbatana, 119, 123, 124.
Ecclesiastes, 18, 32.
Eden, 11, 40, 45-50, 108.
Edmundson, George, 252-253, 382.
Egypt, 64-66, 70-71, 87, 141-142, 180-184, 191-192, 211.
Egyptian gods, 64-66, 180-184, 191-192.
Eikon Alethine. See Milton, *Eikonoklastes.*
Eikon Episte, 325.
Eleale, 112.
Eliot, T. S., 361, 382.
Elysian Fields, 46, 60.
Emilia, 126.
Emmet, 84.
Enna, field of, 108-109.
Enoch, book of, 213.
Epicycles, 162.
Episcopacy, conflict with Puritans, 219-220; scandals of clergy, 224; enemy of true religion, 148-149, 226-227; Satan the leader, 233-235; autocratic rule, 268-269; reform of, 273-280, 288-291; defended, 294-301; origin of, 302-306; and schism, 306-309.
Erasmus, Desiderius, *Encomium Moriae,* xi; and *Comus,* 242-250; youth, 245-246; Stoics, 245-246; wisdom, 246-247; 382.
Ercoco, 119-120.
Ethiopia, 85, 110.
Ethiop Line, 108.

Euphrates, 46, 49, 123, 124, 206-207.
Euripides, 160.
Eurus, 46, 79, 121.
Eve, 42-43, 87-88, 175, 232.
Exact Collection, 328, 331, 343, 345, 348, 349.
Ezekiel, 48, 209.

FABLES, 60-61.
Faction, 147-149.
Fairies, 157.
Fall, 33-34, 43, 152-155, 159.
Fate, 43.
Fig Tree, Indian, 39, 52, 87-88.
Figgis, John N., 382.
Firmament, 11, 28-30.
Firth, Sir Charles, 39, 40, 45, 57, 382.
Fletcher, H. F., ix, 26-27, 29, 33, 382.
Flood, 52-55.
Florida, 45.
Folly, parentage, 243; prime factor in life, 244-246; and sobriety, 246-247.
Fortune, 42-43.
Frazier, J. G., 184, 382.
French, J. Milton, viii, 382.
Fruit, 58.
Fuller, Thomas, *A Pisgah-Sight of Palestine,* 102, 115-117, 202-214, 382.

GADES, 125, 126.
Galicia, 96, 106.
Galileo, 163.
Gallia, 125, 126.
Ganges, river, 90-91, 117.
Gardiner, S. G., 286, 383.
Gaster, Theodore, 55.
Gath, 112, 210-211.
Gaza, 112, 210-211.
Gehenna, 201-202.
Geography, 94-95.
Gerson, Ben, 24, 29-30.
Gibeah, 221, 226-227.
Gilbert, A. H., 39, 50, 64, 95, 96, 103, 112, 383.
Gill, Alexander, 131.
Globes, 95.

God, as orthodox creator, 3, 6-9, 12, 14; qualities of in *P. L.*, 15-16; plan of creation, 19-21; creation natural, 22-24; and light, 27-28; and the universe, 30-32, 44; and man's creation, 32-34, 43; and ambition, 41-42; and fortune, 42-43; sons of, 53; and law, 56, 61-62; and Satan, 56-58, 151, 157, 214-215, 231-239; and Jacob's dream, 115; and marriage, 145-146; unworthy servants, 147-148; his Love, 151-152; man's Fall, 153-159; his secrets, 164-165; his worship, 165, 172, 248-249; defiance of, 168-169, 201-204, 206-211; his City, 188-189; his angels, 197-198.

Golden Chain, 151-152.
Golden Rule. See John Canne.
Gondibert, 37.
Goodwin, John, 225-226, 230, 235, 383.
Gorgades, 90.
Gorgons, 90, 143, 200.
Gottfried, Rudolph, 383.
Grand Atlas, 120, 383.
Great Mother, 190.
Greek Gods, 184-188, 192-197.
Green, C. C., 383.
Greenlaw, Edwin, viii, 4, 18, 383.
Grierson, Sir H. J. C., viii, 135, 136, 175, 383.
Griffins, 57-58, 84-85.
Grimes, Ethog, 238.
Guiana, 39.

HALCYON, 82-83.
Hale, W. T., 268, 282.
Hall, Joseph, 101, 269, 282, 369-374.
Haller, W., ix-x, 218, 294, 357, 389.
Hamath, 114.
Hanford, J. H., vi, viii, ix, x, 130, 131, 133, 141, 143, 144, 170, 179, 252, 293, 325, 383-384.
Haran, 48.
Harlow, V. T., 39.
Hartwell, K. E., 384.
Healey, John, 188, 189.
Hebrus, 101.
Hecate, 191, 194.

Hecatompylos, 123, 124.
Heimbach, Peter, 95, 102.
Helena, 141-142.
Heliopolis, 73.
Henderson, Alexander, 239-240, 384.
Herodotus, 46, 192.
Hesebon, 36, 112, 203, 204, 205.
Hesiod, *Theogony*, 185-188, 198, 384.
Hesperides, 60, 90, 99-100, 164.
Heylyn, Peter, 39, 94, 232, 384.
Heywood, Thomas, 222, 384.
Hinnom, valley of, 201, 202.
Hippocrates, twins of, 351-352.
Hircania, 123, 124.
History, 37-38, 39, 63, 361.
History of the Parliament of England. See Thomas May.
History of the World. See Sir Walter Raleigh.
Hobbes, Thomas, 38.
Holland, Philemon, 74, 101.
Holyhead, 103.
Holy Spirit, 3, 14, 15, 17, 21-23.
Homer, ix, 46, 61, 86, 94, 136, 141-142, 151-152, 354.
Horonaim, 112, 113, 205.
Horton, 131, 132-133, 139.
Horus, 181, 182.
Hotham, Sir John, 343.
Hughes, M. Y., 136, 368.
Hull, 343-344.
Humanism, vi, 139.
Hydraspes, 73, 90-91, 117, 118.

IDEA, 19-20, 23, 31.
Idleness, 132-133, 138-139.
Ignatius, 304, 358.
Imaus, 117-118.
Immortality of the Soul, 156.
India, 90, 118, 123, 124, 125, 128.
Ingoldsby, William, 232-233.
Ireland, 345-348.
Irenaeus, a martyr, 293; as witness, 294-295; rank of, 297-298.
Isaiah, 48.
Isis, 37, 64-65, 180, 181, 183, 191-192.

JABOC, 203-204.
Jacob, 115.
James, Margaret, 384.

Jansson, *Atlas*, 101-102, 120, 121, 122.
Japhet, 152.
Jericho, 116.
Jeroboam, 115-116.
Jerome, 22, 201, 208, 297, 301.
Jerusalem, 116, 201, 202.
Job, 134, 136.
Jones, R. F., 354, 384.
Jordan, 59-60, 114, 203, 204.
Josephus, Flavius, *Jewish Antiquities*, 54, 384.
Jupiter, 60, 66, 72, 101, 187, 190, 194, 208.

KEIGHTLEY, Thomas, 384.
Kelley, Maurice, 384.
Kepler, Johann, 163.
King, Edward, 133.
King's Cabinet, 349.
Knights, L. C., 176, 384.

LANDOR, W. S., 242.
Land's End. *See* Belerium.
Lapland witches, 77, 200.
Lares, 198-199.
Larson, Martin A., 21, 385.
Lauder, William, 37, 385.
Law, 56, 61-62.
Leach, A. F., x, 385.
Lemmi, C. W., 10, 385.
Lemnos, 101.
Lemures, 198-199.
Leontius, 303.
Levant, 121.
Leviathan, 81.
Lhuyd, Humphrey, 103-104.
Libecchio, 121.
Light, 8, 12, 25-28, 164.
Lockwood, Laura E., 96.
Lop, desert, 118, 142.
Lovejoy, A. O., 30, 35, 152, 176, 385.
Lowenhaupt, W. H., 324-325, 330, 332, 334, 338, 339, 340, 342, 349, 350, 351, 352, 353, 360, 385.
Lowes, John L., 365.
Lucifer. *See* Satan.
Luz, 115.
Lymnos, 104.

McCOLLEY, Grant, ix-x, 159-161, 179-180, 207-208, 212, 216, 363, 385.
Magellan, 99-100.
Man, creation of, 12, 32-33; soul, 14, 32; in nature, 31-32; his reason, 33; his will, 33-34; his frailty, 43; depravity of, 53, 54, 92-93, 164; loneliness, 145-147.
Man, isle of, 105.
Manoa, 174.
Maps, Milton's use of, 94-128; Milton recommends, 95; and Milton's poetic inspiration, 94, 96, 126-127.
Margiana, 92, 124.
Marriage, 133-134, 145-147.
Marshall, Stephen, 223-224, 233, 385.
Martyrs, 288.
Masson, David, ix-x, 103, 357, 368, 385.
Matter, original, 14, 16, 17.
Mausbach, Joseph, 189, 385.
May, Thomas, *History of the Parliament of England*, 326; and *Eikonoklastes*, 326-340; courtiers and clergy, 326-327; King enemy of Parliament and people, 327-329; King and papists, 327-330; citizens and Parliament, 332-333; King and Strafford, 333-337; King's expeditions, 337-338; crown jewels, 339; 385.
Melancholy, in seventeenth century, 129; dangers of, 129-130; definition of, 130; excessive study, 131-132; death, 133; marriage, 134; politics, 134-135; and *L'Allegro*, 136-138; and *Il Penseroso*, 138-139; and *Comus*, 141-143; and *P. L.*, 150-173; personal note in *P. L.*, 175-176.
Melinde, 119, 120.
Memphis, 71, 91, 192.
Mercator, *Atlas*, 15, 17, 23-24, 25, 26, 34, 35; Verity on, 96; Africa, 120; winds, 122; 360; 385-386.
Meroe, 73, 88-89, 125-126.
Mesopotamia, 46, 49, 50.
Metz, Rudolf, 11, 386.
Michael, 42, 114, 172, 173, 213.

Milton, John, misconceptions regarding, v; true character, vi; and his age, vi-vii; controversy regarding, vii-x; and orthodoxy, 3-4; originality of, 35, 37; misogyny of, 53; and pagan mythology, 60; condemns greed, 92-93; interest in geography, 95-96; melancholy of, 129-176; a tireless student, 130-132; marriage of, 133-134; blindness of, 134, 149-150; purpose in *L'Allegro* and *Il Penseroso*, 136-139; and faction, 147-149; melancholy in *P. L.*, 150-173; old age, 172-175; as church reformer, 270; style of, 280-281; answers Digby, 283, 286, 291-292; attacked, 293-301; praise of Lord Brooke, 301-302; debt to Lord Brooke, 306-309; his and Canne's views of monarchy compared, 311-322; method of writing, 325-326, 340, 353; opinion of Hall, 373.

Works: *Ad Patrem*, 132; *Animadversions upon the Remonstrants Defence*, 101, 269; *Apology against a Pamphlet call'd A Modest Confutation*, 269; *Apology for Smectymnuus*, 148; *Areopagitica*, 167; *At a Vacation Exercise*, 103; *Brief History of Moscovia*, 95; *Colasterion*, 147; *Commonplace Book*, 36, 40, 188, 218, 269, 386; *Comus*, moly, 86-87; intemperance, 92; Bacchus, 100-101; and melancholy, 141-143; sources of, 242-243; and *Encomium Moriae*, 243-249; *De Doctrina Christiana*, 4, 13-15, 32, 63, 159; *Defensio Secunda*, 134, 218; *De Spherarum Concentu*, 152; *Doctrine and Discipline of Divorce*, 145-146, 357; *Eikonoklastes*, relation to *Eikon Alethine*, 324-325, 352; debt to May's *History*, 326-340; use of *Declarations*, 340-350; Milton's integrity, 353, 359-360; *Epitaphium Damonis*, 143-145; *Epitaph on the Marchioness of Winchester*, 140; *First Academic Exercise*, 139-140; *History of Britain*, 74, 103, 362-363; *Il Penseroso*, 138-141; *In Quintum Novembris*, 139; *L'Allegro*, 136-141; quoted, 157; *Lycidas*, dolphins, 79; Orpheus, 101; geography in, 103-107; personal feeling in, 144; the Wolf, 368; *Of Education*, 95; *Of Prelatical Episcopacy*, 272-273; reply to, 293-301; date of, 293-294; Irenaeus discredited, 294-296; bishops as witnesses, 296-297; rank of bishops, 297-298; used by Lord Brooke, 302-306; *Of Reformation*, 268, 294; refutation of Digby's *Speech*, 282-292; dramatic character of, 291-292; 386; *On the Morning of Christ's Nativity*, 85-86, 177, 180, 184, 199, 211; *Paradise Lost*, Milton's culture, vii; and Homer, ix; Renaissance commonplaces in, ix; and rabbinical commentaries, x; story of creation, 3-35; and the hexamera, 4; and the *Zohar*, 24; and Rashi's commentary, 26-27; light, 27-28; *scala naturae*, 30-32; and history, 38; ambition, 42; and Raleigh's *History*, 41-63; stars, 44; and Diodorus's *History*, 64-74; Egyptian gods, 65; Nyseian Isle, 66; Arabia, 68; the sun, 69-70; Serbonian Bog, 70; pyramids, 71; Bel, 71; Babel, 72; and Pliny's *History*, 75-93; Ptolemaic system, 75-76; winds, 78-79; serpents, 80-81; cranes and pygmies, 82; fig tree, 88; Serica, 90-91; and maps, 107-123, 126-127; Palestine, 111; Jacob's dream and heavenly stairs, 115; Jeroboam's idolatry, 116; vulture's flight, 117; Serbonian Bog, 119; winds, 121-123; precise mental images, 127-128; melancholy theme, 150-173; cosmography, 159-164; temperance, 167; and Plutarch's *Moralia*, 181-185; and *The City of God*, 188-200; and Purchas's *Pilgrimage*, 201-213; and Fuller's *Pisgah-Sight*, 202-213; and contemporary views of Belial and Satan, 223-241; *Paradise Regained*, 62, 71, 91-92, 116, 123-126, 156, 167, 169, 170, 221-222; *Private Correspondence*,

131, 243, 386; *Ready and Easy Way to Establish a Free Commonwealth*, 149; *Reason of Church Government*, 147-148, 251-252, 270-271, 302, 306-310; *Samson Agonistes*, 127, 251-264; *Sixth Academic Exercise*, 243; *Tenure of Kings and Magistrates* and *The Golden Rule*, 311-323; principles of, 311-312; Seneca quoted, 312; obedience conditional, 313-314; king's power limited, 315-316; people's sovereignty, 316-317; king accountable, 317, 320, 386; *Tetrachordon*, 146-147.

Milton Memorial Lectures, 386.

Minerva, 143, 194.

Mirth, 136-138.

Moab, 112, 201-202, 203-206.

Moloch, 36, 111, 201-202.

Moly, 86-87.

Mombaza, 119, 120.

Mona, isle of, 103-105.

Mons Scandali, 116, 202.

Montgomery Shire, 102.

Moon, 75-76, 158, 163-164, 180, 191, 194, 199, 200.

More, Henry, *Conjectura Cabbalistica*, 11-13, 386.

Moreh, 114.

Moses, 4, 5, 6, 13, 19, 25, 35, 48, 113.

Mount Amara, 108, 110.

Mount Calvary, 116.

Mount Carmel, 114.

Mount Casius, 70-71, 119.

Mount Hermon, 114.

Mount Lebanon, 102, 116, 213.

Mount Olivet, 116.

Mount Rhodope, 90.

Mount St. Michael, 106-107.

Mount Senir, 114.

Mount Sinai, 35, 113.

Mozambic, 68, 118.

Muse, Milton's, v, 3, 20-21, 35, 171-172.

Mysteries, divine, 164-165.

Mythology, and Scripture, 60.

NAAMAN, 117.

Namancos, 96, 106.

Nebo, 36, 112, 203-204.

Necessity, 42-43.

Negus, 119-120.

Neo-Platonism, 4, 7, 18-19, 30-31, 35.

Nepenthes, 87, 136, 141-142.

Nero, 350-351.

Newton, Thomas, 29, 37, 38-39, 50, 178-179, 207, 222.

Nicolson, Marjorie, 4, 12, 128, 156, 386-387.

Night, 10, 15, 18, 186.

Nightingale, 83.

Nile, 66, 108, 181, 182.

Nimrod, 50-51, 55-56.

Nineveh, 92, 123.

Ninus, 46, 123.

Niphates, 124.

Nisibis, 123, 124.

Noah, 54.

Nordenskiöld, A. E., 387.

North, F. J., 126, 387.

Norumbega, 121.

Notus, 121.

Novus Atlas, 101-102, 387.

Nyseian Isle, 39, 66-67, 96, 108.

OLDFATHER, C. H., 63-64.

Ophir, 36, 57, 119.

Oracles, 177, 211.

Oreb, 116.

Origen, 214.

Orontes, river, 108, 110.

Orpheus, 101.

Ortelius, Abraham, *Theatre of the World*, xi; Galicia, 96; maps and history, 97-98; merits of, 98; Magellan, 99-100; Sabrina, 102; Mona, 105; Belerium, 106; Namancos, 106; and places compared with Eden, 108-111; Pelorus, 109; grove of Daphne, 110; Palestine, 111-112; Imaus, 117-118; Arabia, 118-119; Serbonian Bog, 119; Abyssinia, 119-120, 361-362, 387.

Osgood, C. G., vi.

Osiris, 37, 64-65, 181-183, 191-192.

Ovid, 8, 17, 46, 195, 199, 354.

Oxus, river, 120, 124.

PADAN-ARAN, 115.
Paganism, idolatry, 177-217; decline of, 177; Milton's catalog of, 178; source of catalog in *P. L.*, 178-180; part of literary background, 180-217; Egyptian, 180-184, 191-192; Greek and Roman, 184-188, 192-200; Gentile, 200-213.
Palestine, 111.
Palm trees, 47, 116.
Pan, 46, 177.
Pandora, 152.
Paneas, fount of Jordan, 59-60.
Papias, 299.
Paquin, 98-99, 119.
Paradise, 45-50, 107-111.
Parergon, 98, 100, 124, 126.
Parker, Henry, 351-352.
Parker, W. R., 252, 254, 264, 387.
Parliament, 326, 327-329, 330, 331, 340-341, 343-344, 346-349.
Patterson, F. A., 47, 368.
Pattison, Mark, 218.
Peck, H. W., 63, 387.
Pelorus, 109.
Peor, 204.
Perkins, William, 358-359, 387.
Persepolis, 92, 123, 124.
Persia, 91-92.
Pessimism, 135, 149-151, 174, 175, 176.
Pharaoh, 59.
Pharphar, river, 117, 212-213.
Phillips, Edward, 147, 181, 188, 387.
Phillips, Philip Lee, 387.
Philosophy, 5-6, 11-13, 62-63.
Phlegraean Fields, 128.
Phoenicians, 197, 207.
Phoenix, 39, 73, 85.
Photius, 303-304.
Pisgah, 102, 204-206.
Planets, 76-77, 161-162.
Plato, 5, 7, 19, 21, 31, 35, 171, 248-249.
Pliny, *Natural History* and *P. L.*, 38-39, 75-93; fig tree, 52; Ptolemaic system, 75-76; winds, 78-79; dolphins, 79-80; serpents, 80; cranes and pygmies, 81; nightingale, 83; griffins, 84-85; phoenix, 85; halcyons, 85-86; moly, 86-87; Meroe, 88-89; Taprobane, 89; 361; 387.
Plotinus, 30.
Plutarch, *Moralia* and *P. L.*, 181-185, 387.
Polycarpus, 294-298.
Polydamna, 142.
Ponent, 121.
Portents, 78.
Praise of Folly. See Erasmus.
Praz, Mario, xi, 242, 361, 388.
Priapus, 195, 216.
Prideaux, Humphrey, 128.
Pritchard, John P., 388.
Proserpina, 108-109, 193, 196.
Psalms, 150.
Ptolemaic System, 75, 159-160.
Ptolemy, *Geographia*, 96-97, 111, 122, 124, 388.
Purchas, Samuel, *Pilgrimage*, 15-35; accounts of creation, 5; first act of creation, 22; light, 26, 28; man, 32-33, 35; Eden, 49-50; Mount Amara, 110-111; pagan gods, 201-214; Moloch, 201-202; Chemosh, 204; Thammuz, 209-210; Dagon, 211-212, 388.
Puritanism, v-vi; concept of history, 39; taste of, 219-220; faith of, 229; views of Belial and Satan, 222-241; and Bible, 272-273; 277; 364; 373.
Pygmies, 81-82.
Pyramids, 38, 71, 91.

QUARLES, Francis, *Historie of Samson* and *S.A.*, 253-264; realism of, 251, 254; Samson's mission, 259; Delila's stratagems, 261-262; contrast with, 264; 365; 388.
Quiller-Couch, Sir Arthur, 388.
Quiloa, 119, 120.

RABBA, 36, 111, 201, 202, 205.
Rabbinical commentaries, ix, 4, 21, 24, 26-27, 29-30, 33.
Raleigh, Sir Walter, his style and Milton's, 16; reputation, 39; *Cabinet-Council*, 40; *History of the World*, 15-35; God, 16; first act

of creation, 22; light, 25, 27; sun, 25-26; firmament, 29; man, 32-33; Adam, 33-34; stars, 44; site of Eden, 45-50; Flood, 54-55; Nimrod, 56; law, 56; Satan, 57; Arimaspi, 57; Busiris, 59; pagan gods, 201-211; history, 361; 388.
Raphael, 3, 15-16, 76, 78, 85, 161, 163, 213.
Rashi, 26-27, 33.
Reason, 62.
Recreation, 136-139.
Redemption, 34, 151, 159, 175-176.
Reed, Amy L., 130.
Religion, vi, 3-4, 35, 127-128, 147-149, 170, 219-220, 239, 253, 269, 271, 277-278, 280-281, 301-302, 354-355, 366-367.
Reno, vale of, 126.
Rhea, 66, 67, 108, 184, 186.
Rimmon, 117, 212-213.
Robbins, F. E., 5-6, 388.
Robin Goodfellow, 157.
Rome, 125, 197, 268, 368, 369, 370, 373.
Ross, Alexander, 179-180, 215-217, 363.

SABA, 68-69, 87, 118.
Sabrina, 102-103.
Samarchand, 119, 120.
Samoyed, 121.
Samson, xi, 174, 211, 251, 252, 254, 259, 260.
Sandys, George, *Relation of a Journey*, 94, 109, 119, 128, 179, 201, 388.
Santayana, George, 220.
Sarmatiae, 126.
Satan, ambition, 41-42; methods, 57, 156-157; and griffin, 57; and vulture, 90, 96, 117-118; shape of, 156; power of, 171; nature of, 214-215; in contemporary pamphlets, 231-241; agents of, 233; 364.
Saturn, 10, 60, 129, 144, 192-193, 201.
Saurat, Denis, 18, 145, 388.
Scala naturae, 30-31.
Schism, 306-308.
Scylla, 89, 109-110.

Sechem, 114.
Sedgwick, William, 240.
Selden, John, 116.
Seleucia, 49, 92, 123, 124.
Seleucus, 50.
Seneca, 312.
Seon, 112, 203-206.
Serapis, 191, 192.
Serbonian Bog, 70-71, 119.
Serica, 90, 117-118.
Serpent. *See* Satan.
Serpents, 58, 80-81.
Serraliona, 121.
Severn. *See* Sabrina.
Shinar, 49, 50.
Sibma, 112, 204-206.
Sicily, 109.
Sidonian virgins, 206-207.
Sin, 151, 170, 190, 215.
Sinarum Regio, 99.
Sirocco, 121.
Smart, J. S., 126.
Smectymnuus, 224.
Smith, George, 229.
Sodom, 221.
Sofala, 119.
Sogdiana, 92, 123, 124.
Solomon, 202, 206, 207, 208.
Sons of Belial. *See* Belial.
Sons of God, 52-53, 230.
Sorek, 211.
Soul, 7, 12, 13, 14, 19, 30-32, 61-62, 248-249.
South Sea, 99-100.
Spenser, Edmund, 18, 177, 242, 355.
Spirits, 14, 30, 58, 60, 142, 155-158.
Spring, eternal, 46-47.
Stars, 44, 76-77, 164.
Stebbing, William, 389.
Stern, Alfred, 389.
Stoics, 242, 245-246.
Stoll, E. E., 135, 389.
Strabo, 47, 94, 192, 389.
Strafford, Lord, 333-335.
Study, 130-132, 138-140.
Sumatra, 89.
Sun, created, 25-26; effects of, 69-70; ruler, 75; masculine, 78; center of universe, 161-162, 163.
Susa, 123, 124.
Susiana, 124.
Syene, 88, 125.
Sylvester, Joshua. *See* Du Bartas.

Symmons, Edward, 235.
Syrtis, 73, 90.

TACITUS, 58, 104-105.
Tanais, river, 90.
Taprobane, 88-89, 125.
Tartaria, 96, 99.
Tasso, Torquato, 242.
Taylor, G. C., ix-x, 8-9, 33, 55-56, 389.
Telassar, 48, 49.
Tempe, vale of, 90.
Temperance, 166-167.
Temple, Thomas, 225, 389.
Teredon, 49, 123, 124.
Terra Moriath, 116.
Tertullian, 155, 190, 304, 305.
Tesiphon, 123, 124.
Thaler, Alwin, 389.
Thammuz, 184, 208-210.
Theatre of the World. See Abraham Ortelius.
Thebes, 38, 73, 142.
Theocritus, 136, 195.
Theodoret, 304.
Thompson, Edward, 40, 389.
Thompson, E. N. S., 94, 95, 96, 389.
Thone, 141-142.
Thrascias, 79, 121.
Thyrsis, 141, 143-145.
Tigris, river, 46, 49, 108.
Tillyard, E. M. W., vi, ix, 34-35, 134, 139, 141, 175-176, 218, 252, 356, 361, 389.
Times Literary Supplement, 55, 127.
Titans, 186-187.
Todd, Henry, 222.
Tophet, 201-202.
Tree of Knowledge, 51-52.
Trevelyan, G. M., 267, 389.
Trinity, 21.
Triton, river, 66, 108.
Tuvil, Daniel, 241.
Typhon, 181-183, 187-188, 191-192.
Tyranny, 50-51, 55-56, 59, 149, 312-314, 317-318, 320.

Tyre, 37, 49.
Tyrrhenia, 100.

"ULYSSES ERRORES," 100.
Urania, 20-21.
Uriel, 69, 213.

VENUS, 76-77, 186, 190, 193.
Verity, A. W., 38-39, 82, 94, 95-96, 222.
Vesta, 193.
Vicars, John, 238.
Victoria, 99-100.
Virgil, 5, 22, 23, 61, 178, 199, 354.
Vives, J. L., vii, 136, 188-189, 190-200.
Vulcan, 101.
Vulture, 117-118.

WAR, condemned, 42, 55, 93, 154, 167-169.
Warburton, William, 178.
Whales, 81.
Wilkins, Bishop, x.
Will, 33-34, 43, 158-159.
Willey, Basil, viii, 355, 389.
Williams, Arnold, 4, 389.
Winds, 78-80, 121-122.
Wine, 166, 243.
Wisdom, 12, 20-21.
Wolves, 218, 279, 368-374.
Woman, 43, 53, 133-134, 145-147, 334-335.
Wonderfull Woorkmanship of the World. See Lambertus Danaeus.
Wood, George A., 389.
Word, 6, 17.
Wordsworth, William, 132.
World, disputed origin of, 4-7; created ex nihilo, 7, 9, 19; finite, 7; infinite, 163-164. See also Cosmography.

ZEPHON, 46, 155.
Zephyr, 79, 121.
Zeus, 186-187.
Zohar, 18, 20-21, 24, 355.